D1688126

Learning English

PASSWORD ORANGE 6

Grundkurs

Unterrichtswerk für Gesamtschulen
und andere differenzierende Schulformen

von
Anette Christiani
Irene Gagel
Margaret Gutmann
Geraldine Greenhalgh
Norbert Köhn
Annegret Preker-Franke
Dietmar Schlinkmann
Stephen Speight
Ulf Degen
Dorothea Nadzeika-Humbaraci

Ernst Klett Verlag
Stuttgart Düsseldorf Leipzig

Learning English – Password Orange 6 Grundkurs
für Klasse 10 an Gesamtschulen und anderen differenzierenden Schulformen

von
Anette Christiani, Dortmund; Irene Gagel, Berlin; Geraldine Greenhalgh, Gägelow; Margaret Gutmann, Berlin; Norbert Köhn, Mettmann; Annegret Preker-Franke, Bielefeld; Dietmar Schlinkmann, Bochum; Stephen Speight, Arnsberg; Ulf Degen, Braunschweig; Dorothea Nadzeika-Humbaraci, Elmshorn
unter besonderer Mitwirkung von
William Sears, Stuttgart

Beratende Mitarbeit:
Karl Otto Herd, Gelnhausen

Visuelle Gestaltung:
Christian Dekelver, Weinstadt; Arne Drescher, Stuttgart;

Kassetten und CDs zu diesem Band

Begleitkassette zum Schülerbuch (Klettnummer 546768)
Begleit-CD zum Schülerbuch (Klettnummer 546793)
Für zu Hause und für den Unterricht, mit *Topic*texten und Liedern. Lieferung durch jede Buchhandlung oder, wo dies auf Schwierigkeiten stößt, zuzüglich Portokosten per Nachnahme vom Verlag.

Kassette zum Hörverstehen (Klettnummer 546769)
CD zum Hörverstehen (Klettnummer 546794)
Für den Unterricht mit den Hörverstehenstexten zu den *Topics* im *Schülerbuch* und *Workbook*, zu den *Klassenarbeiten* und den *Materialien zur Freiarbeit*. Lieferung ausschließlich direkt an Lehrerinnen und Lehrer, Schulstempel erforderlich.

Software zu diesem Band
Passend zu diesem Band wird es multimediale Lernprogramme geben. Die Programme werden abwechslungsreiche Übungsformen zu Wortschatz und Grammatik bieten – unterstützt durch Text, Bild und Ton.

1. Auflage   A 1 $^{5\ 4}$ | 2005

Alle Drucke dieser Auflage können im Unterricht nebeneinander benutzt werden, sie sind untereinander unverändert. Die letzte Zahl bezeichnet das Jahr des Druckes.

© Ernst Klett Verlag GmbH, Stuttgart 2000. Alle Rechte vorbehalten.
Internetadresse: http://www.klett-verlag.de

Redaktion: Mark Borrill, Birgit Piefke-Wagner
             Birgit Gruber (Assistenz)

Herstellung: Eckhard Schultze
Layout: Christian Dekelver, Weinstadt
Satz: DTP-Verlag
Umschlaggestaltung: Christian Dekelver, Weinstadt
Reproduktion: Repro Maurer GmbH, Tübingen
Druck: Druckerei Appl, Wemding
ISBN: 3-12-546760-8

Zum Aufbau von Band 6

Hier erhältst du einen Einblick in den Aufbau des sechsten und letzten Bandes von *Password Orange* Grundkurs. Du wirst dich schnell zurechtfinden. Band 6 ist wie Band 5 aufgebaut.

Das Buch hat fünf Topics (siehe Inhaltsverzeichnis, Seite 4–9). Topic bedeutet, dass alles unter einem bestimmten Thema steht.

Jede Topic besteht aus folgenden Teilen:

Einführungsseiten

Am Anfang jeder Topic steht eine Doppelseite mit Bildmaterial zur Einführung ins jeweilige Thema.

Teil A und Teil B

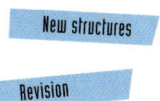

Jede Topic besteht aus zwei Teilen (**A** und **B**), die einen Text (*Reading Corner*) und Aufgaben unter den Rubriken *Words and phrases, Revision* und *New structures* enthalten.

Strategy page

In der Mitte der Topic zwischen dem A- und B-Teil findest du eine *strategy page* mit Tipps zu Fertigkeiten, die du im Umgang mit Texten, dem Wörterbuch usw. brauchst.

Let's check

Am Ende jeder Topic kommt eine *Let's check*-Seite. Hier wiederholst du den neuen Stoff der Topic.

Grammar (ab Seite 82)
Hier kannst du Regeln und Erklärungen zur Grammatik, nach Topics geordnet, nachschlagen und lernen.

Vocabulary (ab Seite 91)
Hier findest du die neuen Wörter jeder Topic.

Dictionary (E-D) (ab Seite 119)
Hier kannst du englische Wörter nachschlagen, die du vergessen hast (es sind alle da von *Password Orange* 1 bis *Password Orange* 6).

Dictionary (D-E) (ab Seite 150)
Das ganze umgekehrt – alle Wörter aus *Password Orange* 1 bis *Password Orange* 6, deutsch-englisch.

Wichtig, wichtig, wichtig!!!

1. Die Reihenfolge der Topics ist beliebig. Es steht euch völlig frei, ob ihr das Buch in der Reihenfolge 1–3–5–4–2 oder 5–1–2–4–3 oder ganz anders durchnehmen wollt. Das ist möglich, weil für jede Topic nur die Vokabeln und Grammatik vorausgesetzt werden, die du bis zum Ende der neunten Klasse gelernt hast.

2. Die beiden folgenden Zeichen verweisen auf andere Stellen im Buch:

   Strategy page 12

   Dieser Pfeil bedeutet, dass du auf Seite 12 eine Arbeitsstrategie findest, die dir die Arbeit an dem Text oder der Übung erleichtert, den/die ihr gerade bearbeitet.

   G3 | p.89

   Dieser Pfeil weist auf die entsprechende Seite im Grammatikanhang hin, auf der die aktuelle Grammatik erklärt bzw. wiederholt wird.

3. Vielleicht möchtet ihr oder eure Lehrerin/euer Lehrer ein Projekt zwischendurch machen. Warum nicht? Im Anhang **Projects** (ab Seite 71) findet ihr allgemeine Angaben zur Projektarbeit und konkrete Ideen für Projekte zu den Topics 2 und 4.

Jetzt hast du den Durch- und Überblick auch für das letzte Jahr mit Password Orange!

INHALTSVERZEICHNIS

	Textsorte	Lernschwerpunkte	Seite

TOPIC 1 — AS AMERICAN AS ...

Photo double page		Comparing life in the U.S.A. and Germany	10

A

Reading corner No time to be real teenagers	Extract from magazine interview	Teenage life in the U.S.A.	12
Revision When Pitt called Lindy	Dialogue	**Revision:** word order	14
Words and phrases Being a teenager in the U.S.A.	Statistics	Talking about statistics	15
Strategy page Reading strategies		Six tips to help with reading	16

B

Words and phrases In the arcade	Dialogue	Some everyday slang	17
Reading corner Cool	Short story	Reading a short story	18
Reading corner About the text		Talking about the story	20
Let's check		Revision	21

	Textsorte	Lernschwerpunkte	Seite

TOPIC 2 GETTING INVOLVED

Picture double page		Talking about a dangerous situation	22

A

Reading corner			
Two incidents	Newspaper/ magazine articles	Two sides of a topic Finding the main points, discussion	24
Words and phrases			
Chat Radio London	Radio phone-in	Making opposites	26
New structures			
Reports		**The passive** (past simple)	27
Strategy page			
Collecting and organizing ideas		Preparing for written work	28

B

Revision			
Speak out for your rights		**Revision:** subsititute verbs (past simple)	29
Reading corner			
Hungry for justice	Story/newspaper	Following a story in two different types of text	30
Words and phrases			
How to react to discrimination	Fact box	What to do if you're treated unfairly	32
Let's check		**Revision**	33

	Textsorte	Lernschwerpunkte	Seite

TOPIC 3 BREAKING DOWN BARRIERS

Photo double page		Talking about Europe	34

A

New structures They came from all over Europe	Registration forms	**Since and for**	36
Words and phrases Where are we going to eat?	Dialogue	Talking about food	37
Reading corner The streets of Niederburg	Story	A story about a difficult situation Finding an end to a story	38
Strategy page What to do when you don't know a word		Strategies for describing things	40

B

Words and phrases Eurotraining	Dialogues	Using fillers	41
Revision The first morning	Dialogues	**Revision:** questions	42
Reading corner On the building site	Story	Retelling a story	43
Let's check		**Revision**	45

	Textsorte	Lernschwerpunkte	Seite

TOPIC 4 LOVE WORRIES

Photo double page		Guessing what people are thinking and saying	46

A

Reading corner All about love	Extract from a book for teens	Talking about advice	48
Words and phrases A love-hate letter	Letter	Making adjectives	50
Revision Problems	Dialogue	**Revision:** negatives in past/present simple	51
Strategy page How to write a poem	Poems	Strategies for writing poems	52

B

Words and phrases Heartline	Personal ads	Adjectives for describing people	53
Reading corner Love, truth and lies	Story	A story with a complicated structure	54
Reading corner About the text		Looking at character	56
Let's check		Revision	57

	Textsorte	Lernschwerpunkte	Seite

TOPIC 5 YOU'RE GOING TO MAKE IT!

Photo double page		Talking about classmates	58

A

Words and phrases			
A few years later	Dialogue	Making telephone calls in English	60
Words and phrases			
Jobs for the boys – and the girls!	Survey	Doing a survey on jobs	61
Reading corner			
Florian meets Joanne	Story	Meeting new people Making a time line for the story	62
Strategy page			
Listening		How to prepare yourself, making notes	64

B

Revision			
Boss for a day	Photo story	**Revision:** reported speech	65
Reading corner			
A problem at the stadium	Picture story	Reworking information	66
Reading corner			
A page of poems	Poems	Write your own poem	68
Let's check		Revision	70

TOPIC 2/4 〈PROJECTS〉

Allgemeine Hinweise zur Projektarbeit	72
Topic 2 Project ideas	74
A project: People who made a difference	76
Topic 4 Project ideas	78
A project: Photo love story	80
Grammar	82
Vocabulary	91
Dictionary (English-German)	119
List of names	145
Dictionary (German-English)	150
Song lyrics	172
List of irregular verbs	176

Zeichenerklärung

> Auf der Begleitkassette/CD zum Schülerbuch (Klettnummer 546768/546793) verfügbar.
>
> Auf der Kassette/CD zum Hörverstehen (Klettnummer 546769/546794) verfügbar. Die Texte sind im Begleitbuch für den Unterricht (Klettnummer 546763) und im Skriptheft (Klettnummer 546761) abgedruckt.
>
> 〈 〉 fakultative Teile/Elemente
>
> ▶ Der Dreieckspfeil weist auf komplexere Aufgaben/Aufgabenteile hin, die sich auch zur Differenzierung nach oben eignen.
>
> GX | p.XX   Der Hinweispfeil verweist auf Erklärungen im Grammatikanhang.
>
> Strategy page XX   Der Hinweispfeil verweist auf Hilfen zur Bearbeitung der Aufgaben.

1 AS AMERICAN AS ...

CONTENTS
- teenage life in the U.S. — p. 12/13
- a story: being part of a group — p. 18/19
- strategy page: reading — p. 16
- revision: word order with adverbial phrases — p. 14
- words and phrases: slang — p. 17
- words and phrases: statistics — p. 15

... cruising around your hometown.

... keeping fit.

DON'T LET THE CRIMINALS WIN! FIGHT FOR YOUR RIGHT TO OWN A GUN!

... owning a gun.

Comparing life in the U.S.A. and Germany

AS AMERICAN AS ...

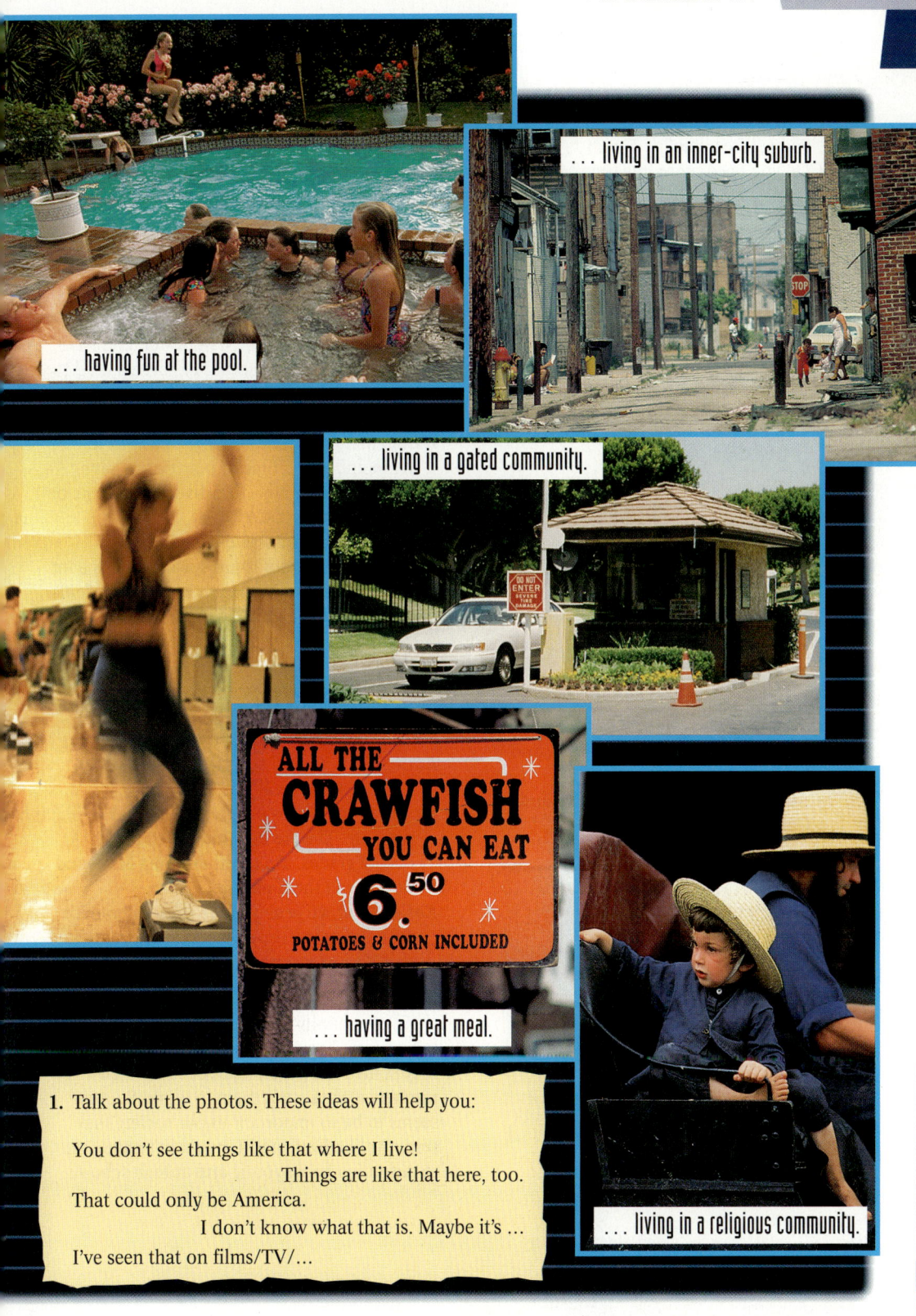

1

... having fun at the pool.

... living in an inner-city suburb.

... living in a gated community.

ALL THE
CRAWFISH
YOU CAN EAT
$6.50
POTATOES & CORN INCLUDED

... having a great meal.

... living in a religious community.

1. Talk about the photos. These ideas will help you:

You don't see things like that where I live!
　　　　　　Things are like that here, too.
That could only be America.
　　　　I don't know what that is. Maybe it's ...
I've seen that on films/TV/...

Comparing life in the U.S.A. and Germany

11

Reading corner
1A AS AMERICAN AS ...

1. Before you read, think:
   a) Why don't some teenagers have enough free time?
   b) Do you need more free time?

   Strategy page 16

2. Are these sentences right or wrong? Correct the wrong sentences.
   a) 1. Katie's parents are divorced.
      2. Her neighborhood is watched by a security guard.
      3. Katie's parents take her everywhere.
      4. Lindy and Katie have a lot of free time.

   b) 1. Janet can walk around where she likes.
      2. She has been hurt by a gang before.
      3. Janet and Coralee do not have much time for their school assignments.
      4. Their moms and dads give them all the money they need.

3. Look at the title again.
   a) What makes it difficult for Katie and Lindy to be 'real teenagers'?
   b) And how is it difficult for Janet and Coralee?

FACT BOX

Headlines from newspapers in the U.S.A. and Germany:

Survey says 40% of American teenagers feel threatened by violence.

Neuere Untersuchungen: Mehrzahl der 15-Jährigen hat Angst vor Gewalt

4. Do you feel threatened by violence? Have you experienced any violence yourself?

I feel/don't feel safe on my way to ...
One day I saw ...   ...

No time to be real teenagers

What is life like for American teenagers today? To answer this question Herald reporter Jon Rosco talked to young people all over the U.S.

I began with Katie and her best friend Lindy, from the middle-class neighborhood of Falls Church, Virginia.

Katie: We live in a gated community ...
Lindy: ... so when you go in or out, you have to pass a security guard. My parents used to take me everywhere, but now I'm sixteen and they have given me my own car.
Katie: Me, too. I get on really well with my mom and dad. Some of our friends have problems at home – like divorced parents or parents who argue a lot.
Lindy: But the atmosphere among the students in school is just great. It helps a lot if you have problems and the other students are interested and listen to you.
Katie: That's right. And there are a lot of things to do at our school. As well as classes there are so many activities and clubs.
Lindy: But the teachers are often too strict. They just never stop!
Katie: Yeah, they always say things like, "You snooze, you lose!".
Lindy: And my parents give me a lot of pressure. They're only interested in my school grades. We're either doing Math and Science all the time ...
Katie: ... or we're getting up early to practice with the swim team. I sometimes get so tired that it's just not much fun.

Katie and Lindy know that they are lucky. The gated community is a good neighborhood, with safe streets. They also do well in school, but they sometimes get stressed because their teachers always want them to work. Success seems to be so important in our society that students like Katie and Lindy don't have time to just enjoy being young and at high school.

AS AMERICAN AS ... Reading corner

1A

After that I talked to Janet and Coralee, from the inner-city suburb of Potrero Hill, San Francisco. Janet and Coralee are also sixteen, but both have divorced parents. They would probably be happy to have Katie and Lindy's problems.

Janet: I sometimes feel I'm a prisoner in my own home. There are girls from school who would beat you up if you walked through their territory, or looked at them in a funny way on the bus.

Coralee: Yeah, that's true. People from a gang have hurt me and my friends. You always think to yourself, dang, I could get killed for no reason.

Janet: Most of the kids at our school have divorced parents or live with their mothers. A few years ago our school was a real help, but now there aren't any after-school programs.

Coralee: And we don't get any money from home, either. If we want anything, we have to get a job after school to pay for it.

Janet: So it's sometimes hard to find time to do our assignments.

Coralee: ... or just go somewhere and hang around with our friends!

Janet and Coralee come from poor families. They seem to be surrounded by violence and they are always worried. Also, they have to work to get money and their schoolwork suffers. They know that without a high school diploma it's going to be hard to get a good job. Like Katie and Lindy, but for very different reasons, Janet and Coralee don't have time to be real teenagers.

▶ 5. What would Katie and Lindy say about kids like Janet and Coralee? And vice versa?

It must be awful for them, because ...   They are so lucky, because ...

6. Jon Rosco also interviewed Matt, a boy from Grand Junction, Nebraska. Listen to the tape of the interview and find the right answers.

   a) Matt's parents work as farmers / run a grocery store / have a clothes store.
   b) At the weekends the kids like to play basketball / go to the movies / have parties.
   c) They also like to go swimming / cruising / ice-skating.
   d) To buy alcoholic drinks you have to be 16 / 18 / 21.
   e) Matt thinks that life in Grand Junction is boring / exciting / interesting.

Revision 1A

AS AMERICAN AS ...

When Pitt called Lindy

"Hello?"

"Hi, is that Lindy?"

Monday	– swim practice
Tuesday	– do assignments
Wednesday	– saxophone lesson
Thursday	– horseback riding club
Friday	– theater club
Saturday	– help Dad (country club)
Sunday	– church (Mom and Dad)

Monday	– do assignments
Tuesday	– dancing lesson
Wednesday	– tennis
Thursday	– go canoeing
Friday	– football practice
Saturday	– help Mom (shopping)
Sunday	– church (Mom and Dad)

1. Look at the two plans. Say who does what extra activity, and when. *Start like this:*
   Lindy has swim practice on Monday.
   On Tuesday ...

   G2/3 | p. 85

2. a) Pitt calls Lindy because he wants a date. Read and listen to the start of the phone call.

   Lindy: Hello?
   Pitt: Hi, is that Lindy? It's me, Pitt.
   Lindy: Pitt? Oh yeah, hi, Pitt.
   Pitt: Okay. Now, Lindy, you know the movie that started in town, 'A Fool in Love'?
   I was thinking, hey, would you like to see it – er – with me? Monday night, maybe?
   Lindy: Wow, Pitt, that would be just great! Oh, but I can't come on Monday. I have swim practice. How about Tuesday?
   Pitt: Tuesday. Wonderful! No, wait a minute! There's something about Tuesdays ... that's it, I have my dancing lesson then. Lindy, can you come on Wednesday ...

   b) Finish the dialogue with a partner. When will Lindy and Pitt see the movie?

   How about ...?   Maybe I could miss ...
   Can you come on ...?

⟨3.⟩ 'Friday on my mind' by Gary Moore. Listen. What will the singer do on Friday? Make a list.

Word order

AS AMERICAN AS ... | Words and phrases

1A

Being a teenager in the U.S.A.

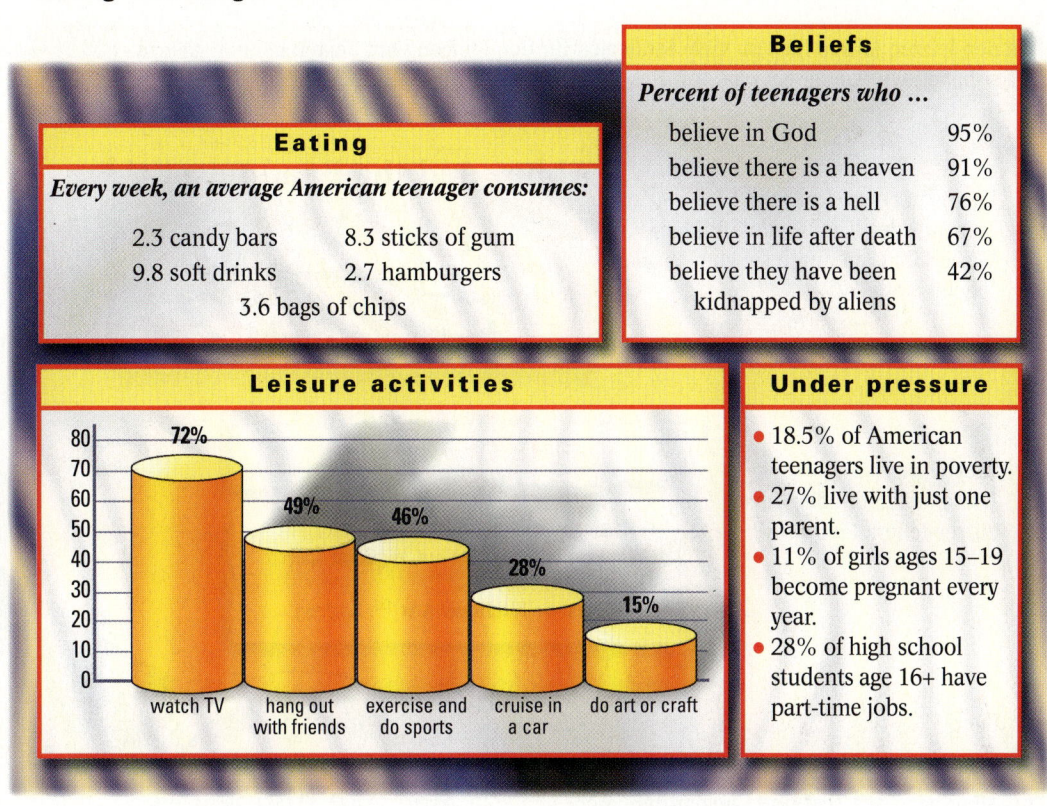

Eating

Every week, an average American teenager consumes:

2.3 candy bars   8.3 sticks of gum
9.8 soft drinks   2.7 hamburgers
3.6 bags of chips

Beliefs

Percent of teenagers who ...

believe in God	95%
believe there is a heaven	91%
believe there is a hell	76%
believe in life after death	67%
believe they have been kidnapped by aliens	42%

Leisure activities

- watch TV: 72%
- hang out with friends: 49%
- exercise and do sports: 46%
- cruise in a car: 28%
- do art or craft: 15%

Under pressure

- 18.5% of American teenagers live in poverty.
- 27% live with just one parent.
- 11% of girls ages 15–19 become pregnant every year.
- 28% of high school students age 16+ have part-time jobs.

1. a) Use these phrases to talk about the statistics. (Not the 'eating' statistics.)

almost	half a quarter	three quarters
more than	a third	two thirds
less than	one/two/three ... out of ten	

Start like this: Almost two out of ten American teenagers live in poverty.

b) Work in a group. Do a survey in your class about the same food as in the American 'eating' statistic. Then find the averages.

c) Compare the 'eating' statistics with your group. *Start like this:* An American teenager ...

That's	more than	we eat/drink.
	about the same as	
	less than	

Talking about statistics

15

Strategy page 1

AS AMERICAN AS ...

READING STRATEGIES

In den letzten Jahren hast du viele Strategien für den Umgang mit Texten kennen gelernt. Hier haben wir wieder ein paar für dich aufgeführt.

1. Bevor du einen Text liest.
   Siehe dir den Titel und die Bilder an.
   Was erfährst du durch sie vom Text?
   Mache Notizen!

   Abbey and the Band to split!

   THE BAND

2. 'Key words'.
   Diese helfen dir, den Text zu verstehen. Finde sie!

   THE TWO TOWERS

   Full screen 256 colour VGA graphics.
   Complete musical score and digitized speech and sound effects.
   Distributed by Electronic Arts ™, England

3. Du suchst nach bestimmten Informationen.
   Überfliege den Text und konzentriere dich nur auf die gewünschten Informationen.
   z. B.: Du willst alles über eine Figur in einer Geschichte wissen. Suche nach den Sätzen, die den Namen dieser Figur enthalten.

   Todd can... ...ing ou... ...re a
   the 'co... ...s leaning aga...
   Ralf... and some of Ralf's
   lan... ...o be like him was wh...
   fri... ...
   To... always wanted.
   Ev... ...g about Ralf was coo...
   the... ...
   wa... e spoke, the way he...
   Even... way he lit a ciga... ...e
   normal... ...dressed li... cool.

4. Weitere Tipps.

| Denke an die vielen englischen Wörter, die als Fremdwörter auch im Deutschen verwendet werden, z. B. Look, Feeling, Styling. Das können auch Teile von Wörtern sein, z. B. durchgestylt, einchecken. | Vergiss nicht, dass du oft schon einen Teil des neuen Wortes oder eines ähnlichen Wortes kennst: enjoyment (to enjoy), to equip (equipment), countryside (country) | Denke auch daran, dass du den Inhalt eines Textes verstehen kannst, ohne dass du jedes Wort nachschlagen musst. Markiere farbig, was du schon verstehst! |

Six tips to help with reading

AS AMERICAN AS ... Words and phrases

1B

In the arcade

> Hi, guys, what's up?
> Hi, Ralf!
> Hey! I wanna play.
> No, cut it out. I ain't through yet.
> Yo! How are you doing, Ralf?
> Okay, take it easy fellas!
> See you guys later.
> C'mon, let's get outa here!

1. Find the phrases in the dialogue which mean …

   … Hello, how are you?   … Goodbye.
   … Don't get so excited! … I want to …
   … I haven't finished yet. … Let's go now.
   … Stop that.   … come on …

2. Make a list of the German phrases which **you** use in situations like these.

3. Work with a partner.
   You are angry with your partner about something. Choose two of the English phrases and make a short dialogue.

Some everyday slang

17

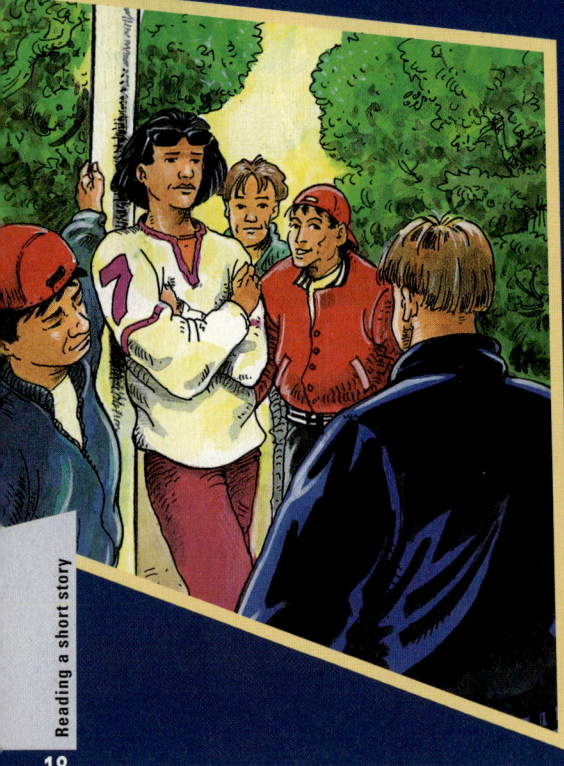

Cool

"Come closer and I'll shoot the crap out of you!" Todd's eyes narrowed as he pulled his shoulders back and stretched out his arm. The gun felt heavy in his hand. It was difficult to keep his arm up. He gazed at the cool-looking figure who stared at him from the mirror and lowered the gun. "Yeah," he thought, "that'll give Ralf the right impression of me – hard ... and cool."

Todd put the gun into the inside pocket of his new dark blue $200 oversized jacket. Thank God his parents had left for the weekend. He could hear his father's voice as he warned him about the family gun. "The gun in this drawer is here for our protection, Todd. Never touch it except in an emergency, when you have to defend yourself or the family." Well, this was sort of an emergency, and he had to defend himself. The guys always laughed at him and he didn't want that again. He would take it with him, just this one time, and make the big impression. Then it would be back in the drawer and his dad would never know. He looked up at the kitchen clock. "God, it's already 10:30!" If he didn't want to be late, he'd have to run.

The night air was cold. Todd's new jacket wasn't as warm as his old one, but that wasn't what counted. He had saved every last cent to buy it and he was really proud. When his mom had seen it she had said, "It's twice your size, Todd, and you look like some kid from the ghetto. You can't wear it!" So his jacket always stayed in the closet ... when his parents were around. As he pulled the jacket tighter around him, he felt the cold metal of the gun through the pocket. Todd was a bit uneasy. What if something went wrong? No, nothing could happen, he'd made sure of that.

Todd came to the park where all the 'cool kids' hung out. He saw Ralf, who was leaning against a lamppost, and some of Ralf's friends. To be like him was what Todd had always wanted. Everything about Ralf was cool – the way he spoke, the way he walked, the way he lit a cigarette. Even if he was dressed like some normal twerp, he'd still look cool. As he walked towards the group, someone said, "Hey, here comes the twerp." He pretended not to hear, but his face turned red. "Twerp?" he thought. He'd show 'em. The gun inside his pocket made him feel strong. Todd pulled back his shoulders and walked over to the group. "What's up?" he asked in his coolest voice. Ralf looked down at him with a half-smile on his face. "Well, looks like we got a problem again tonight, little brother," he said. "Why don't you just go back home, so you don't get hurt." He turned away from Todd and gazed over at the other side of the park.

Through the darkness Todd could see several figures who were walking in their direction. He knew that there were sometimes fights in the park at night. "Was that the 'problem'?" Todd thought and then he saw his chance. "I've got something that'll scare the shit out of 'em," he said. He put his hand into his inside pocket and pulled out the gun. There was a moment of silence. "Where did you get it?" There was admiration in Ralf's voice. Todd felt taller and stronger than he had ever felt before. "From home. It's ours," he said proudly. "Let me see," said Ralf. He looked at it carefully, then smiled. "This'll show the bastards once and for all who's got the say in this park." He looked over towards the figures who were now watching them about 30 yards away. Ralf moved a couple of feet away from his group and called out, cool and commanding. "You wanna play with this for a change, you cowards?" He pointed the gun into the darkness. Ralf was standing there with his arm outstretched and his shoulders pulled back, just like Todd had imagined. Todd took in every word, every movement.

Suddenly there was an explosion. Everyone jumped back. With a look of shock and disbelief, Ralf dropped Todd's gun, then staggered and fell. He lay still in a pool of blood. Shocked, Todd knelt down beside his idol. Then he looked up in desperation and saw the shining metal of another gun. It was pointing in his direction. "God damn!" he screamed. "The gun wasn't even loaded!"

The end of the story

Reading corner 1B

AS AMERICAN AS ...

About the text

1. Finish these sentences to say what happened in the story.
   a) Todd took his dad's gun. He wanted to ...
   b) He put on his new jacket, which he could only wear when ...
   c) He went to the park where Ralf and his friends ...
   d) Ralf and his friends were having problems with ...
   e) Todd proudly showed his gun to Ralf, who ...
   f) Ralf took the gun and pointed it at ...
   g) But suddenly there was an explosion. Ralf ...
   h) A guy from the other group had shot Ralf because ...

2. Explain the sentence 'No, nothing could happen. He'd made sure of that.' (l. 34–35)

3. a) Which phrases fit Todd and which fit Ralf? Make a grid.

   wants to be cool.
   is commanding.
   is like an older brother.
   worries about what other people think of him.
   doesn't like being late.
   does everything in a cool way.
   wants to make a big impression.
   wants to end the argument.

Todd	Ralf
wants to be cool.	...

   b) Now read out all the sentences which fit each person. Do they say everything about them? If not, add more sentences to each list.

4. a) Why did Todd save all his money to buy the jacket?
   b) What clothes are 'cool' in Germany? (How much do you have to pay for 'cool' clothes?)

▶ 5. Could something like this story happen in Germany, too? Work with a partner and say why or why not.

6. Look at these statements from Internet pages about guns in the U.S.A.

   1. In most states, people who want to buy a gun have to wait five days. That's stupid! Most criminals don't buy their guns!

   2. In California, more kids die in shootings than in traffic accidents.

   3. 36,000 Americans are killed in gun incidents every year.

   4. 75% of Americans want to have the right to carry a gun for protection.

   5. Only 11% of gun owners have ever used their guns for protection.

   6. Americans are allowed to carry hidden guns in 31 states. That's dangerous.

   a) Which statements are 'for' the right to own a gun and which are 'against'? Does everyone in the class agree?
   b) Collect the opinions in your class. Should people be allowed to own and carry a gun?

   Strategy page 16

AS AMERICAN AS... Let's check

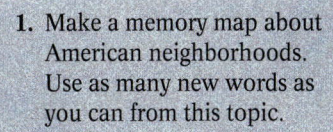

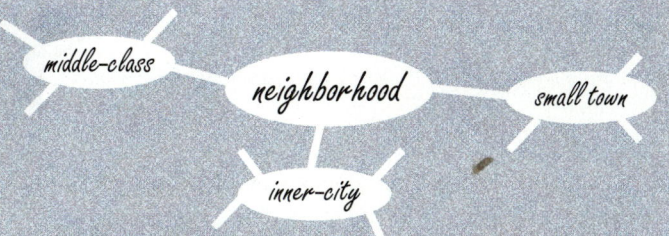

1

1. Make a memory map about American neighborhoods. Use as many new words as you can from this topic.

   middle-class — neighborhood — small town
   |
   inner-city

2. Guns and American teenagers' lives
   Write five sentences about these statistics.

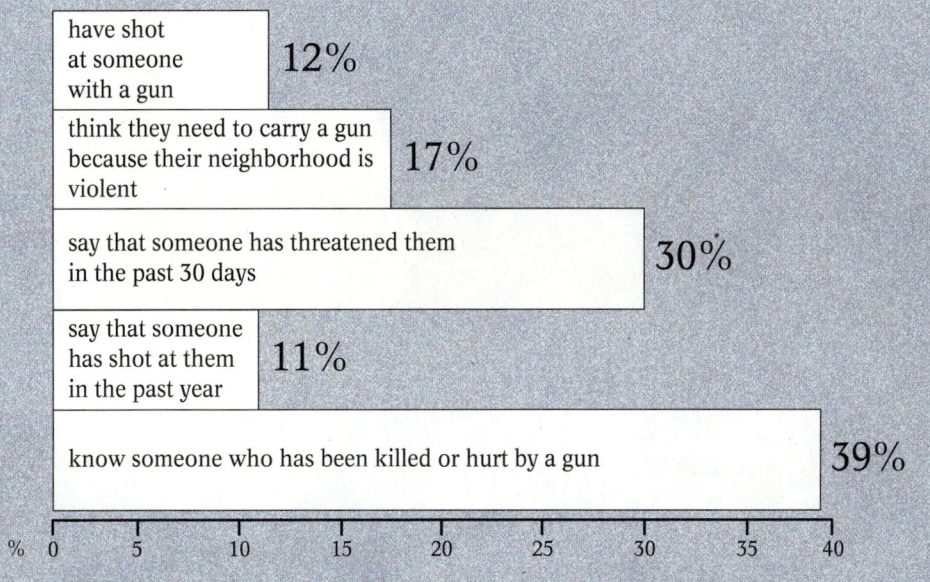

   - have shot at someone with a gun — 12%
   - think they need to carry a gun because their neighborhood is violent — 17%
   - say that someone has threatened them in the past 30 days — 30%
   - say that someone has shot at them in the past year — 11%
   - know someone who has been killed or hurt by a gun — 39%

   Example: More than one out of ten teenagers have shot at someone with a gun.

3. Put the pieces together to make six sentences. If you need help, look back at the topic.

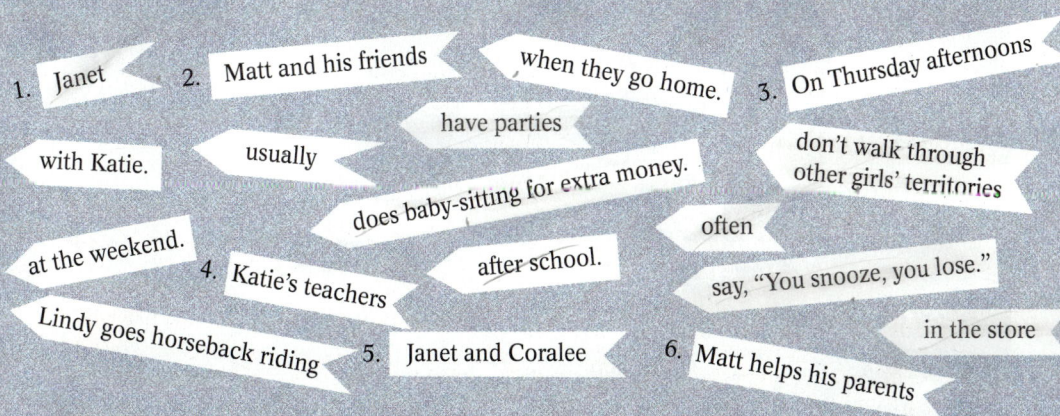

   1. Janet
   2. Matt and his friends
   3. On Thursday afternoons
   4. Katie's teachers
   5. Janet and Coralee
   6. Matt helps his parents

   when they go home.
   with Katie.
   usually
   have parties
   don't walk through other girls' territories
   does baby-sitting for extra money.
   at the weekend.
   often
   after school.
   say, "You snooze, you lose."
   Lindy goes horseback riding
   in the store

   Example: 1. Janet often does baby-sitting for extra money.

The main points of the topic

21

2 GETTING INVOLVED

GETTING INVOLVED

2

CONTENTS

- two violent incidents   p. 24/25
- a true story about discrimination   p. 30/31
- new structures: the passive in the past simple   p. 27
- strategy page: collecting and organizing ideas. p. 28
- revision: substitute verbs in the past simple   p. 29
- words and phrases: making opposites with prefixes   p. 26

1. Work with a partner. Discuss the points below with your partner. Decide on your answers, then present them to the class (pin-board). Look at all of the answers and talk about them in class.

   a) This situation looks dangerous. What shows you that the group of men are aggressive?

   > One has got …   They have all got …
   > … is/are -ing …
   > He looks …   They look …

   b) What do you think is going to happen next?

   > Perhaps he is going to …
   > Maybe they are going to …

   c) What would you do if you were in the situation of the man who is alone?

   > I would feel …
   > I would try to …

Talking about a dangerous situation

Reading corner 2A

GETTING INVOLVED

Two incidents

Read both of these texts first before you look at the exercises.

Rescuer stabbed by violent attacker

LAST NIGHT a young man was stabbed twice in the stomach by a violent attacker when he tried to rescue a woman in a shop doorway. The man is now in Hillcrest Hospital.

Louise Winters, aged 26, was on her way home from work after her late night shift. As she turned the corner into Baker Street, where she lives, a dark-haired man in jeans and a black jacket came out of a shop doorway and grabbed her.

The shop doorway in Baker Street where Louise Winters was attacked

"I was so frightened I couldn't scream," Ms Winters told us. She was pushed back into the shop doorway by the attacker and was told not to struggle. "He held a knife to my throat and said he would kill me if I moved," she continued.

Then a young man appeared on the other side of the street and Ms Winters suddenly found her voice again. She screamed loudly.

"The young man heard my scream and stopped. He shouted something and ran to the doorway. There was a struggle between the two men for a few seconds and then the attacker ran away. The young man was lying on the ground, moaning. I ran to him, and saw that he had blood all over his shirt. My attacker had stabbed him instead of me."

Ms Winters phoned the police from a nearby callbox and stayed with the young man until they arrived. The young man was later identified as Mr Malcolm Sanders, aged 17, of 33, Taunton Way. He was treated immediately by the emergency services and was then taken to hospital. Ms Winters was unhurt but was treated for shock.

Our reporter was able to interview Mr Sanders in hospital for a few moments, late this morning. "I was coming home from the cinema," he said. "Then I heard a horrible scream. I saw a man and a woman in a shop doorway. I knew immediately that the woman was in trouble. The man was tall and looked strong. I didn't think, I just had to do something. Then I felt a terrible pain in my stomach and fell down. That's all I remember. But when I woke up in hospital, I was given some flowers and a beautiful 'thank you' card from a lady called Louise Winters. She's coming to visit me next week."

"This young man saved my life," said Ms Winters. "A lot of people wouldn't want to get involved if they saw somebody in trouble late at night." Ms Winters is correct. Statistics show that only one person in ten would be willing to help someone

---

Two sides of a topic

24

GETTING INVOLVED — **Reading corner 2A**

Got a problem to share? Tell YOUR story here!

I STILL FEEL ASHAMED

I've never wanted to be a hero but I didn't think I was a coward. Now I'm not so sure. I was sitting on the tube last Saturday afternoon. I remember we were at a station when a man got on. He was about forty, and he had blond hair. He went and sat opposite a young guy, who was wearing a denim jacket. A few minutes later the older man said, "Can you take your feet off the seat, please? They're touching my coat." The young man stood up quickly and threatened the other man. "Who do you think you are?" he shouted. "I'm just asking you to move your feet, that's all," the older man said. "Leave me alone or you're in trouble." The young man was red in the face and I think he was drunk. They were both standing up now, and the young man was looking more and more angry. I had the feeling that something terrible was going to happen. I looked around at the other passengers. They were all looking away, reading their newspapers, embarrassed. I wanted to do something, but instead I just looked up at the ads above the window opposite. Suddenly the drunk guy hit the older man in the stomach, really hard. He fell onto a seat and held his stomach. Still nobody did anything. The train was coming into the next station and when the doors opened, the drunk guy got off and just walked away. The older man got up, too, and staggered to the doors. As the train started to move again, I saw him on the platform. He was still holding his stomach. I felt ashamed, and I still feel that way now.

Jeremy Fisher

1. **The facts**
   Louise Winters and Jeremy Fisher both talked to the police about what happened to them. Make a police report card for each incident and fill in the details. You don't need to write full sentences.

   Report card
   Reported by: Louise Winters
   Time of incident: ...
   Place: ...
   What happened: – ...
                  – ...
   Description of suspect: – ...
                           – ...

2. 'You should always get involved when you see this sort of thing.'
   Work with a partner. One person agrees, the other disagrees.
   Use the ideas to make full sentences.

   I agree because
   I disagree because

   - difficult to decide quickly
   - more and more violence
   - you might be attacked, too
   - might be me next time
   - job of the police
   - attackers are often cowards
   - no time to think, just have to do something

▶ 3. A week later Louise went to visit Malcolm in hospital. What did they say to each other? Write a dialogue.

Finding the main points, discussion

Words and phrases — GETTING INVOLVED
2A

Chat Radio London

Chat Radio London is a station with lots of phone-ins, news, advice and information. This evening's phone-in discussion is about young people on school buses.

A lot of kids have a hard time every day before school even starts – on the bus! Phone Chat Radio London and tell us what you think.

On our bus there's a group of older kids who bully the younger ones. The teachers aren't there and the drivers aren't interested. It's unfair!

I really dislike kids who put their bags on the seat next to them. If you can't sit down, it's impossible to do your homework on the bus!

The drivers are really unfriendly and the buses are always too crowded.

I disagree with the last caller. My dad is a bus driver and he is never horrible to kids! He says that the kids are often impolite to him!

1. Opposites.
   Read what the callers say and find all the words which begin with 'un-', 'im-', and 'dis-'. Find the original word for each one and make a grid like this.

Opposites			
original word	un-	im-	dis-
possible	–	impossible	–
...			

2. a) Now use 'un-', 'im-', and 'dis-' to make words which mean the same as the ones on the left.
   Example: false = untrue

   can't be done, false ✓, hate, go away, rude, sad, boring

   im-, un-, dis-

   polite, like, true ✓, appear, happy, interesting, possible

   b) Use each word in a sentence.

Making opposites

GETTING INVOLVED — New structures

2A

Reports

1. Look at the newspaper report on page 24 again.
   a) Find the parts of the text which mean the same as these phrases.
      Example: a violent attacker stabbed a young man twice in the stomach
      a young man was stabbed twice in the stomach by a violent attacker (lines 1–3)

      1. the attacker pushed her back
      2. and told her not to struggle
      3. the police identified the man later as
      4. the emergency services treated him
      5. someone gave him some flowers

   > **Tip**
   > The passive past simple tense
   > was / were + 3rd form

   b) Look at the sentences you found for 1 and 4 again. What word comes before the person who did the action?

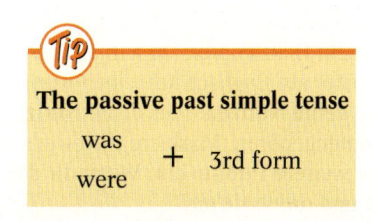

   G4 | p. 86

2. Rosalind Davis works for the Catford Gazette, a local newspaper in London. Every Sunday night Rosalind makes a list of last week's most interesting local stories for the Monday back page.

   a) Look at her notes for this week.

   Monday – A 12-year-old pupil won a Maths prize.
   Tuesday – Somebody stole £48,000 from a bank in Crewe Road.
   Wednesday – The government introduced a tough new law to clean up tube trains.
   Thursday – Camden Allstars beat Catford Cannons 48-44 in a basketball thriller.
   Friday – Marks and Spencer opened a new department store in Lawson Street.
   Saturday – A dog attacked a three-year-old girl in Richmond Park.

   The week in view
   # Last week's BIG stories

   b) Now use the passive past simple tense to write the list as a report.
      Example: On Monday a Maths prize **was won** by a star 12-year-old pupil.

   c) Write a list like Rosalind's for your school or area last week.

3. 'Behind the wall' by Tracy Chapman.
   a) Look at these words and phrases and then listen to the song. Don't look at the lyrics. Six of the words and phrases are in the song. Note them down.

   | struggle | ambulance | screaming | come late | love | bedroom |
   | neighbours | | attack | man and his wife | sleepless night | call the police |

   b) The singer has sleepless nights because of her violent neighbours. She gets involved. Does it help? Give a reason for your answer.

   The passive (past simple)

… Strategy page — GETTING INVOLVED

COLLECTING AND ORGANIZING IDEAS

Diese Strategy page gibt euch Hinweise auf die Vorbereitung schriftlicher Aufgaben. Ihr könnt sie alleine, in Partnerarbeit oder in Gruppen bearbeiten.
Bevor du etwas schreiben kannst (einen Brief, einen kleinen Aufsatz, einen Kommentar oder Ähnliches), musst du deine Ideen und Gedanken sammeln und strukturieren.

1. **Mache Notizen zu deinem Thema.** Notiere alles, was dir zu deinem Thema einfällt, ungeordnet auf ein Blatt Papier. Du kannst dies auf Deutsch tun, aber denke daran, dass du deinen Text später auf Englisch schreiben wirst und die Notizen übersetzen musst.
2. **Ordne deine Notizen.** Lies deine Notizen noch einmal durch und überlege, welche Ideen zusammengehören. Markiere sie jeweils in einer Farbe.
3. **Ordne weitere Punkte ein.** Wenn dir dabei weitere Gedanken zum Thema einfallen, füge sie hinzu und ordne sie ein.
4. **Bestimme die Reihenfolge deiner Notizen.** Schreibe die in einer Farbe markierten Notizen heraus und versuche sie in eine sinnvolle Reihenfolge zu bringen.
5. **Schreibe deine Notizen in richtigen Sätzen aus.** Jetzt kannst du die einzelnen Gedanken ausformulieren. Dabei achte auf die Art von Text, die von dir verlangt wird.

Work with a partner or in groups of three. Look at the opinions about teenagers on school buses on page 26. A magazine has printed them, too.

You have read the article. Now you want to talk about it and say what you think.

Step 1

older kids/younger kids   bags on seats
crowded   impolite   never horrible
can't do homework   unfriendly   bully
drivers   no teachers

Add your own ideas to these.

Step 2

Which ideas belong together?
You can group them in a grid like this:

bullies	homework	drivers	reasons

Step 3

Is your opinion in the grid? If it isn't, note it down.

Step 4

These are the parts of your report:

a) older kids bully younger kids
b) bags on seats
c) drivers and schoolkids
d) reasons
e) your opinion

Are you happy with this order?
If you aren't, change it.

Step 5

You can begin like this:
   I read the article about teenagers on school buses. I think some kids …

Use these phrases, too.

> I think/I don't think/In my opinion…
> I agree with/I disagree with … for the following reasons:
> First of all … secondly/and then …
> finally/last of all
> The real problem is …
> And that's why …

Preparing for written work

GETTING INVOLVED · Revision **2B**

Speak out for your rights

You are going to read a true report about discrimination. Here is some background information.

Until 1964 there was official race discrimination in some parts of the U.S.

1. What was life like for blacks? Look at the pictures and say what blacks …

   had to do.   G5 | p. 87
   weren't able to do.
   weren't allowed to do.

   Examples:
   They had to sit in different waiting rooms.
   They weren't allowed to use the same entrances as whites.

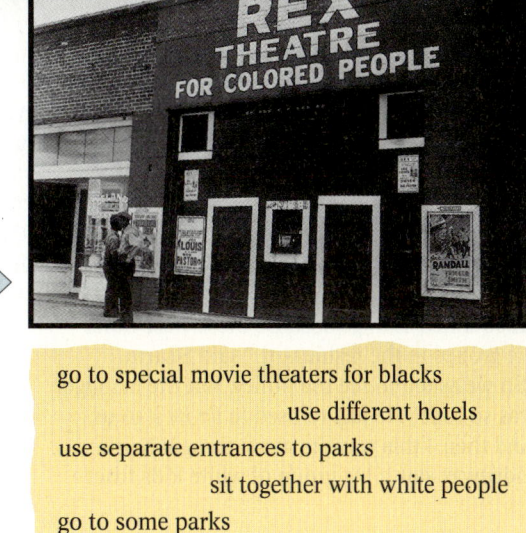

   go to special movie theaters for blacks
   use different hotels
   use separate entrances to parks
   sit together with white people
   go to some parks

This all changed because people got involved, people like Martin Luther King. They fought to get equal rights for black people.

So today there isn't any discrimination against black people in the U.S. Or is there? Look at the next two pages.

← Martin Luther King speaking at a demonstration in Chicago in 1960.

Substitute verbs (past simple)

29

Reading corner — GETTING INVOLVED
2B

Hungry for justice

1. Before you read, look at the pictures and remember what you found out on page 29. What do you think the text is going to be about?

"I still just can't believe it!" Sharra Clausell shouted as she opened the door to her family's apartment in downtown San Jose, California. "Not so loud, Sharra," her brother Kenny told her. "It's after midnight. You'll wake Mom and Dad." But it was too late. "What's up, honey?" their mother called down the hall. "Hey, what's going on here?" asked their father as he came out of the bedroom. "You look real upset, both of you." The children – Sharra was 16 and Kenny 19 – were ordinary teenagers, full of dreams and crazy ideas and everyday problems. But the Clausells knew that tonight something was wrong.

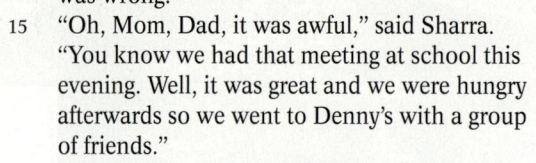

"Oh, Mom, Dad, it was awful," said Sharra. "You know we had that meeting at school this evening. Well, it was great and we were hungry afterwards so we went to Denny's with a group of friends."

"Yeah, we all wanted to celebrate," continued Kenny. "But then the manager stopped us at the door. He said we had to pay a sitting fee before the meal, and that we had to sit in small groups."

"It sounded strange because there were other big groups in the restaurant," said Sharra. "So we asked to see the policy. But the manager was so rude! He just refused to show it to us. And then – this was the worst thing – Kristina Ridgeway saw a big group of white kids from tenth grade at another table. She asked them if they had to pay a sitting fee and they said no. We knew it was discrimination." Sharra's voice was shaking as she ended.

"So what did you do?" asked Mr Clausell. "Oh, we were all angry, but we just walked out. On the way home Kristina told us about how her dad was arrested in the 60s when he ate at a bar for white people. But they just can't treat us like that now, can they?"

The Clausells looked at each other and shook their heads. "No, kids, they can't," said Mrs Clausell. "We're going to call the Ridgeways right now, and together, we're going to do something about this!"

2. Put the sentences into the right order to describe the students' evening.

> They have a meeting at school.   The students feel happy and hungry.
> They go to a restaurant together.   They aren't allowed to sit together.
> There is a large group of white kids.   Their parents want to do something about it.
> Sharra and Kenny arrive home.   They talk to their mom and dad.
> Kristina talks about her dad.   Sharra and her friends walk out.   The manager is very impolite.

Start with: They have a meeting after school.

GETTING INVOLVED   Reading corner
2B

3. Work in groups. Sharra and her friends wrote to the media about what happened. What points did they put in the letter?
   a) Collect your ideas for the letter.
   b) Now write the letter to the San Jose Chronicle Herald Sun.

   > Strategy page 28

▶ 4. Has anything like this ever happened to you or somebody you know? Tell the story. How did you or they react?

5. Now read the newspaper report and find out what happened to the Clausells and their friends.

DISCRIMINATION COSTS DENNY'S $46 MILLION

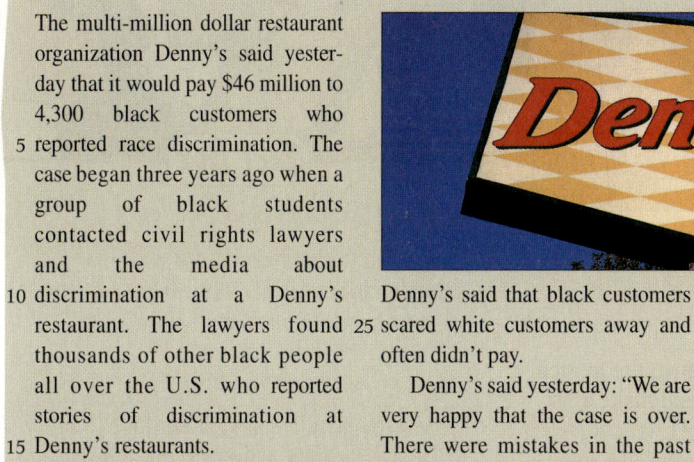

The multi-million dollar restaurant organization Denny's said yesterday that it would pay $46 million to 4,300 black customers who
5 reported race discrimination. The case began three years ago when a group of black students contacted civil rights lawyers and the media about
10 discrimination at a Denny's restaurant. The lawyers found thousands of other black people all over the U.S. who reported stories of discrimination at
15 Denny's restaurants.

A Denny's manager told the lawyers that workers were trained to discriminate against blacks. They could ask them for a sitting
20 fee, give tables to white customers before black customers, or just tell black customers that the restaurant was closed. The reason?

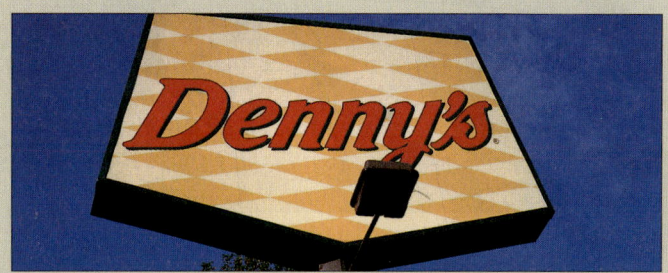

Denny's said that black customers
25 scared white customers away and often didn't pay.

Denny's said yesterday: "We are very happy that the case is over. There were mistakes in the past
30 but Denny's is different now. We will soon have more black managers, and of course black customers are welcome." There were so many bad stories about
35 Denny's that people didn't want to eat there and it was losing money.

Also very happy are Sharra Clausell and her brother Kenny, two
40 of the students from the original case. "We're proud that we finally have justice," she told reporters. "But the case has also changed how we think about America. I didn't
45 think about race discrimination before all this happened, but now it seems to be everywhere. Here's my advice to other teenagers: speak out when you see that something is
50 wrong. Never keep quiet about discrimination!"

6. Look at these headings for each of the four paragraphs in the report. Choose the best heading for each paragraph.

   Paragraph 1
   a) Denny's to pay black students
   b) 4,300 customers reported discrimination

   Paragraph 2
   a) Reasons for discrimination
   b) Trained to discriminate

   Paragraph 3
   a) The case is over
   b) Denny's agrees to change

   Paragraph 4
   a) Proud student tells others to speak out
   b) Sharra and Kenny are happy

7. How has the case changed Sharra? Find the answer in the report.

Words and phrases GETTING INVOLVED

2B

How to react to discrimination

... and don't come back!

Some kids were thrown out of the shopping mall yesterday.

1. What can you do if you think you're treated unfairly? Look at the ideas and make a list of *dos and don'ts*.

   > speak out   collect names of witnesses
   > find out if it's really discrimination
   > stay cool   get angry
   > write a letter to the organization
   > stay quiet and hope it doesn't happen again
   > write to a newspaper
   > be rude to managers   get violent
   > threaten other people physically
   > write down what happened
   > react before you're sure of your rights

dos	don'ts
collect witnesses	...

FACT BOX

Getting justice in the U.S.

The Civil Rights Act of 1964 made discrimination illegal. However, you have to speak out if you're treated unfairly. What is illegal discrimination? Here are some examples:

– A video arcade allows other kids to enter in large groups. Only two black kids can go in together.
– A store's policy is that Hispanic kids are followed by a security guard and other kids are not.
– A teacher says racist things about a student.

2. Sort the ideas in your *dos* list.
   a) What do you do in the situation?
   b) What do you do afterwards?

   > Start like this: First you ...
   >   Then you ...
   >   After that you ...

3. What do you think happened at the mall? Work in groups. Collect ideas, then act the scene at the shopping mall in class.

GETTING INVOLVED   Let's check

2

1. You have heard British English and American English in this topic. But can you hear the difference? Listen to these four people and note down 'BE' or 'AE' for each one.

2. a) Write passive sentences about the people from part A of the topic.

Malcolm	A forty-year-old man	rescue / at night	beat / 44-48
	A three-year-old girl	attack / by / dog	
Louise	Catford Cannons	hit / on the tube	stab / in the stomach

   Start like this: Malcolm was stabbed in the stomach.

   b) Do the same thing with these, from part B.

   Workers at Denny's   give / $46 million
   4,300 black customers   Kristina's dad   arrest / in the 60s   train / to discriminate
   Sharra and her friends   ask / to pay a sitting fee

3. Fill in the gaps with 'un-', 'im-' or 'dis-' and the word at the end.

   a) "It's ... to walk home alone at night in big cities."   (possible)
      "I ...! You just have to be a bit careful."   (agree)
   b) "That poor man! He was really ... that Saturday afternoon."   (lucky)
      "That's right! He wasn't even ... to the other guy."   (polite)
   c) "A lot of bus drivers ... the way teenagers talk to them on the bus."   (like)
      "Yes, but maybe bus drivers are sometimes ..., too."   (friendly)

4. Discrimination.
   Sort the words and phrases into two lists.

   speak out   separate doors
   ...   contact lawyer
   sitting fee fight   tell the press
   treat people unfairly   'whites only'

discrimination	what you can do
sitting fee	...

3 BREAKING DOWN BARRIERS

BREAKING DOWN BARRIERS

CONTENTS
- a misunderstanding?   p. 38/39
- two girls on a building site   p. 43/44
- revision: answering questions   p. 42
- strategy page: when you don't know a word   p. 40
- new structures: for and since   p. 36
- words and phrases: food   p. 37
- words and phrases: fillers   p. 41

1. Travelling in Europe, now and in the past. Talk about the photos.

   Now   you can …
            you don't have to …

   In the past   you had to …
               you weren't allowed to …

2. Write down five questions for a quiz about Europe. Use these and your own ideas.

   What's the fastest way to get from … to … ?

   What colours are in …'s flag?

   What country's capital city is …?

   What country has … as its car nationality plate?

   …

⟨3.⟩ 'Single' by Pet Shop Boys. Listen. Which of these is not mentioned in the song?

the singer's hotel   his computer

his mobile phone   going to the airport

Talking about Europe

35

New structures 3A

BREAKING DOWN BARRIERS

Niederburg jetzt auf Marathon-Weltkarte

Halbmarathon in Niederburg

Im Rahmen unseres internationalen Stadtfestes, mit seiner nunmehr 10-jährigen Tradition, findet am Sonntag, dem 4. Mai, der 1. Niederburger Halbmarathon statt. Dieser einzigartige Laufwettbewerb über ca. 21 km wurde gemeinsam mit unseren Partnern in England und Frankreich geplant. Die Europäische Union unterstützt diese Aktion mit einer erheblichen Summe.

Unsere Anzeigenkampagne hat eine wahre Anmeldelawine ausgelöst. Wir rechnen mit über 600 Teilnehmern. Seit Wochen e...

They came from all over Europe

There were registration forms for the half marathon in lots of magazines for runners and on the Internet. Three of the forms looked like this:

Name: Wayne Evans
Address: 34 Dunraven Road, Swansea, Wales
Age: 16
Running experience: I have been in training for 18 months now. I have run three half marathons since last summer. But I haven't run in a race outside Britain yet. When I am 18 I'd like to take part in a full marathon. I am looking forward to meeting runners from Germany and other countries.

```
Name: Maria Sanchez
Address: 127 Calle de las Carmelas, Salamanca, Spain
Age: 17
Running experience: I have been a member of the local
athletics club for six years and junior ten thousand
metres champion for the last two years. I have taken
part in competitions in France for two years - the
last one was a half marathon. I have been in training
since last spring.
```

Name: Kirsten Sørensen
Address: Husbyvej 19, Fjerritslev, Denmark
Age: 17
Running experience: I have jogged with my dad since I was little. Since last autumn I have been more serious about my running. I often run about 15 km and would like to try a longer race.

1. Look at what the runners say about their experience. Find the sentences with 'since' and 'for'. Make a grid, like this:

since	for
since last summer	...

TIP

since/for = seit
since 1995 = seit 1995 ← Zeitpunkt
for two weeks = seit zwei Wochen ← Zeitraum

G6 | p. 88

2. Who do you think will do best in the half marathon? Why?

3. Make a registration form for an international competition or festival. It can be like the forms on this page. Your partner has to fill in the form.
   Here are some ideas ...

   ... for the competition or festival:

   Battle of the bands   Swimming competition

   23rd international
   go-karting festival   ...   Mastercook

   ... for the 'experience' part of the form:

I have	played ... swum cooked been go-karting ...	since ... for ...

Since and for

BREAKING DOWN BARRIERS **Words and phrases**

3A

Where are we going to eat?

Wir empfehlen heute:

Spätzle mit Rostbraten
Sauerbraten mit Beilagen
Gulasch mit Reis
Schweinshaxe
Kutterscholle mit Salzkartoffeln
Eiskarte

Zum Schwarzen Ferkel

RESTAURANT ISTAMBUL

McDo

CHINA GARDEN

POSEIDON-GRILL

Bella Italia

Maria Sanchez is staying with Corinna Neumann. Corinna is a member of the TV Niederburg and is going to take part in the race, too. Two days before the race they go into town together for a meal.

Corinna: Where would you like to eat, Maria? You're our guest, so you can choose.
Maria: I'm in Germany, so I would like to try some German food, please – but I don't know any of the words. What is or are Spätzle, please?
Corinna: Spätzle – well, they're a kind of pasta – noodles.
Maria: Mmm. That sounds good. But how about Rostbraten?
Corinna: That's beef which is cooked in a special way.

chicken, pork, beef, fish, gravy, potatoes, rice, pasta, carrots, peas, beans, cabbage

1. Continue the conversation with a partner.
   Maria asks about the other dishes on the board. How can Corinna answer? Use the list of food words.

2. a) Think of the meals which you like – and make a menu for a restaurant.
   b) Work with a partner. Ask about the dishes on his/her menu. Can he/she explain what they are?

Waiter! What's this fly doing in my soup?

I think it's doing the breast stroke!

Strategy page 40

Talking about food

37

Reading corner 3A — BREAKING DOWN BARRIERS

The streets of Niederburg

Wayne felt great after the half marathon. Forty-fifth place, out of six hundred runners! He could hardly believe it. And in the evening after the race there was a big party for all the runners. That was good fun, too. He talked for a long time to a very friendly German girl, Corinna. And there was also a Danish girl, Kirsten, and Maria from Spain. Maria was staying with Corinna's family.

The next day Wayne went to the town centre. He had agreed to meet the three girls and a couple of guys from Berlin outside the Arbeitsamt in the main square at eleven o'clock. He was a bit early, so he just walked from street to street. Germany was so clean and tidy, and there were so many pretty old buildings, not like in Swansea! And the people were so kind. It was amazing how everyone in Germany learned English at school and could speak it so well. Wayne laughed as he thought of his French lessons at school. He hadn't tried very hard and now he couldn't even remember how to say 'hello'. Somebody else laughed, too, and Wayne looked up. Three lads – short hair, jeans, T-shirts, big boots – were standing in front of him. They were looking at him, and they weren't smiling. Suddenly Wayne felt a bit nervous. He looked round and saw that he wasn't in the town centre any more. Or at least there weren't any shops in this street. He didn't really know where he was. It was a narrow street, more like an alley. Wayne saw that there were some garages at the end of it. It wasn't a pretty street. It was a dead end.

"Er, hi," began Wayne. "Do you speak English? I'm sort of lost. I'm looking for the town centre, er, the Arbeitsamt?"

A story about a difficult situation

One of them was behind him now. Wayne looked round and saw that there was nobody else in the little street. "Arbeitsamt?" said one of them. Then he said something in German to the others and they all laughed. Wayne laughed, too, but suddenly the others all stopped. The three – were they boys or men? – came nearer, and the one in front of him said something else in German, and pointed at Wayne. He was talking half to Wayne, half to the others. Wayne thought he understood the word 'job'. Then he noticed the design on one of the German guys' T-shirt. He didn't like it. Was that a knife in the taller one's jeans pocket?

Perhaps they hadn't got jobs, Wayne thought. Perhaps they thought he wanted a job here! He said quickly, "Hey, listen, don't get me wrong. I'm not trying to find a job here, no, of course not. I can't speak German or anything, that would be crazy. No, I'm just here for a few days, for the half marathon, you know? I wanted to meet some friends outside the Arbeitsamt, in the main square. And now I'm lost."
Wayne stopped. Nobody said anything.
"Look, don't get me wrong. I'm from South Wales. There are no jobs there, either, no future. There's nothing to do except hang around on the streets. It's the same thing, do you know what I mean? Do you understand?"

The three German guys looked at him, and then at each other. Silence. Wayne didn't even know if they understood English. He didn't know what to do. "Look, I'm not a fighter, me. Okay? If you want to beat me up, just do it, yeah? Are you going to do that?"

1. Finish the sentences to make a summary of the story.
   Example: a) Wayne is happy because he was forty-fifth in the race.

   a) Wayne is happy because ... (line 2)
   b) He enjoys ... (lines 3–6)
   c) He is going to meet his friends ... (lines 10–13)
   d) But then he sees ... (lines 24–26)
   e) He doesn't know ... (lines 30–31)
   f) He tells them that he is trying to ... (lines 36–37)
   g) They think that he ... (lines 40–48)
   h) Wayne tells them that he isn't..., he is just ... (lines 55–58)
   i) At the end he tells them that they can ... (lines 72–73)

2. What does the story tell us about Wayne? Make notes about him in a grid.

Wayne	
sport:	running
languages:	...
home town:	...
ideas about Germany:	...
...	

3. Work in a group of three or four. Make a radio play or a film scene of the story. First collect your ideas. Then write the dialogue. Start at the moment Wayne sees the three German guys. What did they say to him? What will they say and do when Wayne asks his question at the end? (Remember – the story can have a happy ending!)

▶ 4. "There will always be trouble between the young people who live in a place and the young tourists who come to visit it."
   Do you agree? Give a reason for your answer.

Strategy page 3 — BREAKING DOWN BARRIERS

WHAT TO DO WHEN YOU DON'T KNOW A WORD

Wenn du in einem Gespräch bist und ein Wort nicht kennst, kannst du nicht einfach in einem Wörterbuch nachschlagen. Aber das ist kein Grund, plötzlich zu schweigen. Wenn du diese Strategien übst, bist du gut gewappnet, wenn du ein unbekanntes Wort brauchst. Hier geht es nicht darum, stilistisch feines Englisch zu sprechen, sondern sich verständlich auszudrücken.

1. **Personen- und Gegenstandsbeschreibung**
   Hierzu kannst du folgende Wendungen gebrauchen:

   … the stuff which … (für etwas, was man nicht zählen kann z. B. Flüssigkeiten, Stoffe usw.)
   Example: (Schnee) There was a lot of the white stuff which falls in winter.

   … the thing/things (you need) to … (für etwas, was man zählen kann)
   Example: (Messer) Can I have the thing you need to cut meat?

   … the tool/tools (you use) to … (für Werkzeuge)
   Example: (Hammer) Please give me the tool you use to hit nails.

   … equipment (you need) to … (für technische Gegenstände, Ausrüstungen usw.)
   Example: (Warndreieck) We haven't got the equipment you need to put on the road when your car won't go.

2. **Unbekannte Begriffe**
   Umschreibe sie mit einem Relativsatz (mit *who, which*).
   Examples: (Vegetarier) He's someone who doesn't eat meat.
   (Zahnbürste) I've forgotten the thing which I use to clean my teeth.

3. **Adjektive**
   Versuche das Gegenteil verneint auszudrücken.
   Example: (schmutzig) My shoes are not clean.

4. **Schwierige Sachverhalte**
   Sag's mit dir ganz vertrauten Verben
   (do, make, take, bring, go, get, have, find, see, say, give, think etc.).
   Examples: Unsere Lehrerin hat uns ihre Zustimmung verweigert.
   Our teacher said that we couldn't do it.
   Ich will mich im Restaurant über das Essen beschweren.
   I want to say that the food wasn't good.

Now try to find an alternative for the German word in these sentences.

1. I need a … er … (Säge).
2. Oh, no! Where's my … er … (Geldbeutel)?
3. Can I have some … er … (Möbelpolitur) for this table?
4. Kirsten was … er … (ruhig) … before the half marathon.

BREAKING DOWN BARRIERS — Words and phrases

3B

Eurotraining

The Eurotraining scheme is for young people from European countries who are doing their apprenticeship. They get the chance to do work experience for six weeks somewhere in Europe. So they get training and they can also meet young people from other countries. Usually most of them know English from school.

Alassio is a seaside town in Northern Italy. Some young people are going to work together on a large building site.

1. Listen. Four teenagers are at the hostel where they are going to stay while they are on the scheme.

   a) What are their names?
   b) Where are they from?

2. On the way to the pizzeria Patrick asks Kathleen about her journey.

   Patrick: Well , what was so awful about your journey?
   Kathleen: You know , it took nearly two days. The train from Waterford to Dublin was late and I almost missed my plane to Milan. Anyway , I was the last person on the plane and everyone looked at me sort of angrily.
   Patrick: Oh yes, I know that feeling. But you got to Milan okay?
   Kathleen: Right! Anyway , the plane was late. And when we finally landed, I couldn't get to the station in time for the train to Alassio.
   Patrick: But there was another train, wasn't there?
   Kathleen: Yeah, the next day. Sleeping in a station isn't fun, you know !
   Patrick: Oh, I see . You poor thing!
   Kathleen: And the train this morning kind of stopped at every station from Milan to Alassio, you know what I mean ?
   Patrick: Well , here's the pizzeria.

   ### Füllwörter (fillers)

   In der gesprochenen Sprache findest du (im Dialog markiert) einige Ausdrücke, die keine spezielle Bedeutung haben. Sie dienen unter anderem dazu, Denkpausen zu überbrücken. Wenn du diese Füllwörter beim Sprechen verwendest, klingen die Gespräche natürlicher.

   Make a list of the fillers in the dialogue for the next exercise.

3. Work with a partner. Read this dialogue. Add some fillers in five or six places to make it sound more natural. Then act the dialogue in class.

   Meike: Antanas, what job do you do on building sites?
   Antanas: I'm an electrician. What about you?
   Meike: I'm a plumber.
   Antanas: What's that? What do you have to do?
   Meike: I put in the pipes for washbasins, baths and toilets.
   Antanas: But that's not a job for a girl! You have to be strong and it's a dirty job.
   Meike: That's not really true any more. Lots of pipes are made of plastic these days. And you can always wash the dirt off! Plumbing is very technical these days. You need to be able to think!
   Antanas: I don't think …
   Meike: Yes, **that's** your problem!

Revision 3B

BREAKING DOWN BARRIERS

The first morning

It is the first morning at the building site. The people on the scheme are talking to Signora Nencini, the programme coordinator. Now they have the chance to ask her some questions.

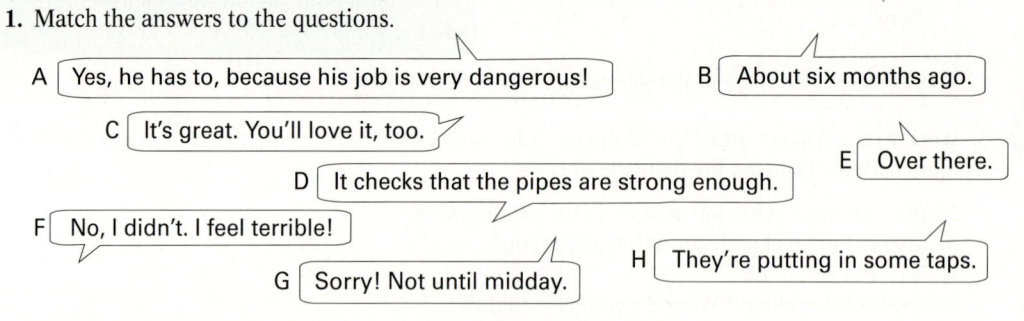

1. Does that man always wear those funny clothes?
2. When did the building work start?
3. Psss! Meike? Did you sleep well?
4. What are those plumbers doing?
5. Where are the toilets?
6. What does that machine do?
7. When do we have lunch?
8. Do you like working here?

1. Match the answers to the questions.

   A Yes, he has to, because his job is very dangerous!
   B About six months ago.
   C It's great. You'll love it, too.
   D It checks that the pipes are strong enough.
   E Over there.
   F No, I didn't. I feel terrible!
   G Sorry! Not until midday.
   H They're putting in some taps.

2. Imagine you are doing work experience on an international scheme. Write down four or five questions to ask on the first morning.

   work on Saturdays?   have a nice breakfast?
   lunch break?   that big machine over there?   ...

On the building site

After the meeting, Signora Nencini took Meike and Kathleen to meet Signor Santoni, the foreman.
"Come with me, then," he said. "I'll show you where you are going to work."
They went through the building site to some bathrooms. "Okay, this morning you can put these taps in. Come to me when you've finished." He turned to go.
"Hey, wait a minute," said Meike. "We haven't got any tools!"
"Tools?" Signor Santoni frowned. "Okay, come with me."
They walked all the way back through the building site to his office. Signor Santoni opened a cupboard and gave them some spanners. "Okay now?"
"Er, no," said Kathleen. "Can you show us how to put the taps in? We haven't worked on an Italian building site before. Perhaps it's different."
Signor Santoni sighed and looked at his watch. "Let's go, then, quickly," he said, and they walked through the building site again. One of the workers called out something in Italian and Signor Santoni laughed and shouted back. Somehow Kathleen and Meike knew that they were talking about them.

"And it went on like that all day," said Meike that evening in the hostel. She and Kathleen were telling their story to Patrick and Antanas. "The worst bit was when we finished those stupid little taps. We stood outside his office for half an hour before he came out. Then he looked at the taps, said they were wrong and we had to do them all again."
"I'm sure there was nothing wrong with them the first time," said Kathleen. "I've never felt so embarrassed – or so angry. I don't want to go back to that building site. I can't work for six weeks with a man like that! I just want to go home."
"Why don't you tell Signora Nencini about it?" suggested Antanas. "Maybe she could help."
"That will just make more trouble," said Meike. "What can she change? He just doesn't like us."
"Yes, and I don't like him," added Kathleen. "I didn't like him right from the first moment. He thinks he's Mr Perfect!"
"But if you go home now, what will your firms say?" asked Patrick. "Won't you get into trouble?"
"Yes, you're right," said Meike. "I'm so angry. I know we can learn a lot here. It's all good experience."
"And we're not just here to work on the building site," added Patrick. "There's so much to do after work and at the weekends."
"Why don't you try to talk to Santoni?" asked Antanas. "I'm sure he saw that you were angry. Perhaps he isn't happy about the situation."
"I don't know," said Kathleen. "I just don't know …"

Reading corner — BREAKING DOWN BARRIERS
3B

When Meike and Kathleen arrived the next day, they couldn't find Signor Santoni anywhere. Then they heard a voice behind them.
"Why are you two just standing here?" It was Signor Santoni.
"We didn't know what to do," said Kathleen.
"Well, the next time you don't know what to do," he shouted, "you ask somebody if you can help. Okay?"
Signor Santoni took them to another bathroom and showed them some taps. "You know how to put in Italian taps now, I think?" He began to walk away.
Meike and Kathleen looked at each other.
"Signor Santoni! I think there's a problem!" Kathleen called out.
Signor Santoni stopped and turned round with a nasty smile. "A problem? Have you forgotten the tools again?"
Meike and Kathleen knew it was now or never. So Kathleen took a deep breath. "Actually, the problem is you," she said. "Why are you so mean the whole time? It's not fair. We want to learn something here and we want to do something useful, too."

"It was a really difficult discussion," Kathleen said quietly as she talked to the other trainees that night. "He just didn't know what to say."
"But then he talked about the building site and the work there. It seems that he has so much work and he doesn't really want any trainees at all. We're his first girl trainees and he just isn't sure what we can do." Meike was happier now. "Maybe it *is* difficult for him!"
"We agreed to start again, and after that he was more helpful," added Kathleen.
"And you don't want to go home, Kathleen?" asked Patrick.
"No, I don't," she answered. "I'm going to make the best of it!"

1. Look at what Kathleen and Meike thought during the two days. Which thoughts did they have on the first day and which thoughts did they have on the second day? Find the places in the text.

> He isn't in his office. Where is he?   Oh, so it's because he's busy!
> What are we going to do about that man?   They're laughing at us!   That's enough! It's time to talk!
> Maybe he's not so bad.
> He really loves himself!
> Oh, no! Not taps again!
> We can't do it without a spanner!   I want to go home!

Example: 'He really loves himself.' That's the first day, line 49.

2. That night Kathleen phoned her dad and told him about Signor Santoni. What did she say? Write the dialogue with a partner and act the conversation as a role play.
(Remember! You aren't allowed to look at each other. You are on the phone!)
These are the things which Kathleen should talk about:

- what happened on the first day
- what they said to Antanas and Patrick
- the discussion with Santoni
- how Kathleen feels now

Start like this: *Kathleen:* Hi, Dad, it's great here but we had a problem with the foreman …
Dad: Really? Tell me all about it …

▶ 3. Imagine you had to work with someone who is a problem. What would you do about the problem? Some ideas:
He/She is lazy and you have to do all of the work.
He/She makes a lot of mistakes.
When something goes wrong, he/she says you did it.

BREAKING DOWN BARRIERS   Let's check

3

1. Choose eight European countries. Make a grid like this and fill it in.

Country	Main language	Capital city	Food/music/…
…	…	…	…

2. Make a memory map about food. Put 'food' in the middle and use three or four of these group words.

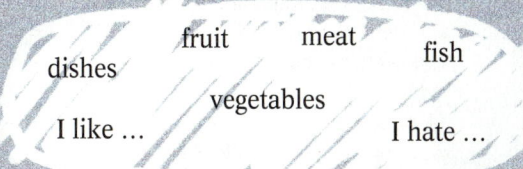

   dishes   fruit   meat   fish
   vegetables
   I like …   I hate …

3. Look at page 36 again and finish the sentences.

   a) 1. Kirsten has been serious about her running since …
      2. Wayne has been in training for …
      3. He has run in three half marathons since …
      4. Maria has been a champion for …

   b) 1. Maria has been a member of her athletics club ◆ six years.
      2. Maria has taken part in competitions ◆ two years.
      3. She has been in training ◆ last summer.
      4. Kirsten has jogged with her dad ◆ she was a little girl.

4. You guessed it! A few months later Corinna goes to visit Wayne in Swansea. What can she say in the situations when she doesn't know the English word?

   a) frech — This is my little sister. She's …

   b) Stoppuhr — Let's go to the stadium. Have you got …

   c) Rollo — Hey, Wayne, we don't have these at home. We have … er …

   d) Serviette — This is delicious, Mrs Evans. But can I have a …

The main points of the topic

4 LOVE WORRIES

CONTENTS
- advice about love — p. 48/49
- the first date — p. 54/55
- revision: negatives — p. 51
- strategy page: how to write a poem — p. 52
- words and phrases: adjectives — p. 50/53

Guessing what people are thinking and saying

46

LOVE WORRIES

4

1. Guess what the people in each photo are thinking or saying.

2. What do you think happens next in each photo? Work with a partner. Choose a photo and note down your ideas. Discuss them in class.

Guessing what people are thinking and saying

47

Reading corner
4A
LOVE WORRIES

1. You've got a date or you know you're going to see someone who you like. What do you worry about? Here are some suggestions. Choose one (or think of your own idea). Write it on a piece of paper. Collect them and hang them up in your class.

I worry about	how when where what	to wear. to go. to say (…) to be at home. …

2. Right or wrong? Check Letty's advice in the text.
   a) Enjoy flirting even if you don't like the person who is doing it. (l. 12–15)
   b) Wait until someone asks you for a date. (l. 18–19)
   c) Don't go to the zoo on a first date. (l. 26–28)
   d) Always try to be as cool as you can on a first date. (l. 30)
   e) You'll never know when you fall in love. (l. 47–50)
   f) Never stop trying to get the loved one back. (l. 60)

All about love

This is an extract from a book by Ros Asquith. In it Letty Chubb, a fifteen-year-old girl, gives advice about teenage relationships.

Ros Asquith — The Teenage Worrier's Guide to Love

F is for flirting

Flirting is like tickling. It's a game where you both know the rules. Flirting is often done without words. Then you twitch all those little eye muscles or touch someone on the arm. Flirting is one of the best things in the world when it comes from someone you like. It is very unwelcome, or just boring from someone you don't like. If that person doesn't stop it, tell a teacher or your parents.

D is for dating

It's easy to get a date. Just ask. The object of your desire will say 'yes' or 'no'. However, remember that some parents are very strict. So some girls (me, for example) are only allowed out one or two evenings a year. But don't give up. Wear comfortable clothes, but do your best if it is someone you really like. No anoraks, rain hats or cycling shorts.
Think about where to go. As a first date, two tickets for the rugby final or the spider house at the zoo may not be the best thing …
Both boys and girls worry about what to say on a first date. Don't try to be too cool. A few grunts were okay for James Dean and Sylvester Stallone but you need the hair, the face, the car and the money, too. Questions like 'Do you like string?' are very sweet, but they land you in a one-word-reply-situation.
If you can't think of anything to say and you're not interested in what your date is saying then you aren't getting on.

Talking about advice

LOVE WORRIES   Reading corner
4A

L is for love

Aaaaaaaaaaaaaaah.
Or Arrrrrrrrrrrrrrrrrrgh.
It depends on your mood.
Most days I alternate
between aaaaaaaaaaaaaah
and arrrrrrrrrrrrrrrrrgh.
If you are worried
about falling in love,
do not worry, you will
know when it happens.
It is not like that feeling you
get when you kiss a popstar poster when you
are twelve. It is more like sunrises and
volcanoes and other parts of the planet. If only
we all loved each other, we could dance, sing,
kiss and sip strawberry milkshakes there all day
near the palm trees and waterfalls etc.

Aaaaaah! Arrrgh!

B is for breaking up

Sadly, part of love is that it ends.
Don't try too much to get the loved one back.
If they want to come back, they will. Play some
very sad music very loudly and slowly tear up
all photos, letters, etc. of your loved one. Put
these on a bonfire (not in your room). Or
maybe keep one photo to show your
grandchildren and remind you of your lucky
escape. Don't listen to people who tell you
your loved one is a worm. What does that say
about you? Avoid places you went to together,
if you can. They will only make you think of the
loved one. After a period of mourning, crying,
talking on your phone to your best friend
(except if she stole your man) etc. you are
ready for phase two. Do something new and
challenging – train to be an
astronaut, start playing
volleyball or the violin
(but avoid sad songs!)
And NEVER play your
father's copy of
The Righteous Brothers'
song 'You've lost that
loving feeling'.

3. Look at what Letty says about breaking up.
   a) Make notes about what she suggests.

breaking up	
you shouldn't	you should
try too much to get the loved one back …	…

   b) Say what you would do after breaking up.
      Example: I would cry all day.
               I would …

▶ 4. In her books about teenage problems
     Letty's advice is in alphabetical order.
     Why is there a different order here?

⟨5.⟩ 'Love's unkind' by Donna Summer.
    a) Why is love unkind in the song?
       1. The girl has finished with her
          boyfriend.
       2. The girl loves a boy but he loves
          her best friend.
       3. The boyfriend has finished with
          the girl.
    b) Look at the song lyrics on page 174.
       Listen to the song again and note the
       missing words (◆ in the text).

Talking about advice

Words and phrases — 4A — LOVE WORRIES

A love-hate letter

Looking for a love letter or a hate letter? Try this.

passion ['pæʃn] Leidenschaft
in fact [ɪn 'fækt] tatsächlich
total ['təʊtl] völlig
boredom ['bɔːdəm] Langeweile
the more … the more   je mehr … desto mehr
habit ['hæbɪt] Angewohnheit
gracefully ['greɪsfʊlɪ] würdevoll, charmant
resemblance [rɪ'zemblns] Ähnlichkeit
to pretend [prɪ'tend] so tun, als ob

Dear …
I'm writing to say that my passion for you has disappeared. In fact my total BOREDOM grows every day. The more I think of you, the more
5 boring you seem. Unfortunately, the more I feel this way, so the more I must tell you openly that I never wanted to ask you to marry me. Our last date showed me there's no way on earth
10 I could spend my LIFE with you! Your terrible habits would make me sick. I really mean it. I only hope you understand gracefully and won't say you want to marry me! You really are
15 without any resemblance to the wonderful person I first thought you were. I can't pretend that I am waiting for your answer.

Now read it again, and leave out every other line! (3, 5, 7 etc.)

1. How can people be, feel or behave?
   Put the parts of the words together – they are all in the love-hate letter.

rib	won	ing	open		ter	der	
ly	le	grace	ly	ful		ful	bor

   Example: boring

2. You know more words than you think! Add either the ending -ous, -able, -ful or -less to each of these words to make a new word. (Some of the words can have more than one ending.) Look in your dictionary for help.

adventure ✔	murder	use	pain	drink	like
help		hope		enjoy	price

   Make a grid like this in your exercise book.

-ous	-able	-ful	-less
adventurous	–	–	–

Making adjectives

LOVE WORRIES Revision
4A

Problems

Letty often talks to her grandma when she has a problem. (People who like giving advice often have problems, too!)

Letty: Oh, Grandma, I'm so fed up with boys.
Grandma: Why is that, Letty?
Letty: Well, I had a terrible date yesterday evening. It was really awful. He smoked all the time and you know how I hate cigarettes! And he didn't want to go to the disco. So we went to the cinema instead.
Grandma: But the cinema's a good place for a date, isn't it?
Letty: Well, it usually is. But he didn't have any money so I paid for both of us. Yuk! We sat in the back row and he said he didn't like the film.
Grandma: Did you like it?
Letty: Of course I didn't. It was a thriller, not a love story! But the worst thing was, he didn't try to kiss me, he didn't even try to hold my hand. And when we got home, … he didn't ask me out again!
Grandma: There, there, Letty. But why didn't you ask him, dear? Maybe he was just shy.
Letty: I don't want a shy boyfriend!
Grandma: Well, what do you want?
Letty: Oh, Grandma, I only know what I don't want …

1. Say what went wrong. Look at the text. Find the negative things about the evening. Write them down in negative sentences.
   Example: The boy didn't want to go to the disco.

The boy		want to go to the disco.
He		…
Letty	didn't	…
She		…
…		

Remember! negatives

+	−
I want	I don't want
she wants	she doesn't want
I liked	I didn't like
he liked	he didn't like

G7 p. 89

2. a) What doesn't Letty want/like/enjoy?

   want   a shy boyfriend   thrillers
       like   …
   enjoy   cigarettes   paying on dates

   Example:
   She doesn't want shy boyfriends.

   b) Look back at Letty's advice about relationships on pages 48/49. What else doesn't she like?

3. Write about a terrible day or date which you or a friend had. Don't forget to use the past simple. These questions will help you to sort your ideas: When was it? Who were you with? Where did you go? What happened? What did you do/the other person do?

Negatives in past/present simple

Strategy page 4 — LOVE WORRIES

HOW TO WRITE A POEM

Bin ich ein Dichter? Keine Angst, es ist leichter, als du denkst. Mit wenigen Worten lässt sich oft viel sagen. Zum Beispiel:

> Love is like a trip to the moon.
> Love is like a cake with chocolate cream.
> Love is like a deep blue river.
> Love is like a safari.

Ist das ein Gedicht? Es reimt sich gar nicht! Sieh dir an, was gleich ist. Richtig! Die ersten vier Wörter jeder Zeile sind gleich. Das kannst du auch! Probiere, indem du überlegst, wie die Liebe für dich sein kann oder womit du sie vergleichen kannst.

1. Collect ideas:
   a) Love is like a …
   b) Love is like rid**ing** on a tiger.
   walk**ing** in the rain.
   …

Now it's your turn! Write a poem with four lines. Use either a) or b) or both.

2. Too easy? Here is a poem with five lines:

> **She**
> She seems to be
> Like waves beneath the sun
> Happy and calm
> On the surface
> But sometimes she wants to break out
>   like waves on a windy day.

Try to write a poem like that. Write it about someone you know. You can change parts of the poem. Here are some ideas:

He/She
He/She seems to be
Like …   (Here you need to compare.)
… and …   (You need two adjectives here.)
On the surface
But sometimes he/she wants to …   (Write about what he/she likes to do best.)
Like …   (You need to compare again here.)

3. Or perhaps you want to write a poem with rhymes. Here is an example:

> I was curious
> Our love was true
> Now I'm furious
> Where are you?

Try it yourself. You can use these rhymes. Write short sentences and mix the pairs of rhymes.

love	sad	hate	flirting	fine	heart[2]
dove[1]	mad	wait	hurting	mine	smart

[1] **dove** [dʌv] weiße Taube; [2] **heart** [hɑːt] Herz

Strategies for writing poems

LOVE WORRIES — **Words and phrases**

4B

1. People often use abbreviations in ads. Before you read these ads, match these abbreviations from the ads with their long forms.

n/s	g.s.o.h.	would like to meet	good sense of humour	non-smoker
a.l.a.	5'7"	y.o.	all letters answered	
w.l.t.m.	no.	number	years old	five feet seven inches (about 1 metre 70)

   Start like this: I think ... must be ...

HEARTLINE

MEETING NEW PEOPLE HAS NEVER BEEN EASIER

A
ATTRACTIVE girl, 18, blond, blue-eyed, tall, looking for genuine guy, 18–20 with g.s.o.h., must like pubs, clubs, music.
Box no. 5267

B
Wanted urgently, girl 16–20 years, who is good-looking and slim, for fun and maybe more with tall, dark-haired, fit guy, 20 y.o.
Box no. 5339

C
NICE-LOOKING girl, 17, 5'3", w.l.t.m. special bloke for fun at weekends. Must be honest and reliable and enjoy life. Serious replies only, please.
Box no. 5441

D
CRAZY male, 19, n/s, short fair hair, brown eyes, likes football, tennis, seeks serious female for friendship at first, a.l.a.
Box no. 5617

2. Who put which ad in Heartline?

   Nick    Katie
   Tony    Tina 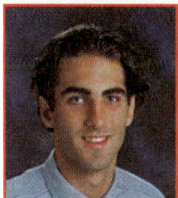

   Start like this: Nick put in ad ...

3. Looks and character. Find the words which the people use in their ads and make lists.

looks	character
attractive	genuine
...	...

4. Now write your own ad for Heartline. Use some of the abbreviations (from exercise 1) and the words from exercise 3 to describe yourself 'honestly'.

Meeting new people – SAFETY TIPS

1. Always meet in a public place. Always tell another person about the meeting.
2. Never go in a car with the person before you really know him/her.
3. Don't worry about being careful. If the person is genuine, he/she will understand.

Adjectives for describing people

Reading corner 4B — LOVE WORRIES

Love, truth and lies

My new jeans! Where are they? Of course, in the ironing basket. Into the jeans and T-shirt, jacket over shoulder, casual. Only ten minutes to go. Gosh, I'm nervous. Right, one last look in the mirror. Hair? Okay, more or less. But what about that spot? Let's squeeze … Got it! Oh, but now I've got a thick lip.

An hour later in Blue Moon Cafe.

"… the prototype was developed in 1993. There were problems with the transmission," Steve explained to Linda.

Rubbish, a load of rubbish. Why do you learn all that rubbish at school, but not what to say in a situation like this?

She's adorable.

His heart was beating faster than a plane at maximum speed.

Linda tried not to yawn. Then smiled.

All wrong. It was months before Linda would even look at me. I know what my problems are; I'm boring, my arms and legs are too long and thin, no trace of a beard, let alone hairs on my chest. *And spots! In all the worst places, and where everybody can see them! Oh, no! Why did you knock over your drink, you idiot? Now she'll see that you're nervous.*

She picked up his glass and cleaned the table with a serviette.

Okay now, tell her that she has lovely hands. They're so small and fragile. Oh no, I'm sweating. I'll smell. No, wait, it's okay. I had that shower before I came out. Why is she looking at me like that? Because I'm behaving like a complete idiot, that's why!

"I don't think that anybody can teach you. You have to learn for yourself," she said.

"What? The transmission?" He was baffled.

"No, I mean what to say on a first date." Then she took his hand, which was much too big, and held it against her cheek. And as he opened his mouth to speak, she put her finger to his lips.

"Shhh," she said and smiled.

● ● ●

"**Hi, mate,** how was it last night?" asked Jason.
"Well, what do you think?" Steve said.
He casually put a fag in the left corner of his mouth. Then he pulled a lighter out of his jeans jacket and slowly lit his fag.
Jason, Derek and Michael, his mates, would ask him again and again about last night's date with Linda. It was natural. He stared at his fag for a few moments. Then he looked at them.
"Well, are you going out with her or didn't it work out?" Jason wanted to know.
"You mean, like with you and Georgia last week?" Steve shot back. "Anyway, what's it got to do with you?"
Derek grinned, "So nothing happened, Stevie-lad! Well, never mind, mate, she didn't look that good, anyway."
"Yeah, nice body, shame about the face," said Jason with a cheeky grin. Michael and Derek looked at each other and started to laugh.

Steve knew that he had to say something.
"What makes you think nothing happened? Of course, we're going out together. We met, we talked and then she wanted it straight away," he heard himself say but it sounded phony.
"What do you mean, mate?" asked Michael. "Did you …?"
"Of course," Steve interrupted, "what do you think? She has been after me for ages!"
His voice sounded cool and tough. He flicked his fag end in the air, kicked it and it landed near a waste bin.

He had often met Linda 'quite by chance' on his bike. He knew where she lived, where she went. Oh God! He had been jealous when she had spoken to that smart bloke on the street. But then he found out from Michael's sister, that it was Linda's cousin, that was all. Steve had stopped football training and started basketball, just because she played handball at the same time and they sometimes ran into each other.

And then, last night, Linda had been so sweet, but nothing had happened except for a kiss and holding hands. And that had seemed enough, almost too much. Something must be wrong with him.

"Hey, mate, tell us about it! Was it good?" Jason wanted to know. "Did you … all the way?" "Sure," Steve heard himself say, "what do you think?"

But what was he going to say when they wanted to know the juicy details? Whatever was he going to say?

Reading corner — LOVE WORRIES

About the text

1. Put these sentences in the right order.

   a) Steve meets his mates the next day.
   b) Steve is nervous before he meets Linda.
   c) Derek, Jason and Michael want to know about Steve's date.
   d) Steve and Linda get closer.
   e) Steve doesn't know what to say to Linda.
   f) Steve doesn't tell his mates the truth.

2. Collect all the information about Steve from the text.
   Sort it. You can use these headings:

how he looks	how he feels	how he behaves
arms/legs too thin	nervous	cool

3. Work with a partner. Why does Steve do these things?

   a) He talks about planes. (l. 9–11)
   b) He smokes his cigarette slowly. (l. 46–52)
   c) He tries to flick his fag in the air. (l. 74–76)
   d) He lies to his mates. (l. 70–73, 92–95)

4. Write a summary of the story. The sentences from exercises 1 and 3 and your notes from 2 can help you. Remember to use connecting words (at first, then, because etc.).

5. The next day Linda comes round to Steve's house. She knows he has talked to his mates.

   a) Listen to the two dialogues. Which dialogue do you think took place?
      Dialogue A or Dialogue B?

   ▶ b) Say why you chose A or B.
      Start like this: I chose ... because ...

   These ideas can help you:

   A She's upset,
      ... but she knows what boys are like.
      ... but she knows that Steve likes her.
      ...

   B She's angry,
      ... because Steve said awful things about her.
      ... because she liked Steve.

LOVE WORRIES   Let's check

4

1. **All about love**
   Find more words that could be part of Letty's alphabetical advice.
   Start like this: A is for agony aunts/anoraks/…
   B is for babies/boys/…
   C is for …
   …

2. 'My best friend is a helpful, wonderful person.'
   Use the adjectives from the 'words and phrases' pages in this topic to describe three or four people you know. Use two or more adjectives for each person.

   | best friend | mother | father | brother | sister | teacher | … |

3. These people are unhappy about something. Make negative sentences.
   Example: a) He doesn't want to go to the party.

   a) want to go/party 
   b) like/loud music 
   c) enjoy/fast food
   d) need/help 
   e) like/cigarettes 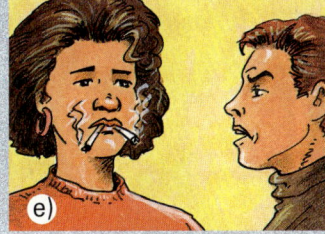
   f) love/any more 

4. Some love stories don't have a happy ending. Write a short poem to say what didn't happen.

   He | didn't kiss me goodnight.
   She | only said goodbye.
        | didn't …
        | only …

   hold my hand   say he/she was sorry
   want to see me again   …

5. Find as many 'relationship' words as you can. Always start with the last letter of the word before.

   relationship people exciting g…

The main points of the topic

57

5 YOU'RE GOING TO MAKE IT!

The members of the 10th class are 'enjoying' their last day at this German school ...

CONTENTS

- just a holiday romance? p. 62/63
- Florian saves the day p. 66/67
- revision: reported speech p. 65
- strategy page: listening p. 64
- a page of poems/write a poem p. 68/69
- words and phrases: telephoning p. 60
- words and phrases: jobs p. 61

... entlassen eure Lehrer euch nun in das Leben und wünschen euch für eure Zukunft Erfolg im Beruf und vergesst nicht: „Nur wer fleißig an sich arbeitet, wird es im Leben zu etwas bringen" ...

Das hab' ich schon 10-mal gehört!

Wo hat der bloß seine grässliche Krawatte gekauft?

Hoffentlich wird das heute Abend nicht genauso langweilig!

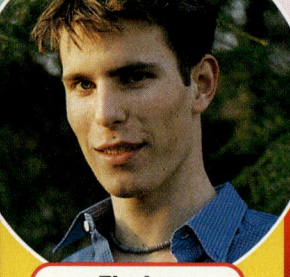

Florian

Is going out with Eleni. Not the best at school and never wants to meet his English teacher again. Good with his hands. A bit shy, but nice. Don't play pool with him, you won't get out alive. Wants to train as a mechanic.

Sabine

You can always go to her when you have a problem. (So don't jump off that bridge, talk to Sabine instead!) Computer freak, bluest eyes in class (says Werner), wants to travel the world and do a million different things before she gets old.

Christian

Was he born with a cigarette in his mouth? He's only got skateboarding and music on his mind (has got a collection of more than 200 CDs). First one to get his driving licence (but only because he did year 10 twice). The future? Who knows ...

Talking about classmates

58

YOU'RE GOING TO MAKE IT!

5

1. Work with a partner. Which of the four classmates would you ask for help in each of these situations, and why?

   a) Your parents won't let you stay out later than ten o'clock, even at weekends. You are getting fed up with it, and you don't know what to do.
   b) Great! You and some friends are going to organize a disco. But you need some help with the music.
   c) Oh, no! Aren't parents awful? You are not allowed to have a surprise party for your boyfriend or girlfriend in your living-room. Where can you have the party?
   d) Your horrible 13-year-old cousin is coming to stay. He thinks he's brilliant at every sport. Who can help you to teach him a lesson?

   You can start like this: For this problem I would ask … because …

2. Each of you writes his or her name on a sheet of paper and gives it to the person on the left. So you will get a sheet from the person on your right. Now write something positive in a sentence about the person on the sheet. Then give the sheet to the person on your left. Do the same thing until the sheet with your name on it comes back to you.
   Do you agree with the sentences on it?!

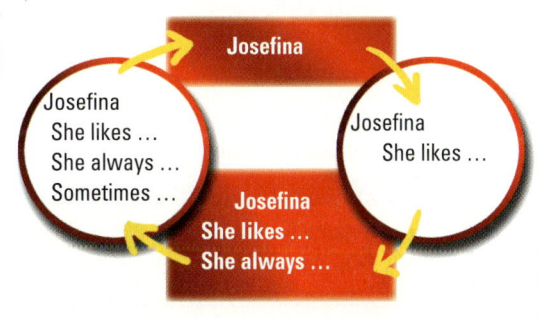

Eleni

Sometimes helps out in her parents' Greek restaurant, organized last year's class party – fantastic! Is crazy about Florian, hates rap music. Often finds school boring and can't wait to get out into the real world.

Josefina
She likes …
She always …
Sometimes …

Josefina
She likes …

Josefina
She likes …
She always …

3. What will life be like for the four classmates in five years' time? These key words will help you to write down your ideas: love, job, need English, live in …, happy. Keep these ideas for later in the topic. Start like this:
   Maybe Florian will … because he …

Talking about classmates

Words and phrases — YOU'RE GOING TO MAKE IT!

5A

A few years later

Eleni is working in the office of an engineering firm now. One lunch-time she is alone in the office.

Eleni: Maschinenbau Matador, hier Nikitas.
Customer: Oh, er, hello, it's Richard Bettingham
5 calling. Do you speak English?
Eleni: Yes, sir, how can I help you?
Customer: Well, I met your Bettina Schmidt at the trade fair last year. I'd like to come and see her next week. I wonder if you can help me …
10 *Eleni:* I'll just put you through to Frau Schmidt. Can you hold the line, please?

A few moments later …
Eleni: I'm sorry, sir, Frau Schmidt isn't in the office at the moment. Can you give me your
15 name again, and your number? I'll ask her to ring you back later.
Customer: Yes, of course. My name is Bettingham.
Eleni: Can you spell that for me, please?
Customer: B E T T I N G H A M. And the number
20 in England is 0332 231859.
Eleni: Thank you, Mr Bettingham. I'll leave a message and Frau Schmidt will call you.
Customer: Thank you very much! Goodbye.
Eleni: You're welcome. Goodbye!

1. Telephone calls in English. Look at the dialogue again and find the phrases.

   a) You are the caller.
      How do you …
      1. … say who you are?
      2. … ask for help?

   b) You are answering the phone. What do you say if …
      1. … you want to put the caller through to somebody else?
      2. … you want the caller to wait?
      3. … you want the caller's details?
      4. … you aren't sure how to write a word?

2. a) Work with a partner. Act out Eleni's dialogue with Mr Bettingham, but change the sentences and names which are highlighted. Use these or your own ideas:

Choose a name for the firm and say who you are.	Choose a name which isn't German, and a telephone number.	Say who can help the caller.
– Well, there's a problem with a bill. – We ordered two machines from you last month. – One of your machines is giving us a lot of trouble.		– It's nearly twice as much as we expected. – I've got some questions about delivery. – Could someone come over and help us?

b) Now act out the dialogue. Sit back to back. You are not allowed to look at each other!

Jobs for the boys – and the girls!

Remember Sabine, the computer freak? She lives in a small flat now, with her two-year-old daughter. Life isn't always easy for them, but Sabine is able to work at home and earn money,
5   with her computer. Sabine designs and updates websites for companies and individuals. The local education office sent Sabine this information about the 'top ten jobs' for English teenagers. They wanted to put it on their
10 website. Sabine had to translate it, too.

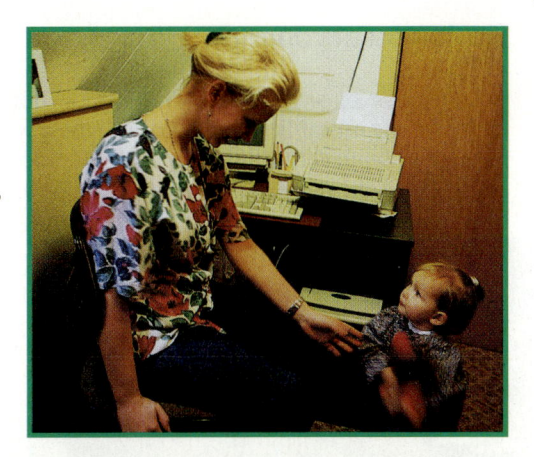

1. Some of the jobs you know already. Some you can guess. Look up the others in a dictionary.

Top ten jobs

Boys	points	position	Girls	points	position
car mechanic	47	1	fashion designer	52	1
electrician	31	2	air hostess	49	2
bricklayer	31	2	photographer	42	3
decorator	25	4	hairdresser	34	4
aviation engineer	25	4	programmer	29	5
programmer	17	6	veterinary nurse	24	6
sound engineer	16	7	nursery nurse	19	7
bank clerk	13	8	bank clerk	17	8
baker	11	9	(surgery) receptionist	12	9
(male) nurse	5	10	dental nurse	5	10

2. Work in pairs – a boy and a girl.
   The phrases in the box can help you.
   a) Boys ask girls about the girls' jobs and girls ask boys about the boys' jobs.
   b) Girls ask boys about the girls' jobs and boys ask girls about the boys' jobs.

   > *Examples:* What does a … do?
   > Would you like to be a …?
   > – A … has to …
   > – Yes, I would/No, I wouldn't because …

3. Do a survey to find out what the most popular jobs are in your class.
   a) Make a list of ten popular jobs. (You will probably need to use a dictionary.)
   b) Each boy and girl gives ten points for his or her first choice, nine for the second choice, and so on.
   c) Now write two top ten lists for your class, one for boys and one for girls.
   d) Look at the two lists. What is different?

4. a) Prepare an e-mail about the results of your survey.
   b) Ask your teacher to send the e-mail to iecc@stolaf.edu. From there it will go to 5500 other schools, and you are sure to get lots of re-mails.

Reading corner — YOU'RE GOING TO MAKE IT!

Florian meets Joanne

When Florian left school, his final report was not very good. He really wanted to be a car mechanic for one of the big car firms, but of course there was no hope. So he started work with a small car repairer, in September. The pay was terrible, and so was the work. He left when the summer came, and spent all his money on a holiday in Majorca. His old school friend, Christian, was working in a bar there for the summer.

One day Florian was lying on the beach. Suddenly the wind blew a beachball towards him, and a girl in a yellow bikini followed it. Florian sat up and picked up the ball.

"Hello," he said. "Is this yours?"

"Yes. Can I have it back, please?"

Florian was usually very shy. But something inside him made him say, "It's too hot to play ball. Stay here and talk to me." And something inside the girl made her say, "Okay." She threw the ball back to her friends and sat down next to Florian.

"Are you having a good holiday?" Florian asked.

"Yes – great! You too, I bet. Where are you staying?"

"I'm on the camping site."

"I'm in a hotel with some friends. We're here for a week."

"Where are you from? You must be English."

"Yes – I'm from Manchester."

"I'm German, from Düsseldorf."

"I did guess you were from Germany."

Later it all seemed like a dream to Florian. The girl's name was Joanne. She worked in a big do-it-yourself store. Florian told Joanne about his awful job in Düsseldorf.

"So now I'm ready for something different," he said.

"Well," said Joanne, half seriously. "How about this? My boss is looking for someone for the plant hire section."

That was where people came to hire machines – cement mixers, mini-tractors, that sort of thing. They needed someone who could check and repair the machines when they came back in.

"I don't know," Florian said. "Maybe I could do the job. I wasn't much good at school, but I like repairing machines. The problem is my English. I hated English at school."

"Don't worry, Florian. It will get better."

That evening Joanne phoned her boss and told him about Florian.

"Well, he sounds okay. Of course, he's welcome to come for an interview. Why not?" he said. But Joanne was worried. "What should I tell Florian?" she thought. "It would be terrible if he went all the way to Manchester and didn't get the job. How do I know that he's got a chance? I know, I've got an idea …"

Next day, Florian and Joanne met again. Joanne didn't say anything about the phone call.

She wanted to hire a motor boat, and Florian liked the idea. Joanne seemed to know the man who looked after the boats, but Florian didn't think about it.

Off they went across the bay. The sun was shining, and Florian was happy. "I've thought about that job again," he said. "I don't know if I'll get it but I want to try." Suddenly the motor coughed and stopped. Florian pulled the cord, but nothing happened.

"Well," Joanne said with a smile. "What now, Mr Fixit?"

Florian looked around for tools. Just an old spanner. He opened the cover and looked at the motor. Everything seemed to be all right. He undid one of the sparking plugs. It was dry.

YOU'RE GOING TO MAKE IT! **Reading corner**

5A

No petrol? He shook the tank. There was lots of petrol. But it wasn't getting to the motor. Then he remembered something. Petrol tanks for outboard motors have a little screw to let air
80 into the tank – and the screw was done up tight. He undid it, and there was a hissing noise. He pulled the cord and the motor started. When they gave the boat back, Joanne and the man smiled at each other.
85 "Komisch," Florian thought. But he soon forgot all about it.
That evening Joanne phoned her boss again. And a week later Florian went to England for an interview. Joanne met him at Manchester
90 Piccadilly station.
"I never thought I'd come to England," he smiled at Joanne as they walked along the platform. "But maybe this is where my future is. Sometimes life just surprises you …"

1. Make a time line for the story. Copy the grid and fill in what happened.

When?	September	next summer	windy day	that evening	next day	that evening	one week later
What happened?	Florian started work	…	…	…	…	…	…

2. a) "I know, I've got an idea." What was Joanne's idea? Choose the answer which you think is right.

    1. Joanne did something to the motor when Florian wasn't looking.
    2. The boat owner didn't put any petrol in the tank.
    3. Joanne asked the boat owner to do something to the petrol tank.

   b) Give a reason for your answer.
      I'm sure that … because …

   ▶ c) Now write the missing part of the story – your answer to a) – as a short dialogue.

3. You are on holiday and you want to meet new people. How are you going to get to know them? Look again at the questions Joanne and Florian asked each other (lines 18 to 25). Find other things to talk about and make a dialogue with a partner. The ideas in the box will help you with your questions and answers. Be careful. You will need to use different tenses.

| already done/seen? | work? | still at school? | alone here? |
| with friends/family? | here long? | going to stay long? |

Making a time line for the story

63

Strategy page 5
YOU'RE GOING TO MAKE IT!

LISTENING

Es ist besonders schwierig, Texte zu verstehen, die man nur einmal hört. Deshalb sollte man die Chance nutzen, das Hörverstehen an Texten zu üben, die man mehrmals abspielen kann. So wird es mit der Zeit auch leichter, Texte sofort zu verstehen. Hier sind ein paar Tipps.

1. **Was wirst Du hören?**
   Überlege dir im Voraus, welche Art von Informationen (z. B. Zahlen, Ortsnamen, Firmennamen, Uhrzeiten usw.) der Text wohl enthalten wird.

2. **Versuche nicht jedes Wort zu verstehen.**
   Du kannst das Wesentliche verstehen, ohne jedes Wort zu kennen.

3. **Worum geht es hier?**
   Nach dem ersten Zuhören versuche in einem Satz zu schreiben, um was es hier geht.

4. **Notiere Schlüsselwörter.**
   Höre den Text noch einmal an. Da sie wichtig sind, werden Schlüsselwörter oft besonders betont, oder sie liegen am Satzende (nach ihnen kommt also eine Pause). Manchmal werden sie sogar ein wenig langsamer gesprochen. Du kannst sie kurz notieren. Dabei ist die Rechtschreibung im Moment nicht wichtig. Du kannst sie nachher prüfen.

5. **Ergänze deine Notizen.**
   Beim nächsten Hören versuche ein oder zwei Wörter zu den schon notierten Schlüsselwörtern dazuzuschreiben.

---

1. Eleni came back from the lunch break today and there were some messages on the answering machine. A few of them were from England. Use the tips to listen and make notes about the calls. Write down your notes in a grid, like this:

	information	keyword	other words
first call	(Name of firm, telephone number)		

2. Over to you
   a) Record some messages on an 'answering machine'. (You can use a cassette recorder.)
      Examples:
      You want to go to the cinema with your friends. Suggest a time and place to meet.
      You left something at a friend's house. You want to come and collect it.
      You are sorry that you forgot someone's birthday.

   b) Play the messages to your partner. Can he or she understand them? (Your partner can use a grid like the one above.)

   c) Can your partner reply to the messages?

YOU'RE GOING TO MAKE IT! — Revision SB

Boss for a day

What has happened to Christian since he left school? Well, he has had some bad times (he had to sell the CDs) as well as good times. Maybe he'll never be rich, but he is still smiling. Last summer he worked in Majorca and this summer he is helping out on a camping site on the south coast of England. Today his boss, Mrs Wilson, is away, and Christian is alone in the office. Some of the campers have problems. Look at the photos.

1. What does Christian tell Mrs Wilson? Start like this: "First a woman came in. She said she couldn't put up her tent."

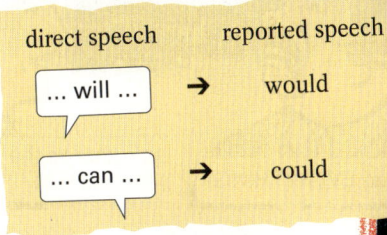

direct speech	reported speech
... will ... →	would
... can ... →	could

G8 p. 90

2. 'To have and to have not' by Billy Bragg.
   a) Listen. Which of these words describe the song best?

   sad   optimistic
   angry   dreamy
   pessimistic happy

   b) "The system has failed you, don't fail yourself!" (Last verse) What does that mean?
      1. You're not going to make it.
      2. Maybe things are hard, but you should still believe in yourself.
      3. If you don't make it, it will be because of the system, not you.

Speech bubbles (photo strip):

- I can't put up my tent! — Okay, I'll help you.
- I have some sand for the camping site. Where do you want it? — You can put it in the sandpit.
- I can't find my key for the toilet block. — You can have another key, but you'll have to pay for it.
- We need a new gas bottle. — Okay, I'll bring one over.
- Hi, Christian, did anything happen while I was away? — Er, yes, Mrs Wilson.

Reported speech

65

Reading corner
YOU'RE GOING TO MAKE IT!

A problem at the stadium

1. "That's fine, Mr Mills."

Florian started work in the plant hire section. He liked the job, and he was good at it. He spent most of his evenings with Joanne.

2. One Friday evening the phone rang ...
"Florian, there is a problem down at the United ground. Can you come up, please?"

Florian wanted to go to the pub with Joanne and her friends, but he couldn't tell the boss that. He called Joanne to say he was going to be late, and went to the boss's office.

3. "So they've got this problem with the big mowers. Do you think you can fix them?"
"Well, I can try."

There was a match between United and Arsenal the next day. Because of all the rain, the grass was very long, and now they couldn't start any of the three big mowers. Florian raced down to the stadium on his moped.

4. "I've tried EVERYTHING!"
"Let's charge the batteries first."

Florian went to the shed where they kept the mowers. The groundsman had tried to start the mowers again and again, and now the batteries were flat.

5. "You say they were all okay last week?"
"Yes. I don't understand it. Why should three mowers go wrong at the same time?"
"It must be the same problem in all three."

What could the problem be? Florian asked if the groundsman had put petrol in all the mowers. He had, on Thursday. In all three of them.

6. "Is this the drum?"
"Yes – omygod! Diesel!"

There was diesel in all the mowers. And petrol engines don't work with diesel in them! Florian started to clean the pipes, tanks and filters. He thought about Joanne and the others in the nice, warm pub.

YOU'RE GOING TO MAKE IT! — Reading corner

5B

7 Thanks, lad. All this on a Friday evening, too!
Well, I ... I was just doing my job.

8 And at the game ...
THANK YOU FLORIAN

And a big thank you to Florian Scheller, from Germany. Florian works for DIY Direct, and he gave up his Friday evening to repair our mowers. Thank you, Florian!

Florian repaired the mowers. The groundsman said he would tell the manager about it and cut the grass early next morning before the game. Now it was too late to see Joanne.

So Florian had his big moment, and there was a cheque in the post for him on Monday morning.

1. The reason why
    a) Why did the boss phone Florian?
       Example: a) Because there was a problem at United's ground.
    b) Why did they have to cut the grass?
    c) Why couldn't they do it?
    d) Why did Florian charge the batteries?
    e) Why did all the mowers go wrong at the same time?
    f) Why did United say thank you to Florian?

2. A reporter from the local paper came to interview Florian at work. She was very smart, and Florian felt shy in his oily overalls. Before she talked to Florian the reporter made some notes.

    Tip
    questions
    past simple   present simple
    ... did ...   ... do/does ...
                    ... are/is ...

    a) Write the notes as questions.
    b) Act out the interview with a partner. (Remember that the reporter is very cool, and Florian is very nervous!)

    Interview with Florian Scheller
    — when/come to England?   — how old?
    — where/learn English?   — how/find the problem?
    — like job?   — how/get job?

3. Look at these headlines from a local newspaper. Change the one you like best so that it fits Florian's story. Or you can find your own headline.

    Trevor saves the day!
    Roger the postman in Monday morning drama!
    Homestead Hotel says, "Thank you, Jane!"

▶ 4. Write the reporter's article about Florian. Use your headline from exercise 3 as the title.

Reworking information

Reading corner 5B — YOU'RE GOING TO MAKE IT!

A page of poems

1

DREAMS

Hold fast to dreams
For if dreams die
Life is a broken-winged bird
That cannot fly.

Hold fast to dreams
For when dreams go
Life is a barren field
Frozen with snow.

Langston Hughes

2

Reach out

and look
at this world
differently
it's easier

Upside Down

Ronald Keen

3

LIFE

Love
Ice cream
Friends
Enjoy!

4

Yesterday is history
Tomorrow a mystery
Today is a gift
That's why it's called the present!

5

All I can be is the perfect mother to my child,
All I can be is the wind, very wild.
I am stronger than a horse,
That's because I use my great force.
I am the changing sea,
But I will not change for anyone but me.

Tina Goodnow, 17

YOU'RE GOING TO MAKE IT! — Reading corner 5B

> **TIP**
> 1. Your poem doesn't have to have rhymes.
> 2. Your poem doesn't have to have full sentences.
> 3. Your poem can be as long and as short as you want.
> 4. You can put the words together in your poem just as you want.
> 5. There is no such thing as a right and a wrong poem.
>
> Strategy page 52

1. Write your own poem like 3. LIFE. Here are some ideas for titles:

LOVE   HOPE   NOW   YOUTH

2. Poem 1 is called "Dreams". You can write a poem about "Dreams". It isn't very difficult.

a) Collect words about "Dreams for the future". Make a memory map, too. The words and phrases in the box will start you off.

b) Put the words into groups. It's easier to do this with a memory map.

c) Now you can make your own poem. Look at the tips, too.

> home   job   flat   sad
> relationships   happy   help people
> travel/see other countries
> friends   be a good friend   car

3. You can write a poem like number 5. Take the subject "Friendship".

a) Collect words about this subject.

b) Start each line with the words "All I can …".

c) After this you will need verbs like "be, give, have, hope, want, wish". Then finish the sentence with ideas from your list of words.

> You can also start your lines with:
> I am …
> That's because …

Write your own poem

69

Let's check 5
YOU'RE GOING TO MAKE IT!

1. **The four school leavers**
   a) You know a lot about the four classmates now. Draw a grid like the one below and fill in all the details. (Check back in the topic if you're not sure.)

	job	lives in …	uses English?	happy?	love?
Florian					
Sabine					
…					

   b) Look again at what you wrote about the four characters at the start of the topic (page 59, exercise 3). Who guessed the best?

2. **Words from the topic**
   Work in a small group, or alone. Look through the topic.
   a) How many names of jobs can you find? Write them down in alphabetical order.

   b) Look at these drawings. Find the English words for these tools and pieces of equipment. (They are all in the topic.)

⟨PROJECTS⟩

Allgemeine Hinweise zur Projektarbeit   72

A	*Planung*	*Planning*
B	*Erarbeitung im Team*	*Team work*
C	*Präsentation*	*Presentation*
D	*Nachbereitung*	*Feedback*

TOPIC 2   Project ideas   74

A project: People who made a difference   76

TOPIC 4   Project ideas   78

A project: Photo love story   80

Projects — ALLGEMEINE HINWEISE

Projektarbeit ist Teamarbeit! Alle, die an einem Projekt teilnehmen, sind gemeinsam an der Herstellung eines Produkts beteiligt. Das kann ein gemeinsamer Vortrag sein, eine Informationswand, ein Poster, eine Zeitung, ein Theaterstück, ein Hörspiel, ein Videoclip oder auch ein Film. Hier noch einmal zur Erinnerung das ABC eines Projekts, damit euer Vorhaben auch ein voller Erfolg wird.

A Planung — Planning

– Arbeit im Klassenverband:

Themenfindung	– Einigt euch auf ein Projektthema. (Projektideen findet ihr auf den folgenden Seiten.)
Brain storming	– Schreibt alles auf, was euch zu dem Thema einfällt. – Wo ergeben sich Unterthemen?
Gruppeneinteilung	– Teilt euch in Gruppen auf: Wer kann zu welchem Unterthema mit wem gut zusammenarbeiten? – Überlegt mit eurem Lehrer/eurer Lehrerin, ob ihr an eurem Projekt auch noch in anderen Fachunterrichtsstunden arbeiten könnt, z. B. für ein Medienprojekt auch im Kunstunterricht. – Überlegt, ob ihr eure Projekte auch mit jüngeren Jahrgängen durchführen könnt.
Arbeits- und Zeitplan	– Stellt einen Arbeits- und Zeitplan auf.

Weniger ist oft mehr!

B Erarbeitung im Team — Team work

– Arbeit in Kleingruppen:

Materialsammlung	– Wo und womit könnt ihr mehr über euer Thema herausfinden? • In der Bibliothek, in Zeitschriften, durch Befragungen, im Internet … – Klärt, welches Material ihr braucht und wer was besorgen kann. • Nachschlagewerke, Bastelmaterial, Tonpapier, Requisiten, Fotoapparat, Kassettenrekorder, Videorekorder, Videokamera, Filme … – Sichtet euer gesammeltes Material gemeinsam.
Rollen- und Aufgabenverteilung im Team	– Ordnet es in weitere Unterthemen und entscheidet, wer was bearbeitet. – Stellt einen Arbeits- und Zeitplan für euer Team auf. – Meldet euch rechtzeitig an, wenn ihr noch in anderen Räumen außer eurem Klassenraum arbeiten müsst. (z. B. wann ist der Computerraum frei?)
Präsentationsvorbereitung	– Verteilt Rollen und Aufgaben für die Präsentation. – Denkt daran, dass jedes Teammitglied bei der Präsentation Aufgaben je nach seinen Fähigkeiten übernehmen soll.

Haltet euch an Absprachen!

ALLGEMEINE HINWEISE — Projects

C Präsentation / Presentation

– Im Klassenverband

Anschauungsmaterial	– Stellt Vokabeln vor, die ihr bei der Projektarbeit gelernt habt. – Benutzt möglichst viel Anschauungsmaterial, um eure Präsentation abwechslungsreicher zu gestalten (Fotos, Karten, Musikausschnitte, etc.).
Generalprobe Präsentation	– Macht eine 'Generalprobe' für euren Vortrag. – Tragt möglichst frei vor. Schaut eure Zuhörer dabei an. – Unterstützt das, was ihr sagt, durch Mimik und Gestik.

Gestaltet eure Präsentation möglichst abwechslungsreich!

TIP

Eine Projektvorstellung ist das Ergebnis einer gelungenen Gruppenarbeit. Jeder von euch hat besondere Fähigkeiten und Stärken. Nutzt diese für eure Präsentation.

– Wer gut planen und organisieren kann, stellt den Arbeits- und Zeitplan auf, erinnert Mitschüler daran, etwas mitzubringen usw.
– Wer keine Scheu hat, frei zu sprechen, trägt vor oder leitet die mündliche Präsentation.
– Wer gut malen und zeichnen kann, übernimmt die Regie bei der künstlerischen Gestaltung der Gruppenergebnisse.
– Wer mathematische Talente hat, übernimmt die Erstellung und das Errechnen von Statistiken.
– Ein schauspielerisches Talent lässt sich einbringen, indem man die Präsentation als Gespräch oder Interview darbietet oder etwas szenisch darstellt.
– Musikbegeisterte übernehmen die Auswahl von Songs oder gestalten die musikalische Untermalung der Vorführung.
– Wer gut mit Menschen umgehen kann, vermittelt bei Unstimmigkeiten.

D Nachbereitung / Feedback

– Im Team und im Klassenverband

Interessierte Fragen	– Stellt als Zuschauer am Ende des Vortrags Fragen, wenn ihr etwas nicht verstanden habt oder mehr wissen wollt. (Dafür ist es hilfreich während des Vortrags kurze Notizen zu machen.)
Konstruktive Kritik	– Sagt auch, was euch besonders gut gefallen hat. – Was hätte noch besser gemacht werden können?
Dokumentation	– Dokumentiert am Ende eures Projekts, wer welche Fähigkeiten eingebracht hat und wie ihr mit eurer Arbeit zufrieden seid.
Weitere Präsentationen	– Überlegt, wo und wann das Projekt noch präsentiert werden könnte: Schulfest, Basar, Mittagspause, Elternabend …

Seid faire Zuschauer und Zuhörer! Sprecht auch ein Lob aus!

Projects 2 — GETTING INVOLVED

Do a survey

People are often aggressive because they are afraid or worried. What are people your age most afraid of? Do a survey about it. Collect ideas. Look at the examples and find more ideas.

What do you really worry about?

Age: _____

Sex:
- [ ] male
- [ ] female

Where do you live?
- [ ] village
- [ ] small town
- [ ] big city

	often	never	sometimes
1. Illness			
2. Losing a friend			
3. Being poor			
4. Bad marks at school			

Do a survey in other schools.
Now ask the same questions in English via e-mail or Internet to teenagers in English-speaking countries.
Compare the survey with yours and find differences.
Write about your results in your school magazine.

Tip
If you want to send questionnaires or other information to schools in foreign countries, send an e-mail to:
iecc-projects@stolaf.edu

More project ideas:

Prejudices

A lot of people have prejudices because they don't know much about other people.
Get to know teenagers in other countries.
Start an e-mail project.
Find e-mail pals and start friendships with as many foreign teenagers as you can. Find out what you have in common. Talk about your family, your favourite activities, your friends, your dreams.

Treated unfairly?

Do a survey
What do kids in your school do when they feel that they are treated unfairly?
Collect ideas. (Look at page 32.)
Make a questionnaire with these ideas.
Send your questionnaire to an English or American school via e-mail (see the tip).
Find out about any differences.

GETTING INVOLVED | Projects 2

Posters against violence

A school in England has got a problem with violence. So the head teacher and some of the other teachers have organized a competition. You have to design a poster against violence and bullying.
Take part in the competition.

– Use pictures from magazines for your poster.
– Find slogans:

> Bully-free school
> Help others and they'll …
> Get involved. Don't …
> Talk about it.

Last week a girl got bullied at our school by ten boys. Nine were just watching.

Well, what's your excuse?

Martin Luther King Day

The Americans celebrate Martin Luther King Day on the third Monday in January. Organize a Martin Luther King Day at your school. Find out more about Martin Luther King Jr. in books and through the Internet. Find information about   his life.
                                         his ideas/dreams.
What have his ideas got to do with your life?

Scenes from real life

Has someone treated you unfairly?
Have you been the victim of violence?
Write a short play or the scene where it happened.
You can present it as a play, as a radio play or as a video production.

Projects 2 — GETTING INVOLVED

People who made a difference

Do a project about a special person. It can be a famous person or someone who is in the news. Perhaps there's someone special in your family or among your friends.

Melba Pattillo Beals

Why we chose Melba Pattillo Beals
We think Melba Pattillo Beals is a hero because she had the courage to stand up for her rights and fight racism when she was only 15 years old.

The background to the story
Before 1954 black and white students went to different schools in the U.S.A. In 1954 the U.S. Supreme Court made a law which banned racial segregation in public schools. But a lot of all-white schools in the South still didn't allow black students to go there.

Melba's story
In 1957 Melba was 15 years old and dreamed of going to college and later to university. The best high school in her hometown – Little Rock, Arkansas – was Central High, and she wanted to be one of the first black teenagers to go there.

September 3rd was her first day at Central High. She and eight other black students arrived at the school but the National Guard wouldn't let them go in. On September 25th the nine black students were escorted into Central High by troops of the U.S. Army.

Although life wasn't easy for Melba at Central High, she worked hard and went to college and university.
After that she worked as a journalist and TV reporter.
In her book 'Warriors Don't Cry', she tells her story. The German title of the book is 'Niemand darf mich weinen sehen'.

In September 1997 she came back to Central High together with the eight others. This time they were welcomed by President Clinton.

Amina, Thommy, Kemal, Bettina, Frank, Maria

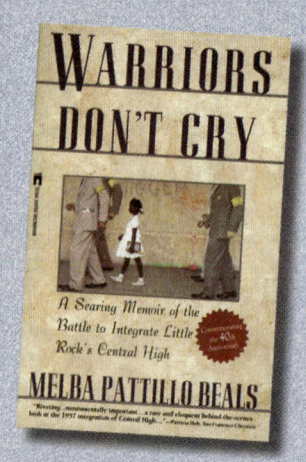

GETTING INVOLVED — Projects 2

Selim

A VERY SPECIAL PERSON

In the picture on the right you can see my friend Selim. That's me in the picture on the left. Selim sits next to me at school and he is a very special friend.

When we meet at school in the morning, he always says: "Gimme five!" And I clap his hand. Every morning it's the same ritual.
We have a lot of fun together. He doesn't push my wheelchair, he always walks next to me so we can look at each other when we talk. We can talk about anything and everything. For him I'm just like all the other kids in our class. He isn't different with me and that's very special.
When other kids are mean to me, I get very angry. Selim always stays calm and talks quietly to them.

Sebastian

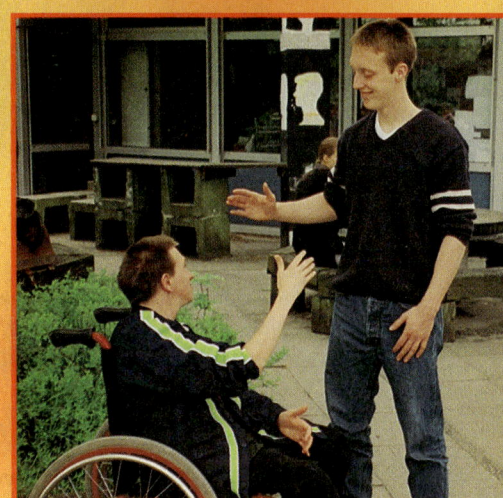

Some ideas for your project:

1. Find out and write about other people who made a difference in history, e. g.: Martin Luther King Jr., Rosa Parks, Jackie Robinson.

2. Do a project on people who have made a difference in your life, school or town.

3. You can do something about people who you have read about in newspapers and magazines or know about from TV.

4. – Say why you chose the person.
   – Give a short biography.
   – Give an example of what the person did that made a difference.
   – Use at least two photos.

Tip

Heroes on the internet.
You can find out more about public and private heroes at: www.myhero.com
You can make your own homepage about your hero there, too.

Projects 4 — LOVE WORRIES

Send your love

Be my Valentine. February 14th is Valentine's Day, but every day is the right day to send a card to a loved one.

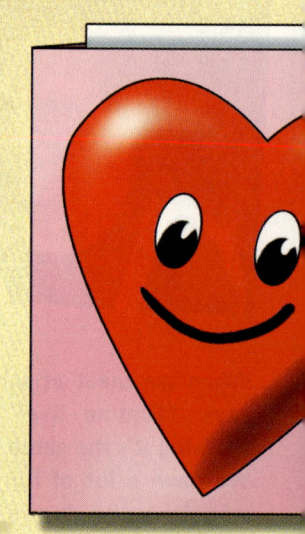

More cards and love poems

Write love poems. For ideas see page 52.
If you want to write a poem with the name of your loved one, here is another idea. Start each line of your poem with a letter of her/his name. Now make a nice card for it.

How to make a card for your love poems

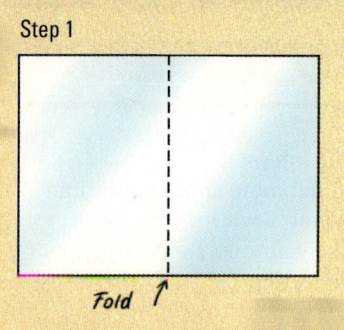

Step 1
Cut out a piece of light cardboard, (for a normal envelope use size A5), and fold it.

Step 2
Draw a heart, not larger than a postcard, on another piece of cardboard and cut it out.

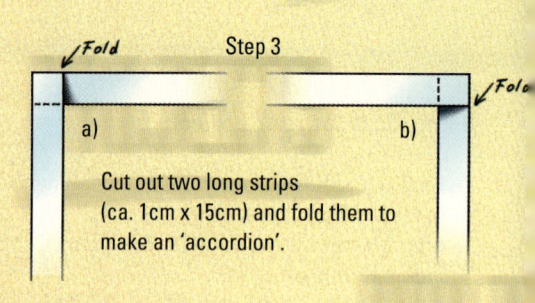

Step 3
a) b)
Cut out two long strips (ca. 1cm x 15cm) and fold them to make an 'accordion'.

LOVE WORRIES

Projects 4

Make Valentine cards and give them to friends. Either try to be very romantic or funny. Here are some ideas:

I want to share
♥ my life with you.
♥ a … with you.
♥ …

You are
♥ the sunshine of my life.
♥ my …

When I see you, I feel
♥ very happy.
♥ …

When I think of you,
♥ it warms my heart.
♥ I can't …
♥ my knees …

I dream of
♥ holding you close.
♥ touching …
♥ …

I want to
♥ go out with you.
♥ …

Tip
Make a lot of cards and poems with popular names.
Sell them at a school fete or bazaar.

Step 4

My heart beats for YOU

Love at first sight
Arrows hit me
Under an oak tree
Rhythm of love
All I can think of is you

Glue the 'accordion' to the heart and glue the other side of it to the card, so that the heart pops out when you open the card.

More project ideas:

Love poems in print

Write love poems and send them to an English teenage magazine.
Address:
Sugar, 16-18 Berners Street
London UK   W1P3DD

Or publish them on the web.
Here are the addresses of teenage e-zines:
www.lovepoems.com/index.html
www.thewebpost.com/lovepoems.htm
www.cyberteens.com/ctmain.html
www.teenvoices.com (click on "Love poems", only for girls)
Read the love poems which have been published there.

Guide to boys / Guide to girls

There are two kinds of guides you can make:
1. Boys make a guide to boys for girls.
   Girls make a guide to girls for boys.
Here you give advice about feelings and characters.
2. Boys give other boys tips on girls.
   Girls give other girls tips about boys.
For example:
– What to say on dates.
– How to know that she/he loves you.
– What girls will never understand about boys.
– What boys will never understand about girls.

Love songs

Present your favourite love songs.
Bring a cassette of your favourite love song.
Write down the lyrics and make a quiz for your classmates.
Say which are your favourite lines.
Make a new love song with all the favourite lines in class.

Projects 4: LOVE WORRIES

Photo love story

Have you got any good ideas for a photo love story? Here is an example:

Title:
This boy is mine

Characters:
Sophie, her friend Tina, the new pupil Matt, teacher Mr Dean, classmates

this boy is

1
Hello.
This is Matt Spencer. Matt, you can sit next to Ben.

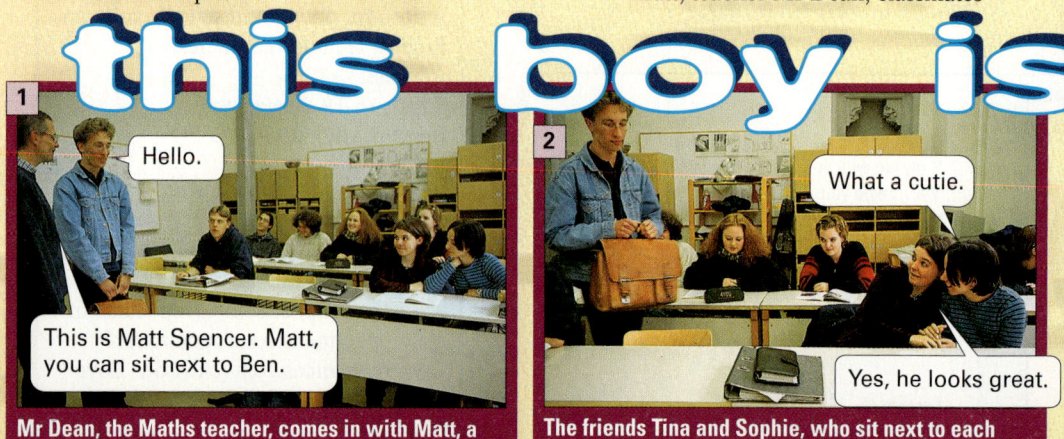

Mr Dean, the Maths teacher, comes in with Matt, a new boy. He tells Matt to sit next to Ben.

2
What a cutie.
Yes, he looks great.

The friends Tina and Sophie, who sit next to each other, like the new boy. They think he looks cute.

3
Well done, Sophie. Another A.
Thank you, Sir.

Mr Dean gives back the Maths test. Sophie has done well again.

4 During the break.
Can I copy that from you? We didn't do that at my old school.
What about tomorrow at 5 p.m.
Good idea.

During the break Matt asks Sophie to help her with his Maths. They agree to do their homework together.

5 After homework.
I liked you from the first moment, Sophie.
I really like you, Matt. but I have to baby-sit that evening.

After Sophie has helped Matt with his homework, he asks her to go with him to Ben's party on Saturday.

6

LOVE WORRIES · Projects 4

Work in groups and finish the story.

- What happens in each photo and what happens at the end of the story?
- Write the text which goes under each photo.
- Decide what to put in the speech bubbles.
- Copy the photos 6–9 and put in the speech bubbles.
- Take a photo or do a drawing for the last picture.

Make your own photo story:

Decide who does what in your group.
Who is going to write the texts (under the photos and in the speech bubbles)?
Who is going to organize the scenes?
Who is going to take the photos?
Who is going to put the photos and the texts together?

TIP

1. Write the texts under the photos in the present simple not in the past simple.
2. You can put information about place and time in the photos:
   Next day. Five minutes later. When Tim's dad has gone out. At Samantha's house. In the tent. etc.
3. When you organize the photos, don't forget you need space for the speech bubbles.
4. Use a Polaroid camera or a digital camera with a computer. You can see the results more quickly.

GRAMMAR

Jeder Grammatikabschnitt (G) gehört zu einer bestimmten Seite vorne in den Topics; diesen Seitenverweis `page 17` findest du rechts oben vor jedem Abschnitt.

Die Grammatikseiten helfen dir beim Englischlernen.
Du kannst sie benutzen,
- wenn du Hausaufgaben machst,
- wenn du dich auf eine Klassenarbeit vorbereitest,
- wenn du nicht sicher bist, warum ein Grammatikphänomen so ist,
- wenn du eine Übersicht brauchst, z. B. wie in G1.

Von besonderer Hilfe ist:

– Vorsicht! Hier musst du besonders aufpassen.

Grammatical terms

Grammatischer Begriff	Englisch	Englisches Beispiel
Adjektiv/Eigenschaftswort	adjective	This homework is **easy**.
Adverb/Umstandswort	adverb	The baby cried **easily**.
Artikel	article	
bestimmter Artikel	definite article	Your book is on **the** table.
unbestimmter Artikel	indefinite article	That's **a** good idea/**an** idea!
bejaht G7	positive	She often **goes** swimming.
direkte Rede G8	direct speech	"I'm hungry."
each other	each other	Sonia and David like **each other**.
Ersatzverb G5	substitute verb	**have to, be allowed to,** etc.
Fragewort	question word	**Who?, What?, Where?** etc.
Gegenwart G1	present tense	
einfache Gegenwart	present simple	School finish**es** at 3 o'clock.
Verlaufsform der Gegenwart	present progressive	Today **I'm going** by bus.
Genitiv (wessen-Fall)	genitive	
	s-genitive	Debby is **Gary's** friend.
	of-genitive	the photo **of** a dog
Grundform/Infinitiv/ 1. (Verb-)Form G1, G7	infinitive	to **play,** to **live,** to **be**
Häufigkeitsadverb G3	adverb of frequency	I **never** get up late.
Hauptsatz	main clause	..., **I'd buy a big house.**
Hilfsverb G3	modal verb	I **can't** help you.
If-Satz	if-sentence	
if-Satz mit *will*	if-sentence with 'will'	**If** it **rains**, we'**ll stay** at home.
if-Satz mit *would*	if-sentence with 'would'	**If** it **rained**, we **would stay** at home.
Imperativ/Befehlsform	imperative	**Give** me your book, please.
Indirekte Rede G8	reported speech	**Tracey says she likes hockey.**

Grammar

Grammatischer Begriff	Englisch	Englisches Beispiel
-ing-form G1	-ing-form (gerund)	**cooking, having, swimming**
-ing-form als Objekt	-ing-form as object	I like **cooking**.
-ing-form als Subjekt	-ing-form as subject	**Cooking** is fun.
Konjunktion/Bindewort	connecting word	**and, or, because, when** etc.
Kurzform	short form	**I'm, they'll, she's got, we'd** etc.
Langform	long form	**I am, they will, she has got, we would** etc.
nichtzählbares Substantiv	uncountable noun	**bread, butter** etc.
Objekt/Satzergänzung	object	She must clean **the cage**.
Partizip Perfekt/ 3. (Verb-)Form G1, G4, G6	past participle	She has **made** tea.
Passiv/Leideform G4	passive	English **is spoken** here.
Perfekt G1, G6	present perfect	Greg **has** just **broken** his leg.
Personalpronomen/ persönliches Fürwort	personal pronoun	**I, you, he, she, it, we, they**
Plural/Mehrzahl	plural	two **girls**; child**ren**; m**en**
Possessivpronomen/ besitzanzeigendes Fürwort	possessive pronoun	**my, your, his, her** etc.
Präposition/Verhältniswort	preposition	**in** the park; **on** the table
Reflexivpronomen	reflexive pronoun	**myself, yourself, themselves** etc.
regelmäßiges Verb G7	regular verb	**work, look, invite**
Relativpronomen	relative pronoun	**who, which**
Relativsatz	relative clause	… **who isn't** here.
Satz ohne Relativpronomen	contact clause	Choose a story **you like**.
Signalwort G6	signal word	**sometimes, just, yesterday** etc.
1. Steigerungsform	comparative	**bigger, more boring**
2. Steigerungsform	superlative	**biggest, most boring**
Subjekt/Satzgegenstand G4	subject	**The bike** is in the shop.
Substantiv/Hauptwort	noun	**book, girl, cousin**
unregelmäßiges Verb G7	irregular verb	**be, go, come** etc.
Verbform G1	form of the verb	**be, was, been**
Vergangenheit	past tense	
einfache Vergangenheit/ 2. (Verb-)Form G1, G7	past simple	I **watched** televison yesterday.
Verlaufsform der Vergangenheit G1	past progressive	They **were walking** in the park when it started to rain.
verneint G7	negative	She **doesn't go** swimming.
Wunsch äußern	I'd like to … /I want to …	**I'd like to/want to** see Big Ben.
zählbares Substantiv	countable noun	**apple, bottle**
Zeitform G1	tense	**present progressive, past simple** etc.
Zukunft/Futur	future tense	
going to-Futur	going to-future	**I'm going to watch** TV.
will-Futur G1	will-future	They **will like** it.

Grammar

TOPIC 1

G1 **Verbformen: Übersicht**
Making the forms of the verb

a) **Hauptverben** – das Beispiel *take*

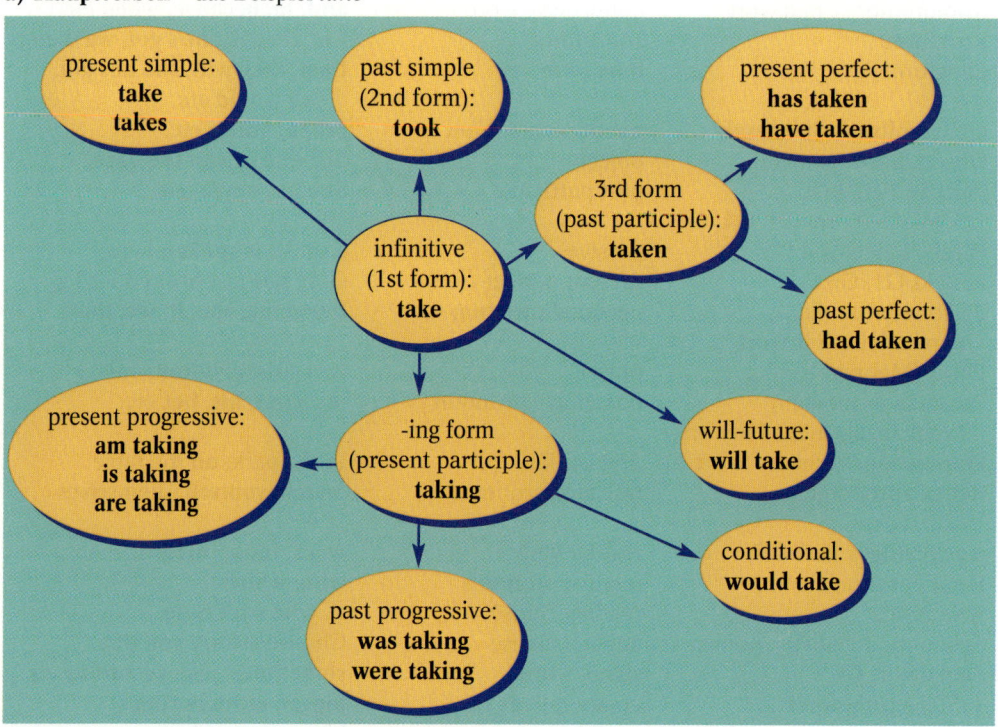

- present simple: **take / takes**
- past simple (2nd form): **took**
- present perfect: **has taken / have taken**
- 3rd form (past participle): **taken**
- infinitive (1st form): **take**
- past perfect: **had taken**
- present progressive: **am taking / is taking / are taking**
- -ing form (present participle): **taking**
- will-future: **will take**
- conditional: **would take**
- past progressive: **was taking / were taking**

b) *be*   Das Verb *be* ist immer etwas **Besonderes**.

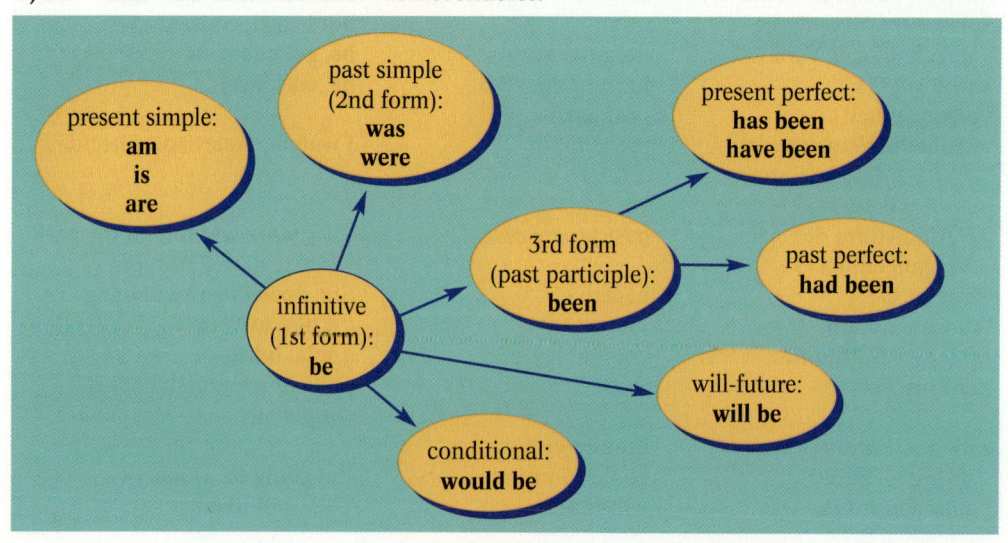

- present simple: **am / is / are**
- past simple (2nd form): **was / were**
- present perfect: **has been / have been**
- 3rd form (past participle): **been**
- infinitive (1st form): **be**
- past perfect: **had been**
- will-future: **will be**
- conditional: **would be**

Grammar 1

G2 **Die Stellung von Orts- und Zeitangaben im Satz**
The position of adverbial phrases in a sentence

Seite 14

Orts- und Zeitangaben stehen im Englischen meistens am Ende des Satzes.
Die Ortsangabe steht immer vor der Zeitangabe.

> **O**rt vor **Z**eit

	Ortsangabe	Zeitangabe
Most of my friends meet	at the mall.	
I often take my mother's car		at the weekend.
We went shopping	at Christina mall	on Saturday afternoon.
Tracy's brother took me	home	after the party.

We went shopping ... — *... at Christina mall ...* — *... on Saturday afternoon.*

G3 **Die Stellung von Adverbien der Häufigkeit**
The position of adverbs of frequency

Seite 14

Adverbien der Häufigkeit *(always, often, sometimes, usually, never)* drücken aus, wie oft etwas geschieht. Sie stehen meistens vor dem Hauptverb.

	Hilfsverb	Adverb	Hauptverb	
Jon		sometimes	works	in a store after school.
We		always	got up	before 9 on holiday.
Sarah	doesn't	often	go out	in the evening.
I	have	never	been	to the U.S.A.
Todd	will	never	forget	that accident.

Es gibt Ausnahmen beim Verb *be*. Bei einfachen Formen von *be* (*am, is, are, was, were*) stehen Adverbien der Häufigkeit hinter dem Verb.

> Das Verb *be* ist immer etwas **B**esonderes.

	Form von *be*	Adverb	
It	is	sometimes	difficult to find a part-time job.
Violence	was	never	a problem when I was at school.

Grammar 2

TOPIC 2

G4 **Gebrauch und Bildung der Passivform im *past simple***   Seite 27
Using and making the passive form in the *past simple*

Manchmal kann man sich entscheiden, ob man etwas mit einer Aktivform oder einer Passivform sagen möchte.

Das **Aktiv** wird verwendet, wenn man betonen möchte, <u>wer</u> etwas getan hat.	A dog **attacked** a three-year-old girl. *Ein Hund griff ein 3-jähriges Mädchen an.*
Das **Passiv** wird benutzt, wenn man betonen will, <u>was</u> getan wurde.	A three-year-old girl **was attacked**. *Ein 3-jähriges Mädchen wurde angegriffen.*

Man kann betonen, wer etwas gemacht hat. Dazu braucht man das Wörtchen *by*:

Den **Verursacher** der Handlung schließt man dann mit *by* an.	A three-year old girl was attacked **by a dog**.

Das Passiv wird aus einer Form von *be* und der 3. Form des Verbs gebildet.

Passivform im *past simple*

was / were	+ 3. Form

Passivform im *past simple*

Subjekt	Form von *be*	3. Form		Verursacher	
Two schoolgirls	were	attacked		by a dog.	... wurden von einem Hund angegriffen.
They	were	taken	to hospital.		Sie wurden ... gebracht.
One of the girls	was	reported	to have serious injuries.		Es wurde berichtet, dass ...
The dog	was	put	to sleep	by a vet.	... wurde von einem Tierarzt eingeschläfert.

Grammar 2

G5 **Ersatzverben im *past simple***   Seite 29
Substitute verbs in the *past simple*

a) *must* (muss, musst, müsst, müssen) kann nur im *present simple* verwendet werden.

> I've missed the bus. Now I **must** walk home. (Now I **have to** walk home.)
> Ich habe den Bus verpasst. Jetzt muss ich zu Fuß nach Hause gehen.

Das *past simple* wird mit dem Ersatzverb *have to* gebildet.

> I missed the bus. So I **had to** walk home.
> Ich verpasste den Bus. Also musste ich zu Fuß nach Hause gehen.

> We had enough sandwiches. So we **didn't have to** go to a snack bar.
> Wir hatten genügend Sandwiches. Also mussten wir nicht in eine Snackbar gehen.

b) *can* (kann, kannst, könnt, können) wird nur im *present simple* gebraucht.

> The castle is open. We **can** visit it.
> Das Schloss ist geöffnet. Wir können es besichtigen.

Für das *past simple* benutzt man *could* oder die Ersatzverben
be able to (können) oder *be allowed to* (dürfen).

Ersatzverben im *past simple*	
Form von *be*	
was wasn't were weren't	able to allowed to

The castle was open. So we could/were able to visit it.
     Also konnten wir es besichtigen.

But we couldn't/weren't allowed to take any photos.
     Aber wir durften keine Fotos machen.

There was a shop. So I could/was able to buy some postcards.
     Ich konnte also Postkarten kaufen.

Manchmal ist es wichtig zu unterscheiden, ob man etwas konnte oder durfte.
Dann ist es gut, dass man es mit *be able to* und *be allowed to* machen kann.

> Sorry, I couldn't come to your party last Friday.

> I know the weather was bad but everybody else came!

> I wanted to be there but I wasn't allowed to go out.

Grammar

TOPIC 3

G6 **Gebrauch** von *since* und *for*
Using *since* and *for*

Seite 36

Das *present perfect* wird verwendet für Handlungen, die in der Vergangenheit stattgefunden haben. Die Folge ist wichtig für die Gegenwart.
Signalwörter: *since, for, never, not ... yet, just,... ever ...?, all my life*

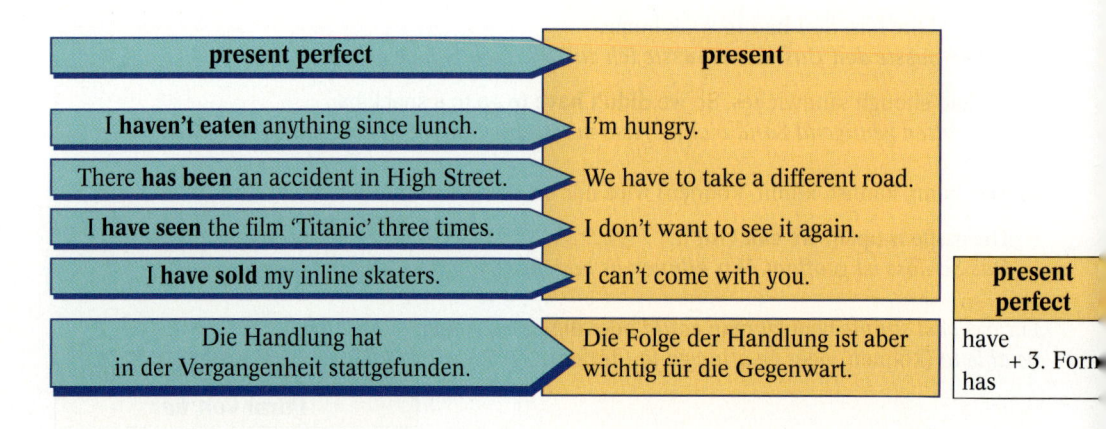

present perfect	present
I **haven't eaten** anything since lunch.	I'm hungry.
There **has been** an accident in High Street.	We have to take a different road.
I **have seen** the film 'Titanic' three times.	I don't want to see it again.
I **have sold** my inline skaters.	I can't come with you.
Die Handlung hat in der Vergangenheit stattgefunden.	Die Folge der Handlung ist aber wichtig für die Gegenwart.

present perfect
have / has + 3. Form

Zeitangaben mit *since* und *for* werden häufig im *present perfect* verwendet.

present perfect	Zeitangabe
I haven't eaten anything	since breakfast.
Caroline has been in the football club	for 3 years.
We haven't seen Debbie	for a long time.

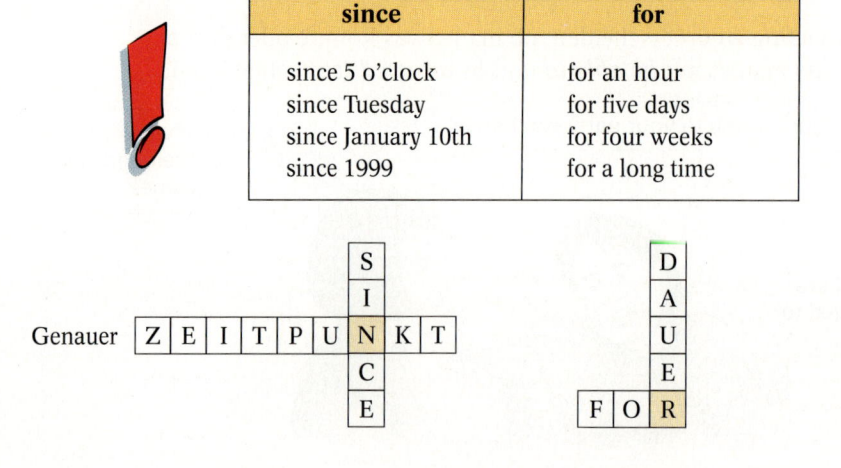

since	for
since 5 o'clock	for an hour
since Tuesday	for five days
since January 10th	for four weeks
since 1999	for a long time

Genauer Z E I T P U N K T   (SICHE down)   F O R (DAUER down)

Grammar 4

TOPIC 4

G7 Verneinte Sätze im *present simple* und *past simple*
Negative sentences in the *present simple* and *past simple*

Seite 51

a) Hauptverben

Bei Hauptverben wie *play*, *go* oder *have* werden verneinte Sätze im *present simple* mit *don't* oder *doesn't* gebildet.

> **Verneinung im *present simple***
> don't
> doesn't +1. Form

present simple	
bejaht	**verneint**
I **speak** English and German. My parents **drink** tea for breakfast. Brian **plays** the guitar.	I **don't speak** Italian. They **don't drink** coffee. But he **doesn't play** very well.

Verneinte Sätze im *past simple* bildet man bei Hauptverben wie *play*, *go* und *have* mit *didn't*.

> **Verneinung im *past simple***
> didn't + 1. Form

past simple	
bejaht	**verneint**
I **waited** 30 minutes for my boyfriend. We **went** to the disco. I **asked** him for a date.	But I **didn't wait** at the right bus stop. We **didn't go** to the cinema. He **didn't ask** me.

> **2. Form (past simple)**
>
> Regelmäßige Verben: Verb + -ed   Unregelmäßige Verben: 2. Form (s. Seite 176)

a) Verb *be*

Bei Formen des Verbs *be (am, is, are, was, were)* werden verneinte Sätze ähnlich wie im Deutschen durch *not* gebildet.

bejaht	verneint
present simple	
I'**m** in love with Sandra. Ben **is** still at school. My parents **are** really great.	I'**m not** in love with Tina. Sorry, he **isn't** at home. They **aren't** very strict.
past simple	
It **was** a very nice evening. There **were** a lot of people in town.	But it **wasn't** a good film. Too much violence and horror. There **weren't** many people in the cinema.

Grammar

TOPIC 5

Seite 65

G8 Indirekte Rede / Reported speech

Man verwendet häufig die indirekte Rede um mitzuteilen, was jemand gesagt hat.

Speech bubble 1: This is John Davies, caravan 44b. I have a big problem. I ...

Speech bubble 2: Mrs Davies? Your husband just called. He said that he had a big problem. He ...

Bei der indirekten Rede wird die Zeitform verändert.

Direkte Rede	Indirekte Rede
present simple	**past simple**
"I **have** a big problem." „Ich habe ein großes Problem."	Your husband said that he **had** a big problem. Ihr Mann sagte, er habe/hätte ein großes Problem.
"I **don't have** enough money for a taxi." „Ich habe nicht genug Geld für ein Taxi."	He said he **didn't have** enough money for a taxi. Er sagte, er habe/hätte nicht genug Geld für ein Taxi.
will ('ll)/won't	**would/wouldn't**
"**I'll** wait for her in the car park." „Ich werde auf dem Parkplatz auf sie warten."	He said that he **would** wait for you in the car park. Er sagte, er werde/würde auf dem Parkplatz auf Sie warten.
"I **won't** go home without her." „Ich werde nicht ohne sie nach Hause gehen."	He said he **wouldn't** go home without you. Er sagte, er werde/würde nicht ohne Sie nach Hause gehen.

Sätze der indirekten Rede leitet man meist durch bestimmte Verben ein. Das Wort *that* kann weggelassen werden.

Verb + (that)
He said (that)
He thought (that)

Verb + Person + (that)
He told me (that)

VOCABULARY

Das Vokabular jeder einzelnen der insgesamt fünf Topics schließt an das Vokabular von Band 5 an. Das hat den Vorteil, dass die Reihenfolge der Topics beliebig wählbar ist. Jede Topic hat ein kleines Inhaltsverzeichnis, das dir zeigt, was du nach der Bearbeitung dieser Lerneinheit kannst.

Innerhalb der Topic wird das Vokabular in gewohnter Weise der Reihe nach aufgelistet. Dabei kommt es natürlich vor, dass Vokabeln aus Topic 1 in Topic 2 oder einer anderen Topic noch einmal aufgeführt werden, aber das ist ja für euch nicht weiter schlimm. Wenn die Vokabel schon sitzt, brauchst du sie nicht mehr zu lernen.

Die Vokabeln erscheinen im gewohnten Kleid:
heaven: fett gedruckt sind die Wörter, die du unbedingt lernen musst.
°*to threaten:* Kringel vor einem in Schrägschrift gedruckten Wort bedeutet: musst du wieder erkennen, wenn es wieder auftaucht.
⟨3⟩ on my mind: Spitzklammer vor einer Übung weist auf freiwillige, zusätzliche Übungen und freiwilliges Vokabular hin.

Zusätzlich zur deutschen **Übersetzung** bieten wir dir Beispielsätze, Bilder und Erklärungen in der **Mittelspalte.** Sie sollen dir eine Hilfe beim Lernen und Anwenden der neuen Wörter sein. Mit *Pronunciation!, Spelling!* und *Stress!* machen wir dich auf Besonderheiten aufmerksam.

Selbstverständlich steht neben jedem neuen Wort die **Lautschrift,** die dir bei der Aussprache hilft. Bist du bei der Aussprache eines Lautzeichens unsicher, schlage nach auf Seite 92.

Band 6 enthält zahlreiche **Originaltexte,** die manchmal viele neue Vokabeln enthalten. Alle neuen Wörter dieser Texte stehen in einem Kasten. Du brauchst sie aber nicht unbedingt alle zu lernen. Die für dich wichtigen Vokabeln werden unter dem jeweiligen Kasten noch einmal fett gedruckt aufgeführt. Und wie du schon weißt: fett gedruckte Wörter müssen gelernt werden.

Das Vokabular zu den Projekten findest du im Anschluss an das Vokabular von Topic 5. Wenn du **Projektarbeit** betreibst, musst du natürlich auch die neuen Wörter lernen, die das Projekt betreffen.

Richtige Vokabelfreaks kommen auch auf ihre Kosten, denn zu jeder Topic bieten wir in einem Kasten tolle Spiele rund ums Vokabular an. Mit jedem Spiel vertiefen sich deine Vokabularkenntnisse. Vokabeln behält man spielend. Also, los geht's!

Alle englischen Wörter außerhalb der Kästen stehen dir zusätzlich in einer alphabetischen Liste, dem **Dictionary,** ab Seite 119 zur Verfügung. Du findest dort auch alle Wörter aus den Bänden 1–5. An das Dictionary schließt sich ab Seite 150 eine **Deutsch-englische Wortliste** an.

Folgende Abkürzungen und Zeichen werden im Vokabular benutzt:

sb.	somebody	*AE*	American English
sth.	something	*BE*	British English
e.g.	for example	⟷	das Gegenteil von
ugs.	umgangssprachlich	=	gleichzusetzen mit
sl.	slang	~	Tilde ersetzt die neue Vokabel
pl.	plural		
sg.	singular		

Vocabulary

Englische Lautzeichen (English sounds)

Selbstlaute (Vowels)

- [ɑː] car, father; ähnlich wie in *Bahn*
- [ʌ] number, bus, mother; ähnlich wie in *nass*
- [e] yes, pen, friend; ähnlich wie in *nett*
- [ə] a sticker; ähnlich wie in *bitte*
- [ɜː] girl, her, turn
- [æ] bag, cat, that
- [ɪ] it, a bit, six; ähnlich wie in *Kind*
- [iː] she, see, please; ähnlich wie in *tief*
- [ɒ] on, dog, what; ähnlich wie in *Kopf*
- [ɔː] door, four, morning
- [ʊ] put, look; ähnlich wie in *Schutt*
- [uː] you, two, blue; ähnlich wie in *du*

Doppellaute (Diphthongs)

- [aɪ] nice, five, bye; ähnlich wie in *kein*
- [aʊ] now, pound; ähnlich wie in *Frau*
- [eə] there, chair, their
- [eɪ] name, say, table
- [ɪə] here, clear
- [ɔɪ] boy; ähnlich wie in *Scheune*
- [əʊ] no, go, show
- [ʊə] you're

Mitlaute (Consonants)

- [j] yes, you; wie das deutsche *j* in *ja*
- [l] let's, blue, school, twelve
- [g] get, glass, wie in *Gold*, *gerade*
- [ŋ] morning; wie in si*ng*en, kein [g] sprechen!
- [ŋg] English; wie [ŋ], jedoch mit nachfolgendem [g]
- [r] ruler, radio, red
- [s] see, sister, class; stimmloses, d. h. hartes *s* wie in *reißen*
- [z] is, dogs, cars; stimmhaftes, d. h. weiches *s* wie in *brausen*
- [ʒ] television; wie in *Jalousie* und *Gelee*
- [dʒ] German, orange; wie in *Dschungel*
- [ʃ] she, fish; wie in *Tisch*
- [tʃ] teacher, child; wie in *deutsch*
- [ð] the, this, mother; stimmhafter, d. h. weicher Laut
- [θ] thank you; stimmloser, d. h. harter Laut
- [v] vet, of; wie in *Wasser*
- [w] one, what, sandwich
- [ː] bedeutet, dass der vorangehende Laut lang ist, z. B. blue [bluː]
- ['] bedeutet, dass auf der folgenden Silbe die Hauptbetonung liegt, z. B. hello [həˈləʊ]
- [ˌ] bedeutet, dass auf der folgenden Silbe die Nebenbetonung liegt, z. B. exercise book [ˈeksəsaɪz ˌbʊk]
- [‿] zwischen zwei Wörtern bedeutet, dass man den letzten Laut des ersten Wortes zum nächsten Wort hinüberzieht, z. B. come on [kʌm‿ˈɒn]

Das englische Alphabet (The English alphabet)

a [eɪ]	b [biː]	c [siː]	d [diː]	e [iː]	f [ef]	g [dʒiː]	h [eɪtʃ]	i [aɪ]
j [dʒeɪ]	k [keɪ]	l [el]	m [em]	n [en]	o [əʊ]	p [piː]	q [kjuː]	r [ɑː]
s [es]	t [tiː]	u [juː]	v [viː]	w [ˈdʌbljuː]	x [eks]	y [waɪ]	z [zed]	

Vocabulary 1

TOPIC 1   As American as ...

statistics [stə'tɪstɪks]		Statistik
to cruise [kru:z]	*Spelling!* = to drive around in a car	herumfahren
hometown ['həʊmtaʊn]	= the town where you live or come from	Heimatstadt
to keep fit [ˌki:p 'fɪt]	I run every morning to ~.	sich fit halten
to own [əʊn]	Most car drivers ~ a car.	besitzen
inner-city ['ɪnə ˌsɪti]	= in the center of a big town	innerstädtisch
gated community ['geɪtɪd kə'mju:nəti]		bewachte Siedlung, meistens ummauert und mit kontrolliertem Eingang
crawfish ['krɔ:fɪʃ]		Langusten
all the crawfish [ˌɔ:l ðə 'krɔ:fɪʃ]		so viele Langusten wie
potato [pə'teɪtəʊ]	What french fries are made from.	Kartoffel
corn [kɔ:n]		*hier:* Mais
included [ɪn'klu:dɪd]		inbegriffen
religious community [rɪ'lɪdʒəs kə'mju:nəti]	*Pronunciation!* = people who live together and believe the same things	Religionsgemeinschaft

READING CORNER

No time to be real teenagers

°**Herald** ['herəld]		Zeitung
middle-class [mɪdl'klɑ:s]		Mittelklasse-
Falls Church ['fɒls tʃɜ:tʃ]		Ortschaft in Virginia
Virginia [vɜ:'dʒɪnɪə]		Bundesstaat in den U.S.A.
to pass [pɑ:s]		vorbeigehen an
security guard [sɪ'kjʊərəti gɑ:d]	*Pronunciation!* A ~ always stands outside the White House.	Sicherheitsangestellte/r
My parents used to take me everywhere. [maɪ 'peərənts ju:st tʊ 'teɪk mi ˌ'evrɪweə]		Meine Eltern brachten mich früher überall hin.
atmosphere ['ætməˌsfɪə]	*Stress!* The ~ at the party was great. Everybody had a lot of fun.	Stimmung
among [ə'mʌŋ]	There were many children ~ the visitors.	unter
to snooze [snu:z]	= to sleep for a short time	dösen
pressure ['preʃə]	Kids are often under ~ before important tests.	Druck
to get stressed [get 'strest]	Many people ~ when they have too much work to do.	gestresst werden
society [sə'saɪəti]	= all the people who live in a country	Gesellschaft
to enjoy being young [ɪn'dʒɔɪ bi:ɪŋ 'jʌŋ]		es genießen, jung zu sein
Potrero Hill [pɒ'trerəʊ ˌhɪl]		Stadtteil von San Francisco
San Francisco [sæn frænˌsɪskəʊ]		Stadt in Kalifornien
territory ['terətəri]	= an area	Revier
gang [gæŋ]		Bande
dang *(sl.)* [dæŋ]		*ugs.* verdammt

Vocabulary

1

after-school ['ɑːftə skuːl]	= when school is over	nachschulisch
assignment [ə'saɪnmənt]	*Spelling!* = homework	(Haus-) Aufgabe
to **surround** [sə'raʊnd]	= to stand around sb. or sth.	umzingeln
violence ['vaɪələns]	When people fight and hurt or kill sb. you call that ~.	Gewalt
to **suffer** ['sʌfə]	Some people ~ from headaches when they work on the computer too long.	leiden
diploma [dɪ'pləʊmə]	When you finish school you get a ~.	Abschluss
4 °to **threaten** ['θretn]	= to say you will do sth. terrible to sb.	drohen, bedrohen
°to **feel threatened** [fiːl 'θretnd]	In a war, people ~.	sich bedroht fühlen
°to **experience** [ɪk'spɪərɪəns]	When you go abroad you can ~ a lot.	erleben
5 °*vice versa* [ˌvaɪsɪ'vɜːsə]	*Pronunciation!*	umgekehrt
6 **Grand Junction** [grænd 'dʒʌŋtʃən]		Stadt in Nebraska
Nebraska [nɪ'bræskə]		Bundesstaat in den U.S.A.
grocery store ['grəʊsərɪ stɔː]	= a place where you can buy food and drinks	Lebensmittelgeschäft
alcoholic [ˌælkə'hɒlɪk]	Beer is an ~ drink.	alkoholisch

A REVISION

When Pitt called Lindy

horseback riding *(AE)* ['hɔːsbæk ˌraɪdɪŋ]	= horseriding *(BE)*	Reiten
country club ['kʌntrɪ klʌb]		*Klub auf dem Land, oft mit Sportmöglichkeiten*
2 **fool** [fuːl]	= a stupid person	Narr/Närrin
in love [ɪn 'lʌv]	It's a wonderful feeling to be ~.	verliebt
to **miss** [mɪs]	"I always enjoy swim practice. I don't want to ~ it."	ausfallen lassen

⟨3⟩ **on my mind** [ɒn maɪ 'maɪnd] in meinem Kopf | **Gary Moore** [gærɪ 'mʊə] *irischer Sänger*

A WORDS AND PHRASES

Being a teenager in the U.S.A.

average ['ævərɪdʒ]	The ~ age of pupils who leave school is 16.	durchschnittlich
to **consume** [kən'sjuːm]	= to use or eat	verbrauchen
candy bar ['kændɪ bɑː]		(Schoko-)Riegel
stick of gum [stɪk əv 'gʌm]		Streifen Kaugummi
chips *(AE)* [tʃɪps]		Kartoffelchips
belief [bɪ'liːf]		Glaube
heaven ['hevn]	= the place where people want to be after they have died	Himmel
hell [hel]	↔ heaven	Hölle
alien ['eɪljən]	= a being from another planet	Außerirdische/r
leisure ['leʒə]	= free time	Freizeit
to **exercise** ['eksəsaɪz]	= to train	sich fit halten
to **do sports** [duː 'spɔːts]		Sport betreiben

Vocabulary 1

craft [krɑːft]		Handwerk, Kunstgewerbe
poverty ['pɒvəti]	poor – ~	Armut
pregnant ['pregnənt]	= what you are in the nine months before you have a baby	schwanger
1 **less than** ['les ðæn]	He waited ~ five minutes for her. Then he went alone.	weniger als
a third [ə 'θɜːd]	= 1/3	ein Drittel
three out of ten ['θriː ˌaʊt əv ten]		drei von zehn
°**average** ['ævərɪdʒ]		*Durchschnitt*

STRATEGY PAGE

Reading strategies

to **split** [splɪt]		sich teilen, sich spalten
enjoyment [ɪn'dʒɔɪmənt]	to enjoy → ~	Freude
to **equip** [ɪ'kwɪp]	~ → equipment	ausrüsten

B WORDS AND PHRASES

In the arcade

arcade [ɑː'keɪd]	An ~ is a place where people go to play games.	Spielhalle
What's up? *(sl.)* [wɒts 'ʌp]		*ugs.* Wie geht's?
wanna = want to *(sl.)* ['wɒnə]		*ugs.* will
Cut it out! *(sl.)* [kʌt ɪt 'aʊt]	= Stop it!	*ugs.* Hör auf!
ain't = haven't *(sl.)* [eɪnt]		*ugs.* habe nicht
through *(sl.)* [θruː]		*ugs.* fertig
Yo! *(sl.)* [jəʊ]		*ugs.* Hallo!
How are you doing? *(sl.)* ['haʊ ɑː jə 'duːɪŋ]		*ugs.* Wie geht's?
Take it easy! *(sl.)* ['teɪk ɪt 'iːzɪ]		*ugs.* Bleib ruhig.
fellas = fellows *(sl.)* ['feləz]		*ugs.* Jungs
See you guys later. *(sl.)* ['siː juː gaɪz 'leɪtə]		*ugs.* Bis bald.
C'mon = come on *(sl.)* [kʌm 'ɒn]		*ugs.* Komm mit.
outa = out of *(sl.)* ['aʊt ə]		*ugs.* raus

Vocabulary 1

READING CORNER

Cool

English	German	English	German
I'll shoot the crap out of you! (sl.) [aɪl 'ʃuːt ðə 'kræp ˌaʊt ˌəv juː]	ugs. Ich werde euch zusammenschießen.	He'd show 'em. (sl.) [hiːd 'ʃəʊ ˌəm]	ugs. Er würde es ihnen zeigen.
to narrow ['nærəʊ]	sich verengen	half-smile ['hɑːf smaɪl]	Halblächeln
to stretch out [stretʃ 'aʊt]	herausstrecken	darkness ['dɑːknɪs]	Dunkelheit
to feel [fiːl]	hier: liegen	direction [dɪ'rekʃn]	Richtung
to keep up [kiːp 'ʌp]	hoch halten	at night [æt 'naɪt]	nachts
to gaze ['geɪz]	anstarren	to scare [skeə]	erschrecken
cool-looking ['kuːl 'lʊkɪŋ]	‚cool' aussehend	... that'll scare the shit out of 'em (sl.) ['ðætl 'skeə ðə ʃɪt ˌaʊt ˌəv ˌəm]	ugs. ... was sie zu Tode erschrecken wird
to stare [steə]	starren	silence ['saɪləns]	Schweigen
to lower ['ləʊə]	senken	admiration [ˌædmə'reɪʃn]	Bewunderung
inside pocket [ˌɪn'saɪd 'pɒkɪt]	Innentasche	bastard ['bɑːstəd]	Bastard
oversized ['əʊvəsaɪzd]	in Übergröße	once and for all ['wʌns ænd fɔːr ˌ'ɔːl]	ein für allemal
Thank God. [θæŋk 'gɒd]	Gott sei Dank.	yard [jɑːd]	Yard (0,91 m)
to warn [wɔːn]	warnen	a couple of [ə 'kʌpl ˌəv]	ein paar
drawer ['drɔːə]	Schublade	commanding [kə'mɑːndɪŋ]	befehlshaberisch
protection [prə'tekʃn]	Schutz	for a change [fɔːr ə 'tʃeɪndʒ]	zur Abwechslung
emergency [ɪ'mɜːdʒənsɪ]	Notfall	coward ['kaʊəd]	Feigling
to defend [dɪ'fend]	verteidigen	to point [pɔɪnt]	zielen
sort of ['sɔːt ˌəv]	so was wie	outstretched [ˌaʊt'stretʃt]	ausgestreckt
to save [seɪv]	sparen	to take in [teɪk ˌ'ɪn]	aufnehmen
every last cent ['evrɪ lɑːst 'sent]	jeder Pfennig	movement ['muːvmənt]	Bewegung
size [saɪz]	Größe	explosion [ɪk'spləʊʒn]	Knall, Explosion
some [sʌm]	irgend so ein/e	disbelief [ˌdɪsbɪ'liːf]	Unglaube
ghetto ['getəʊ]	Ghetto	to stagger ['stægə]	schwanken, taumeln
to be around [bɪ ˌə'raʊnd]	anwesend sein	still [stɪl]	regungslos
tight [taɪt]	eng	blood [blʌd]	Blut
uneasy [ʌn'iːzɪ]	unruhig, unbehaglich	to kneel down [niːl 'daʊn]	sich niederknien
to make sure of [meɪk 'ʃɔːr ˌəv]	sich versichern	beside [bɪ'saɪd]	neben
to lean [liːn]	sich anlehnen, lehnen	idol [aɪdl]	Idol
lamppost ['læmppəʊst]	Straßenlaterne	desperation [ˌdespə'reɪʃn]	Verzweiflung
cigarette [ˌsɪgə'ret]	Zigarette	shining ['ʃaɪnɪŋ]	glänzend
to dress ['dres]	anziehen	God damn! [gɒd 'dæm]	Verdammt nochmal!
twerp (sl.) [twɜːp]	ugs. Hohlkopf	to load [ləʊd]	laden
to pretend [prɪ'tend]	so tun, als ob		
to turn red [tɜːn 'red]	rot werden		

to **gaze** ['geɪz]	= to look at sb. or sth. for a long time	anstarren
to **stare** [steə]	= to look wide-eyed	starren
to **lower** ['ləʊə]	= to put down	senken
inside pocket [ˌɪn'saɪd 'pɒkɪt]		Innentasche
oversized ['əʊvəsaɪzd]	When sth. is too big it's ~.	in Übergröße
Thank God. [θæŋk 'gɒd]	~. We've found the money!	Gott sei Dank
to **warn** [wɔːn]	The police ~ed the people because there was bomb.	warnen
drawer ['drɔːə]		Schublade
protection [prə'tekʃn]	to protect – ~	Schutz
emergency [ɪ'mɜːdʒənsɪ]	Pronunciation! When people are hurt in an accident it's an ~.	Notfall
to **defend** (oneself) [dɪ'fend]	When sb. attacks you you can try to ~ yourself.	(sich) schützen

Vocabulary 1

sort of ['sɔːt‿əv]		irgendwie
to **save** [seɪv]		sparen
size [saɪz]	to spend ⟷ ~ What ~ are your jeans? – Oh, they're XXL.	Größe
tight [taɪt]	The jacket is too ~. I can't wear it any more.	eng
to **lean** [liːn]		sich anlehnen
cigarette [ˌsɪɡəˈret]	*Stress!*	Zigarette
to **pretend** [prɪˈtend]		so tun, als ob
to **turn red** [tɜːn ˈred]	Shy people often ~.	rot werden
darkness [ˈdɑːknɪs]	dark – the ~ There was ~ when they went through the tunnel.	Dunkelheit
direction [dɪˈrekʃn]	= the way you go or drive	Richtung
at night [æt ˈnaɪt]	~ you must turn on the light.	nachts
to **scare** [skeə]		erschrecken
silence [ˈsaɪləns]	= when everything is quiet	Schweigen
admiration [ˌædməˈreɪʃn]	= when you like sth. very much	Bewunderung
once and for all [ˈwʌns‿ænd fɔː‿ˈɔːl]	I tell you ~: Leave me alone!	ein für allemal
a couple of [ə ˈkʌpl‿əv]	= some	ein paar
for a change [fɔːr‿ə ˈtʃeɪndʒ]		zur Abwechslung
coward [ˈkaʊəd]	*Pronunciation!* = sb. who is afraid of everything	Feigling
movement [ˈmuːvmənt]		Bewegung
explosion [ɪkˈspləʊʒn]	to explode – an ~	Knall, Explosion
still [stɪl]	When sth. doesn't move it's ~.	regungslos
blood [blʌd]	~ is red and runs through your body.	Blut
to **kneel down** [niːl ˈdaʊn]		sich niederknien
beside [bɪˈsaɪd]	= next to	neben
idol [ˈaɪdl]	= a person or thing that everybody loves	Idol
desperation [ˌdespəˈreɪʃn]	When you don't know what to do you feel ~.	Verzweiflung
God damn! [ˈɡɒd ˈdæm]		Verdammt nochmal!
to **load** [ləʊd]	When a gun is ~*ed* you must be very, very careful with it.	laden

READING CORNER

About the text

6 **shooting** [ˈʃuːtɪŋ]	to shoot – the ~	Schießerei
incident [ˈɪnsɪdənt]		Vorfall
hidden [ˈhɪdn]		versteckt
°*opinion* [əˈpɪnjən]		*Meinung*

LET'S CHECK

2 **violent** [ˈvaɪələnt]	Sb. who wants to fight with other people is ~.	gewalttätig
to **threaten** [ˈθretn]		bedrohen

Vocabulary 1/2

Connections

In dieser Topic hast du Verben gelernt, die eine bestimmte Präposition nach sich ziehen. Diese Präpositionen musst du immer unbedingt mitlernen. Hier eine kleine Übung dazu: Ordne die richtige Präposition dem richtigen Verb zu.

to beat	out
to stretch	up
to keep	down
to gaze	towards
to make sure	in
to walk	of
to take	up
to kneel	at

Wenn ihr zu mehreren lernt, könnt ihr einen Schritt weitergehen und euch das englisch-deutsche *Dictionary* in diesem Buch vornehmen: Sammelt weitere Verben, zu denen eine bestimmte Präposition gehört. Ihr könnt daraus ein Wettspiel machen – wer ordnet die meisten Präpositionen fehlerfrei zu? (Passt auf: Bei manchen Verben passen verschiedene Präpositionen, z. B. passt bei *to look* sowohl *after* als auch *for* als auch *up*.)

In dieser Topic tauchen einige neue Vokabeln auf, die aus zwei Wörtern zusammengesetzt sind. Im folgenden Kasten findest du sechzehn Einzelwörter – finde heraus, welche acht neuen Vokabeln sich dahinter verbergen! (Achtung: Manche werden mit, manche ohne Bindestrich geschrieben.)

| inner | security | after | bar | middle | candy | pocket | country |
| club | store | class | grocery | city | guard | school | inside |

TOPIC 2 GETTING INVOLVED

to **get involved** [gɛt ɪnˈvɒlvd]		sich engagieren
violent [ˈvaɪələnt]	*Stress!* Sb. who wants to fight with other people is ~.	gewalttätig
incident [ˈɪnsɪdənt]		Vorfall
discrimination [dɪˌskrɪmɪˈneɪʃn]	*Stress!* When some people or groups of people aren't allowed to do the same things as the others because of their colour or religion.	Diskriminierung
prefix [ˈpriːfɪks]		Vorsilbe
°*to decide on* [dɪˈsaɪd ɒn]		auswählen, sich entscheiden für
°*to present* [prɪˈzent]		präsentieren, zeigen
°*pinboard* [ˈpɪnbɔːd]		Pinnwand
aggressive [əˈgresɪv]	*Stress!*	aggressiv

Vocabulary 2

A READING CORNER

Two incidents

rescuer ['reskjʊə]	Retter/in	blood [blʌd]	Blut
to stab [stæb]	niederstechen, mit einem Messerstich verletzen	nearby [nɪə'baɪ]	nahe gelegen
attacker [ə'tækə]	Angreifer/in	to identify [aɪ'dentɪfaɪ]	die Identität feststellen, identifizieren
Hillcrest ['hɪlkrest]	Name eines Stadtteils	Malcolm Sanders [ˌmælkəm 'sændəs]	Name
late night shift ['leɪt naɪt 'ʃɪft]	Spätschicht	Taunton Way [ˌtɔːntn 'weɪ]	Straßenname
Baker Street ['beɪkə striːt]	Straßenname	emergency services [ɪ'mɜːdʒənsi 'sɜːvɪsɪz]	Notdienst
dark haired ['dɑːk heəd]	dunkelhaarig	unhurt [ʌn'hɜːt]	unverletzt
to struggle ['strʌgl]	hier: sich wehren	lady ['leɪdi]	Dame
throat [θrəʊt]	Kehle	to get involved [get ɪn'vɒlvd]	verwickelt werden
to continue [kən'tɪnjuː]	fortfahren	in trouble [ɪn 'trʌbl]	in Schwierigkeiten
to appear [ə'pɪə]	erscheinen	to be correct [bɪ kə'rekt]	Recht haben
struggle ['strʌgl]	Kampf	statistic [stə'tɪstɪk]	Statistik
to moan [məʊn]	stöhnen		

dark-haired ['dɑːk ˌheəd]		dunkelhaarig
to **struggle** ['strʌgl]		hier: sich wehren
to **continue** [kən'tɪnjuː]	= to go on	fortfahren
to **appear** [ə'pɪə]	Suddenly he ~ed at the party.	erscheinen
struggle ['strʌgl]	= a fight	Kampf
to **moan** [məʊn]	He felt so terrible that he couldn't speak. He just lay on his bed and ~ed.	stöhnen
blood [blʌd]	~ is red and runs through your body.	Blut
nearby [nɪə'baɪ]		nahegelegen
to **identify** [aɪ'dentɪfaɪ]	= to find out who sb. is	die Identität feststellen
emergency services [ɪ'mɜːdʒənsi 'sɜːvɪsɪz]	After an accident you should call the ~ for help.	Notdienst
unhurt [ʌn'hɜːt]	Nobody could believe it. He was ~ after the accident.	unverletzt
lady ['leɪdi]	= a (fine) woman	Dame
in trouble [ɪn 'trʌbl]	"You must help me! I'm ~!"	in Schwierigkeiten
statistics [stə'tɪstɪks]		Statistik

A READING CORNER

I still feel ashamed

to **feel ashamed** [fiːl ə'ʃeɪmd]		sich schämen
coward ['kaʊəd]	*Pronunciation!* = sb. who is afraid of doing sth.	Feigling
station ['steɪʃn]	= where an underground train stops	Haltestelle
opposite ['ɒpəzɪt]	*Stress!* The bathroom is ~ the bedroom.	gegenüber
denim ['denɪm]	Jeans are made of this.	Jeansstoff
seat [siːt]		Sitz
coat [kəʊt]		Mantel
to **threaten** ['θretn]	He ~ed him with a knife. It was terrible.	bedrohen

99

Vocabulary

2

drunk [drʌŋk]	If you drink too much beer, you get ~.	betrunken
passenger ['pæsɪndʒə]	= sb. who takes a bus, a train or a taxi	Fahrgast, Passagier
to **stagger** ['stægə]	Sometimes people ~ when they have drunk too much beer.	schwanken
platform ['plætfɔ:m]	You stand there when you wait for a train.	Bahnsteig
1 **suspect** [sə'spekt]	Who is the murderer? There are five ~s.	Verdächtige(r)

A WORDS AND PHRASES

Chat Radio London

Chat Radio London [tʃæt ˌreɪdɪəʊ 'lʌndən]		erfunderner Radiosender
station ['steɪʃn]	Kiss FM is a ~ which only plays pop music.	Sender
phone-in ['fəʊn_ɪn]	= a sort of radio programme	Rundfunkprogramm, an dem sich Hörer per Telefon beteiligen können
advice [əd'vaɪs]	= help or a tip	Rat
to **dislike** ['dɪslaɪk]	⟷ to like	nicht mögen, verabscheuen
impossible [ɪm'pɒsəbl]	It's ~ to walk to the moon.	unmöglich
crowded ['kraʊdɪd]	When a disco is ~ too many people are there.	*hier:* überfüllt
impolite ['ɪmpəlaɪt]	⟷ polite	unhöflich
1 **original** [ə'rɪdʒənl]	Nobody could read the ~letter. It was too old.	Original-, ursprünglich
2 **false** [fɔ:ls]	= wrong	falsch

A NEW STRUCTURES

Reports

Catford Gazette [ˌkætfəd gə'zet]		*Zeitung*
Camden Allstars [ˌkæmdn 'ɔ:lstɑ:s]		*erfundener Name einer Basketballmannschaft*
Catford Cannons [ˌkætfəd 'kænəns]		*erfundener Name einer Basketballmannschaft*
Crewe Road [kru: 'rəʊd]		*Straßenname*
to **introduce** [ˌɪntrə'dju:s]	= to use or to show sth. for the first time	einführen
Marks and Spencer [ˌmɑ:ks ənd 'spensə]		*engl. Geschäftskette*
Lawson Street ['lɔ:sən stri:t]		*Straßenname*
Richmond Park ['rɪtʃmənd pɑ:k]		*Park in London*
⟨3⟩ **Tracy Chapman** [ˌtreɪsɪ 'tʃæpmən]	*Sängerin*	
	lyric ['lɪrɪk]	Liedtext
	sleepless ['sli:plɪs]	schlaflos

Vocabulary 2

STRATEGY PAGE

Collecting and organizing ideas

opinion [ə'pɪnjən]	= what you think of sb. or sth. What's your ~ of the new teacher?	Meinung
°**to group** [gruːp]		gruppieren
first of all ['fɜːst‿əv‿ɔːl]	first, ~ …	erstens, zuallererst
secondly ['sekəndlɪ]		zweitens
last of all ['lɑːst‿əv‿ɔːl]		zuletzt

REVISION

Speak out for your rights

to **speak out** [spiːk‿'aʊt]	= to fight for/against sth.	sich für/gegen etwas aussprechen
discrimination [dɪskrɪmɪ'neɪʃn]		Diskriminierung
race [reɪs]		Rasse
1 **entrance** ['entrəns]	= where you go in	Eingang
separate ['sepəreɪt]	Men and women often use ~ toilets.	getrennt
Martin Luther King ['mɑːtɪn luːθə ˌkɪŋ]		amerik. Bürgerrechtler
equal ['iːkwəl]	= the same	gleich

READING CORNER

Hungry for justice

justice ['dʒʌstɪs]	= when sth. is fair	Gerechtigkeit
apartment *(AE)* [ə'pɑːtmənt]	= flat	Wohnung
San Jose [sæn ˌhəʊ'zeɪ]		*Stadt in Kalifornien*
downtown San Jose [daʊntaʊn sæn ˌhəʊ'zeɪ]		in der City von San Jose
honey ['hʌnɪ]	"Bears like ~." – "And I like you, ~."	Honig, *hier:* Schätzchen
ordinary ['ɔːdnrɪ]	= normal	gewöhnlich, normal
dream [driːm]	to dream – the ~	Traum
everyday problem ['evrɪdeɪ ˌprɒbləm]		Alltagsproblem
afterwards ['ɑːftəwədz]	First we went to the cinema. ~ we met our friends.	hinterher
Denny's ['deniːz]		*erfundener Name einer Restaurantkette*
sitting fee ['sɪtɪŋ fiː]		Platzgebühr
policy ['pɒləsɪ]		*hier:* Geschäftsbedingungen
to **refuse** [rɪ'fjuːz]	When you show or say that you don't want to do sth. Children sometimes ~ to do what their parents tell them.	sich weigern
to **shake** [ʃeɪk]	When it's cold people often ~.	zittern
bar [bɑː]	A place where you can eat snacks.	Snackbar

Vocabulary 2

They can't ..., can they? [ðeɪ 'kɑːnt ... 'kæn ðeɪ]	~ come to the party, ~?	Sie können nicht ..., nicht wahr?
right now [raɪt 'naʊ]		jetzt sofort
3 **Chronicle Herald Sun** [ˌkrɒnɪkl 'herəld sʌn]		*Tageszeitung*
4 °**to react** [rɪ'ækt]		reagieren
5 **organization** [ɔː gənaɪ'zeɪʃn]		*hier:* Konzern
case [keɪs]	Who is the murderer? That ~ is very interesting.	Fall
to contact ['kɒntækt]		ansprechen, Kontakt aufnehmen
civil right [sɪvl 'raɪt]	Black people in America didn't have the same ~s as white people 200 years ago.	Bürgerrecht
lawyer ['lɔːjə]	*Pronunciation!* = sb. who knows a lot about laws and helps other people	Rechtsanwalt/Rechtsanwältin
to **discriminate against** [dɪ'skrɪmɪneɪt ə,genst]	*Stress!* Restaurants and shops sometimes ~ black people.	diskriminieren
to **scare away** ['skeə ə'weɪ]	He ~ d ~ the wolf with a gun. Everybody was very happy.	verjagen

B WORDS AND PHRASES

How to react to discrimination

to **react (to)** [rɪ'ækt]	When he heard the lies he ~ed angrily.	reagieren (auf)
act [ækt]	= a law	Gesetz
Civil Rights Act [sɪvl 'raɪts ækt]		*Bürgerrechtsakte von 1964*
video arcade ['vɪdɪəʊ ɑː'keɪd]	= a place where you can play video games	Videospielhalle
policy ['pɒlɪsɪ]		Politik, Grundsatz
security guard [sɪ'kjʊərətɪ gɑːd]		Sicherheitsangestellte/r
racist ['reɪsɪst]		rassistisch
to **throw out** [θrəʊ 'aʊt]	They ~ the man ~ because he was drunk.	herausschmeißen
1 **witness** ['wɪtnɪs]	Sb. who sees an accident is a ~. *Pronunciation!*	Zeuge/Zeugin
to **threaten physically** ['θretn 'fɪzɪkəlɪ]		mit roher Gewalt drohen

Vokabeln versenken

Ihr kennt wahrscheinlich alle das sehr alte und beliebte Spiel „Schiffe versenken". Im Folgenden sollt ihr keine Schiffe, sondern Vokabeln versenken. Das Spiel wird paarweise gespielt. Beide Spieler zeichnen auf ein großes Blatt Papier (am besten kariert) ein großes Quadrat, das waagerecht und senkrecht jeweils 15 kleine Quadrate umfasst. Die Waagerechte erhält die Zahlen 1 bis 15, die Senkrechte die Buchstaben A bis O.

1	2	3	4	5	6	7	8	9	10	11	12	13	14	15	
															A
															B
				s	t	a	b								C
															D
															E
															F
															G
															H
															I
															J
															K
															L
															M
															N
															O

Nun tragt ihr in euer Quadrat, ohne dass die/der andere es sehen kann, senkrecht, waagerecht oder diagonal Wörter ein, die ihr in dieser Topic gelernt habt – und zwar ein Wort mit vier, eins mit fünf, eins mit sechs, eins mit sieben und eins mit acht Buchstaben. Setzt euch einander gegenüber und beginnt, mit Fragen herauszufinden, wo sich die Wörter der/des anderen befinden. *C5? – Yes. An S.* Ihr tragt das S in euer Quadrat ein und dürft nochmals fragen. *C6? – Yes, a T.* So geht's weiter, bis ihr als Antwort *No, sorry.* bekommt, dann ist die/der andere dran. Wer findet zuerst alle Wörter?

TOPIC 3 BREAKING DOWN BARRIERS

to **break down** [breɪk 'daʊn]	*Pronunciation!*	niederreißen
barrier ['bærɪə]		Barriere
building site ['bɪldɪŋ saɪt]		Baustelle
filler ['fɪlə]		Füllwort
2 **nationality plate** [ˌnæʃə'nælɪtɪ pleɪt]	D	Nationalitätenschild
⟨3⟩ Pet Shop Boys ['pet ʃɒp bɔɪz]	*engl. Pop-Duo*	to **mention** ['menʃən] erwähnen

Vocabulary

3

A NEW STRUCTURES

They came from all over Europe

registration [ˌredʒɪˈstreɪʃn]		Anmeldung
form [fɔːm]		Formular
registration form [ˌredʒɪˈstreɪʃn fɔːm]	When you want to become a member of a club you must put your name and address on a ~.	Anmeldeformular
marathon [ˈmærəθən]		Marathon
runner [ˈrʌnə]		Läufer/in
Wales [weɪlz]		Wales
to **be in training** [bɪ ɪn ˈtreɪnɪŋ]		trainieren
to **take part** [teɪk ˈpɑːt]	Did you ~ in the race? – Yes, and I won it!	teilnehmen
Salamanca [ˌsæləˈmæŋkə]		*Stadt in Spanien*
Spain [speɪn]		Spanien
athletics [æθˈletɪks]	*Pronunciation! Spelling!*	Athletik
champion [ˈtʃæmpjən]	= the winner of a race or match	Champion
France [frɑːns]		Frankreich
to **jog** [dʒɒg]		joggen
autumn [ˈɔːtəm]		Herbst
battle [bætl]		Kampf
international [ˌɪntəˈnæʃnl]		international
mastercook [ˈmɑːstəkʊk]	= sb. who cooks very, very well	Meisterkoch/köchin

A WORDS AND PHRASES

Where are we going to eat?

pork [pɔːk]		Schweinefleisch
beef [biːf]		Rindfleisch
gravy [ˈgreɪvi]		Soße
pasta [ˈpæstə]	Not only Italians like to eat ~.	Pasta, Teigware
potato [pəˈteɪtəʊ]	What french fries are made from.	Kartoffel
carrot [ˈkærət]		Mohrrübe, Karotte
bean [biːn]		Bohne
pea [piː]		Erbse
cabbage [ˈkæbɪdʒ]		Kohl
noodle [nuːdl]		Nudel
1 **dish** [dɪʃ]	= a meal	Gericht
2 **waiter** [ˈweɪtə]		Ober/Kellner
fly [flaɪ]		Fliege
to **do the breast stoke** [duː ðə ˈbrest strəʊk]		brustschwimmen

A READING CORNER

The streets of Niederburg

hardly [ˈhɑːdli]	I ~ learnt my vocabulary but the test was okay.	kaum
a couple of [ə ˈkʌpl əv]	= some	ein paar
square [skweə]	= an open area in a town, e.g. *Trafalgar* ~	Platz
tidy [ˈtaɪdi]	When your room is ~ your mother is happy.	ordentlich

Vocabulary 3

pretty [ˈprɪtɪ]		hübsch
kind [kaɪnd]	= nice	nett
lad [læd]	= guy	Bursche
at least [æt ˈliːst]		zumindest
narrow [ˈnærəʊ]	= not very wide	eng
alley [ˈælɪ]	= a small street	Gasse
dead end [dedˈend]		Sackgasse
I'm sort of lost. [aɪm ˈsɔːt əv lɒst]	Can you tell me the way to the station? I think ~.	Ich habe mich irgendwie verlaufen.
design [dɪˈzaɪn]		Muster, Design
to **get sb. wrong** [get sʌmbədɪ ˈrɒŋ]		jdn. falsch verstehen
no jobs either [nəʊ ˈdʒɒbz aɪðə]		auch keine Jobs
future [ˈfjuːtʃə]	When you talk about the year 2080 you talk about the ~.	Zukunft
silence [ˈsaɪləns]	= when everything is quiet; when nobody says anything	Schweigen
fighter [ˈfaɪtə]	to fight – a ~	Kämpfer/in

STRATEGY PAGE

What to do when you don't know a word

tool [tuːl]		Werkzeug/Gerät
alternative [ɔːlˈtɜːnətɪv]	*Pronunciation! Stress!*	Alternative

WORDS AND PHRASES

Eurotraining

eurotraining [ˈjʊərəʊtreɪnɪŋ]		*Beispiel für ein europäisches Trainingsprogramm für junge Leute*
scheme [skiːm]	= a program	Programm
apprenticeship [əˈprentɪʃɪp]	To learn a job you have to do an ~.	Lehre
Alassio [əˈlæsɪəʊ]		*Stadt in Norditalien*
1 **hostel** [ˈhɒstl]	= a hotel for young people or students	Wohnheim
while [waɪl]	~ he was writing a letter she had a bath.	während
2 **Waterford** [ˈwɔːtəfəd]		*Stadt in Irland*
Dublin [ˈdʌblɪn]		*Hauptstadt Irlands*
to **miss** [mɪs]	I must go now. I don't want to ~ my train.	verpassen
Milan [mɪˈlæn]		Mailand, *Stadt in Italien*
sort of [ˈsɔːt əv]		irgendwie
station [ˈsteɪʃn]	Let us meet at the ~.	Bahnhof
in time [ɪn ˈtaɪm]	= not late	rechtzeitig, pünktlich
There was ..., wasn't there? [ðeə ˈwɒz ... ˈwɒznt ðeə]	~ a car crash, ~?	Es gab ..., nicht wahr?
kind of [ˈkaɪnd əv]		irgendwie
3 **electrician** [ˌɪlekˈtrɪʃn]	*Stress!* An ~ repairs radios, TVs or telephones.	Elektriker/in
What about you? [wɒt əˈbaʊt ˈjuː]	I don't like fish. ~?	Und du? Wie ist es bei dir?
plumber [ˈplʌmə]		Installateur/in
pipe [paɪp]	Water is delivered to your house through ~s.	Rohr

Vocabulary

3

washbasin ['wɒʃbeɪsn]		Waschbecken
bath [bɑːθ]		Badewanne
these days ['ðiːz deɪz]	~ many people have mobile phones.	heute, heutzutage
to **wash off** [wɒʃ 'ɒf]		abwaschen
dirt [dɜːt]		Schmutz
technical ['teknɪkl]		technisch

REVISION

The first morning

	coordinator [kəʊˈɔːdɪneɪtə]	*Pronunciation!*	Koordinator/in, Organisator/in
1	**midday** ['mɪdeɪ]	= the time when you have your lunch (12 a.m.)	Mittag
	to **put in** [pʊt 'ɪn]		installieren
2	°*international* [ɪntəˈnæʃənl]		*international*

READING CORNER

On the building site

	foreman ['fɔːmən]	= sb. who tells the workers what they have to do	Polier, Vorarbeiter
	spanner ['spænə]		Schraubenschlüssel
	to **suggest** [səˈdʒest]	I ~ we go swimming. What do you think?	vorschlagen
	right from the first moment ['raɪt frɒm ðə fɜːst 'məʊmənt]	I didn't like him ~. That was a real problem.	vom ersten Moment an
	perfect ['pɜːfɪkt]	*Stress!*	perfekt
	to **take a deep breath** [teɪk ə 'diːp breθ]		tief Luft einholen
	actually ['æktʃʊəli]	~ I'd like to watch that film. What about you?	eigentlich
	trainee [treɪˈniː]	= sb. who is learning a job	Auszubildende/r
	helpful ['helpfʊl]	A dictionary can be very ~.	hilfsbereit
3	**lazy** ['leɪzi]		faul

LET'S CHECK

dishes ['dɪʃɪz]	After a meal someone has to wash the ~.	Geschirr

---

Play with phonetics [ˌwɒts ðə 'wɜːd]?

In dieser Topic kommen einige Wörter vor, die es so oder ähnlich auch im Deutschen gibt, allerdings ist die Aussprache nicht immer in beiden Sprachen gleich. Um die englische Aussprache zu trainieren, findest du im folgenden Kasten die neuen Wörter in Lautschrift. Um welche Vokabeln handelt es sich?

[kəʊˈɔːdɪneɪtə]	[ɪntəˈnæʃənl]	['bæriə]	['tʃæmpjən]
[æθˈletɪks]	[ɔːlˈtɜːnətɪv]	['pæstə]	['nuːdl]
[dɪˈzaɪn]	[ɪlekˈtrɪʃn]	['pɜːfɪkt]	

Wenn euch Lautschrift Spaß macht: Eine/r von euch nimmt sich Topic 1 vor, die/der andere Topic 2. Schreibt einige Wörter in Lautschrift und lasst euch überraschen, ob eure Partnerin/euer Partner herausfindet, welche Wörter ihr ausgewählt habt.

Vocabulary 4

TOPIC 4 — LOVE WORRIES

advice [əd'vaɪs]	I've got a problem. Perhaps you can give me some ~.	Ratschlag, Tipp
poem ['pəʊɪm]		Gedicht

READING CORNER

All about love

extract ['ekstrækt]	Auszug	to sip [sɪp]	schlürfen
flirting ['flɜːtɪŋ]	Flirten	strawberry ['strɔːbəri]	Erdbeere
tickling ['tɪklɪŋ]	Kitzeln	milkshake ['mɪlkʃeɪk]	Milchshake
to twitch [twɪtʃ]	zucken	palm tree ['pɑːm triː]	Palme
muscle ['mʌsl]	Muskel	waterfall ['wɔːtəfɔːl]	Wasserfall
unwelcome [ʌn'welkəm]	unwillkommen	breaking up [breɪkɪŋ ˌʌp]	Auseinandergehen
dating ['deɪtɪŋ]	eine Verabredung treffen, sich verabreden	to end [end]	aufhören
		loved one ['lʌvd wʌn]	Angebetete/r
object ['ɒbdʒɪkt]	Objekt	to tear up [teər ˌʌp]	zerreißen
desire [dɪ'zaɪə]	Begierde	bonfire ['bɒnˌfaɪə]	Feuer
to be allowed out [bɪ ə'laʊd ˌaʊt]	fort dürfen	grandchildren ['grænˌtʃɪldrən]	Enkelkinder
night [naɪt]	*hier:* Abend	to remind [rɪ'maɪnd]	erinnern
to give up [gɪv ˌʌp]	aufgeben	lucky ['lʌki]	glücklich
comfortable ['kʌmfətəbl]	bequem	escape [ɪ'skeɪp]	Flucht
rugby final ['rʌgbi 'faɪnl]	Endspiel der Rugby-Meisterschaften	worm [wɜːm]	Wurm
		to avoid [ə'vɔɪd]	vermeiden
grunt [grʌnt]	Grunzen	period ['pɪəriəd]	Zeit
string [strɪŋ]	Schnur	to mourn [mɔːn]	trauern
reply [rɪ'plaɪ]	Antwort	phase [feɪz]	Teil
to get on [get ˌɒn]	miteinander auskommen, zusammen passen	challenging ['tʃælɪndʒɪŋ]	herausfordernd
		astronaut ['æstrənɔːt]	Astronaut/in
mood [muːd]	Laune	volleyball ['vɒlibɔːl]	Volleyball
to alternate ['ɔːltəneɪt]	wechseln	violin [ˌvaɪə'lɪn]	Geige
to fall in love [fɒl ɪn 'lʌv]	sich verlieben	copy ['kɒpi]	Exemplar
sunrise ['sʌnraɪz]	Sonnenaufgang	The Righteous Brothers [ðə 'raɪtʃəs ˌbrʌðəs]	*Pop-Duo aus den 60er Jahren*
volcano [vɒl'keɪnəʊ]	Vulkan		

Ros Asquith [ˌrɒz 'æskwɪθ]		*engl. Cartoonistin, Fotografin, Autorin und Journalistin*
flirting ['flɜːtɪŋ]	She enjoys ~ with the men in the company.	Flirten
muscle ['mʌsl]		Muskel
unwelcome [ʌn'welkəm]	welcome ⟷ ~	unwillkommen
dating ['deɪtɪŋ]	~ is very important when you like sb. very much and want to meet him/her again.	Verabredungen treffen
object ['ɒbdʒɪkt]		Objekt
desire [dɪ'zaɪə]	= when you want sth. very much	Begierde
to be allowed out [bɪ ə'laʊd ˌaʊt]	Teenagers are always very angry when they aren't ~.	fort dürfen
night [naɪt]	I went to the cinema last ~. It was super.	*hier:* Abend
to give up [gɪv ˌʌp]	He has given up football. He is too old.	aufgeben
comfortable ['kʌmfətəbl]	Stress! Is that chair ~?	bequem
James Dean [ˌdʒeɪmz 'diːn]		*amerik. Kultfilmstar der 50er Jahre*

Vocabulary

4

reply [rɪˈplaɪ]	= an answer	Antwort
to **get on** [getˈɒn]	They are always arguing because they don't ~.	miteinander auskommen, zusammen passen
mood [muːd]	= the way you feel	Laune, Stimmung
to **fall in love** [ˌfɔːl ɪn ˈlʌv]		sich verlieben
sunrise [ˈsʌnraɪz]		Sonnenaufgang
to **sip** [sɪp]	When coffee is too hot, some people ~ it.	schlürfen
strawberry [ˈstrɔːbərɪ]		Erdbeere
milkshake [ˈmɪlkʃeɪk]		Milchshake
palm tree [ˈpaːm triː]		Palme
waterfall [ˈwɔːtəfɔːl]		Wasserfall
breaking up [breɪkɪŋ ˈʌp]	= ending a friendship	Schluss machen
to **end** [end]	= to finish/to stop	aufhören
grandchildren [ˈɡrænˌtʃɪldrən]	The children of your children will be your ~.	Enkelkinder
to **remind** [rɪˈmaɪnd]	That song ~s me of our holiday.	erinnern
lucky [ˈlʌkɪ]		glücklich
escape [ɪˈskeɪp]		Flucht
worm [wɜːm]		Wurm
to **avoid** [əˈvɔɪd]	You should ~ the sun. It's not good for your skin.	vermeiden
to **mourn** [mɔːn]	During the months after sb. has died you ~.	trauern
astronaut [ˈæstrənɔːt]	*Stress!* = sb. who travels in a spaceship	Astronaut/in
volleyball [ˈvɒlɪbɔːl]		Volleyball
violin [ˌvaɪəˈlɪn]		Geige
1 **suggestion** [səˈdʒestʃən]		Vorschlag
3 to **suggest** [səˈdʒest]	I ~ we go swimming. What do you think?	vorschlagen

⟨5⟩ **unkind** [ʌnˈkaɪnd]	*hier: gemein*	**lyric** [ˈlɪrɪk]	Liedtext
Donna Summer [ˈdɒnə ˈsʌmə]	*Diskosängerin, die in den 70er Jahren sehr erfolgreich war.*		

A WORDS AND PHRASES

A love-hate letter

passion [ˈpæʃn]		Leidenschaft
in fact [ɪn ˈfækt]		tatsächlich
total [ˈtəʊtl]	*Stress!*	völlig
boredom [ˈbɔːdəm]		Langeweile
the more ... the more [ðə ˈmɔː ... ðə ˈmɔː]		je mehr ... desto mehr
habit [ˈhæbɪt]	Smoking is a bad ~.	Angewohnheit
graceful [ˈɡreɪsfʊl]		würdevoll
resemblance [rɪˈzembləns]		Ähnlichkeit
to **pretend** [prɪˈtend]	"I don't like Grandma's present." – "Well, when you see her, ~ that you like it."	so tun, als ob
°*every other line* [ˌevrɪ ˈʌðə ˌlaɪn]		*jede zweite Zeile*
°to **behave** [bɪˈheɪv]		*sich benehmen*

Vocabulary 4

A REVISION

Problems

to **smoke** [sməʊk]		rauchen
cigarette [ˌsɪɡəˈret]		Zigarette
instead [ɪnˈsted]	I didn't like the film on TV so I read a comic ~.	stattdessen
Yuk! [jʌk]		Ätzend!
back row [ˈbæk rəʊ]	When you sit in the ~ of a cinema you sometimes can't see everything.	hinterste Reihe
to **ask sb. out** [ˈɑːsk sʌmbədɪ ˈaʊt]		sich mit jemandem verabreden

STRATEGY PAGE

How to write a poem

	safari [səˈfɑːrɪ]	On a ~ people hunt wild animals.	Safari
1	**tiger** [ˈtaɪɡə]		Tiger
	rain [reɪn]		Regen
2	**wave** [weɪv]		Welle
	beneath [bɪˈniːθ]		unter
	calm [kɑːm]	= not nervous	ruhig
	surface [ˈsɜːfɪs]	The ~ of the sea is sometimes calm. Then it's nice to swim.	Oberfläche
	to **break out** [breɪk ˈaʊt]	Sometimes wild animals ~ of the zoo.	ausbrechen
3	**curious** [ˈkjʊərɪəs]	A ~ person wants to know everything.	neugierig
	dove [dʌv]		weiße Taube
	heart [hɑːt]		Herz

B WORDS AND PHRASES

Heartline

1	°*abbreviation* [əˌbriːvɪˈeɪʃn]	*Pronunciation!*	*Abkürzung*
	non-smoker [ˌnɒnˈsməʊkə]		Nichtraucher
	attractive [əˈtræktɪv]	*Stress!* = good-looking	attraktiv
	blue-eyed [ˈbluː aɪd]		blauäugig
	genuine [ˈdʒenjʊɪn]	*Pronunciation!*	natürlich
	urgent [ˈɜːdʒənt]	I'd like to speak to Mr Miller at once. It's ~.	dringend
	slim [slɪm]		dünn, schlank
	bloke [bləʊk]	= guy	Typ
	reliable [rɪˈlaɪəbl]	When sb. is ~ you can count on him/her.	verlässlich
	fair [feə]		blond
	to **seek** [siːk]	= to look for	suchen
	friendship [ˈfrendʃɪp]	when you are friends with sb.	Freundschaft
	safety [ˈseɪftɪ]	safe – ~	Sicherheit

Vocabulary 4

B READING CORNER

Love, truth and lies

truth [truːθ]	Wahrheit	lip [lɪp]	Lippe
lie [laɪ]	Lüge	fag (sl.) [fæg]	ugs. Zigarette
ironing [ˈaɪənɪŋ]	Bügelwäsche	lighter [ˈlaɪtə]	Feuerzeug
casual [ˈkæʒʊəl]	lässig	natural [ˈnætʃrəl]	natürlich
ten minutes to go [ˈten ˌmɪnɪts tə ˈgəʊ]	noch zehn Minuten	to stare [steə]	starren
to squeeze [skwiːz]	ausdrücken	to go out with sb. [gəʊ ˈaʊt wɪð ˌsʌmbədɪ]	mit jdm. ausgehen
thick lip [θɪk ˈlɪp]	dicke Lippe	to work out [wɜːk ˈaʊt]	klappen
prototype [ˈprəʊtəʊtaɪp]	Prototyp	lad [læd]	Junge
transmission [trænzˈmɪʃn]	Getriebe, Antrieb	never mind [ˈnevə ˈmaɪnd]	macht nichts
rubbish [ˈrʌbɪʃ]	Quatsch	shame about the face [ˈʃeɪm əˈbaʊt ðə ˈfeɪs]	schade um das Gesicht
load [ləʊd]	Haufen	straight away [streɪt əˈweɪ]	sofort
maximum [ˈmæksɪməm]	höchst		
to yawn [jɔːn]	gähnen	phony [ˈfəʊnɪ]	unecht
trace [treɪs]	Spur	for ages [fɔːr ˈeɪdʒɪz]	seit einer Ewigkeit
beard [bɪəd]	Bart	to flick [flɪk]	schnipsen
let alone … [let əˈləʊn]	geschweige denn …	fag end [fæg ˈend]	Kippe
chest [tʃest]	Brust	to kick [kɪk]	treten
to knock over [nɒk ˈəʊvə]	umwerfen	quite by chance [ˈkwaɪt baɪ ˈtʃɑːns]	ganz zufällig
idiot [ˈɪdɪət]	Idiot	jealous [ˈdʒeləs]	eifersüchtig
serviette [ˌsɛːvɪˈet]	Serviette	to run into sb. [rʌn ˈɪntʊ ˈsʌmbədɪ]	jdn. zufällig treffen
lovely [ˈlʌvlɪ]	schön	all the way [ˈɔːl ðə weɪ]	den ganzen Weg
fragile [ˈfrædʒaɪl]	zart	juicy [ˈdʒuːsɪ]	pikant
to sweat [swet]	schwitzen	whatever [wɒtˈevə]	was bloß
to smell [smel]	riechen		
to behave [bɪˈheɪv]	sich benehmen		
baffled [ˈbæfld]	verdutzt		
cheek [tʃiːk]	Wange		

truth [truːθ] — Wahrheit
lie [laɪ] — Lüge
ironing [ˈaɪənɪŋ] — *Pronunciation!* — Bügelwäsche

casual [ˈkæʒʊəl] = cool — lässig
ten minutes to go [ˈten ˌmɪnɪts tə ˈgəʊ] = ten more minutes — noch zehn Minuten
rubbish [ˈrʌbɪʃ] — Oh, no, that's ~. I didn't say that. — Quatsch
to yawn [jɔːn] — When you're tired you ~. — gähnen
trace [treɪs] — Where is the murderer? There isn't any ~ of him. — Spur

beard [bɪəd] — Bart
chest [tʃest] — Brust
idiot [ˈɪdɪət] — *Stress!* = a very stupid person — Idiot
lovely [ˈlʌvlɪ] = very nice — schön
fragile [ˈfrædʒaɪl] — *Pronunciation!* Sth. that can break easily is ~. — zart

to sweat [swet] — When it's hot you ~. — schwitzen
to smell [smel] — That ~s terrible. What is it? Fish? — riechen
to behave [bɪˈheɪv] — The football fans ~d very well. Everybody was happy. — sich benehmen

cheek [tʃiːk] — Wange
lip [lɪp] — Lippe
fag (sl.) [fæg] — ugs. Zigarette

Vocabulary 4

lighter [ˈlaɪtə]		Feuerzeug
natural [ˈnætʃrəl]		natürlich
to **go out with sb.** [gəʊ ˈaʊt wɪð ˌsʌmbədɪ]	= to be sb.'s girlfriend/boyfriend	mit jdm. ausgehen
never mind [ˈnevə ˈmaɪnd]	Sorry, I forgot your book. – Oh, ~. I don't need it today.	macht nichts
straight away [streɪt əˈweɪ]	= at once	sofort
for ages [fɔː ˈeɪdʒɪz]	= for a long time	seit einer Ewigkeit
quite by chance [ˈkwaɪt baɪ ˈtʃɑːns]	We didn't plan it. It happened ~.	ganz zufällig
jealous [ˈdʒeləs]	= you want to have sth. that sb. else has. Tom is ~ of Peter's girlfriend.	eifersüchtig
to **run into sb.** [rʌn ˈɪntʊ ˈsʌmbədɪ]	Oh, I met Linda. I ran into her in town.	jdn. zufällig treffen
all the way [ɔːl ðə ˈweɪ]	~ the bus driver listened to this terrible radio programme. I hated it!	den ganzen Weg
whatever [wɒtˈevə]	~ is he doing?	was bloß

READING CORNER

About the text

3 to **lie** [laɪ]	= when you say sth. that's not right.	lügen
5 to **come round** [kʌm ˈraʊnd]		vorbeikommen
to **take place** [teɪk ˈpleɪs]	Where is the party going to ~? – Oh, I think at Joanne's.	stattfinden

LET'S CHECK

4 to **kiss sb. goodnight** [ˌkɪs ˌsʌmbədɪ gʊdˈnaɪt]		jdm. einen Gutenachtkuss geben

---

Activity card game

Für dieses Spiel musst du dich mit mehreren Leuten zusammentun. Schreibt 20 Vokabeln jeweils auf eine Karteikarte oder ein Stück Papier und legt diese Karten mit dem Gesicht nach unten auf einen Stapel. Weitere 20 Karten, die so genannten *Activity*-Karten, markiert ihr auf einer Seite jeweils rot, grün oder blau.
Die rot markierten Karten bedeuten: Auf Englisch erklären!
Die grün markierten Karten bedeuten: Malen (also ohne Worte!)
Die blau markierten Karten bedeuten: Gestik und Mimik (also auch ohne Worte!)
Diese Karten legt ihr ebenfalls mit dem Gesicht nach unten auf einen Stapel.
Nun teilt euch in zwei Gruppen. Die/Der Erste zieht eine Karte vom Vokabelstapel und eine vom *Activity*-Stapel und hat nun 30 Sekunden Zeit, um die Vokabel, die sie/er gezogen hat, entsprechend der gezogenen *Activity*-Karte ihrer/seiner Gruppe zu erklären. Wenn die Gruppe den Begriff innerhalb der vorgegebenen Zeit errät, gibt's dafür einen Punkt. Dann ist die andere Gruppe dran. Na, wer gewinnt?

Vocabulary

TOPIC 5 — YOU'RE GOING TO MAKE IT!

to **make it** ['meɪk ɪt]	I've worked so hard for the test. I'm sure I'll ~.	es schaffen
romance [rəʊ'mæns]		Romanze, Liebesgeschichte
to **save** [seɪv]		retten
to **go out with sb.** [gəʊ 'aʊt wɪð ˌsʌmbədɪ]	= to be sb's girlfriend/boyfriend	mit jdm. ausgehen
pool [puːl]		Poolbillard
to **jump off** [dʒʌmp 'ɒf]		herunterspringen
instead [ɪn'sted]		stattdessen
freak [friːk]	= a fan	Fan
cigarette [ˌsɪgə'ret]	Stress!	Zigarette
skateboarding ['skeɪtbɔːdɪŋ]		Skateboard fahren
on his mind [ɒn hɪz 'maɪnd]		in seinem Kopf
collection [kə'lekʃn]		Sammlung
driving licence ['draɪvɪŋ ˌlaɪsns]	You need a ~ to drive a car.	Führerschein
future ['fjuːtʃə]		Zukunft
Greek [griːk]		griechisch
to **organize** ['ɔːgənaɪz]		organisieren
1 **surprise** [sə'praɪz]		Überraschung
to **teach sb. a lesson** ['tiːtʃ ˌsʌmbədɪ ə 'lesn]	Sometimes pupils ~ a new pupil ~.	jdm. eine Lektion erteilen
°**sheet of paper** [ʃiːt əv 'peɪpə]		Blatt Papier
°**in five years' time** [ɪn 'faɪv jɪəz teɪm]		in fünf Jahren

A — WORDS AND PHRASES

A few years later

engineering firm [ˌendʒɪ'nɪərɪŋ fɜːm]	= a company that makes machines	Maschinenbaufirma
trade fair ['treɪd feə]	Companies show the things they sell at a ~.	Messe
I wonder if you can ... [aɪ 'wʌndə ɪf juː kæn]	~ phone the doctor for me. I'm feeling so terrible.	Können Sie vielleicht ...
to **put sb. through** [pʊt ˌsʌmbədɪ 'θruː]	= to connect sb. with sb.	jdn. durchstellen
to **hold the line** [həʊld ðə 'laɪn]	= to wait a moment on the phone	warten (während eines Telefonats)
to **leave a message** [liːv ə 'mesɪdʒ]	Would you like to ~ for Mr Smith? – No, thanks, I'll call again later.	eine Nachricht hinterlassen
You're welcome. [jʊə 'welkʌm]		Gern geschehen.
2 **bill** [bɪl]	When you've bought sth. you get a ~.	Rechnung
to **order** ['ɔːdə]	In a bar you can ~ a drink.	bestellen
back to back [ˌbæk tʊ 'bæk]		Rücken an Rücken

Vocabulary 5

A WORDS AND PHRASES

Jobs for the boys – and the girls

to **design** [dɪˈzaɪn]	Before you can make e.g. a car you must ~ it.	entwerfen
to **update** [ˈʌpdeɪt]		aktualisieren
website [ˈwebsaɪt]	= a page on the Internet	Seite im Internet
individual [ɪndɪˈvɪdjʊəl]		Einzelperson
education office [ˌedjuːˈkeɪʃn ˌɒfɪs]		Schulamt
to **translate** [trænsˈleɪt]	= to put a text e.g. from English into German	übersetzen
remail [ˈriːmeɪl]	= an answer to your e-mail	Antwortmail

B READING CORNER

Florian meets Joanne

final [ˈfaɪnl]	= the last	End-
hope [həʊp]	"I haven't found my watch." – "Well, don't give up ~."	Hoffnung
repairer [rɪˈpeərə]	to repair – a ~	Instandsetzer/in
pay [peɪ]	= the money you get for your work	Bezahlung
Majorca [məˈdʒɔːkə]		Mallorca
bar [bɑː]		Bar
beachball [ˈbiːtʃbɔːl]		Strandball
bikini [bɪˈkiːnɪ]		Bikini
something made him say ... [ˈsʌmθɪŋ meɪd hɪm ˈseɪ]		etwas zwang ihn zu sagen ...
I bet [aɪ ˈbet]		Ich denke, ich wette
camping site [ˈkæmpɪŋ saɪt]		Campingplatz
Manchester [ˈmæntʃɪstə]		Stadt in Mittelengland
I did guess ... [aɪ ˈdɪd ges]	~ he was her new boyfriend. Did you know?	Ich hab's mir gedacht ...
do-it-yourself store [duːˌɪt jɔːˈself stɔː]		Heimwerkermarkt
plant hire section [ˈplɑːnt haɪə ˈsekʃn]		Abteilung für Baumaschinenvermietung
cement mixer [sɪˈment mɪksə]		Betonmischer
tractor [ˈtræktə]		Traktor
motor boat [ˈməʊtəbəʊt]		Motorboot
bay [beɪ]	= a part of the coast with a beach and cliffs	Bucht
motor [ˈməʊtə]	Every car has a ~.	Motor
to **cough** [kɒf]	*Pronunciation!* If you smoke too much, you have to ~.	husten
cord [kɔːd]		Schnur
Mr Fixit [ˌmɪstə ˈfɪksɪt]		Herr Allesreparierer
tool [tuːl]		Werkzeug
spanner [ˈspænə]		Schraubenschlüssel
cover [ˈkʌvə]		Deckel, Haube
to **undo** [ˌʌnˈduː]	*Stress!*	lösen
sparking plug [ˈspɑːkɪŋ plʌg]		Zündkerze

113

Vocabulary

5

petrol ['petrəl]	A car won't move without ~.	Benzin
tank [tæŋk]		Tank
outboard motor [,aʊtbɔːd 'məʊtə]		Außenbordmotor
screw [skruː]		Schraube
done up tight [dʌn ʌp 'taɪt]	A bottle should always be ~.	fest zugeschraubt
hissing ['hɪsɪŋ]	When you open a bottle you sometimes hear a ~ noise.	zischend
Manchester Piccadilly ['mæntʃɪstə ˌpɪkə'dɪlɪ]		Hauptbahnhof von Manchester
station ['steɪʃn]		Bahnhof, Haltestelle
to surprise [sə'praɪz]	Oh, they really ~ed me. And it was such a great party!	überraschen

STRATEGY PAGE

Listening

°**answering machine** ['ɑːnsərɪŋ mə'ʃiːn]	When you go out, you can turn on your ~.	Anrufbeantworter
°**to suggest** [sə'dʒest]	I ~ we go swimming. What do you think?	vorschlagen

B REVISION

Boss for a day

camper ['kæmpə]	= sb. who lives and sleeps in a tent	Camper
sandpit ['sændpɪt]	Children like to play in a ~.	Sandkasten
toilet block ['tɔɪlɪt ˌblɒk]		Toilettenanlage
gas [gæs]		Gas
over ['əʊvə]	When the concert was ~ everybody left the hall.	vorbei
while [waɪl]	~ he was writing a letter she had a bath.	während

⟨2⟩ Billy Bragg [ˌbɪlɪ 'bræg]	kritischer britischer Sänger/Songschreiber	**pessimistic** [ˌpesɪ'mɪstɪk] **system** ['sɪstəm] **to fail** [feɪl]		pessimistisch System versagen, scheitern
optimistic [ˌɒptɪ'mɪstɪk] **dreamy** ['driːmɪ]	optimistisch verträumt			

B READING CORNER

A problem at the stadium

United [jʊ'naɪtɪd]		Manchester United, Fußballclub
ground [graʊnd]		(Fußball-)Platz
mower ['məʊə]		(Rasen-)Mäher
to fix [fɪks]	= to repair	reparieren
Arsenal ['ɑːsənl]		Name einer Londoner Fußballmannschaft
rain [reɪn]		Regen
grass [grɑːs]		Gras
to race [reɪs]	= to hurry	eilen
moped ['məʊped]		Moped

Vocabulary

5

to **charge** [tʃɑːdʒ]		aufladen
battery [ˈbætərɪ]	You need ~ies for your walkman.	Batterie
groundsman [ˈgraʊndzmæn]		Platzwart
flat [flæt]		entladen, leer
to **go wrong** [gəʊ ˈrɒŋ]	Help! My computer is ~ing wrong. What can I do?	kaputtgehen
drum [drʌm]	Restaurants use a lot of oil. So they buy it in large ~s.	Tonne
omygod [əʊmɪˈgɒd]	Spelling!	Oh mein Gott!
diesel [ˈdiːzl]		Diesel
pipe [paɪp]		Rohr
filter [fɪltə]	When you make coffee, you put the coffee in a paper ~.	Filter
lad [læd]		mein Junge *(Anrede)*
to **cut the grass** [kʌt ðə ˈgrɑːs]	In winter you needn't ~.	das Gras mähen
DIY [ˌdiː_aɪ ˈwaɪ]	*Pronunciation!*	Do-it-yourself
DIY Direct [ˌdiː_aɪ waɪ daɪˈrekt]		Name einer Firma
to **give up sth.** [gɪv_ˈʌp ˌsʌmθɪŋ]	Some people find it very difficult to ~ drinking.	auf etwas verzichten
cheque [tʃek]	Spelling!	Scheck
2 **oily** [ˈɔɪlɪ]	People who repair cars are often ~.	ölverschmiert
overalls [ˈəʊvərɔːlz]	You should wear ~ when you repair a car or a bike.	Arbeitsanzug
3 °**headline** [ˈhedlaɪn]		*Schlagzeile*
to **save** [seɪv]		retten
postman [ˈpəʊstmæn]	= he brings the letters to people's homes	Postbote
drama [ˈdrɑːmə]		Drama
Homestead Hotel [ˌhəʊmsted həʊˈtel]	*Pronunciation!*	*Hotelname*

READING CORNER

A page of poems

fast [fɑːst]		*hier:* fest
broken-winged [ˈbrəʊken wɪŋd]		mit gebrochenem Flügel
cannot [ˈkænɒt]	= long form of can't	kann nicht
barren [ˈbærən]		öd
field [fiːld]	Cows spend the summer outside in a ~.	Feld
frozen [frəʊzn]	Ice cream is made of ~ milk.	gefroren
Langston Hughes [ˈlæŋstən ˌhjuːs]		*amerik. Schriftsteller*
to **reach out** [riːtʃ_ˈaʊt]		die Hände ausstrecken
upside down [ˈʌpsaɪd daʊn]	To get the shampoo out of the bottle, you have to turn it ~.	auf den Kopf gestellt
mystery [ˈmɪstərɪ]		Geheimnis
gift [gɪft]	= a present	Geschenk
perfect [ˈpɜːfɪkt]	*Stress!*	perfekt
horse [hɔːs]		Pferd
great [greɪt]		groß
force [fɔːs]	= power	Macht

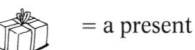

Vocabulary 5

    but [bʌt]   *hier:* außer
2 °*future* ['fju:tʃə]   *Zukunft*
   °*to start sb. off* [sta:t   *jdm. mit dem Anfang*
    'sʌmbədɪ‿ɒf]   *helfen*

LET'S CHECK

1 **school leaver** ['sku:l ˌli:və]   = sb. who has just finished school   Schulabgänger/in
2 °*drawing* ['drɔ:ɪŋ]   *Zeichnung*

Description of a milkman

Auch in dieser letzten Topic sollt ihr aktiv mit den Vokabeln umgehen – ein bisschen kniffelig, aber dafür umso spannender.

Dieses Spiel spielt ihr am besten in einer größeren Gruppe oder aber sogar mit der ganzen Klasse. Es werden zwei Gruppen gebildet, die gegeneinander antreten.

Zur Vorbereitung: Jede Gruppe sucht fünf Begriffe aus dieser Topic (oder dem englisch-deutschen *Dictionary* hinten im Buch) aus und schreibt sie jeweils auf ein Blatt oder eine Karteikarte. Zusätzlich müssen auf der Karte drei Wörter angegeben werden, die bei der Erklärung des Wortes auf keinen Fall verwendet werden dürfen.

Beispiel:
milkman (zu umschreibendes Wort)
1. *cow*
2. *white*
3. *drink*

Wenn ein/eine Spieler/in der gegnerischen Gruppe nun den Begriff *milkman* zieht, muss er/sie ihn erklären, ohne die Wörter *cow*, *white* und *drink* zu benutzen (die Einzelbestandteile *milk* und *man* sind natürlich auch tabu). Wenn er/sie es schafft und die Gruppe den Begriff errät, gibt's einen Punkt für die Gruppe. Danach wird gewechselt, und die andere Gruppe ist dran.

Wenn ihr zum ersten Mal spielt, könnt ihr es euch etwas leichter machen und euch darauf einigen, nur Wörter aus dem Wortfeld *jobs* zu nehmen. Das macht es einfacher.

PROJECT 2 / GETTING INVOLVED

Do a survey

aggressive [ə'gresɪv]	aggressiv	friendship ['frendʃɪp]	Freundschaft
illness ['ɪlnɪs]	Krankheit	in common [ɪn 'kɒmən]	gemeinsam
via ['vaɪə]	über, durch	dream [dri:m]	Traum
to get to know [get tu: 'nəʊ]	kennen lernen		

Posters against violence

violence ['vaɪələns]	Gewalt	excuse [ɪks'kju:s]	Entschuldigung
head teacher ['hed ˌti:tʃə]	Schuldirektor/in	victim ['vɪktɪm]	Opfer
to design [dɪ'zaɪn]	entwerfen	to present [prɪ'zent]	präsentieren
slogan ['sləʊgən]	Slogan	production [prə'dʌkʃn]	Produktion

Vocabulary

People who made a difference

among [əˈmʌŋ]	unter	National Guard [ˈnæʃənl ˈɡɑːd]	Nationalgarde, Armee unter der Kontrolle des Bundesstaats
Melba Pattillo Beals [melbə ˌpəˈtɪləʊ biːls]	amerik. Journalistin und Autorin		
courage [ˈkʌrɪdʒ]	Mut		
racism [ˈreɪsɪzəm]	Rassismus	to escort [ɪˈskɔːt]	begleiten
Supreme Court [sʊˈpriːm ˌkɔːt]	Oberstes Gericht	army [ˈɑːmɪ]	Armee
to ban [bæn]	verbieten	troops [truːps]	Truppen
racial segregation [ˈreɪʃl ˌseɡrɪˈɡeɪʃn]	Rassentrennung	college [ˈkɒlɪdʒ]	College
		journalist [ˈdʒɜːnəlɪst]	Journalist/in
university [juːnɪˈvɜːsətɪ]	Universität	warrior [ˈwɒrɪə]	Krieger
Little Rock [lɪtl ˈrɒk]	Hauptstadt von Arkansas	President Clinton [ˌprezɪdənt ˈklɪntən]	Amerikanischer Präsident
Arkansas [ˈɑːkənsɔː]	Bundesstaat in den U.S.A.		

Selim

"Gimme five!" [ˌɡɪmɪ ˈfaɪv]	Begrüßungsritual, bei dem man sich gegenseitig die rechte Hand schlägt.	Jackie Robinson [ˌdʒækɪ ˈrɒbɪnsən]	amerik. Bürgerrechtler und Sportler
ritual [ˈrɪtʃʊəl]	Ritual	biography [baɪˈɒɡrəfɪ]	Biografie
calm [kɑːm]	ruhig	private [ˈpraɪvɪt]	privat
Rosa Parks [ˌrəʊsə ˈpɑːks]	amerik. Bürgerrechtlerin	homepage [ˈhəʊmpeɪdʒ]	erste Seite einer Webseite

PROJECT 4 / LOVE WORRIES

Send your love

Valentine [ˈvæləntaɪn]	St. Valentin	advice [ədˈvaɪs]	Rat
Valentine's Day [ˈvæləntaɪnz deɪ]	Valentinstag	bazaar [bəˈzɑː]	Basar
		character [ˈkærəktə]	Persönlichkeit
accordion [əˈkɔːdjən]	Akkordeon	classmate [ˈklɑːsmeɪt]	Klassenkamerad
arrow [ˈærəʊ]	Pfeil	e-zine [ˈiːziːn]	Zeitschrift im Internet
cardboard [ˈkɑːdbɔːd]	Karton		
envelope [ˈenvələʊp]	Briefumschlag	guide [ɡaɪd]	Führer
heart [hɑːt]	Herz	in print [ɪn ˈprɪnt]	veröffentlicht
oak [əʊk]	Eiche	quiz [kwɪz]	Quiz
poem [ˈpəʊɪm]	Gedicht	school fete [skuːl ˈfeɪt]	Schulfest
loved one [ˈlʌved wʌn]	Angebete/r	sunshine [ˈsʌnʃaɪn]	Sonnenschein
rhythm [ˈrɪðəm]	Rhythmus	to go out with sb. [ɡəʊ ˈaʊt wɪð ˈsʌmbədɪ]	mit jdm gehen
size [saɪz]	Größe		
strip [strɪp]	Streifen	to publish [ˈpʌblɪʃ]	veröffentlichen
to fold [fəʊld]	falten	to warm [wɔːm]	erwärmen
to glue [ɡluː]	kleben	web [web]	Netz
to pop out [pɒp ˈaʊt]	hervorspringen		

Vocabulary

Photo Love Story

cutie	*hier:* süßer Kerl	drawing ['drɔːɪŋ]	Zeichnung
to baby-sit ['beɪbɪsɪt]	babysitten	Polaroid camera [pəʊləˈrɔɪd ˌkæmərə]	Sofortbildkamera
to do well [duː 'wel]	eine gute Note bekommen	space [speɪs]	Platz
digital ['dɪdʒɪtl]	Digital-	speech bubble ['spiːtʃ ˌbʌbl]	Sprechblasen

A WORLD MAP

jumbo jet ['dʒʌmbəʊ ˌdʒet]	Jumbojet	fleet [fliːt]	Flotte
Sydney Cove [ˌsɪdnɪ' kəʊv]	Bucht von Sydney	lip [lɪp]	Lippe
convict ['kɒnvɪkt]	Gefangene/r	King Philip [kɪŋ 'fɪlɪp]	König Philip
voyage ['vɔɪɪdʒ]	Reise	bad luck [bæd 'lʌk]	Pech
obviously ['ɒbvɪəslɪ]	offensichtlich	to travel the world [ˌtrævl ðə 'wɜːld]	um die Welt reisen
South Africa [ˌsaʊθ ˈæfrɪkə]	Südafrika	equator [ɪ'kweɪtə]	Äquator
Aborigine [ˌæbə'rɪdʒənɪ]	Ureinwohner/in Australiens	rum [rʌm]	Rum
to discover [dɪs'kʌvə]	entdecken	sugar ['ʃʊgə]	Zucker
eventually [ɪ'ventʃʊəlɪ]	schließlich, endlich	cotton [kɒtn]	Baumwolle
		to emigrate ['emɪgreɪt]	auswandern
folks [fəʊks]	*ugs.:* Leute	Irish ['aɪrɪʃ]	irisch
horn [hɔːn]	Horn	potato [pə'teɪtəʊ]	Kartoffel
silly ['sɪlɪ]	Dummkopf	Great Famine [greɪt 'fæmɪn]	Große Hungersnot
independent [ɪndɪ'pendənt]	unabhängig		
India ['ɪndɪə]	Indien	to cough [kɒf]	husten
to rhyme [raɪm]	reimen	Industrial Revolution [ɪn'dʌstrɪəl revə'luːʃən]	Industrielle Revolution
greyish ['greɪɪʃ]	gräulich	trade [treɪd]	Handel
to sail [seɪl]	segeln	Portuguese [pɔːtʃʊ'giːz]	Portugiese, Portugiesin
to conquer ['kɒnkə]	erobern		
Norman ['nɔːmən]	Normanne	Triangular Trade [traɪ'æŋgjʊlə treɪd]	Dreieckshandel
William the Conqueror ['wɪljəm ðə 'kɒnkərə]	*William, der Eroberer*	slave [sleɪv]	Sklave, Sklavin
Ireland ['aɪələnd]	Irland	friendship ['frendʃɪp]	Freundschaft
to finish off [ˌfɪnɪʃ ˈɒf]	erledigen	to discover [dɪs'kʌvə]	entdecken
off (Scotland) [ɒf]	vor, auf der Höhe von (Schottland)	Columbus [kɒ'lʌmbəs]	Kolumbus
		alias [eɪ'lɪəs]	alias
storm [stɔːm]	Sturm	Chris Colón [krɪs kɒ'lɒn]	Christoph Kolumbus
Drake [dreɪk]	*Sir Francis Drake, Seefahrer*		
		Declaration of Independance [dekləˈreɪʃn əv ɪndɪ'pendəns]	Unabhängigkeitserklärung
to kicked in the pants [get ˈkɪkd ɪn ðə 'pænts]	einen Tritt in den Hintern bekommen	Alaska [ə'læskə]	Alaska
Armada [ɑː'mɑːdə]	Die Spanische Armada		

DICTIONARY (ENGLISH-GERMAN)

In dieser alphabetischen Wortliste ist das gesamte Vokabular von *Password Orange 1–6* enthalten. Namen werden in einer gesonderten Liste nach dem Vokabular aufgeführt.
– Das Zeichen ° vor einer Angabe bedeutet, dass das Wort zum rezeptiven Wortschatz zählt. Es muss in seiner Bedeutung wieder erkannt werden.
– Das Zeichen ⟨ ⟩ bei einer Angabe weist darauf hin, dass das Wort fakultativ ist, d. h. freiwillig zu lernen. Dazu gehören auch Wörter aus authentischen Texten.
– Das Zeichen * bedeutet, dass es sich um ein unregelmäßiges Verb handelt, das in der Liste der unregelmäßigen Verben auf S. 176 nachgeschlagen werden kann.

A

'A' [eɪ] *beste Note in englischsprachigen Ländern*
a [ə] ein/eine
  a bit [ə 'bɪt] ein bisschen
  a few [ə 'fjuː] ein paar
  a lot [ə 'lɒt] viel, eine Menge
  a lot of [ə 'lɒt ˌəv] viele, eine Menge
  a must [ə 'mʌst] ein Muss, unbedingt erforderlich
  a week [ə 'wiːk] pro Woche
° **abbreviation** [əˌbriːvɪ'eɪʃn] Abkürzung
to be **able to** [bɪ 'eɪbl tuː] können
⟨**Aborigine**⟩ [ˌæbə'rɪdʒəni] Ureinwohner/in Australiens
about [ə'baʊt] °über; ungefähr; wegen
  What about …? [wɒt ə'baʊt] Wie wäre es mit …?
° **above** [ə'bʌv] oben
abroad [ə'brɔːd] im Ausland
absence ['æbsəns] Fehlen, Abwesenheit
accident ['æksɪdnt] Unfall
⟨**accordion**⟩ [ə'kɔːdjən] Akkordeon
act [ækt] Gesetz
to **act** [ækt] spielen, darstellen
action ['ækʃn] Action; °Bewegung
activity [æk'tɪvəti] °Beschäftigung, Aktivität; Freizeitbeschäftigung
actor ['æktə] Schauspieler
actress ['æktrɪs] Schauspielerin
actually ['æktʃʊəli] eigentlich
ad (= **advertisement**) [əd('vɜːtɪsmənt] Anzeige
to **add** [æd] °addieren; hinzufügen
address [ə'dres] Adresse, Anschrift
° **adjective** ['ædʒɪktɪv] Adjektiv
admiration [ˌædmə'reɪʃn] Bewunderung
adorable [ə'dɔːrəbl] bezaubernd, hinreißend
adult ['ædʌlt] Erwachsene/r
advantage [əd'vɑːntɪdʒ] Vorteil
° **adventure** [əd'ventʃə] Abenteuer
° **adverb** ['ædvɜːb] Adverb
advert ['ædvɜːt] Werbung

to **advertise** ['ædvətaɪz] werben
advice [əd'vaɪs] Rat; Ratschlag, Tipp
to be **afraid** [bɪ ə'freɪd] Angst haben
after-school ['ɑːftə skuːl] nachschulisch
after ['ɑːftə] nach
  after that [ˌɑːftə 'ðæt] danach
afternoon [ˌɑːftə'nuːn] Nachmittag
afterwards ['ɑːftəwədz] hinterher
again [ə'gen] noch einmal, wieder
against [ə'genst] gegen
age [eɪdʒ] Alter
  for ages [fɔː 'eɪdʒɪz] seit einer Ewigkeit
  the aged [ðiː 'eɪdʒɪd] die alten Menschen, die Alten
agency ['eɪdʒənsi] Agentur
aggressive [ə'gresɪv] aggressiv
ago [ə'gəʊ] vor *(Zeitangabe)*
agony aunt ['ægəni ˌɑːnt] Kummerkastentante
to **agree** [ə'griː] zustimmen
  to agree on sth. [ə'griː ɒn] sich auf etwas einigen
to **aim** [eɪm] zielen
ain't = haven't *(sl.)* [eɪnt] *ugs.* habe nicht
air [eə] Luft
airport ['eəpɔːt] Flughafen
alcoholic [ˌælkə'hɒlɪk] alkoholisch
⟨**alias**⟩ ['eɪliəs] alias
alien ['eɪljən] Außerirdische/r
alike [ə'laɪk] gleich
alive [ə'laɪv] lebendig
all the way [ɔːl ðə 'weɪ] den ganzen Weg
  all the crawfish [ˌɔːl ðə 'krɔːfɪʃ] so viele Langusten wie
all [ɔːl] alle
° all around [ˌɔːl ə'raʊnd] überall
  all over [ˌɔːl 'əʊvə] überall (in)
  all the time [ˌɔːl ðə taɪm] die ganze Zeit
  first of all ['fɜːst ˌəv ɔːl] erstens, zuallererst
  last of all ['lɑːst ˌəv ɔːl] zuletzt
alley ['æli] Gasse
alligator ['ælɪgeɪtə] Alligator
to **allow sb. to do sth.** [ə'laʊ sʌmbədi tə 'duː ˌsʌmθɪŋ] jdm. etwas erlauben
to be **allowed to** [bɪ ə'laʊd tə] dürfen
to be **allowed out** [bɪ ə'laʊd aʊt] fort dürfen
almost ['ɔːlməʊst] fast
alone [ə'ləʊn] allein
alphabet ['ælfəbet] Alphabet
° **alphabetical** [ˌælfə'betɪkl] alphabetisch
already [ɔːl'redi] schon, schon mal
also ['ɔːlsəʊ] auch
alternative [ɔːl'tɜːnətɪv] Alternative
although [ɔːl'ðəʊ] obwohl
always ['ɔːlweɪz] immer
a.m. [eɪ 'em] morgens (0-11:59 Uhr)
amazing [ə'meɪzɪŋ] erstaunlich
ambulance ['æmbjʊləns] Krankenwagen
  ambulance woman ['æmbjʊlns ˌwʊmən] Sanitäterin
American [ə'merɪkən] Amerikaner/in; amerikanisch
  Native American [ˌneɪtɪv ə'merɪkən] Ureinwohner/in Amerikas (Indianer/in)
among [ə'mʌŋ] unter
an [ən] ein/eine *(vor Vokalen)*
and [ænd] und
  And that's that! [ænd ˌðæts 'ðæt] Schluss! Basta!
angry ['æŋgri] ärgerlich, wütend
animal ['ænɪml] Tier
  animal home ['ænɪml ˌhəʊm] Tierheim
annoying [ə'nɔɪɪŋ] lästig, nervig
anorak ['ænəræk] Anorak
another [ə'nʌðə] ein/e weitere/s/r;
° noch ein/e/er
answer ['ɑːnsə] Antwort
to **answer** ['ɑːnsə] (be)antworten
  to answer the telephone [ˌɑːnsə ðə 'telɪfəʊn] ans Telefon gehen
° **answering machine** ['ɑːnsərɪŋ mə'ʃiːn] Anrufbeantworter
any ['eni] etwas; (irgend)ein/e
  not … any [nɒt … 'eni] kein/e
  not … any more [nɒt … eni 'mɔː] nicht mehr

Dictionary

anybody [ˈenɪˌbɒdɪ] (irgend)jemand
anything [ˈenɪθɪŋ] (irgend)etwas
  anything else [ˌenɪθɪŋ ˈels] (irgend)etwas anderes
anyway [ˈenɪweɪ] sowieso; überhaupt
Anyway, ... [ˈenɪweɪ] Jedenfalls, ... Egal, ...
anywhere [ˈenɪweə] irgendwo
apartment (*AE*) [əˈpɑːtmənt] Wohnung
to **appear** [əˈpɪə] erscheinen
apple [ˈæpl] Apfel
  apple pie [ˌæpl ˈpaɪ] (gedeckter) Apfelkuchen
to **apply** [əˈplaɪ] sich bewerben
apprentice [[əˈprentɪs] Lehrling
apprenticeship [əˈprentɪʃɪp] Lehre
April [ˈeɪprɪl] April
° **A&R man** [eɪˌɒnˈɑː mæn] Talentsucher und Künstlerbetreuer
arcade [ɑːˈkeɪd] Spielhalle
area [ˈeərɪə] Gegend, Nachbarschaft
to **argue** [ˈɑːgjuː] (sich) streiten
argument [ˈɑːgjʊmənt] Argument, Auseinandersetzung; °Streit
arm [ɑːm] Arm
armchair [ˈɑːmtʃeə] Sessel
⟨**army**⟩ [ˈɑːmɪ] Armee
around [əˈraʊnd] um, herum
° all around [ɔːlˌəˈraʊnd] überall
  around here [əˈraʊnd hɪə] hier in der Umgebung
  to get around [getˌəˈraʊnd] herumkommen, sich umsehen
  to hang around [hæŋˌəˈraʊnd] herumhängen
  to look around [lʊkˌəˈraʊnd] sich umsehen
  to shake around [ʃeɪkˌəˈraʊnd] hin und her schütteln
to **arrange** [əˈreɪndʒ] ausmachen, vereinbaren
to **arrest** [əˈrest] festnehmen
to **arrive** [əˈraɪv] ankommen
⟨**arrow**⟩ [ˈærəʊ] Pfeil
Art [ɑːt] Kunst (*Schulfach*); Kunst
article [ˈɑːtɪkl] Artikel, Bericht; Gegenstand, Gebrauchsartikel
artist [ˈɑːtɪst] Künstler/in
as ... as [əz ... əz] so ... wie
as [æz] als
Asian [ˈeɪʃn] Asiat/in, asiatisch
to **ask** [ɑːsk] fragen
  to ask for [ˈɑːsk fə] um ... bitten
  to ask sb. out [ˈɑːsk sʌmbədɪˌˈaʊt] sich mit jemandem verabreden
asleep [əˈsliːp] schlafend, eingeschlafen
  to be asleep [əˈsliːp] schlafen
  to fall asleep [fɔːlˌəˈsliːp] einschlafen

asphalt [ˈæsfælt] Asphalt
Assembly [əˈsemblɪ] Versammlung
  assembly hall [əˈsemblɪ ˌhɔːl] Schulhalle, Aula
assignment [əˈsaɪnmənt] (Haus-)Aufgabe
assistant [əˈsɪstənt] Verkäufer/in
astronaut [ˈæstrənɔːt] Astronaut/in
(**at**) **recess** (*AE*) [rɪˈses] (in der) Pause
at [æt] auf, beim
  at a time [ætˌəˈtaɪm] auf einmal
  at all [ætˌˈɔːl] überhaupt
  at first [ət ˈfɜːst] zuerst
  at home [ət ˈhəʊm] zu Hause
  at least [ət ˈliːst] °wenigstens, mindestens; zumindest, jedenfalls
  at once [ət ˈwʌns] sofort
  at school [ət ˈskuːl] in der Schule
  at that moment [ət ðæt ˈməʊmənt] in diesem Augenblick
  at the back [ət ðə ˈbæk] hinten
  at the cinema [ət ðə ˈsɪnəmə] im Kino
  at the front [ət ðə ˈfrʌnt] vorne
° at the top of [ət ðə ˈtɒp əv] oben auf
  at the weekend [ət ðə ˌwiːˈkend] am Wochenende
  at work [ət ˈwɜːk] bei der Arbeit
  at ... o'clock [ət wɒn ...] Uhr
athletics [æθˈletɪks] Athletik
atmosphere [ˈætməˌsfɪə] Stimmung
  heart **attack** [ˈhɑːtˌətæk] Herzinfarkt
to **attack** [əˈtæk] angreifen
attendance office [əˈtendənsˌˈɒfɪs] *Sekretariat, das sich um Fälle häufig unentschuldigten Fehlens kümmert*
attic [ˈætɪk] Dachboden
attractive [əˈtræktɪv] attraktiv
auction [ˈɔːkʃn] Auktion, Versteigerung
auctioneer [ˌɔːkʃəˈnɪə] Auktionator/in
August [ˈɔːgəst] August
aunt [ɑːnt] Tante
  agony aunt [ˈægənɪˌɑːnt] Kummerkastentante
Australia [ɒˈstreɪljə] Australien
Australian [ɒˈstreɪljən] Australier/in
Austrian [ˈɒstrɪən] Österreicher/in, österreichisch
autograph [ˈɔːtəgrɑːf] Autogramm
automatic [ˌɔːtəˈmætɪk] automatisch
autumn [ˈɔːtəm] Herbst
average [ˈævərɪdʒ] Durchschnitt
  average [ˈævərɪdʒ] durchschnittlich
to **avoid** [əˈvɔɪd] vermeiden

away [əˈweɪ] weg
  to throw away [θrəʊˌəˈweɪ] wegwerfen
awful [ˈɔːfʊl] furchtbar; fürchterlich

B

baby [ˈbeɪbɪ] Baby
  ⟨to baby-sit⟩ [ˈbeɪbɪsɪt] babysitten
  baby-sitter [ˈbeɪbɪˌsɪtə] Babysitter/in
  baby-sitting [ˈbeɪbɪˌsɪtɪŋ] Babysitting
back [bæk] Rücken
  at the back [ət ðə ˈbæk] hinten
  back garden (*BE*) [bæk ˈgɑːdn] Garten hinter dem Haus
  back row [ˈbæk rəʊ] hinterste Reihe
  back to back [ˌbæk tʊ ˈbæk] Rücken an Rücken
back [bæk] zurück
  to get back [get ˈbæk] zurückkommen, zurückkehren
background [ˈbækgraʊnd] Hintergrund
backstroke [ˈbækstrəʊk] Rückenschwimmen
backyard (*AE*) [bækˈjɑːd] Garten hinter dem Haus
bad [bæd] schlecht
  ⟨bad luck⟩ [bæd ˈlʌk] Pech
bag [bæg] (Schul)tasche; Beutel, Sack; Tüte
ball [bɔːl] (Tanz-) Ball
  ball park (*AE*) [ˈbɔːl pɑːk] Baseballplatz
ballet [ˈbæleɪ] Ballett
balloon [bəˈluːn] Heißluftballon
ballooning [bəˈluːnɪŋ] Ballonfahren
⟨to **ban**⟩ [bæn] verbieten
band [bænd] Musikband
  heavy metal band [ˈhevɪ ˈmetl bænd] Heavymetal-Band
bank [bæŋk] Bank
  bottle bank [ˈbɒtl bæŋk] *Sammelstelle für Altglas*
  food bank [ˈfuːd bæŋk] *Sammelstelle für Essensspenden*
bar [bɑː] Bar; Snackbar; Theke
Bar-B-Q (= barbecue) [ˈbɑːbɪkjuː] Grillparty
bargain [ˈbɑːgɪn] Gelegenheitskauf, Schnäppchen
to **bark** [bɑːk] bellen
barman [ˈbɑːmən] Typ hinter der Theke
barren [ˈbærən] öd
barrier [ˈbærɪə] Barriere
baseball [ˈbeɪsbɔːl] Baseball

basket ['bɑːskɪt] Korb
basketball ['bɑːskɪtbɔːl] Basketball
bass guitar ['beɪs gɪˈtɑː] Bassgitarre
bath [bɑːθ] Badewanne
bathroom ['bɑːθrʊm] Badezimmer
battery ['bætrɪ] Batterie
battle [bætl] Kampf
bay [beɪ] Bucht
⟨**bazaar**⟩ [bəˈzɑː] Basar
BC (= **Before Christ**) [biːˈsiː] v. Chr.
to **be*** [biː] sein
 ° Be careful! [bɪ ˈkeəfʊl] Pass auf!
 to be able to [bɪ ˈeɪbl tuː] können
 to be afraid [bɪ əˈfreɪd] Angst haben
 to be allowed out [bɪ əˈlaʊd aʊt] fort dürfen
 to be allowed to [bɪ əˈlaʊd tə] dürfen
 to be asleep [bɪ əˈsliːp] schlafen
 to be born [bɪ ˈbɔːn] geboren werden
 to be fed up with [bɪ fed ˈʌp wɪð] die Nase voll haben von
 to be fed up with sb. [bɪ fed ˈʌp wɪð ˈsʌmbədɪ] von jdm. die Nase voll haben
 to be good at [bɪ ˈgʊd ət] etwas gut können, gut sein in
 to be homesick [bɪ ˈhəʊmsɪk] Heimweh haben
 to be in training [bɪ ɪn ˈtreɪnɪŋ] trainieren
 ° to be interested in [bɪ ˈɪntrɪstɪd ɪn] interessiert sein an
 to be lucky [bɪ ˈlʌkɪ] Glück haben
 to be mad about [bɪ ˈmæd əˌbaʊt] verrückt nach etwas sein
 to be patient [bɪ ˈpeɪʃnt] Geduld haben
 to be proud of oneself [bɪ ˈpraʊd əv wʌnˈself] stolz auf sich sein
 to be recycled [bɪ riːˈsaɪkld] wiederverwertet werden
 to be right [bɪ ˈraɪt] Recht haben
 to be scared [bɪ ˈskeəd] Angst haben
 to be sorry [bɪ ˈsɒrɪ] Leid tun
 to be wrong [bɪ ˈrɒŋ] Unrecht haben
beach [biːtʃ] Strand
beachball ['biːtʃbɔːl] Strandball
bean [biːn] Bohne
koala **bear** [kəʊˈɑːlə beə] Koalabär
beard [bɪəd] Bart
 to **beat up** [biːt ˈʌp] zusammenschlagen
 to **beat*** [biːt] schlagen
 to get a beating [get ə ˈbiːtɪŋ] verprügelt werden
beautiful ['bjuːtɪfʊl] schön, wundervoll
because [bɪˈkɒz] weil
to **become*** [bɪˈkʌm] werden

 to become involved [bɪˈkʌm ɪnˈvɒlvd] verwickelt werden
bed [bed] Bett; Flussbett
 bed and breakfast place [ˌbed ən ˈbrekfəst ˌpleɪs] Frühstückspension
bedroom ['bedrʊm] Schlafzimmer
beef [biːf] Rindfleisch
beer [bɪə] Bier
 ° beer mat ['bɪə mæt] Bierdeckel
before [bɪˈfɔː] vor; vorher, zuvor; schon einmal
to **begin*** [bɪˈgɪn] anfangen, beginnen
to **behave** [bɪˈheɪv] sich benehmen
behind [bɪˈhaɪnd] hinter
being ['biːɪŋ] Wesen
belief [bɪˈliːf] Glaube
to **believe** [bɪˈliːv] glauben
 to believe in [bɪˈliːv ɪn] an etwas glauben
below [bɪˈləʊ] unten/unterhalb;
 ° unter
beneath [bɪˈniːθ] unter
beside [bɪˈsaɪd] neben
best [best] beste/r/s
 best wishes [ˌbest ˈwɪʃɪz] herzliche Grüße
I **bet** [aɪ ˈbet] Ich denke, ich wette
to **bet*** [bet] wetten
better ['betə] besser
 to get better at sth. [get ˈbetər ət] in etwas besser werden
between [bɪˈtwiːn] zwischen
bicycle ['baɪsɪkl] Fahrrad
big [bɪg] groß
 big-headed [ˌbɪg ˈhedɪd] eingebildet
bike [baɪk] Fahrrad
 by bike [baɪ ˈbaɪk] mit dem Fahrrad
 mountain bike ['maʊntɪn ˌbaɪk] Mountainbike
 racing bike ['reɪsɪŋ ˌbaɪk] Rennrad
 trekking bike ['trekɪŋ ˌbaɪk] Trekkingbike
bikini [bɪˈkiːnɪ] Bikini
bill [bɪl] Rechnung
⟨**biography**⟩ [baɪˈɒgrəfɪ] Biografie
Biology [baɪˈɒlədʒɪ] Biologie (*Schulfach*)
bird [bɜːd] Vogel
birth [bɜːθ] Geburt
 date of birth [ˌdeɪt əv ˈbɜːθ] Geburtsdatum
birthday ['bɜːθdeɪ] Geburtstag
bit [bɪt] Stück, Teil
a **bit** [ə ˈbɪt] ein bisschen
bitter ['bɪtə] bitter
black [blæk] schwarz
block [blɒk] (Häuser-) Block; Podest
bloke [bləʊk] Typ

blond [blɒnd] blond
blood [blʌd] Blut
bloody ['blʌdɪ] blutig
to **blow*** [bləʊ] blasen
 to blow off [bləʊ ˈɒf] wegblasen
blue [bluː] blau
 blue-eyed ['bluː aɪd] blauäugig
board [bɔːd] Tafel
 on board [ɒn ˈbɔːd] an Bord
boardgame ['bɔːdgeɪm] Brettspiel
boardwalk ['bɔːdwɔːk] Uferpromenade
boat [bəʊt] Boot, Schiff
body ['bɒdɪ] Körper
 half of a body ['hɑːf əv ə 'bɒdɪ] eine halbe Körperlänge
bone [bəʊn] Knochen
book [bʊk] Buch
 picture book ['pɪktʃə ˌbʊk] Bilderbuch
bookshop ['bʊkʃɒp] Buchhandlung
° **bookworm** ['bʊkwɜːm] Bücherwurm
boomerang ['buːməræŋ] Bumerang
boot [buːt] Stiefel
booter [buːtə] *Händler/in auf dem Flohmarkt*
 hiking **boots** ['haɪkɪŋ ˌbuːts] Wanderschuhe
border ['bɔːdə] Grenze
bored [bɔːd] gelangweilt
boredom ['bɔːdəm] Langeweile
boring ['bɔːrɪŋ] langweilig
to be **born** [bɪ ˈbɔːn] geboren werden
to **borrow** ['bɒrəʊ] borgen, ausleihen
boss [bɒs] Boss, Chef/in
both [bəʊθ] beide
bottle ['bɒtl] Flasche
 bottle bank ['bɒtl bæŋk] *Sammelstelle für Altglas*
to **bottle** [bɒtl] in Flaschen abfüllen
bottom ['bɒtəm] Boden
to **bounce off** [baʊns ˈɒf] abprallen
bowling alley ['bəʊlɪŋ ˌælɪ] Kegelbahn
box [bɒks] Schachtel
 box office ['bɒks ˌɒfɪs] (Theater-/Kino-) Kasse
 telephone box ['telɪfəʊn bɒks] Telefonzelle
boy [bɔɪ] Junge
boycott ['bɔɪkɒt] Boykott
boyfriend ['bɔɪfrend] Freund
brake [breɪk] Bremse
to **brake** [breɪk] bremsen
brave [breɪv] mutig
Brazilian [brəˈzɪljən] brasilianisch
bread [bred] Brot
breadwinner ['bredˌwɪnə] Brötchenverdiener/in

Dictionary

break [breɪk] Pause
to **break*** [breɪk] (zer)brechen
  to break down [breɪk ˈdaʊn] niederreißen; zusammenbrechen
  to break into [breɪk ˈɪntʊ] einbrechen, hineingelangen
  to break out [breɪk ˈaʊt] ausbrechen
  to break up [breɪk ˈʌp] zerbrechen
breakfast [ˈbrekfəst] Frühstück
  to have breakfast [hæv ˈbrekfəst] frühstücken
breaking up [breɪkɪŋ ˈʌp] Schluss machen
bridge [brɪdʒ] Brücke
the **bright lights** [ðə ˈbraɪt laɪts] der Glanz der Großstadt
bright [braɪt] glänzend
brilliant [ˈbrɪljənt] fantastisch, echt klasse!
bring-and-buy sale [brɪŋ ən ˈbaɪ ˌseɪl] eine Art Flohmarkt
to **bring*** [brɪŋ] bringen; mitbringen
British [ˈbrɪtɪʃ] britisch
brochure [ˈbrəʊʃə] °Broschüre; Prospekt
broken-winged [ˈbrəʊkən wɪŋd] mit gebrochenem Flügel
brother [ˈbrʌðə] Bruder
brown [braʊn] braun
°**bubble** [ˈbʌbl] (Luft-, Seifen-) Blase
budgie [ˈbʌdʒi] Wellensittich
to **build*** [bɪld] bauen
building [ˈbɪldɪŋ] Gebäude
  building site [ˈbɪldɪŋ saɪt] Baustelle
bully [ˈbʊli] Schläger, Rabauke
to **bully** [ˈbʊli] einschüchtern, schikanieren
bus [bʌs] Bus
  bus stop [ˈbʌs ˌstɒp] Bushaltestelle
  by bus [baɪ ˈbʌs] mit dem Bus
  on the bus [ɒn ðə ˈbʌs] im Bus
  to catch a bus [ˈkætʃ ə bʌs] einen Bus erreichen, kriegen
bush [bʊʃ] Busch
bushman [ˈbʊʃmən] Buschmann
business [ˈbɪznɪs] Unternehmen, Firma
  It's none of her business. [ɪts ˈnʌn əv hɜː ˈbɪznɪs] Das geht sie nichts an.
  music business [ˈmjuːzɪk ˈbɪznɪs] Musikbranche
busy [ˈbɪzi] beschäftigt, stark befahren
but [bʌt] aber, außer
  But it's no good. [bʌt ɪts nəʊ ˈgʊd] Aber es ist sowieso egal.
butler [ˈbʌtlə] Butler
butter [ˈbʌtə] Butter

to **buy*** [baɪ] kaufen
I get a real **buzz** out of it. [aɪ get ə rɪəl ˈbʌz aʊt əv ɪt] Das törnt mich total an.
by [baɪ] bis
  by bike [baɪ ˈbaɪk] mit dem Fahrrad
  by bus [baɪ ˈbʌs] mit dem Bus
  by the end [baɪ ðɪ ˈend] am Ende
  By the way, … [baɪ ðə ˈweɪ] Übrigens, …
Bye! [baɪ] Tschüs!
  Bye for now [ˈbaɪ fə ˌnaʊ] Tschüs, bis zum nächsten Mal!

C

cabbage [ˈkæbɪdʒ] Kohl
cafe [ˈkæfeɪ] Café
cafeteria [ˌkæfɪˈtɪərɪə] Kantine
cage [keɪdʒ] Käfig
cake [keɪk] Kuchen
call [kɔːl] Anruf, Telefongespräch
to **call** [kɔːl] anrufen; rufen
  to make a telephone call [meɪk ə ˈtelɪfəʊn ˌkɔːl] einen Anruf tätigen
callbox [ˈkɔːlbɒks] Telefonzelle
caller [ˈkɔːlə] Anrufer/in
to **calm down** [kɑːm ˈdaʊn] sich beruhigen
calm [kɑːm] ruhig
video **camera** [ˌvɪdɪəʊ ˈkæmrə] Videokamera
camper [ˈkæmpə] Camper
camping site [ˈkæmpɪŋ saɪt] Campingplatz
  to go camping [gəʊ ˈkæmpɪŋ] zelten gehen
can [kæn] Blechdose, Aludose
  garbage can (AE) [ˈgɑːbɪdʒ kæn] Mülleimer
can [kæn] können
can't …, either [ˈkɑːnt … ˈaɪðə] kann auch nicht
Canadian [kəˈneɪdjən] kanadisch
candle [ˈkændl] Kerze
candy bar [ˈkændɪ bɑː] (Schoko-)Riegel
cannot [ˈkænɒt] kann nicht
canoe [kəˈnuː] Kanu
canoeing [kəˈnuːɪŋ] Kanufahren
I can't stand … [aɪ ˌkɑːnt ˈstænd] Ich kann … nicht ausstehen.
°**cap** [kæp] Kappe
capital [ˈkæpɪtl] Hauptstadt
captain [ˈkæptɪn] Kapitän
car [kɑː] Auto
  car park [ˈkɑː pɑːk] Parkplatz, Parkhaus
card [kɑːd] Karte, Spielkarte
  cash card [ˈkæʃ kɑːd] Bankkarte
  identity card [aɪˈdentɪtɪ ˌkɑːd] (Personal-) Ausweis

⟨**cardboard**⟩ [ˈkɑːdbɔːd] Karton
career [kəˈrɪə] berufliche Laufbahn
  °careers officer [kəˈrɪəz ˈɒfɪsə] Berufsberater/in
careful [ˈkeəfʊl] vorsichtig, sorgfältig
  °Be careful! [bɪ ˈkeəfʊl] Pass auf!
carpet [ˈkɑːpɪt] Teppich
carrier [ˈkærɪə] Gepäckträger
carrot [ˈkærət] Mohrrübe, Karotte
to **carry** [ˈkærɪ] tragen
carton [ˈkɑːtn] Karton, Pappschachtel
cartoon [kɑːˈtuːn] °Comic; Zeichentrickfilm
case [keɪs] Fall
cash card [ˈkæʃ kɑːd] Bankkarte
cassette [kəˈset] Kassette
  cassette recorder [kəˈset rɪˌkɔːdə] Kassettenrekorder
castle [ˈkɑːsl] Schloss
casual [ˈkæʒʊəl] lässig
cat [kæt] Katze
to **catch*** [kætʃ] fangen
  to catch a bus [ˈkætʃ ə bʌs] einen Bus erreichen, kriegen
  to catch up [kætʃ ˈʌp] einholen
  to catch up with [kætʃ ˈʌp wɪð] aufholen
cattle [ˈkætl] Vieh
to **cause** [kɔːz] verursachen
CD (= compact disc) [siː ˈdiː] Compact Disc
  CD player [siː ˈdiː ˌpleɪə] CD-Player
  CD-ROM [siːdiːˈrɒm] CD-ROM
to **celebrate** [ˈselɪbreɪt] feiern
celebration [ˌselɪˈbreɪʃn] Feier
cellar [ˈselə] Keller
cement mixer [sɪˈment mɪksə] Betonmischer
recycling **center** [riːˈsaɪklɪŋ ˈsentə] Wiederaufbereitungsanlage
  Youth Center (AE) [ˈjuːθ sentə] Jugendzentrum
°**centimeter** (AE) [ˈsentɪˌmiːtə] Zentimeter
centre [ˌsentə] Zentrum
  city centre [ˌsɪtɪ ˈsentə] Stadtmitte, Innenstadt
  shopping centre [ˈʃɒpɪŋ ˌsentə] Einkaufszentrum
  sports centre [ˈspɔːts ˌsentə] Sportzentrum
certificate [səˈtɪfɪkət] Urkunde
°**chain** [tʃeɪn] Kette
chair [tʃeə] Stuhl
challenger [ˈtʃælɪndʒə] Herausforderer, Herausforderin
champion [ˈtʃæmpjən] Champion
chance [tʃɑːns] Chance, Gelegenheit
  quite by chance [ˈkwaɪt baɪ ˈtʃɑːns] ganz zufällig

change [tʃeɪndʒ] Wechsel
for a change [fɔːr ə ˈtʃeɪndʒ] zur Abwechslung
to **change** [tʃeɪndʒ] sich ändern, wechseln; umsteigen
changing room [ˈtʃeɪndʒɪŋ ˌrʊm] Umkleideraum
character [ˈkærəktə] Charakter; °Figur, Person (in Buch, Film, Geschichte); ⟨Persönlichkeit⟩
to **charge** [tʃɑːdʒ] aufladen
charity [ˈtʃærəti] Wohltätigkeitsverein
chart [tʃɑːt] Hitliste, Charts
to **chase** [tʃeɪs] jagen
chat line [ˈtʃæt laɪn] Chatline (*eine Online-Gesprächsrunde*)
to **chat** [tʃæt] plaudern, klönen, quatschen
to **chat sb. up** [tʃæt ˈʌp] jdn. anmachen
cheap [tʃiːp] billig
to **cheat** [tʃiːt] schummeln, mogeln
cheated [ˈtʃiːtɪd] betrogen
to **check** [tʃek] (über-) prüfen; °überprüfen
checklist [ˈtʃeklɪst] Checkliste
cheek [tʃiːk] Wange
cheeky [ˈtʃiːki] frech
to **cheer up** [tʃɪər ˈʌp] aufmuntern
cheerful [ˈtʃɪəfʊl] fröhlich, gutgelaunt
cheerleader [ˈtʃɪəliːdə] Cheerleader
cheese [tʃiːz] Käse
Chemistry [ˈkemɪstri] Chemie (*Schulfach*)
cheque [tʃek] Scheck
chest [tʃest] Brust
chicken [ˈtʃɪkɪn] Hähnchen
chihuahua [tʃɪˈwɑːwə] Chihuahua
child [tʃaɪld] Kind
childhood [ˈtʃaɪldhʊd] Kindheit
children (*pl.*) [ˈtʃɪldrən] Kinder
chips [tʃɪps] Kartoffelchips (*AE*); Pommes frites (*BE*)
chocolate [ˈtʃɒklɪt] Schokolade
choice [tʃɔɪs] Wahl
choir [ˈkwaɪə] Chor
to **choose*** [tʃuːz] °(aus)wählen, (sich) aussuchen; wählen
Christian [ˈkrɪstʃən] Christ/in, christlich
Christmas [ˈkrɪsməs] Weihnachten
Christmas Day [krɪsməs ˈdeɪ] 1. Weihnachtstag
Christmas Eve [krɪsməs ˈiːv] Heiligabend
Father Christmas [ˌfɑːðə ˈkrɪsməs] Nikolaus
Merry Christmas! [ˌmeri ˈkrɪsməs] Fröhliche Weihnachten!
church [tʃɜːtʃ] Kirche

cigarette [ˌsɪɡəˈret] Zigarette
cinema [ˈsɪnəmə] Kino
°**circle** [ˈsɜːkl] Kreis
city [ˈsɪti] Stadt, Großstadt
city centre [ˌsɪti ˈsentə] Stadtmitte, Innenstadt
civil right [sɪvl ˈraɪt] Bürgerrecht
to **clap** [klæp] klatschen
class [klɑːs] (Schul)klasse; Kurs; Schulstunde (*AE*)
to cut classes [kʌt ˈklɑːsɪz] Stunden ausfallen lassen, schwänzen
⟨**classmate**⟩ [ˈklɑːsmeɪt] Klassenkamerad
classroom [ˈklɑːsrʊm] Klassenzimmer
to **clean** [kliːn] sauber machen
to clean up [kliːn ˈʌp] aufräumen, sauber machen
clean [kliːn] sauber
to do sth. clean [duː sʌmθɪŋ ˈkliːn] etwas schnell und schmerzlos tun
clever [ˈklevə] schlau, klug
cliff [klɪf] Klippe
climate [ˈklaɪmət] Klima
to **climb** [klaɪm] klettern
rock **climbing** [ˈrɒk klaɪmɪŋ] Klettern
to **clobber sb.** (*sl.*) [ˈklɒbə] *ugs.* jdn. fertig machen
clock [klɒk] Uhr
clock radio [klɒk ˈreɪdiəʊ] Radiowecker
to **close** [kləʊz] zumachen, schließen
close [kləʊs] nah; genau
closed [kləʊzd] geschlossen
closet (*AE*) [ˈklɒzɪt] Schrank
clothes (*pl.*) [kləʊðz] Kleidung, Kleider
cloud [klaʊd] Wolke
club [klʌb] Klub, Verein
Young People's Club [jʌŋ ˈpiːplz ˌklʌb] Jugendklub
youth club [ˈjuːθ klʌb] Jugendklub
clue [kluː] Hinweis, Spur
C'mon = come on (*sl.*) [kʌm ˈɒn] *ugs.* kommt!
coach [kəʊtʃ] Reisebus
coast [kəʊst] Küste
coat [kəʊt] Mantel
°**code** [kəʊd] Code, Geheimschrift
coffee [ˈkɒfiː] Kaffee
coin [kɔɪn] Münze
coke [kəʊk] Coca-Cola
cola [ˈkəʊlə] Cola
cold [kəʊld] kalt
collar [ˈkɒlə] Kragen
to **collect** [kəˈlekt] abholen; sammeln
collection [kəˈlekʃn] Sammlung
⟨**college**⟩ [ˈkɒlɪdʒ] College

colony [ˈkɒləni] Kolonie
°**color** (*AE*) [ˈkʌlə] Farbe
to **color** (*AE*) [ˈkʌlə] färben
colorful (*AE*) [ˈkʌləfʊl] bunt, farbenprächtig
colour (*BE*) [ˈkʌlə] Farbe
°What colour is it? [wɒt ˈkʌlər ɪz ɪt] Welche Farbe hat es?
°**column** [ˈkɒləm] Spalte
to **come*** [kʌm] kommen
°to come true [kʌm ˈtruː] wahr werden
Come on. [kʌm ˈɒn] Los, komm! Gehen wir!
I'm coming to that. [aɪm ˈkʌmɪŋ tʊ ˈðæt] Das wollte ich gerade erzählen.
to come in [kʌm ˈɪn] hereinkommen
to come round [kʌm ˈraʊnd] vorbeikommen
to come up to [kʌm ˈʌp tə] zu jdm. kommen, auf jdn. zukommen
comedy [ˈkɒmədi] Komödie
comfortable [ˈkʌmfətəbl] bequem
comic [ˈkɒmɪk] Comic(heft)
commercial [kəˈmɜːʃl] Werbespot
to **communicate** [kəˈmjuːnɪkeɪt] sich unterhalten
communication [kəˌmjuːnɪˈkeɪʃn] Kommunikation
community [kəˈmjuːnəti] Gemeinschaft
company [ˈkʌmpni] Firma
°to **compare** [kəmˈpeə] vergleichen
competition [kɒmpɪˈtɪʃn] Wettkampf, Wettbewerb
to **complain** [kəmˈpleɪn] beschweren
complete [kəmˈpliːt] vollständig
comprehensive school [kɒmprɪˈhensɪv ˌskuːl] Gesamtschule
computer [kəmˈpjuːtə] Computer
computer game [kəmˈpjuːtə ˌɡeɪm] Computerspiel
°**Computers** [kəmˈpjuːtəz] Informatik (*Schulfach*)
to **concentrate** (on) [ˈkɒnsəntreɪt ɒn] sich konzentrieren (auf)
concert [ˈkɒnsət] Konzert
concrete [ˈkɒŋkriːt] Beton
condition [kənˈdɪʃn] Bedingung
conflict [ˈkɒnflɪkt] Konflikt, Schwierigkeit
°to **connect** [kəˈnekt] verbinden
°**connecting words** [kəˈnektɪŋ ˌwɜːdz] Bindewörter
connection [kəˈnekʃn] Verbindung
⟨to **conquer**⟩ [ˈkɒŋkə] erobern
consultant [kənˈsʌltnt] Berater/in
to **consume** [kənˈsjuːm] verbrauchen

contact ['kɒntækt] Kontakt
to contact ['kɒntækt] ansprechen, Kontakt aufnehmen
to contain [kən'teɪn] enthalten
container [kən'teɪnə] Behälter
   plastic container ['plæstɪk kən'teɪnə] Plastikbehälter
to continue [kən'tɪnjuː] fortfahren; °weitermachen
contract ['kɒntrækt] Vertrag
control [kən'trəʊl] Kontrolle
   power control ['paʊwə kən'trəʊl] Leistungsregler
to control [kən'trəʊl] kontrollieren
°conversation [ˌkɒnvə'seɪʃn] Unterhaltung, Gespräch
conveyor belt [kən'veɪə belt] Fließband
convict ['kɒnvɪkt] ⟨Gefangene/r⟩; Sträfling, Strafgefangene/r
cook [kʊk] Koch, Köchin
to cook [kʊk] kochen
cooker ['kʊkə] Herd
cookie ['kʊkɪ] Plätzchen
cool [kuːl] kühl, "cool"
coordinator [kəʊ'ɔːdɪneɪtə] Koordinator/in, Organisator/in
cop (sl.) [kɒp] ugs. Polizist/in
°to copy ['kɒpɪ] abschreiben, kopieren
cord [kɔːd] Schnur
corn [kɔːn] hier: Mais
corner ['kɔːnə] Ecke
   street corner [striːt 'kɔːnə] Straßenecke
cornflakes (pl.) ['kɔːnfleɪks] Cornflakes
to correct [kə'rekt] °berichtigen, korrigieren, verbessern
°correct [kə'rekt] richtig, korrekt
°cost [kɒst] Kosten
to cost [kɒst] kosten
costume ['kɒstjuːm] Kostüm
⟨cotton⟩ ['kɒtn] Baumwolle
to cough [kɒf] husten
could [kʊd] könnte; konnte, konnten
council flat ['kaʊnsl flæt] Sozialwohnung
to count [kaʊnt] zählen
country ['kʌntrɪ] Land
   country club ['kʌntrɪ klʌb] Klub auf dem Land, oft mit Sportmöglichkeiten
countryside ['kʌntrɪsaɪd] Landschaft, Gegend
a couple of [ə 'kʌpl̩ əv] ein paar
⟨courage⟩ ['kʌrɪdʒ] Mut
of course [əv 'kɔːs] natürlich, selbstverständlich
tennis court ['tenɪs kɔːt] Tennisplatz
cousin ['kʌzn] Cousin/Cousine
cover ['kʌvə] Deckel, Haube

to cover ['kʌvə] bedecken
°to cover up [kʌvər'ʌp] zudecken, verdecken
coward ['kaʊəd] Feigling
cowboy ['kaʊbɔɪ] Cowboy
cracked [krækt] zersprungen
craft [krɑːft] Handwerk, Kunstgewerbe
Crash! [kræʃ] Krach!
to crash [kræʃ] abstürzen
crate [kreɪt] Kiste
crawfish ['krɔːfɪʃ] Languste/n
crazy ['kreɪzɪ] verrückt
cream [kriːm] Creme
   ice cream [ˌaɪs 'kriːm] Eis
   sun cream ['sʌnkriːm] Sonnencreme
°cream [kriːm] beige
criminal ['krɪmɪnl] Kriminelle/r
crocodile ['krɒkədaɪl] Krokodil
to cross [krɒs] überqueren
crowd [kraʊd] Menge (Menschen)
crowded ['kraʊdɪd] überfüllt
to cruise [kruːz] herumfahren
cry [kraɪ] Schrei
to cry [kraɪ] schreien; weinen
Cuban ['kjuːbən] Kubaner/in, kubanisch
cup [kʌp] Tasse
cupboard ['kʌbəd] Schrank
curious ['kjʊərɪəs] neugierig
cursor ['kɜːsə] Cursor, Einfügezeichen auf dem Bildschirm
customer ['kʌstəmə] Kunde/Kundin
to cut* [kʌt] schneiden
   to cut classes [kʌt 'klɑːsɪz] Stunden ausfallen lassen, schwänzen
   °to cut out [kʌt'aʊt] ausschneiden
   to cut the grass [kʌt ðə 'grɑːs] das Gras mähen
Cut it out! (sl.) [kʌt ɪt'aʊt] ugs. Hör auf!
cute [kjuːt] süß, niedlich
⟨cutie⟩ süßer Kerl
cycle path ['saɪkl pɑːθ] Radweg
cycling ['saɪklɪŋ] Radfahren
cyclist ['saɪklɪst] Radfahrer/in

D

dad [dæd] Vati, Vater
to damage ['dæmɪdʒ] beschädigen
Damn it! ['dæm ɪt] Verdammt!
dance [dɑːns] Tanz
to dance [dɑːns] tanzen
dancer ['dɑːnsə] Tänzer/in
dancing ['dɑːnsɪŋ] Tanzen
dang (sl.) [dæŋ] ugs. verdammt
danger ['deɪndʒə] Gefahr
dangerous ['deɪndʒrəs] gefährlich
Danish ['deɪnɪʃ] Däne/Dänin,

dänisch
dark [dɑːk] dunkel
   dark-haired ['dɑːk ˌheəd] dunkelhaarig
darkness ['dɑːknɪs] Dunkelheit
darling ['dɑːlɪŋ] Schatz, Liebling
date [deɪt] Datum; Verabredung
   date of birth [ˌdeɪt əv 'bɜːθ] Geburtsdatum
   °tour dates ['tʊə deɪts] Tourdaten
   up to date [ˌʌp tə 'deɪt] auf dem neuesten Stand, modern
dating ['deɪtɪŋ] Verabredungen treffen
daughter ['dɔːtə] Tochter
day [deɪ] Tag
   Christmas Day [krɪsməs 'deɪ] 1. Weihnachtstag
   °day out [deɪ'aʊt] Tagesausflug
   hours a day ['aʊəz ə deɪ] Stunden pro Tag
   these days ['ðiːz deɪz] heute, heutzutage
   °working day ['wɜːkɪŋ deɪ] Arbeitstag
   in the daytime [ɪn ðə 'deɪtaɪm] tagsüber
°to daydream ['deɪdriːm] tagträumen
days a week ['deɪz ə wiːk] Tage pro Woche
dead [ded] tot
   dead end [ded 'end] Sackgasse
dealer ['diːlə] Dealer/in
(Lesley) dear ['lezlɪ ˌdɪə] (Lesley) Liebling, Schatz
Dear ... [dɪə] Liebe/r ...
death [deθ] Tod
December [dɪ'sembə] Dezember
to decide [dɪ'saɪd] sich entschließen
°to decide on [dɪ'saɪd ɒn] auswählen, sich entscheiden für
deck [dek] Deck
to decorate ['dekəreɪt] schmücken
deep [diːp] tief
to defend (oneself) [dɪ'fend] (sich) schützen
delicious [dɪ'lɪʃəs] lecker
to deliver [dɪ'lɪvə] austeilen, austragen, ausliefern
deliverer [dɪ'lɪvərə] Lieferant/in
delivery [dɪ'lɪvərɪ] (Aus-) Lieferung
denim ['denɪm] Jeansstoff
department store [dɪ'pɑːtmənt ˌstɔː] Kaufhaus, Warenhaus
to depend on [dɪ'pend ɒn] abhängen von
to describe [dɪ'skraɪb] beschreiben
description [dɪ'skrɪpʃn] Beschreibung
design [dɪ'zaɪn] Muster, Design
to design [dɪ'zaɪn] entwerfen
desire [dɪ'zaɪə] Begierde

desk [desk] Schreibtisch
desperation [ˌdespəˈreɪʃn] Verzweiflung
to **destroy** [dɪˈstrɔɪ] zerstören
detail [ˈdiːteɪl] Detail, °Einzelheit; Kleinigkeit
detective [dɪˈtektɪv] Detektiv
detention [dɪˈtenʃn] Nachsitzen
to **develop** [dɪˈveləp] entwickeln
diagram [ˈdaɪəgræm] Diagramm, Schaubild
to **dial** [daɪl] wählen
dialling tone [ˈdaɪlɪŋ ˌtəʊn] Freizeichen
°**dialogue** [ˈdaɪəlɒg] Dialog
diary [ˈdaɪərɪ] Tagebuch
dictionary [ˈdɪkʃnrɪ] Wörterbuch
to **die** [daɪ] sterben
diesel [ˈdiːzl] Diesel
difference [ˈdɪfrns] Unterschied
different [ˈdɪfrənt] anders, verschieden
difficult [ˈdɪfɪkəlt] schwer, schwierig
⟨**digital**⟩ [ˈdɪdʒɪtl] Digital-
dingo [ˈdɪŋgəʊ] Dingo
dining-room [ˈdaɪnɪŋ ˌrʊm] Esszimmer
dinner [ˈdɪnə] Abendessen
dinosaur [ˈdaɪnəsɔː] Dinosaurier
diploma [dɪˈpləʊmə] Abschluss
to **direct** [daɪˈrekt] Regie führen
direct [dɪˈrekt] direkt
 direct speech [daɪˈrekt spiːtʃ] direkte Rede
direction [dɪˈrekʃn] Richtung
dirt [dɜːt] Schmutz
dirty [ˈdɜːtɪ] schmutzig
disabled [dɪsˈeɪbld] behindert
°**disadvantage** [ˌdɪsədˈvɑːntɪdʒ] Nachteil
to **disagree** [ˌdɪsəˈgriː] nicht übereinstimmen
to **disappear** [ˌdɪsəˈpɪə] verschwinden
disappointed [ˌdɪsəˈpɔɪntɪd] enttäuscht
disc [dɪsk] Diskette
°floppy disc [ˈflɒpɪ ˈdɪsk] Diskette
disco [ˈdɪskəʊ] Disko
 ice disco [ˈaɪs ˌdɪskəʊ] Eisdisko
discount [ˈdɪskaʊnt] Diskountladen
⟨to **discover**⟩ [dɪsˈkʌvə] entdecken
to **discriminate against** [dɪˈskrɪmɪneɪt ə ˌgenst] diskriminieren
discrimination [dɪˌskrɪmɪˈneɪʃn] Diskriminierung
°to **discuss** [dɪˈskʌs] diskutieren
discussion [dɪˈskʌʃn] Diskussion, Gespräch
dish [dɪʃ] Gericht
dishes [ˈdɪʃɪz] Geschirr

dishwasher [ˈdɪʃˌwɒʃə] Geschirrspülmaschine
to **dislike** [ˈdɪslaɪk] nicht mögen, verabscheuen
to **divide** [dɪˈvaɪd] teilen
divorce [dɪˈvɔːs] Scheidung
divorced [dɪˈvɔːst] geschieden
Diwali [dɪˈvɑːlɪ] *hinduistisches Fest*
DIY [ˌdiː ˌaɪ ˈwaɪ] Do-it-yourself
DJ (= **disc jockey**) [ˈdiː ˌdʒeɪ] Diskjockey
do-it-yourself store [duː ɪt jɔːˈself stɔː] Heimwerkermarkt
to **do*** [duː] tun, machen
 it'll do (*sl.*) [ɪtl ˈduː] *ugs.* es geht, es reicht
 to do a paper route (*AE*) [duˈə ˈpeɪpə ˌruːt] Zeitungen austragen
 to do sports [duː ˈspɔːts] Sport betreiben
 to do sth. clean [duː sʌmθɪŋ ˈkliːn] etwas schnell und schmerzlos tun
 to do the breast stroke [duː ðə ˈbrest strəʊk] brustschwimmen
 to do the washing-up [duː ðə ˌwɒʃɪŋ ˈʌp] abwaschen
 ⟨to do well⟩ [duː ˈwel] eine gute Note bekommen
 He isn't like anything I do. [hi ˈdʌznt laɪk ˈenɪθɪŋ aɪ duː] Ihm passt nichts, was ich tue.
doctor [ˈdɒktə] Arzt/Ärztin
 at the doctor's [ət ðə ˈdɒktəs] beim Arzt
dog [dɒg] Hund
$ (= **dollar**) [ˈdɒlə] Dollar
done up tight [dʌn ʌp ˈtaɪt] fest zugeschraubt
Don't panic. [dəʊnt ˈpænɪk] Keine Panik!
door [dɔː] Tür
 front door [frʌnt ˈdɔː] Haustür
doorbell [ˈdɔːbel] Türklingel
doorway [ˈdɔːweɪ] Eingangsbereich
dos and don'ts [ˈduːz n ˈdəʊnts] was man tun und was man nicht tun sollte
°**dot** [dɒt] Punkt
double-decker bus [ˌdʌbl dekə ˈbʌs] Doppeldeckerbus
double [ˈdʌbl] doppelt
dove [dʌv] weiße Taube
down [daʊn] herunter, hinunter
 to break down [breɪk ˈdaʊn] zusammenbrechen
 to calm down [kɑːm ˈdaʊn] sich beruhigen
downstairs [ˌdaʊnˈsteəz] unten, nach unten (*im Haus*)
downtown San Jose [ˌdaʊntaʊn sæn ˌhəʊˈzeɪ] in der City von San Jose

drama [ˈdrɑːmə] Drama; Theater, darstellendes Spiel
to **draw*** [drɔː] zeichnen
drawer [ˈdrɔːə] Schublade
°**drawing** [ˈdrɔːɪŋ] Zeichnung
dream [driːm] Traum
to **dream** [driːm] träumen
dreamer [ˈdriːmə] Träumer/in
⟨**dreamy**⟩ [ˈdriːmɪ] verträumt
dress [dres] Kleid
 dress code [ˈdres kəʊd] Kleidungsvorschrift
°to **dress** [dres] anziehen
dressmaker [ˈdresˌmeɪkə] Schneider/in
Dressmaking [ˈdresˌmeɪkɪŋ] Nähkurs (*Schulfach*)
drinks (*pl.*) [drɪŋks] Getränke
 soft drink [sɒft ˈdrɪŋk] alkoholfreies Getränk
to **drink*** [drɪŋk] trinken
to **drive*** [draɪv] fahren
 to drive off [draɪv ˈɒf] wegfahren
driver [ˈdraɪvə] Fahrer/in
Driver's Ed program [ˈdraɪvəz ed ˈprəʊgræm] Fahrschulunterricht
driving licence [ˈdraɪvɪŋ ˌlaɪsns] Führerschein
to **drop** [drɒp] fallen lassen
drug [drʌg] Droge
 drug-dealing [ˈdrʌgˌdiːlɪŋ] Drogendealerei
drum [drʌm] Tonne
drums [drʌmz] Schlagzeug
drunk [drʌŋk] betrunken
to **dry** [draɪ] trocknen
dry [draɪ] trocken
during [ˈdjʊərɪŋ] während
°**Dutch** [dʌtʃ] holländisch

E

⟨**e-zine**⟩ [ˈiːziːn] Zeitschrift im Internet
each [iːtʃ] jede/r/s
 each other [iːtʃ ˈʌðə] sich gegenseitig
°each time [iːtʃ ˈtaɪm] jedes Mal
ear [ɪə] Ohr
early [ˈɜːlɪ] früh
to **earn** [ɜːn] verdienen
earth [ɜːθ] die Erde
Earthling [ˈɜːθlɪŋ] Erdling
easy [ˈiːzɪ] leicht, einfach
 Take it easy! (*sl.*) [ˈteɪk ɪt ˈiːzɪ] *ugs.* Bleib ruhig.
to **eat*** [iːt] essen
edge [edʒ] Rand, Grenze
editor [ˈedɪtə] Herausgeber/in, Redakteur/in
education [ˌedʒʊˈkeɪʃn] Bildung
 education office [ˌedjuːˈkeɪʃn ˌɒfɪs] Schulamt

Dictionary

Eek! [iːk] Ahhh!
egg [eg] Ei
Eid [iːd] *moslemisches Fest*
eight [eɪt] acht
eighteen [ˌeɪˈtiːn] achtzehn
eighth (= **8th**) [eɪtθ] achte/r/s
eighty [ˈeɪtɪ] achtzig
either ... or [ˈaɪðə ... ɔː] entweder ... oder
 can't ..., either [ˈkɑːnt ...ˈaɪðə] kann auch nicht
 wasn't ... either [ˈwɒznt ... ˈaɪðə] war ... auch nicht
electrician [ˌɪlekˈtrɪʃn] Elektriker/in
electricity [ˌɪlekˈtrɪsɪtɪ] Elektrizität
elephant [[ˈelɪfənt] Elefant
eleven [ɪˈlevn] elf
else [els] sonst
 anything else [ˌenɪθɪŋ ˈels] (irgend)etwas anderes
 everyone else [evrɪwʌn ˈels] alle anderen
 what else? [wɒt ˈels] Was sonst? Was noch?
embarrassed [ɪmˈbærəst] verlegen
embassy [ˈembəsɪ] Botschaft
emergency [ɪˈmɜːdʒənsɪ] Notfall
 emergency services [ɪˈmɜːdʒənsɪ ˈsɜːvɪsɪz] Notdienst
⟨**to emigrate**⟩ [ˈemɪgreɪt] auswandern
empty [ˈemtɪ] leer
emu [ˈiːmjuː] Emu
° **encyclopedia** [ɪnˌsaɪkləˈpiːdjə] Enzyklopädie
end [end] Ende
 by the end [baɪ ðɪ ˈend] am Ende
 to end [end] aufhören; °beenden
ending [ˈendɪŋ] °Ausgang, Ende, Schluss; °Schlussteil
energy [ˈenədʒɪ] Energie, Kraft
 systems engineer [ˈsɪstəmz ˈendʒɪˈnɪə] Systemingenieur/in
 engineering firm [ˌendʒɪˈnɪərɪŋ fɜːm] Maschinenbaufirma
English [ˈɪŋglɪʃ] englisch
 in English [ɪn ˈɪŋglɪʃ] auf Englisch
 to enjoy [ɪnˈdʒɔɪ] genießen; Spaß haben
 to enjoy being young [ɪnˈdʒɔɪ biːɪŋ ˈjʌŋ] es genießen, jung zu sein
enjoyment [ɪnˈdʒɔɪmənt] Freude
enough [ɪˈnʌf] genug
to enter [ˈentə] betreten; °eintragen
entrance [ˈentrəns] Eingang
 main entrance [ˌmeɪn ˈentrəns] Haupteingang
entry [ˈentrɪ] Eintritt
⟨**envelope**⟩ [ˈenvələʊp] Briefumschlag
environment [ɪnˈvaɪərnmənt] Umwelt

environmental group [ɪnˌvaɪərənˈmentl gruːp] Umweltgruppe
° **environmentalist** [ɪnˌvaɪərənˈmentəlɪst] Umweltschützer/in
equal [ˈiːkwəl] gleich
⟨**equator**⟩ [ɪˈkweɪtə] Äquator
to equip [ɪˈkwɪp] ausrüsten
equipment [ɪˈkwɪpmənt] Ausrüstung, Anlage
escape [ɪˈskeɪp] Flucht
⟨**to escort**⟩ [ɪˈskɔːt] begleiten
ethnic [ˈeθnɪk] *aus einer sprachlich und kulturell einheitlichen Volksgruppe*
° **European** [ˌjʊərəˈpiːən] europäisch
eurotraining [ˈjʊərəʊtreɪnɪŋ] *Beispiel für ein europäisches Trainingsprogramm für junge Leute*
 Christmas Eve [krɪsməs ˈiːv] Heiligabend
even [ˈiːvn] sogar
° **even if** [ˈiːvn ɪf] auch wenn
evening [ˈiːvnɪŋ] Abend
event [ɪˈvent] Ereignis; Veranstaltung
⟨**eventually**⟩ [ɪˈventʃʊəlɪ] schließlich, endlich
ever [ˈevə] je, jemals; schon einmal
every [ˈevrɪ] jede/r/s/n
° **every day** [evrɪ ˈdeɪ] jeden Tag
° **every other line** [ˌevrɪ ˈʌðə ˌlaɪn] jede zweite Zeile
everybody [ˈevrɪˌbɒdɪ] jede/r, alle
° **everyday life** [ˌevrɪdeɪ ˈlaɪf] Leben im Alltag
 everyday problem [ˌevrɪdeɪ ˈprɒbləm] Alltagsproblem
everyone [ˌevrɪwʌn] jeder, alle
 everyone else [evrɪwʌn ˈels] alle anderen
everything [ˈevrɪθɪŋ] alles
everywhere [ˈevrɪweə] überall (in)
exam [ɪgˈzæm] Klassenarbeit, Prüfung
° **example** [ɪgˈzɑːmpl] Beispiel
excellent [ˈekslənt] ausgezeichnet, hervorragend
except [ɪkˈsept] außer
exchange [ɪksˈtʃeɪndʒ] Austausch
excited [ɪkˈsaɪtɪd] aufgeregt
exciting [ɪkˈsaɪtɪŋ] aufregend, spannend
⟨**excuse**⟩ [ɪkˈskjuːs] Entschuldigung
Excuse me! [ɪkˈskjuːz mɪ] Entschuldigung!
exercise [ˈeksəsaɪz] Übung
 exercise book [ˈeksəsaɪz ˌbʊk] Übungsheft
to exercise [ˈeksəsaɪz] sich fit halten
to expect [ɪkˈspekt] erwarten

expensive [ɪkˈspensɪv] teuer
experience [ɪksˈpɪərɪəns] Erfahrung
° **to experience** [ɪkˈspɪərɪəns] erleben
expert [ˈekspɜːt] Experte/in
to explain [ɪkˈspleɪn] erklären
to explode [ɪkˈspləʊd] explodieren, in die Luft gehen
explosion [ɪkˈspləʊʒn] Knall, Explosion
° **expression** [ɪkˈspreʃn] Ausdruck
extra [ˈekstrə] Extra
eye [aɪ] Auge

F

face [feɪs] Gesicht
° **to make funny faces** [ˈmeɪk fʌnɪ ˈfeɪsɪz] Grimassen schneiden
fact [fækt] Fakt, Tatsache
 in fact [ɪn ˈfækt] tatsächlich
factory [ˈfæktrɪ] Fabrik
fag (*sl.*) [fæg] *ugs.* Zigarette
⟨**to fail**⟩ [feɪl] versagen, scheitern
fair play [feə ˈpleɪ] Fairplay
fair [feə] blond; gerecht, fair
to fall* [fɔːl] fallen
 to fall asleep [fɔːl əˈsliːp] einschlafen
 to fall in love [ˌfɔːl ɪn ˈlʌv] sich verlieben
 to fall out [fɔːl ˈaʊt] herausfallen
 to fall over [fɔːl ˈəʊvə] hinfallen
false [fɔːls] falsch
family [ˈfæməlɪ] Familie
° **family tree** [ˌfæməlɪ ˈtriː] Stammbaum
° **host family** [həʊst ˈfæmlɪ] Gastfamilie
famous [ˈfeɪməs] berühmt
fan [fæn] Fan
to fancy [ˈfænsɪ] Lust haben, mögen
fantastic [fænˈtæstɪk] fantastisch
far [fɑː] weit
farm [fɑːm] Bauernhof
farmer [ˈfɑːmə] Bauer
fast-food place [ˈfɑːstfuːd pleɪs] Schnellimbiss
fast [fɑːst] fest; schnell
fasting [ˈfɑːstɪŋ] Fasten
fat [fæt] dick, fett
father [ˈfɑːðə] Vater
 Father Christmas [ˌfɑːðə ˈkrɪsməs] Nikolaus
fault [fɔːlt] Fehler
favorite (*AE*) [ˈfeɪvrɪt] Lieblings-
favourite (*BE*) [ˈfeɪvrɪt] Lieblings-
fax [fæks] Fax
 fax machine [ˈfæks məʃiːn] Faxgerät
February [ˈfebrʊərɪ] Februar

Dictionary

to get **fed up with** [get fed ˈʌp wɪð] die Nase allmählich voll haben von
to **feed*** [fiːd] füttern
 to be fed up (with sb.) [bɪ fed ˈʌp wɪð ˈsʌmbədɪ] (von jdm.) die Nase voll haben
to **feel*** [fiːl] (sich) fühlen
 to feel ashamed [fiːl əˈʃeɪmd] sich schämen
 to feel sorry [fiːl ˈsɒrɪ fɔː] Leid tun, bedauern
°to feel threatened [fiːl ˈθretnd] sich bedroht fühlen
 to make sb. feel guilty [meɪk ˈsʌmbədɪ fiːl ˈgɪltɪ] jdm. ein schlechtes Gewissen machen
feeling [ˈfiːlɪŋ] Gefühl
fellas = fellows (sl.) [ˈfeləz] ugs. Jungs
female [ˈfiːmeɪl] weiblich
festival [ˈfestəvl] Fest(tag)
a **few** [ə ˈfjuː] ein paar
 quite a few [kwaɪt ə ˈfjuː] etliche
fewer [ˈfjuːə] weniger
field [fiːld] Feld
fifteen [ˌfɪfˈtiːn] fünfzehn
fifth [fɪfθ] fünfte/r/s
fifty [ˈfɪftɪ] fünfzig
fight [faɪt] Kampf
to **fight*** [faɪt] kämpfen, streiten
fighter [ˈfaɪtə] Kämpfer/in
figure [ˈfɪgə] Figur
file [faɪl] Datei; °Karteikasten, Ordner
to **fill** [fɪl] füllen
filler [ˈfɪlə] Füllwort
film [fɪlm] Film
filter [ˈfɪltə] Filter
final [ˈfaɪnl] End-
finally [ˈfaɪnəlɪ] schließlich
to **find*** [faɪnd] finden
 to find out [faɪnd ˈaʊt] herausfinden
 to find one's way around [ˈfaɪnd wʌnz weɪ əˈraʊnd] sich zurechtfinden
fine [faɪn] fein, vornehm
finger [ˈfɪŋgə] Finger
to **finish** [ˈfɪnɪʃ] aufhören, beenden
 ⟨to finish off⟩ [ˌfɪnɪʃ ˈɒf] erledigen
fire [ˈfaɪə] Feuer
 open fire [ˌəʊpən ˈfaɪə] Kamin
fireworks (pl.) [ˈfaɪəwɜːks] Feuerwerk
firm [fɜːm] Firma
first aid [fɜːst ˈeɪd] erste Hilfe
first [fɜːst] erste/r/s; zuerst, als Erste/r/s
 at first [ət ˈfɜːst] zuerst
 first of all [ˈfɜːst əv ɔːl] erstens, zuallererst
fish (sg./pl.) [fɪʃ] Fisch/Fische

fish and chips [fɪʃnˈtʃɪps] Fisch mit Pommes frites
fish stick (AE) [ˈfɪʃ stɪk] Fischstäbchen
fishburger [ˈfɪʃbɜːgə] Fischburger
fishing lake [ˈfɪʃɪŋ ˌleɪk] See zum Angeln
fist [fɪst] Faust
°to **fit** [fɪt] passen zu
fit [fɪt] gesund, stark
°**fitness** [ˈfɪtnɪs] Fitness
 fitness studio [ˈfɪtnɪs ˈstjuːdɪəʊ] Fitnessstudio
five [faɪv] fünf
to **fix** [fɪks] reparieren
flag [flæg] Flagge
flat [flæt] Wohnung
 council flat [ˈkaʊnsl flæt] Sozialwohnung
flat [flæt] entladen, leer
⟨**fleet**⟩ [fliːt] Flotte
flight [flaɪt] Flug; Fahrt
flirting [ˈflɜːtɪŋ] Flirten
float [fləʊt] Floß; Wagen
floor [flɔː] Fußboden; Stockwerk, Etage
°**floppy disc** [ˈflɒpɪ ˈdɪsk] Diskette
flower [ˈflaʊə] Blume
flute [fluːt] Querflöte
fly [flaɪ] Fliege
to **fly*** [flaɪ] fliegen
 to fly off [flaɪ ˈɒf] abfliegen, losfliegen
⟨to **fold**⟩ [fəʊld] falten
⟨**folks**⟩ (sl.) [fəʊks] ugs. Leute
to **follow** [ˈfɒləʊ] folgen; °verfolgen
food [fuːd] Essen
 food bank [ˈfuːd bæŋk] Sammelstelle für Essensspenden
fool [fuːl] Narr/Närrin
to make a **fool** of sb. [ˌmeɪk ə ˈfuːl əv] jdn. veräppeln, jdn. lächerlich machen
foot [fʊt] Fuß; Fuß (Maßeinheit: 30,5 cm)
 on foot [ɒn ˈfʊt] zu Fuß
football [ˈfʊtbɔːl] Fußball
 football match [ˈfʊtbɔːl ˌmætʃ] Fußballspiel
for [fɔː] für
 for a change [fɔːr ə ˈtʃeɪndʒ] zur Abwechslung
 for a time [fɔːr ə ˈtaɪm] eine Zeit lang
 for a week [ˈfɔːr ə ˈwiːk] eine Woche lang
 for ages [fɔːr ˈeɪdʒɪz] seit einer Ewigkeit
 for any reason [fɔːr ˈenɪ ˌriːzn] aus irgendeinem Grund
 for the first time [fɔː ðə ˈfɜːst taɪm] zum ersten Mal
for [fɔː] seit
force [fɔːs] Macht

foreign [ˈfɒrɪn] fremd, ausländisch
foreigner [ˈfɒrɪnə] Fremde/r, Ausländer/in
foreman [ˈfɔːmən] Polier, Vorarbeiter
forest [ˈfɒrɪst] Wald
to **forget*** [fəˈget] vergessen
fork [fɔːk] Gabel
form [fɔːm] Form; Formular
°past form [ˈpɑːst fɔːm] Vergangenheitsform
 registration form [ˌredʒɪˈstreɪʃn fɔːm] Anmeldeformular
°short form [ˈʃɔːt fɔːm] Kurzform
°to **form** [fɔːm] bilden
formal [ˈfɔːml] formell
forty [ˈfɔːtɪ] vierzig
four [fɔː] vier
fourteen [ˌfɔːˈtiːn] vierzehn
fourth [fɔːθ] vierte/r/s
fragile [ˈfrædʒaɪl] zart
freak [friːk] Fan
the **free** [ðə friː] die Freien
free [friː] frei
 free time [ˌfriː ˈtaɪm] Freizeit
freedom [ˈfriːdəm] Freiheit
French [frenʃ] Französisch
 french fries (AE) [frentʃ ˈfraɪs] Pommes frites
fresh [freʃ] frisch
Friday [ˈfraɪdɪ] Freitag
fridge [frɪdʒ] Kühlschrank
fried [fraɪd] gebraten
friend [frend] Freund/in
friendly [ˈfrendlɪ] freundlich
friendship [ˈfrendʃɪp] Freundschaft
frightening [ˈfraɪtnɪŋ] furchterregend
frog [frɒg] Frosch
from [frɒm] aus, von
 from ... to [frɒm ... tʊ] von ... bis (Wochentage)
 where ... from [ˌweə ... ˈfrɒm] woher
at the **front** [ət ðə ˈfrʌnt] vorne
 front door [frʌnt ˈdɔː] Haustür
 in front of [ɪn ˈfrʌnt əv] vor
to **frown** [fraʊn] die Stirn runzeln
frozen [ˈfrəʊzn] gefroren
fruit [fruːt] Obst
full-time [ˈfʊltaɪm] Vollzeit
full [fʊl] ausführlich; voll
fumes [fjuːmz] Abgase
fun [fʌn] Spaß
 Have fun! [hæv ˈfʌn] Viel Spaß!
 That's fun! [ðæts ˈfʌn] Das macht Spaß!
 The fun they had [ðə ˈfʌn ðeɪ hæd] Was für einen Spaß sie hatten!
 to make fun of someone [meɪk ˈfʌn əv] sich über jdn. lustig machen

Dictionary

funny ['fʌnɪ] komisch, merkwürdig; lustig, witzig
furious ['fjʊərɪəs] wütend, rasend
furniture (sg.) ['fɜːnɪtʃə] Möbel
future ['fjuːtʃə] Zukunft

G

gadget ['gædʒɪt] Gerät
game [geɪm] Spiel
  game show ['geɪm ʃəʊ] Spielshow
gang [gæŋ] Bande
° **gap** [gæp] Lücke
garage ['gærɑːdʒ] Garage; Kfz-Werkstatt
garbage (AE) ['gɑːbɪdʒ] Müll, Abfall
  garbage can (AE) ['gɑːbɪdʒ kæn] Mülleimer
garden ['gɑːdn] Garten
  back garden (BE) [bæk 'gɑːdn] Garten hinter dem Haus
gas [gæs] Gas
gated community ['geɪtɪd kə'mjuːnətɪ] bewachte Siedlung, *meistens ummauert und mit kontrolliertem Eingang*
to **gaze** ['geɪz] anstarren
gear [gɪə] Gang
gears [gɪəz] Gangschaltung
Gee! [dʒiː] Mann! Mensch!
genuine ['dʒenjʊɪn] natürlich
Geography [dʒɪ'ɒgrəfɪ] Erdkunde (*Schulfach*)
German ['dʒɜːmən] deutsch
to **get*** [get] bekommen, kriegen; erreichen, gelangen; holen; werden
  to get a beating [get ə 'biːtɪŋ] verprügelt werden
  to get around [get ə'raʊnd] herumkommen, sich umsehen
  to get around the ranch [get ə'raʊnd ðə rɑːntʃ] sich auf der Ranch fortbewegen
  to get away [get ə'weɪ] weg-, fortkommen
  to get back [get 'bæk] zurückkommen, zurückkehren
  to get better at sth. [get betər ət] in etwas besser werden
  to get expelled [get ɪk'speld] von der Schule verwiesen werden
  to get fed up with [get fed ʌp wɪð] die Nase allmählich voll haben von
  to get into a program [get ɪntu ə 'prəʊgræm] in ein Programm gelangen
  to get into trouble [get ɪntʊ 'trʌbl] Schwierigkeiten, Probleme bekommen

  to get involved [get ɪn'vɒlvd] sich engagieren
  to get lost [get 'lɒst] abhauen, verschwinden; sich verlaufen
  to get married [get 'mærɪd] heiraten
  (to get) nasty ['nɑːstɪ] böse, ungemütlich, scheußlich (werden)
  to get off [get 'ɒf] aussteigen
  to get on [get 'ɒn] miteinander auskommen, zusammen passen
  to get on the bus [get ɒn] einsteigen, aufsteigen
  to get on well with [get ɒn 'wel wɪð] gut auskommen mit
  to get on with each other [get ɒn wɪð iːtʃ 'ʌðə] miteinander auskommen
  to get out [get 'aʊt] herausholen
  to get over sth. [get 'əʊvə ˌsʌmθɪŋ] etwas überstehen
  to get paid for sth. [get 'peɪd fɔː ˌsʌmθɪŋ] für etwas bezahlt werden
  to get sb. wrong [get sʌmbədɪ 'rɒŋ] jdm. falsch verstehen
  to get stressed [get 'strest] gestresst werden
° to get there ['get ðeə] dort hinkommen
  ⟨to get to know⟩ [get tu: 'nəʊ] kennen lernen
  to get to no.1 [get tu ˌnʌmbə 'wʌn] die Nummer 1 werden
  to get up [get 'ʌp] aufstehen
  to get used to sth. [get 'juːzd] sich an etwas gewöhnen
  ⟨to get kicked in the pants⟩ [get 'kɪkd ɪn ðə 'pænts] einen Tritt in den Hintern bekommen
gift [gɪft] Geschenk
⟨**"Gimme five!"**⟩ [gɪmɪ 'faɪv] Begrüßungsritual, *bei dem man sich gegenseitig die rechte Hand schlägt.*
girl [gɜːl] Mädchen
girlfriend ['gɜːlfrend] Freundin *(eines Jungen)*
to **give*** [gɪv] geben
  to give up [gɪv 'ʌp] aufgeben
  to give up sth. [gɪv 'ʌp ˌsʌmθɪŋ] auf etwas verzichten
glass [glɑːs] Glas
⟨to **glue**⟩ [gluː] kleben
to **go*** [gəʊ] gehen, fahren
  to go away [gəʊ ə'weɪ] weggehen, verreisen
  to go by [gəʊ 'baɪ] vergehen
  to go by bus [gəʊ baɪ 'bʌs] mit dem Bus fahren
  to go camping [gəʊ 'kæmpɪŋ] zelten gehen
  to go down [gəʊ 'daʊn] heruntergehen; zu Boden gehen

  to go for a walk [gəʊ fər ə 'wɔːk] spazieren gehen
  to go in [gəʊ 'ɪn] hineingehen
  to go on [gəʊ 'ɒn] geschehen, vor sich gehen, los sein; °weitermachen
  to go on a bike trip [gəʊ ɒn ə 'baɪk trɪp] eine Fahrradtour machen
  to go on-line [gəʊ 'ɒnlaɪn] online gehen
  to go out with sb. [gəʊ 'aʊt wɪð ˌsʌmbədɪ] ⟨mit jdm. gehen⟩; mit jdm. ausgehen
  to go over to [gəʊ 'əʊvə tə] herübergehen, zu jdm. gehen
  to go skiing [gəʊ 'skiːɪŋ] Ski laufen gehen
  to go straight on [ˌgəʊ streɪt 'ɒn] geradeaus weitergehen
  to go swimming [gəʊ 'swɪmɪŋ] schwimmen gehen
  to go to bed [gəʊ tə 'bed] ins Bett gehen
  to go well [gəʊ 'wel] gut gehen
° to go with ['gəʊ wɪð] passen zu
  to go wrong [gəʊ 'rɒŋ] kaputtgehen; schief laufen, daneben gehen
go-karting ['gəʊkɑːtɪŋ] Gokart-Fahren
goal [gəʊl] Tor
goalkeeper ['gəʊlˌkiːpə] Torhüter/in
God damn! [gɒd 'dæm] Verdammt nochmal!
gold [gəʊld] Gold
  to pan for gold [pæn fə 'gəʊld] Gold waschen
good [gʊd] brav; gut
  Good morning. [gʊd 'mɔːnɪŋ] Guten Morgen.
  good-looking [gʊd'lʊkɪŋ] gut aussehend
  to be good at [bɪ 'gʊd ət] etwas gut können, gut sein in
  Good pay! [gʊd 'peɪ] Gute Bezahlung!
Goodbye! [gʊd'baɪ] Auf Wiedersehen!
  to kiss sb. goodbye ['kɪs sʌmbədɪ ˌgʊd'baɪ] jdm. beim/zum Abschied einen Kuss geben
gosh [gɒʃ] Ach du Schreck!
° **gossip** ['gɒsɪp] Klatsch, Schwatz
got [gɒt] *see* to get
I've gotten (AE) [aɪv 'gɒtn] *amerikanisch für:* I've got
government ['gʌvnmənt] Regierung
to **grab** [græb] packen
graceful ['greɪsfʊl] würdevoll
grade [greɪd] Klasse; Note
to **grade** (AE) [greɪd] benoten
8th-grader (AE) [eɪtθ 'greɪdə] Achtklässler

graffiti [grəˈfiːtɪ] Graffiti
°**grammar** [ˈgræmə] Grammatik
gran [græn] Oma
grandad [ˈgrændæd] Opa, Großvater
grandchildren [ˈgrænˌtʃɪldrən] Enkelkinder
Grandma [ˈgrænmɑː] Oma, Großmutter
grandmother [ˈgrænˌmʌðə] Großmutter
grandparents [ˈgrænˌpærnts] Großeltern
°**graph** [grɑːf] Grafik
grass [grɑːs] Gras
  to cut the grass [kʌt ðə ˈgrɑːs] das Gras mähen
grateful [ˈgreɪtfʊl] dankbar
gravy [ˈgreɪvɪ] Soße
great-great-grandparents [ˌgreɪtˌgreɪt ˈgrænpeərnts] Ururgroßeltern
great [greɪt] groß; toll, super, prima
Greek [griːk] griechisch
green [griːn] grün
grey [greɪ] grau
  ⟨**greyish**⟩ [ˈgreɪɪʃ] gräulich
°**grid** [grɪd] Raster
grin [grɪn] Grinsen
to **grin** [grɪn] grinsen
grocery store [ˈgrəʊsərɪ stɔː] Lebensmittelgeschäft
ground [graʊnd] (Fußball-)Platz; Grund, Boden
groundsman [ˈgraʊndzmæn] Platzwart
group [gruːp] Gruppe
  environmental group [ɪnˌvaɪərənˈmentl gruːp] Umweltgruppe
°to **group** [gruːp] gruppieren
groupwork [ˈgruːpwɜːk] Gruppenarbeit
to **grow*** [grəʊ] wachsen
  to grow up [grəʊ ˈʌp] aufwachsen
guardsman [ˈgɑːdzmən] Wache, Wachtposten
to **guess** [ges] annehmen, vermuten; erraten
  I did guess ... [aɪ dɪd ges] Ich hab's mir gedacht ...
  I guess ... [aɪ ges] Ich nehme an, Ich vermute, ...
guest [gest] Gast
⟨**guide**⟩ [gaɪd] Führer
guilty [ˈgɪltɪ] schuldig
  to make sb. feel guilty [meɪk ˈsʌmbədɪ fiːl ˈgɪltɪ] jdm. ein schlechtes Gewissen machen
guitar [gɪˈtɑː] Gitarre
  bass guitar [ˈbeɪs gɪˈtɑː] Bassgitarre

  lead guitar [ˈliːd gɪˈtɑː] 1. Gitarre, Leadgitarre
  to play the guitar [ˌpleɪ ðə gɪˈtɑː] Gitarre spielen
stick of **gum** [stɪk əv ˈgʌm] Streifen Kaugummi
gun [gʌn] Pistole
guy [gaɪ] Typ, Kerl
gym [dʒɪm] Turnhalle

H

habit [ˈhæbɪt] Angewohheit
hacker [ˈhækə] Hacker
hair [heə] Haar, Haare
  dark haired [ˈdɑːk ˌheəd] dunkelhaarig
hairdryer [ˈheəˌdraɪə] Fön
half-time [hɑːfˈtaɪm] Halbzeit
half past [ˈhɑːf pɑːst] halb (Uhrzeit)
half of a body [ˈhɑːf əv ə ˈbɒdɪ] eine halbe Körperlänge
halfpipe [ˈhɑːfpaɪp] Halfpipe
hall [hɔːl] Flur
°sentence **halves** [ˈsentəns ˌhɑːvz] Satzhälften
hamburger [ˈhæmbɜːgə] Hamburger
hamster [ˈhæmstə] Hamster
hand [hænd] Hand
handsome [ˈhænsəm] gut aussehend
hang gliding [ˈhæŋ ˌglaɪdɪŋ] Drachenfliegen
to **hang*** [hæŋ] hängen
  to hang around [hæŋ əˈraʊnd] herumhängen
  Hang on, ... [hæŋ ˈɒn] Warte, ...
  to hang out [hæŋ ˈaʊt] sich die Zeit vertreiben
Hanukkah [ˈhænuːkə] jüdisches Fest
to **happen** [ˈhæpn] passieren, geschehen
happy [ˈhæpɪ] glücklich, fröhlich
  Happy birthday! [ˌhæpɪ ˈbɜːθdeɪ] Herzlichen Glückwunsch zum Geburtstag!
hard [hɑːd] schwer, hart
hardly [ˈhɑːdlɪ] kaum
hardware [ˈhɑːdweə] Hardware
has got [hæz ˈgɒt] hat, besitzt
hat [hæt] Hut
to **hate** [heɪt] hassen
to **have*** [hæv] haben
  Have fun! [hæv ˈfʌn] Viel Spaß!
  have got [hæv ˈgɒt] haben, besitzen
  to have a good time [hæv ə ˌgʊd ˈtaɪm] viel Spaß haben
  to have a shower [hæv ə ˈʃaʊə] duschen

  to have breakfast [hæv ˈbrekfəst] frühstücken
  to have lunch [hæv ˈlʌntʃ] zu Mittag essen
  to have to [ˈhæv tʊ] müssen
  What are you having?[ˈwɒt ə ˈjuː ˌhævɪŋ] Was nimmst du?
he [hiː] er
head [hed] Kopf
  ⟨head teacher⟩ [ˈhed ˌtiːtʃə] Schuldirektor/in
to **head for** [ˈhed fə] sich auf den Weg machen zu/nach
°**heading** [ˈhedɪŋ] Überschrift
°**headline** [ˈhedlaɪn] Schlagzeile
headphones (pl.) [ˈhedfəʊnz] Kopfhörer
healthy [ˈhelθɪ] gesund
to **hear*** [hɪə] hören
heart [hɑːt] Herz
  heart attack [ˈhɑːt əˌtæk] Herzinfarkt
heaven [ˈhevn] Himmel
  Thank **heavens!** [θæŋk ˈhevnz] Dem Himmel sei Dank!
heavy [ˈhevɪ] schwer
heavy metal band [ˈhevɪ ˈmetl bænd] Heavymetal-Band
height [heɪt] Körpergröße
heliskiing [ˈhelɪskiːɪŋ] mit dem Hubschrauber zum Abfahrtski geflogen werden
hell [hel] Hölle
Hello. [həˈləʊ] Hallo, Guten Tag.
helmet [ˈhelmɪt] Helm
help [help] Hilfe
  home help [həʊm ˈhelp] Haushaltshilfe
°to ask for help [ɑːsk fə ˈhelp] um Hilfe bitten
to **help** [help] helfen
helper [ˈhelpə] Helfer/in
helpful [ˈhelpfʊl] °hilfreich; hilfsbereit
her [hɜː] ihr/ihre; ihr/sie
here [hɪə] hier
  around here [əˈraʊnd hɪə] hier in der Umgebung
  Here you are. [hɪə juˈɑː] Hier bitte.
hero [ˈhɪərəʊ] Held/in
herself [hɜːˈself] sie/ihr/sich selbst
Hey [heɪ] Ausruf
Hi. [haɪ] Hallo! (zu Freunden)
hidden [ˈhɪdn] versteckt
hide-and-seek [haɪd ənd ˈsiːk] Versteckspiel
to **hide*** [haɪd] (sich) verstecken
high school [ˈhaɪ skuːl] amer. Schulform ab Klasse 9
high [haɪ] hoch
to **highlight** [ˈhaɪlaɪt] hervorheben, herausstellen; °markieren
hiking boots [ˈhaɪkɪŋ ˌbuːts] Wanderschuhe

hill [hɪl] Hügel, Berg
him [hɪm] ihm/ihn
himself [hɪmˈself] er/ihm/sich selbst
Hindu [ˈhɪnduː] Hindu, hinduistisch
to **hire** [ˈhaɪə] leihen, mieten
his [hɪz] sein/seine
Hispanic [hɪˈspænɪk] *(U.S.A.-) Einwanderer mit der Muttersprache Spanisch*
hissing [ˈhɪsɪŋ] zischend
History [ˈhɪstrɪ] Geschichte *(Schulfach);* Geschichte
  The History of Rock Music [ðə ˌhɪstərɪ əv ˈrɒk ˌmjuːzɪk] Die Geschichte der Rockmusik *(Schulfach)*
hit [hɪt] Hit
to **hit*** [hɪt] schlagen
  They won't know what hit them. [ðeɪ ˈwəʊnt nəʊ wɒt ˈhɪt ðəm] Sie werden nicht wissen, wie ihnen geschieht.
hobby [ˈhɒbɪ] Hobby
hockey [ˈhɒkɪ] Hockey
to **hold*** [həʊld] halten
  to hold the line [həʊld ðə ˈlaɪn] warten *(während eines Telefonats)*
  to hold up [həʊld ˈʌp] hoch halten, zeigen
holiday [ˈhɒlɪdeɪ] Urlaub
  holiday flat [ˈhɒlɪdeɪ ˌflæt] Ferienwohnung
  on holiday [ˌɒn ˈhɒlɪdeɪ] im Urlaub
  school holidays [skuːl ˈhɒlɪdeɪz] Schulferien
home [həʊm] nach Hause; Zuhause
  at home [ət ˈhəʊm] zu Hause
  home help [həʊm ˈhelp] Haushaltshilfe
  old people's home [əʊld ˈpiːplz həʊm] Altersheim
home-made [ˈhəʊm meɪd] hausgemacht
⟨**homepage**⟩ [ˈhəʊmpeɪdʒ] *erste Seite einer Webseite*
homeroom *(AE)* [ˈhəʊmruːm] *Zimmer des/r Klassenlehrers/lehrerin*
to be **homesick** [ˈhəʊmsɪk] Heimweh haben
hometown [ˈhəʊmtaʊn] Heimatstadt
homework [ˈhəʊmwɜːk] Hausaufgaben
honest [ˈɒnɪst] ehrlich
honey [ˈhʌnɪ] Honig; Schätzchen
hope [həʊp] Hoffnung
to **hope** [həʊp] hoffen
⟨**horn**⟩ [hɔːn] Horn

horrible [ˈhɒrəbl] furchtbar, schrecklich
horror [ˈhɒrə] Horror
horse [hɔːs] Pferd
horseback riding *(AE)* [ˈhɔːsbæk ˌraɪdɪŋ] Reiten
hospital [ˈhɒspɪtl] Krankenhaus
°**host** [həʊst] Gastgeber
°**host family** [həʊst ˈfæmlɪ] Gastfamilie
hostel [ˈhɒstl] Wohnheim
hot [hɒt] heiß; scharf
hotel [həʊˈtel] Hotel
hour [ˈaʊə] Stunde
  long hours [lɒŋ ˈaʊəz] Überstunden
  hours a day [ˈaʊəz ə deɪ] Stunden pro Tag
house [haʊs] Haus
  semi-detached house [ˌsemɪdɪˌtætʃt ˈhaʊs] Doppelhaushälfte
  terraced house [ˈterəst haʊs] Reihenhaus
housework [ˈhaʊswɜːk] Hausarbeit
how [haʊ] wie
  How are you? [ˌhaʊ ə ˈjuː] Wie geht es dir/euch?
  How are you doing? *(sl.)* [ˈhaʊ aː jə ˈduːɪŋ] *ugs.* Wie geht's?
  how many [ˌhaʊ ˈmenɪ] wie viele
  How many times …? [ˌhaʊ menɪ ˈtaɪmz] Wie oft …?
  how much [haʊ ˈmʌtʃ] wie viel
  How much is/are …? [haʊ ˈmʌtʃ] Wie viel kostet/kosten …?
° how often [haʊ ˈɒfn] wie oft
  how old [haʊ ˈəʊld] wie alt
However, … [haʊˈevə] Jedoch …
to **howl** [haʊl] heulen
hug [hʌg] Umarmung
  sense of **humour** [sens əv ˈhjuːmə] Sinn für Humor
one **hundred** [wʌn ˈhʌndrəd] (ein)hundert
hungry [ˈhʌŋgrɪ] hungrig
to **hunt** [hʌnt] jagen
hunter [ˈhʌntə] Jäger/in
hurrah [hʊˈrɑː] hurra!
to **hurry** [ˈhʌrɪ] eilen, schnell laufen
in a **hurry** [ɪn ə ˈhʌrɪ] eilig
to **hurt*** [hɜːt] verletzen, wehtun
hurt [hɜːt] verletzt, gekränkt
husband [ˈhʌzbənd] Ehemann

I

I [aɪ] ich
  I can't stand … [aɪ ˌkɑːnt ˈstænd] Ich kann … nicht ausstehen.
  I think so. [aɪ ˈθɪŋk səʊ] Ich glaube, ja. Ich denke, ja.

ice [aɪs] Eis
  ice cream [ˌaɪs ˈkriːm] (Speise)eis
  ice disco [ˈaɪs ˌdɪskəʊ] Eisdisko
  ice skating [ˈaɪs ˌskeɪtɪŋ] Schlittschuhlaufen
  ice stadium [ˈaɪs ˌsteɪdɪəm] Eislaufstadion
I'd (= **I would**) **like to** [aɪd ˈlaɪk tə] Ich würde gerne …. Ich möchte …
idea [aɪˈdɪə] Idee, Vorstellung
  no idea [nəʊ aɪˈdɪə] keine Ahnung
ideal [aɪˈdɪəl] ideal
identification [aɪˌdentɪfɪˈkeɪʃn] Identifikation, Ausweispapiere
to **identify** [aɪˈdentɪfaɪ] die Identität feststellen
identity card [aɪˈdentətɪ ˌkɑːd] (Personal-) Ausweis
idiot [ˈɪdɪət] Idiot
idol [ˈaɪdl] Idol
if [ɪf] wenn, falls
° even if [ˈiːvn ɪf] auch wenn
ill [ɪl] krank
illegal [ɪˈliːgl] illegal
⟨**illness**⟩ [ˈɪlnɪs] Krankheit
image [ˈɪmɪdʒ] Eindruck, Bild
to **imagine** [ɪˈmædʒɪn] sich vorstellen
immediately [ɪˈmiːdjətlɪ] sofort
immigrant [ˈɪmɪgrnt] Einwanderer
impolite [ˈɪmpəlaɪt] unhöflich
important [ɪmˈpɔːtnt] wichtig
impossible [ɪmˈpɒsəbl] unmöglich
impression [ɪmˈpreʃn] Eindruck
  to make a good impression [meɪk ə gʊd ɪmˈpreʃn] einen guten Eindruck machen
in [ɪn] in
  in a hurry [ɪn ə ˈhʌrɪ] eilig
  in a mess [ɪn ə ˈmes] durcheinander
  in a muddle [ɪn ə ˈmʌdl] durcheinander
  in a way [ɪn ə ˈweɪ] in gewisser Weise
  in case [ɪn ˈkeɪs] für den Fall
  ⟨in common⟩ [ɪn ˈkɒmən] gemeinsam
  in English [ɪn ˈɪŋglɪʃ] auf Englisch
  in fact [ɪn ˈfækt] tatsächlich
° in five years' time [ɪn ˈfaɪv jɪəz taɪm] in fünf Jahren
  in front of [ɪn ˈfrʌnt əv] vor
  in love [ɪn ˈlʌv] verliebt
  in need [ɪn ˈniːd] in Not
  ⟨in print⟩ [ɪn ˈprɪnt] veröffentlicht
  in the daytime [ɪn ðə ˈdeɪtaɪm] tagsüber
  in the morning [ɪn ðə ˈmɔːnɪŋ] am Morgen, morgens

Dictionary

in the mornings [ɪn ðə 'mɔːnɪŋz] jeden Morgen
in time [ɪn 'taɪm] rechtzeitig, pünktlich
in trouble [ɪn 'trʌbl] in Schwierigkeiten
to log in [lɒɡ_'ɪn] einloggen
inch [ɪntʃ] Inch (engl. Maßeinheit, = 2,4 cm)
incident ['ɪnsɪdənt] Vorfall
included [ɪn'kluːdɪd] inbegriffen
⟨independent⟩ [ɪndɪ'pendənt] unabhängig
Indian ['ɪndjən] Inder/in, indisch
indoors ['ɪndɔːz] innen, im Haus
industrial nation [ɪn'dʌstrɪəl 'neɪʃn] Industrienation
° information [ˌɪnfə'meɪʃn] Information
information centre [ɪnfə'meɪʃn ˌsentə] Verkehrsbüro
inner-city ['ɪnə ˌsɪtɪ] innerstädtisch
insect ['ɪnsekt] Insekt
to insert [ɪn'sɜːt] einwerfen
° inside ['ɪnˌsaɪd] Innenansicht, Innenaufteilung
inside [ˌɪn'saɪd] innen
inside pocket [ˌɪn'saɪd 'pɒkɪt] Innentasche
instead [ɪn'sted] stattdessen
instead of [ɪn'sted_əv] an Stelle von, anstatt
instrument ['ɪnstrʊmənt] Instrument
interest ['ɪntrəst] Interesse
° to be interested in [['ɪntrɪstɪd_ɪn] interessiert sein an
interesting ['ɪntrəstɪŋ] interessant
international [ˌɪntə'næʃənl] international
Internet ['ɪntənet] Internet
° on the Internet [ɒn ðiː_'ɪntənet] im Internet
surfing the Internet ['sɜːfɪŋ ðiː_ 'ɪntənet] im Internet surfen
to surf the Internet ['sɜːf ðiː_ _'ɪntənet] im Internet surfen
to interrupt [ˌɪntə'rʌpt] unterbrechen
interview ['ɪntəˌvjuː] Interview
to interview ['ɪntəˌvjuː] interviewen, befragen
into ['ɪntʊ] in (hinein)
to introduce [ˌɪntrə'djuːs] einführen; sich (jdm.) vorstellen
to invent [ɪn'vent] erfinden
invention [ɪn'venʃn] Erfindung
inventor [ɪn'ventə] Erfinder/in
invitation [ˌɪnvɪ'teɪʃn] Einladung
to invite [ɪn'vaɪt] einladen
to become involved [bɪ'kʌm_ ɪn'vɒlvd] verwickelt werden
⟨Irish⟩ ['aɪrɪʃ] irisch
ironing ['aɪənɪŋ] Bügelwäsche

° irregular [ɪ'reɡjʊlə] unregelmäßig
it [ɪt] es; ihm; ihn
Italian [ɪ'tæljən] Italiener/in, italienisch
its [ɪts] sein/e, ihr/e
It's the way wolves are. [ɪts ðə weɪ wʊlvz_'ɑː] So sind Wölfe.
It's none of her business. [ɪts 'nʌn_ əv hɜː 'bɪznɪs] Das geht sie nichts an.
itself [ɪt'self] es/ihm/sich selbst

J

jacket ['dʒækɪt] Jacke, Jackett
Jamaican [dʒə'meɪkən] jamaikanisch
January ['dʒænjʊərɪ] Januar
Japanese [ˌdʒæpə'niːz] japanisch
jazz [dʒæz] Jazz
jealous ['dʒeləs] eifersüchtig
jeans (pl.) [dʒiːnz] Jeans
Jewish ['dʒuːɪʃ] jüdisch
job [dʒɒb] Arbeit, Aufgabe
to jog [dʒɒɡ] joggen
to join [dʒɔɪn] angehören
joke [dʒəʊk] Witz
° You must be joking! [jʊ ˌmʌst bɪ 'dʒəʊkɪŋ] Du spinnst wohl!
⟨journalist⟩ ['dʒɜːnəlɪst] Journalist/in
journey ['dʒɜːnɪ] Reise
July [dʒʊ'laɪ] Juli
⟨jumbo jet⟩ ['dʒʌmbəʊ ˌdʒet] Jumbojet
jump [dʒʌmp] Sprung
long jump ['lɒŋ ˌdʒʌmp] Weitsprung
to jump [dʒʌmp] springen
to jump off [dʒʌmp_'ɒf] herunterspringen
June [dʒuːn] Juni
jungle ['dʒʌŋɡl] Dschungel
office junior [ˌɒfɪs 'dʒuːnjə] Bürogehilfe, Bürogehilfin
° junior athletics ['dʒuːnjər_ æθ'letɪks] Leichtathletik für Jugendliche
junior reporter ['dʒuːnjə rɪ'pɔːtə] unerfahrene/r Reporter/in
just [dʒʌst] nur, bloß, einfach
Just a moment. [ˌdʒʌst_ə 'məʊmənt] Moment mal!, Ja, gleich!
justice ['dʒʌstɪs] Gerechtigkeit

K

kangaroo [ˌkæŋɡə'ruː] Känguru
karaoke [kærɪ'əʊkɪ] Musik zum Mitsingen

to keep* [kiːp] behalten, halten; führen
to keep fit [ˌkiːp 'fɪt] sich fit halten
key [kiː] Schlüssel
keyboard ['kiːbɔːd] Keyboard
keyword ['kiːwɜːd] Schlüsselwort
kid [kɪd] ugs.: Kind
Are you kidding? [ˌɑː jə 'kɪdɪŋ] Soll das ein Scherz sein?
to kidnap ['kɪdnæp] entführen
to kill [kɪl] töten
killer ['kɪlə] Mörder
° kilogram ['kɪləɡræm] Kilogramm
kilometre ['kɪləˌmiːtə] Kilometer
kind [kaɪnd] Art
You know the kind of thing. [jʊ 'nəʊ ðə kaɪnd_əv ˌθɪŋ] Man kennt das ja.
kind [kaɪnd] nett
kind of ['kaɪnd_əv] irgendwie
to kiss [kɪs] küssen
to kiss sb. goodbye ['kɪs sʌmbədɪ ˌɡʊd'baɪ] jdm. beim/zum Abschied einen Kuss geben
to kiss sb. goodnight [ˌkɪs sʌmbədɪ ɡʊd'naɪt] jdm. einen Gutenachtkuss geben
kitchen ['kɪtʃɪn] Küche
knee [niː] Knie
to kneel down [niːl 'daʊn] sich niederknien
knife, knives [naɪf] Messer
to knock [nɒk] klopfen
to know* [nəʊ] kennen; °wissen
⟨to get to know⟩ [ɡet tuː 'nəʊ] kennen lernen
You know the kind of thing. [jʊ 'nəʊ ðə kaɪnd_əv ˌθɪŋ] Man kennt das ja.
koala bear [kəʊ'ɑːlə beə] Koalabär

L

lab (= laboratory) [læb] Labor
label ['leɪbl] Etikett
lad [læd] Bursche; mein Junge (Anrede)
lady ['leɪdɪ] Dame
lake [leɪk] (der) See
lamp [læmp] Lampe
land [lænd] Land
to land [lænd] landen, ankommen
lane [leɪn] Bahn; °Weg
language ['læŋɡwɪdʒ] Sprache
large [lɑːdʒ] groß
last [lɑːst] letzte/r/s
last of all ['lɑːst_əv ˌɔːl] zuletzt
the very last [ðə 'verɪ lɑːst] der, die, das allerletzte
late [leɪt] spät, zu spät
to stay out late ['steɪ_aʊt 'leɪt] lange/spät wegbleiben
to stay up late [steɪ_ʌp 'leɪt] (abends) lange/spät aufbleiben

Dictionary

See you **later!** [ˌsiː jʊ ˈleɪtə] Bis bald!
to **laugh** (at) [lɑːf (ət)] lachen (über)
law [lɔː] Gesetz
lawyer [ˈlɔːjə] Rechtsanwalt/wältin
lazy [ˈleɪzi] faul
lead guitar [ˈliːd gɪˈtɑː] 1. Gitarre, Leadgitarre
leaf [liːf] Blatt
to **lean** [liːn] sich anlehnen
to **learn** [lɜːn] lernen
at **least** [ət ˈliːst] °wenigstens, mindestens; zumindest
to **leave*** [liːv] (da) lassen; verlassen
to leave a message [liːv ə ˈmesɪdʒ] eine Nachricht hinterlassen
Leave me alone. [ˌliːv miː əˈləʊn] Lass/t mich in Ruhe.
leaves (pl.) [liːvs] Blätter
ledge [ledʒ] (Fels)vorsprung
°**left-hand** [ˈleft hænd] linke/r/s
left [left] links; übrig
on the left [ˌɒn ðə ˈleft] links
leg [leg] Bein
leisure [ˈleʒə] Freizeit
lemonade [leməˈneɪd] Limonade
length [leŋθ] Bahnen
less than [ˈles ðæn] weniger als
lesson [ˈlesn] (Unterrichts)stunde
to teach sb. a lesson [ˈtiːtʃ ˌsʌmbədi ə ˈlesn] jdm. eine Lektion erteilen
to **let*** [let] lassen
let's (= let us) [lets] lass/lasst uns
letter [ˈletə] Brief; °Buchstabe
letterbox [ˈletəbɒks] Briefkasten
lettuce [ˈletɪs] (Blatt)salat
library [ˈlaɪbrəri] Bücherei, Bibliothek
lid [lɪd] Deckel
lie [laɪ] Lüge
to **lie** [laɪ] lügen
to **lie*** [laɪ] liegen; sich legen
life [laɪf] Leben
°everyday life [ˌevrɪdeɪ ˈlaɪf] Leben im Alltag
to **lift** [lɪft] heben, abnehmen
light [laɪt] leicht
light [laɪt] Licht, Lampe
to **light*** [laɪt] anzünden
lighter [ˈlaɪtə] Feuerzeug
the bright **lights** [ðə ˈbraɪt laɪts] der Glanz der Großstadt
to **like** [laɪk] mögen
He doesn't like anything I do. [hi: ˈdʌznt laɪk ˈeniθɪŋ aɪ duː] Ihm passt nichts, was ich tue.
I'd like [aɪd ˈlaɪk] Ich hätte gern
like [laɪk] wie
°like this [laɪk ˈðɪs] so
What is ... like? [wɒt ɪz ... ˈlaɪk] Wie ist ...?

line [laɪn] Reihe; Warteschlange; Zeile
chat line [ˈtʃæt laɪn] Chatline (eine Online-Gesprächsrunde)
telephone line [ˈtelɪfəʊn laɪn] Telefonleitung
lion [ˈlaɪən] Löwe
lip [lɪp] Lippe
lipstick [ˈlɪpstɪk] Lippenstift
liquid [ˈlɪkwɪd] Flüssigkeit
washing-up liquid [ˌwɒʃɪŋ ˈʌp ˈlɪkwɪd] Spülmittel
list [lɪst] Liste
°to **list** [lɪst] auflisten
to **listen** (to) [ˈlɪsn tə] anhören, zuhören
listener [ˈlɪsnə] Zuhörer/in
little [ˈlɪtl] klein
to **live** [lɪv] leben, wohnen
to live off sth. [lɪv ˈɒf] von etwas leben
live [laɪv] live, direkt
living-room [ˈlɪvɪŋ rʊm] Wohnzimmer
to **load** [ləʊd] laden
local [ˈləʊkl] °lokal; örtlich, Lokal-
lock [lɒk] Schloss
to **log in** [lɒg ˈɪn] einloggen
°**logical** [ˈlɒdʒɪkl] logisch
lonely [ˈləʊnli] einsam
long [lɒŋ] lang
long jump [ˈlɒŋ ˌdʒʌmp] Weitsprung
long hours [lɒŋ ˈaʊəz] Überstunden
look [lʊk] Blick
to **look** [lʊk] aussehen; schauen, sehen
to look after [lʊk ˈɑːftə] aufpassen auf
to look at [ˈlʊk ət] ansehen, anschauen
to look for [ˈlʊk fɔː] suchen
to look forward to [lʊk ˈfɔːwəd tuː] sich freuen auf
°to look like [ˈlʊk laɪk] aussehen wie
to look up [lʊk ˈʌp] hochschauen, aufblicken; °nachschlagen
Lord [lɔːd] Herr, Gott; Herr
lorry [ˈlɒri] Lastwagen
to **lose*** [luːz] verlieren
to get **lost** [get ˈlɒst] abhauen, verschwinden; sich verlaufen
a **lot** [ə ˈlɒt] viel, eine Menge
a lot of [ə ˈlɒt əv] viele, eine Menge
°lots more [lɒts ˈmɔː] viel mehr
lots of [ˈlɒts əv] viel/viele
loud [laʊd] laut
love [lʌv] Liebe; meine Liebe (Anrede)
in love [ɪn ˈlʌv] verliebt

Love, ... [lʌv] Liebe Grüße, ...
to fall in love [ˌfɔːl ɪn ˈlʌv] sich verlieben
to **love** [lʌv] lieben
⟨**loved one**⟩ [ˈlʌvd wʌn] Angebete/r
loved [lʌvd] geliebt
lovely [ˈlʌvli] schön
to **lower** [ˈləʊə] senken
luck [lʌk] Glück
⟨bad luck⟩ [bæd ˈlʌk] Pech
lucky [ˈlʌki] glücklich
to be lucky [bɪ ˈlʌki] Glück haben
lunch [lʌntʃ] Mittagessen
lunch-time [ˈlʌntʃtaɪm] Mittag(s)zeit)
packed lunch [pækt ˈlʌntʃ] Lunchpaket
to have lunch [hæv ˈlʌntʃ] zu Mittag essen
⟨**lyric**⟩ [ˈlɪrɪk] Liedtext

M

machine [məˈʃiːn] Automat; Maschine
fax machine [ˈfæks məʃiːn] Faxgerät
mad [mæd] verrückt
to be mad about [ˈmæd əˌbaʊt] verrückt nach etwas sein
magazine [ˌmæɡəˈziːn] Zeitschrift
main [meɪn] Haupt-
main entrance [ˌmeɪn ˈentrəns] Haupteingang
maize [meɪz] Mais
Make a Difference Day [meɪk ə ˈdɪfrns ˌdeɪ] Aktionstag, an dem sich Menschen für einen guten Zweck engagieren
to **make*** [meɪk] machen
to make a fool of sb. [ˌmeɪk ə ˈfuːl əv ˈsʌmbədi] jdn. veräppeln, jdn. lächerlich machen
to make a good impression [meɪk ə gʊd ɪmˈpreʃn] einen guten Eindruck machen
to make a save [ˈmeɪk ə ˈseɪv] einen Schuss abwehren, ein Tor verhindern
to make a telephone call [meɪk ə ˈtelɪfəʊn ˌkɔːl] einen Anruf tätigen
to make fun of someone [meɪk ˈfʌn əv] sich über jdn. lustig machen
°to make funny faces [meɪk ˈfʌni ˈfeɪsɪz] Grimassen schneiden
to make it [ˈmeɪk ɪt] es schaffen
to make sb. feel guilty [meɪk ˈsʌmbədi fiːl ˈgɪlti] jdm. ein schlechtes Gewissen machen
male [meɪl] männlich
mall (AE) [mɔːl] Einkaufszentrum

Dictionary

man [mæn] Mann
manager ['mænɪdʒə] Manager/in
many ['menɪ] viele
  how many [ˌhaʊ 'menɪ] wie viele
map [mæp] Landkarte, Stadtplan
March [mɑːtʃ] März
mark [mɑːk] Note
  On your marks ... [ɒn jə 'mɑːks]
  Auf die Plätze ...
to **mark** [mɑːk] benoten; °markieren, kennzeichnen
market ['mɑːkɪt] Markt
  market square [ˌmɑːkɪt 'skweə] Marktplatz
marriage ['mærɪdʒ] Ehe
married ['mærɪd] verheiratet
to **marry** ['mærɪ] heiraten
  to get married [get 'mærɪd] heiraten
mascot ['mæskət] Maskottchen
Massala [mə'sɑːlə] *pikantes indisches Gericht*
mastercook ['mɑːstəkʊk] Meisterkoch/köchin
° **mat** [mæt] Matte
match [mætʃ] Wettkampf, Match
  football match ['fʊtbɔːl ˌmætʃ] Fußballspiel
° to **match** [mætʃ] zuordnen
matchstick [mætʃstɪk] Streichholz
mate [meɪt] Kumpel
material [mə'tɪərɪəl] Material
Math (AE) [mæθ] Mathe
Maths [mæθs] Mathe(matik)
matter ['mætə] Angelegenheit, Sache
  What's the matter? ['wɒts ðə 'mætə] Was ist los?
May [meɪ] Mai
maybe ['meɪbɪ] vielleicht
me [miː] mir/mich
Me, too. [miː tuː] Ich auch.
meadow ['medəʊ] Wiese
meal [miːl] Mahlzeit
to **mean** [miːn] bedeuten; meinen
mean [miːn] gemein
° **meaning** ['miːnɪŋ] Bedeutung
meat [miːt] Fleisch
  meat pie [ˌmiːt 'paɪ] Fleischpastete
mechanic [mɪ'kænɪk] Mechaniker/in
medal ['medl] Medaille
media ['miːdjə] Medien
to **meet*** [miːt] (sich) treffen
meeting ['miːtɪŋ] Treffen, Verabredung
to **melt** [melt] schmelzen
member ['membə] Mitglied
° **memory** ['memərɪ] Gedächtnis
men (pl.) [men] Männer
⟨to **mention**⟩ ['menʃən] erwähnen
° **menu** [menjuː] Speisekarte
Merry Christmas! [ˌmerɪ 'krɪsməs]
Fröhliche Weihnachten!
mess [mes] fürchterlicher Zustand
  in a mess [ɪnˌə'mes] durcheinander
message ['mesɪdʒ] Nachricht, Botschaft
  to leave a message [liːvˌə 'mesɪdʒ] eine Nachricht hinterlassen
messenger ['mesɪndʒə] Kurier
metal ['metl] Metall
Mexican ['meksɪkn] Mexikaner/in; mexikanisch
mice [maɪs] Mäuse
microphone ['maɪkrəfəʊn] Mikrophon
microwave ['maɪkrəʊweɪv] Mikrowelle
midday ['mɪdeɪ] Mittag
middle ['mɪdl] Mitte
  middle school ['mɪdl skuːl] *amer. Schulform (Klassen 7 und 8)*
  in the middle of the night [ɪn ðə 'mɪdlˌ əv ðə naɪt] mitten in der Nacht
middle-class [ˌmɪdl'klɑːs] Mittelklasse-
midnight ['mɪdnaɪt] Mitternacht
might [maɪt] könnte/n
mile [maɪl] Meile (1,609 km)
milk [mɪlk] Milch
milkman ['mɪlkmən] Milchmann
milkshake ['mɪlkʃeɪk] Milchshake
million ['mɪljən] Million
⟨on my **mind**⟩ [ɒn maɪ 'maɪnd] in meinem Kopf
  on his mind [ɒn hɪz 'maɪnd] in seinem Kopf
  I don't **mind.** [aɪ dəʊnt 'maɪnd] Das macht mir nichts aus. Von mir aus.
  She doesn't mind it. [ʃiː 'dʌznt maɪndˌ ɪt] Es macht ihr nichts aus.
mine [maɪn] Mine
mine [maɪn] meiner, meine, mein, meins
° **mini** ['mɪnɪ] Mini-
minigolf ['mɪnɪgɒlf] Minigolf
minute ['mɪnɪt] Minute
  ten minutes to go ['ten ˌmɪnɪts tə 'gəʊ] noch zehn Minuten
mirror ['mɪrə] Spiegel
to **miss** [mɪs] ausfallen lassen; vermissen; verpassen
° **missing** ['mɪsɪŋ] fehlend
mistake [mɪ'steɪk] Fehler, Irrtum
misunderstood [ˌmɪsʌndə'stʊd] missverstanden
to **mix** [mɪks] mischen
mixed [mɪkst] gemischt
to **moan** [məʊn] stöhnen
mobile phone [ˌməʊbaɪl 'fəʊn] Handy
modal verb ['məʊdl vɜːb] Modalverb
model [mɒdl] Model; Modell, Modell-
° **modeling card** [ˌmɒdlɪŋ'kɑːd] *Kurzfassung der wichtigsten Modeldaten*
modern ['mɒdən] modern
mom (AE) [mɒm] Mutti
moment ['məʊmənt] Moment, Augenblick
  at that moment [ət ðæt 'məʊmənt] in diesem Augenblick
  at the moment [ət ðə 'məʊmənt] gerade, im Augenblick
  Just a moment. [ˌdʒʌstˌə 'məʊmənt] Moment mal!, Ja, gleich!
  right from the first moment ['raɪt frɒm ðə fɜːst 'məʊmənt] vom ersten Moment an
Monday ['mʌndɪ] Montag
money ['mʌnɪ] Geld
  pocket money ['pɒkɪt ˌmʌnɪ] Taschengeld
monster ['mɒnstə] Monster
month [mʌnθ] Monat
mood [muːd] Laune, Stimmung
moon [muːn] Mond
moped ['məʊped] Moped
more [mɔː] mehr
  the more ... the more [ðə 'mɔː ... ðə 'mɔː] je mehr ... desto mehr
  not ... any more [nɒt...enɪ 'mɔː] nicht mehr
morning ['mɔːnɪŋ] Morgen
  Good morning. [gʊd 'mɔːnɪŋ] Guten Morgen.
  in the morning [ɪn ðə 'mɔːnɪŋ] am Morgen, morgens
most [məʊst] die meisten, der/die/das meiste
  most of the time [ˌməʊstˌəv ðə 'taɪm] die meiste Zeit
mother ['mʌðə] Mutter
motor ['məʊtə] Motor
  motor boat ['məʊtəbəʊt] Motorboot
motorbike ['məʊtəbaɪk] Motorrad
motorway ['məʊtəweɪ] Autobahn
mountain ['maʊntɪn] Berg
  mountain bike ['maʊntɪn ˌbaɪk] Mountainbike
to **mourn** [mɔːn] trauern
mouse [maʊs] Maus
mouth [maʊθ] Mund
to **move** [muːv] (sich) bewegen; umziehen
  to move in [muːvˌ'ɪn] einziehen
  to move out [muːvˌ'aʊt] ausziehen
movement ['muːvmənt] Bewegung
movie ['muːvɪ] Film
movies (AE) (pl.) ['muːvɪz] Kino

Dictionary

moving ['muːvɪŋ] Umzug
mower ['məʊə] (Rasen-)Mäher
Mr ['mɪstə] Herr *(Anrede)*
Mrs ['mɪsɪz] Frau *(Anrede)*
much [mʌtʃ] viel
  how much [haʊ 'mʌtʃ] wie viel
  ° too much [ˌtuː 'mʌtʃ] zu viel
  in a **muddle** [ɪnˌə 'mʌdl] durcheinander
mudguard ['mʌdgɑːd] Schutzblech
muesli ['mjuːzlɪ] Müsli
multi-cultural [ˌmʌltɪˌ'kʌltʃrl] multikulturell; aus verschiedenen Kulturen bestehend
mum [mʌm] Mutti, Mutter
murderer ['mɜːdərə] Mörder/in
muscle ['mʌsl] Muskel
museum [mjuː'zɪəm] Museum
Music ['mjuːzɪk] Musik *(Schulfach)*; Musik
  music business ['mjuːzɪk 'bɪznɪs] Musikbranche
musical ['mjuːzɪkl] Musical
musical ['mjuːzɪkl] musikalisch
musician [mjuː'zɪʃn] Musiker/in
  street musician [ˌstriːt mjuː'zɪʃn] Straßenmusikant
Muslim ['mʊslɪm] Moslem; moslemisch
must [mʌst] müssen
  must not [mʌst nɒt] nicht dürfen
  ° You must be joking! [juˌmʌst bɪ 'dʒəʊkɪŋ] Du spinnst wohl!
my [maɪ] mein/meine
myself [maɪ'self] ich/mir/mich selbst
mysterious [mɪ'stɪərɪəs] geheimnisvoll, rätselhaft
mystery ['mɪstərɪ] Geheimnis
  ° mystery place ['mɪstrɪ ˌpleɪs] unbekannter Ort

N

name [neɪm] Name
° to **name** [neɪm] nennen
narrator [nə'reɪtə] Erzähler/in
narrow ['nærəʊ] eng
(to get) **nasty** ['nɑːstɪ] böse, ungemütlich, scheußlich (werden)
industrial **nation** [ɪn'dʌstrɪəl 'neɪʃn] Industrienation
⟨**National Guard**⟩ ['næʃnl gɑːd] Nationalgarde, *Armee unter der Kontrolle des Bundesstaats*
nationality plate [ˌnæʃə'nælɪtɪ pleɪt] Nationalitätenschild
Native American [ˌneɪtɪvˌ ə'merɪkən] Ureinwohner/in Amerikas (Indianer/in)
natural ['nætʃrəl] natürlich
nature ['neɪtʃə] Natur
near [nɪə] in der Nähe von

nearby [nɪə'baɪ] in der Nähe; nahegelegen
nearly ['nɪəlɪ] beinahe
° **necessary** ['nesəsrɪ] notwendig
in **need** [ɪn 'niːd] in Not
to **need** [niːd] brauchen
needn't ['niːdnt] nicht brauchen
° **negative** ['negətɪv] negativ, verneinend
neighbor *(AE)* ['neɪbə] Nachbar/in
neighborhood *(AE)* ['neɪbəhʊd] Wohngegend, Nachbarschaft
neighbour *(BE)* ['neɪbə] Nachbar/in
neighbourhood *(BE)* ['neɪbəhʊd] Wohngegend, Nachbarschaft
nervous ['nɜːvəs] nervös
net [net] Netz
never ['nevə] nie
  never mind ['nevə 'maɪnd] macht nichts
new [njuː] neu
news *(sg.)* [njuːz] Nachricht, Nachrichten
newspaper ['njuːzˌpeɪpə] Zeitung
next [nekst] als Nächste/r/s; nächste/r/s
next to ['nekst tə] neben
nice [naɪs] nett
  Nice to see you. [naɪs tə 'siː jʊ] Schön, dich zu sehen.
niece [niːs] Nichte
night [naɪt] Abend, Nacht
  at night [æt 'naɪt] nachts
  in the middle of the night [ɪn ðə 'mɪdlˌ əv ðə naɪt] mitten in der Nacht
  night out [naɪtˌ'aʊt] ein freier Abend
nine [naɪn] neun
nineteen [ˌnaɪn'tiːn] neunzehn
ninety ['naɪntɪ] neunzig
ninth [naɪnθ] neunte/r/s
no [nəʊ] kein/e; nein
  no idea [nəʊˌaɪ'dɪə] keine Ahnung
  no one ['nəʊwʌn] niemand
  no jobs either [nəʊ 'dʒɒbzˌaɪðə] auch keine Jobs
nobody ['nəʊbɒdɪ] niemand
to **nod** [nɒd] nicken
noise [nɔɪz] Lärm, Geräusch
noisy ['nɔɪzɪ] laut
non-smoker [ˌnɒn'sməʊkə] Nichtraucher
° **Non-Uniform Day** [nɒn 'juːnɪfɔːm ˌdeɪ] Tag ohne (Schul)uniform
non-stop [nɒn 'stɒp] ohne Unterbrechung, nonstop
none [nʌn] keine/n/s
noodle [nuːdl] Nudel
° **noon** [nuːn] Mittag
normal ['nɔːml] normal

⟨**Norman**⟩ ['nɔːmən] Normanne
nose [nəʊz] Nase
not [nɒt] nicht
  not … any [nɒt … 'enɪ] kein/e
  not … any more [nɒt…enɪ 'mɔː] nicht mehr
note [nəʊt] Notiz, Stichwort; Entschuldigung
° to **note down** [nəʊt 'daʊn] notieren, aufschreiben
nothing ['nʌθɪŋ] nichts
  Nothing I do … ['nʌθɪŋˌaɪ 'duː] Nichts, was ich tue, …
notice board ['nəʊtɪs ˌbɔːd]
° Anzeigetafel; schwarzes Brett
to **notice** ['nəʊtɪs] bemerken
November [nəʊ'vembə] November
now [naʊ] nun, jetzt
  right now [raɪt 'naʊ] jetzt sofort
number ['nʌmbə] Zahl
° number chain ['nʌmbə tʃeɪn] Zahlenkette
  to get to no.1 [get tʊ 'nʌmbə 'wʌn] die Nummer 1 werden
nurse [nɜːs] Krankenschwester

O

⟨**oak**⟩ [əʊk] Eiche
object ['ɒbdʒɪkt] Objekt
⟨**obviously**⟩ ['ɒbvɪəslɪ] offensichtlich
o'clock [ə'klɒk] … Uhr *(Zeitangabe)*
October [ɒk'təʊbə] Oktober
° **odd one out** ['ɒd wʌnˌ'aʊt] nicht dazugehöriges Wort
of [ɒv] von
  of course [əv 'kɔːs] natürlich, selbstverständlich
off-line ['ɒf laɪn] nicht an den Computer angeschlossen
  off school [ɒf 'skuːl] nicht in der Schule
to get **off** [getˌ'ɒf] aussteigen
off they go [ɒf ðeɪ 'gəʊ] sie fahren los, los geht's
to **offer** ['ɒfə] anbieten
office ['ɒfɪs] Büro, Sekretariat
  box office ['bɒksˌɒfɪs] (Theater-/Kino-) Kasse
  office junior [ˌɒfɪs 'dʒuːnjə] Bürogehilfe, Bürogehilfin
° careers **officer** [kə'rɪəzˌ'ɒfɪsə] Berufsberater/in
official [ə'fɪʃl] Beamter, Beamtin
⟨**off** (Scotland)⟩ [ɒf] vor, auf der Höhe von (Schottland)
often ['ɒfn] oft
° how often … [haʊˌ'ɒfn] wie oft …
oh [əʊ] null *(bei Telefonnummern und Uhrzeiten)*
oil [ɔɪl] Öl

oil rig ['ɔɪl rɪɡ] Ölförderturm, Ölbohrinsel
oil rig worker ['ɔɪl rɪɡ ˌwɜːkə] Arbeiter/in auf dem Ölförderturm
oily ['ɔɪlɪ] ölverschmiert
okay [əʊ'keɪ] okay, in Ordnung
old [əʊld] alt
old people's home [əʊld 'piːplz həʊm] Altersheim
omelette ['ɒmlɪt] Omelette
omygod [əʊmɪ'ɡɒd] Oh mein Gott!
on [ɒn] auf; für
  on board [ɒn 'bɔːd] an Bord
  on foot [ɒn 'fʊt] zu Fuß
  on her own [ɒn hɜːr ˌ'əʊn] für sich alleine
  on his mind [ɒn hɪz 'maɪnd] in seinem Kopf
  on holiday [ˌɒn 'hɒlɪdeɪ] im Urlaub
  ⟨on my mind⟩ [ɒn maɪ 'maɪnd] in meinem Kopf
  on Saturday [ˌɒn 'sætədɪ] am Samstag, samstags
  on stage [ɒn 'steɪdʒ] auf der Bühne
  on the bus [ˌɒn ðə 'bʌs] im Bus
  on the dole [ɒn ðə 'dəʊl] arbeitslos
  ° on the Internet [ɒn ðiː ˌɪntənet] im Internet
  on the left [ˌɒn ðə 'left] links
  on the radio [ˌɒn ðə 'reɪdɪəʊ] im Radio, auf Sendung
  on the right [ˌɒn ðə 'raɪt] rechts
  on time [ɒn 'taɪm] pünktlich
  on TV [ˌɒn ˌtiː 'viː] im Fernsehen
  on vacation (AE) [ɒn və'keɪʃn] im Urlaub, in den Ferien
  On your marks … [ɒn jə 'mɑːks] Auf die Plätze …
  on your own [ɒn jɔːr ˌ əʊn] alleine, selbst
once [wʌns] einmal
  once and for all ['wʌns ˌænd fɔː ˌ'ɔːl] ein für allemal
one [wʌn] eins
to go on-line [ɡəʊ ˌ'ɒnlaɪn] online gehen
only ['əʊnlɪ] einzige/r; nur
onto ['ɒntʊ] auf
open fire [ˌəʊpən 'faɪə] Kamin
to open ['əʊpn] aufmachen, (sich) öffnen
open ['əʊpn] geöffnet
open-minded [ˌəʊpn'maɪndɪd] aufgeschlossen
opinion [ə'pɪnjən] Meinung
opposite ['ɒpəzɪt] Gegenteil
opposite ['ɒpəzɪt] gegenüber
⟨optimistic⟩ [ˌɒptɪ'mɪstɪk] optimistisch
option ['ɒpʃn] Wahlmöglichkeit
or [ɔː] oder

either … or ['aɪðə … ɔː] entweder … oder
orange juice ['ɒrɪndʒ ˌdʒuːs] Orangensaft
orange ['ɒrɪndʒ] orange
orchestra ['ɔːkɪstrə] Orchester
° order ['ɔːdə] Ordnung; Reihenfolge
to order ['ɔːdə] bestellen
ordinary ['ɔːdnrɪ] gewöhnlich, normal
organization [ɔː ɡənaɪ'zeɪʃn] Konzern
to organize ['ɔːɡənaɪz] organisieren
original [ə'rɪdʒənl] Original-, ursprünglich
other ['ʌðə] andere
Ouch! ['aʊtʃ] Aua!
our ['aʊə] unser/unsere
ours ['aʊəz] unser/e
ourselves [aʊə'selvz] wir/uns selbst
out ['aʊt ˌəv] aus, heraus, hinaus
° day out [deɪ ˌ'aʊt] Tagesausflug
  night out [naɪt ˌ'aʊt] ein freier Abend
  out of ['aʊt ˌəv] aus … heraus
  out the window (AE) [ˌaʊt ðə 'wɪndəʊ] aus dem Fenster
  out there ['aʊt ðeə] da draußen
  three out of ten ['θriː ˌaʊt ˌəv ten] drei von zehn
  to find out [faɪnd ˌ'aʊt] herausfinden
  to get out [ɡet ˌ'aʊt] herausholen
  to hang out [hæŋ ˌ'aʊt] sich die Zeit vertreiben
  to move out [muːv ˌ'aʊt] ausziehen
  to print out [prɪnt ˌ'aʊt] ausdrucken
  to put out [pʊt ˌ'aʊt] herauslegen, aufstellen
  to try out for (AE) [traɪ ˌ'aʊt fə] (für eine Rolle) vorsprechen
outa = out of (sl.) [aʊt ˌə] ugs. raus
outback ['aʊtbæk] der australische Busch, das Hinterland
outboard motor [ˌaʊtbɔːd 'məʊtə] Außenbordmotor
outdoor [aʊt'dɔː] Freiluft-, im Freien
outdoors [aʊt'dɔːz] draußen, im Freien
  the big outdoors [ðə bɪɡ ˌ'aʊtdɔːz] die freie Natur
° outside ['aʊtsaɪd] Außenansicht
outside [aʊt'saɪd] draußen, außerhalb
outsider [ˌaʊt'saɪdə] Außenseiter/in
over ['əʊvə] hinüber; über; vorbei
  all over [ɔːl 'əʊvə] überall (in)
  over there [ˌəʊvə 'ðeə] da drüben
  to take over [teɪk ˌ'əʊvə] beherrschen

  to walk over [wɔːk ˌ'əʊvə] hinübergehen
  to paint over [peɪnt ˌ'əʊvə] überstreichen
overalls ['əʊvərɔːlz] Arbeitsanzug
overboard ['əʊvəbɔːd] über Bord
oversized ['əʊvəsaɪzd] in Übergröße
to own [əʊn] besitzen
own [əʊn] eigene/r/s
owner ['əʊnə] Besitzer/in

P

p = pence (pl.) [pens] Pence (britische Währung)
to pack [pæk] packen
packed lunch [pækt 'lʌnʃ] Lunchpaket
to paddle ['pædl] paddeln
page [peɪdʒ] Seite
pain [peɪn] Schmerz
paint [peɪnt] Anstrich, Farbe
to paint [peɪnt] (an)streichen, malen
to paint over [peɪnt ˌ'əʊvə] überstreichen
pajamas (AE) [pə'dʒɑːməz] Schlafanzug, Pyjama
Pakistani [ˌpɑːkɪ'stɑːnɪ] Pakistani, pakistanisch
pal [pæl] Kumpel, Freund/in
palm tree ['pɑːm triː] Palme
pan [pæn] Schale
to pan for gold [pæn fə 'ɡəʊld] Gold waschen
panic ['pænɪk] Panik
  Don't panic. [dəʊnt 'pænɪk] Keine Panik!
pants (AE) [pænts] Hose
paper ['peɪpə] Papier; Zeitung
paper shop ['peɪpə ʃɒp] Zeitungsladen, -kiosk
° piece of paper [piːs ˌəv 'peɪpə] Stück Papier
° sheet of paper [ʃiːt ˌəv 'peɪpə] Blatt Papier
  to do a paper route (AE) [duː ə 'peɪpə ˌruːt] Zeitungen austragen
paradise ['pærədaɪs] Paradies
paragliding ['pærəɡlaɪdɪŋ] Gleitschirmfliegen
° paragraph ['pærəɡrɑːf] Absatz, Abschnitt
parents (pl.) ['peərənts] Eltern
  single parent ['sɪŋɡl 'peərənt] ein Elternteil, Alleinerziehende/r
park [pɑːk] Park
  ball park (AE) ['bɔːl pɑːk] Baseballplatz
  theme park ['θiːm pɑːk] Freizeitpark

Dictionary

part [pɑːt] Teil
part-time [ˈpɑːttaɪm] Teilzeit
to take **part** [teɪk ˈpɑːt] teilnehmen
° past **participle** [pɑːst ˈpɑːtɪsɪpl] Partizip Perfekt (3. Form des Verbes)
partner [ˈpɑːtnə] Partner/in, Nachbar/in
party [ˈpɑːtɪ] Party, Feier, Fest
pass [pɑːs] Ausweis; Pass
to **pass** [pɑːs] vorbeigehen an
passenger [ˈpæsɪndʒə] Fahrgast, Passagier
passion [ˈpæʃn] Leidenschaft
passport [ˈpɑːspɔːt] Reisepass
° **password** [ˈpɑːswɜːd] Kennwort
past [pɑːst] Vergangenheit
° past **form** [ˈpɑːst fɔːm] Vergangenheitsform
° past **participle** [pɑːst ˈpɑːtɪsɪpl] Partizip Perfekt (3. Form des Verbes)
° past **simple** [ˌpɑːst ˈsɪmpl] einfache Vergangenheit
past [pɑːst] an ... vorbei; nach (Uhrzeit)
pasta [ˈpæstə] Pasta, Teigware
path [pɑːθ] Weg
 cycle path [ˈsaɪkl pɑːθ] Radweg
to be **patient** [bɪ ˈpeɪʃnt] Geduld haben
pay [peɪ] Bezahlung
to **pay*** [peɪ] bezahlen
 to get paid for sth. [get ˈpeɪd fɔː ˈsʌmθɪŋ] für etwas bezahlt werden
P.E. (=**Physical Education**) [piːˈiː] Sport(unterricht)
pea [piː] Erbse
pedal [ˈpedl] Pedal
° to **pedal** [ˈpedl] (Pedale) treten
pedestrian [pɪˈdestrɪən] Fußgänger/in
pen [pen] Füller
 pen pal [ˈpen pæl] Brieffreund/in
pence [pens] Pence (britische Währung)
pencil [ˈpensl] Bleistift
 pencil case [ˈpensl ˌkeɪs] Etui, Federmäppchen
 pencil sharpener [ˈpensl ˌʃɑːpnə] Bleistiftspitzer, Anspitzer
pendant [ˈpendənt] Anhänger
penny farthing [ˌpenɪ ˈfɑːðɪŋ] Hochrad
people (pl.) [ˈpiːpl] Leute, Menschen
 Young People's Club [jʌŋ ˈpiːplz ˌklʌb] Jugendklub
 old people's home [əʊld ˈpiːplz həʊm] Altersheim
percent [pəˈsent] Prozent, %
perfect [ˈpɜːfɪkt] perfekt
to **perform** [pəˈfɔːm] aufführen, spielen

perhaps [pəˈhæps] vielleicht
period (AE) [ˈpɪərɪəd] Schulstunde
person [ˈpɜːsn] Person
personality [ˌpɜːsəˈnælətɪ] Persönlichkeit
⟨**pessimistic**⟩ [ˌpesɪˈmɪstɪk] pessimistisch
pet [pet] Haustier
petrol [ˈpetrəl] Benzin
phone-in [ˈfəʊn ɪn] Rundfunkprogramm, an dem sich Hörer per Telefon beteiligen können
 mobile phone [ˈməʊbaɪl ˈfəʊn] Handy
to **phone** [fəʊn] anrufen
phonecard [ˈfəʊnkɑːd] Telefonkarte
photo [ˈfəʊtəʊ] Foto
 to take photos [teɪk ˈfəʊtəʊz] Fotos machen, fotografieren
° **photograph** [ˈfəʊtəgrɑːf] Foto
° **phrase** [freɪz] Satzteil, Ausdruck
physical [ˈfɪzɪkl] körperlich
Physics [ˈfɪzɪks] Physik (Schulfach)
° to **pick** [pɪk] auswählen
 to pick up [pɪk ˈʌp] aufheben, hochheben
picnic [ˈpɪknɪk] Picknick
picture [ˈpɪktʃə] Bild
 picture book [ˈpɪktʃə ˌbʊk] Bilderbuch
 meat **pie** [ˌmiːt ˈpaɪ] Fleischpastete
piece [piːs] Stück
° piece of paper [piːs əv ˈpeɪpə] Stück Papier
pin [pɪn] Kegel
° **pinboard** [ˈpɪnbɔːd] Pinnwand
pink [pɪŋk] rosa, pink
pint [paɪnt] engl. Maß
pipe [paɪp] Rohr
pizza [ˈpiːtsə] Pizza
pizzeria [pɪtsəˈrɪə] Pizzeria
place [pleɪs] Ort; Platz
 fast-food place [fɑːstˈfuːd pleɪs] Schnellimbiss
 to take place [teɪk ˈpleɪs] stattfinden
 working place [ˈwɜːkɪŋ pleɪs] Arbeitsplatz
plan [plæn] Plan, Skizze
° to **plan** [plæn] planen
plane [pleɪn] Flugzeug
planet [ˈplænɪt] Planet
plant [plɑːnt] Pflanze
 plant hire section [ˈplɑːnt haɪə ˈsekʃn] Abteilung für Baumaschinenvermietung
plastic [ˈplæstɪk] Plastik
 plastic container [ˈplæstɪk kənˈteɪnə] Plastikbehälter
plate [pleɪt] Teller
platform [ˈplætfɔːm] Bahnsteig
play [pleɪ] Theaterstück

 role play [ˈrəʊl pleɪ] Rollenspiel
to **play** [pleɪ] spielen
 to play a trick [pleɪ ə ˈtrɪk] einen Streich spielen
 to play Southend [ˈpleɪ saʊθˈend] gegen Southend spielen
 to play the guitar [ˌpleɪ ðə ɡɪˈtɑː] Gitarre spielen
player [ˈpleɪə] Spieler/in
 record player [ˈrekɔːd ˌpleɪə] Plattenspieler
 (school) **playground** [ˈpleɪɡraʊnd] Schulhof, Spielplatz
playing field [ˈpleɪɪŋ ˌfiːld] Sportplatz
please [pliːz] bitte
pleased [pliːzd] erfreut, zufrieden
plumber [ˈplʌmə] Installateur/in
° **plural** [ˈplʊərəl] Plural, Mehrzahl
p.m. [piːˈem] nachmittags (bei Uhrzeiten)
pocket [ˈpɒkɪt] Tasche
pocket money [ˈpɒkɪt ˌmʌnɪ] Taschengeld
podium [ˈpəʊdɪəm] Podest
poem [ˈpəʊɪm] Gedicht
point [pɔɪnt] Punkt
to **point** [pɔɪnt] zeigen
⟨**Polaroid camera**⟩ [pəʊləˈrɔɪd ˌkæmərə] Sofortbildkamera
police (pl.) [pəˈliːs] Polizei
 police station [pəˈliːs ˌsteɪʃn] Polizeirevier
policeman [pəˈliːsmən] Polizist
policy [ˈpɒləsɪ] Geschäftsbedingungen; Politik, Grundsatz
polite [pəˈlaɪt] höflich
pollution [pəˈluːʃn] Verschmutzung
pony [ˈpəʊnɪ] Pony
pool [puːl] Poolbillard; Schwimmbecken
 swimming pool [ˈswɪmɪŋ ˌpuːl] Schwimmbad
poor [pɔː] arm
pop star [ˈpɒp stɑː] Popstar
 pop group [ˈpɒp ɡruːp] Popgruppe
 pop music [ˈpɒp ˌmjuːzɪk] Popmusik
⟨to **pop out**⟩ [pɒp ˈaʊt] hervorspringen
popcorn [ˈpɒpkɔːn] Popcorn
popular [ˈpɒpjʊlə] beliebt
population [ˌpɒpjʊˈleɪʃn] Bevölkerung
pork [pɔːk] Schweinefleisch
portfolio [ˌpɔːtˈfəʊlɪəʊ] Präsentationsmappe
° **portrait** [ˈpɔːtreɪt] Porträt, Darstellung
⟨**Portuguese**⟩ [pɔːtʃʊˈɡiːz] Portugiese, Portugiesin
position [pəˈzɪʃn] Position

Dictionary

°**positive** ['pɒzətɪv] positiv, bejahend
post office ['pəʊst ˌɒfɪs] Postamt
to **post** [pəʊst] einwerfen, einstecken
postcard ['pəʊstkɑːd] Postkarte
poster ['pəʊstə] Poster, Plakat
postman ['pəʊstmæn] Postbote
potato [pə'teɪtəʊ] Kartoffel
°**pound** [paʊnd] Pfund (Gewicht)
£ 1 = 1 pound [paʊnd] ein Pfund (britische Währung)
poverty ['pɒvətɪ] Armut
power ['paʊwə] Macht, Kraft
power control ['paʊwə kən'trəʊl] Leistungsregler
to **practice** (AE) ['præktɪs] üben
to **practise** (BE) ['præktɪs] üben
to **prefer** [prɪ'fɜː] lieber haben, vorziehen
prefix ['priːfɪks] Vorsilbe
pregnant ['pregnənt] schwanger
prejudice ['predʒʊdɪs] Vorurteil
prescription [prɪ'skrɪpʃn] Rezept (Medikament)
present ['preznt] °Gegenwart; Geschenk
°**present perfect** [ˌpreznt 'pɜːfɪkt] Perfekt
°**present progressive** ['preznt prəʊ'gresɪv] Verlaufsform der Gegenwart
°**present simple** [ˌpreznt 'sɪmpl] einfache Gegenwart
to **present** [prɪ'zent] °präsentieren, zeigen
presentation [ˌpreznˈteɪʃn] Darstellung, Präsentation
president ['prezɪdnt] Präsident/in
pressure ['preʃə] Druck
to **pretend** [prɪ'tend] so tun, als ob
pretty ['prɪtɪ] hübsch
pretty strong [prɪtɪ 'strɒŋ] ziemlich stark
price [praɪs] Preis
primitive ['prɪmɪtɪv] primitiv, einfach
principal ['prɪnsəpl] Rektor/in, Schulleiter/in
to **print** [prɪnt] drucken
to print out [prɪnt ˈaʊt] ausdrucken
prison ['prɪzn] Gefängnis
prisoner ['prɪznə] Gefangene/r
⟨**private**⟩ ['praɪvɪt] privat
prize [praɪz] Preis (den man gewinnt)
probably ['prɒbəblɪ] wahrscheinlich
problem ['prɒbləm] Problem
everyday problem [ˌevrɪdeɪ 'prɒbləm] Alltagsproblem
producer [prə'djuːsə] Produzent
⟨**production**⟩ [prə'dʌkʃn] Produktion

program ['prəʊgræm] Programm, Vorhaben
Driver's Ed program ['draɪvəz ed 'prəʊgræm] Fahrschulunterricht
to get into a program [get ˈɪntʊ ə 'prəʊgræm] in ein Programm gelangen
programme ['prəʊgræm] Programm; Sendung
programmer ['prəʊgræmə] Programmierer/in
programming ['prəʊgræmɪŋ] Programme schreiben
project ['prɒdʒekt] Projekt
prop [prɒp] Requisit
prostitution [ˌprɒstɪ'tjuːʃn] Prostitution
to **protect** [prə'tekt] beschützen
protection [prə'tekʃn] Schutz
proud [praʊd] stolz
to be proud of oneself [bɪ 'praʊd əv wʌn'self] stolz auf sich sein
pub [pʌb] Kneipe
public ['pʌblɪk] öffentlich
public convenience ['pʌblɪk kən'viːnjəns] öffentliche Toilette
⟨to **publish**⟩ ['pʌblɪʃ] veröffentlichen
to **pull** [pʊl] ziehen
pump [pʌmp] Luftpumpe
punk [pʌŋk] Punker/in
pupil ['pjuːpl] Schüler/in
pure [pjʊə] rein, vollkommen
°**purple** ['pɜːpl] violett
purse [pɜːs] Portmonee
to **push** [pʊʃ] schieben
to push off [pʊʃ ˈɒf] sich abstoßen
to push over [pʊʃ ˈəʊvə] umwerfen
to **put*** [pʊt] setzen, stellen, legen
to put in [pʊt ˈɪn] °einsetzen; installieren
to put on [pʊt ˈɒn] anziehen
to put out [pʊt ˈaʊt] herauslegen, aufstellen
°to put right [pʊt ˈraɪt] richtig stellen
to put sb. through [pʊt ˌsʌmbədɪ 'θruː] jdn. durchstellen
to put up [pʊt ˈʌp] aushängen
pyjama trousers (pl.) [pə'dʒɑːmə 'traʊzəz] Schlafanzughose

Q

quarter ['kwɔːtə] Viertel
quarter past ['kwɔːtə ˌpɑːst] Viertel nach (Uhrzeit)
quarter to ['kwɔːtə ˌtə] Viertel vor (Uhrzeit)
quarterback ['kwɔːtəbæk] Spielerposition im American Football

queen [kwiːn] Königin
question ['kwestʃn] Frage
°**questionnaire** [ˌkwestʃə'neə] Fragebogen
to **queue** [kjuː] Schlange stehen, sich anstellen
quick [kwɪk] schnell
quiet ['kwaɪət] ruhig, still
quite a few [kwaɪt ə 'fjuː] etliche
quite by chance ['kwaɪt baɪ 'tʃɑːns] ganz zufällig
°**quiz** [kwɪz] Quiz

R

rabbit ['ræbɪt] Kaninchen
race [reɪs] Rasse; Rennen
speedboat racing ['spiːdbəʊt ˌreɪsɪŋ] Schnellbootfahren
to **race** [reɪs] eilen
⟨**racial segregation**⟩ ['reɪʃl ˌsegrɪ'geɪʃn] Rassentrennung
racing bike ['reɪsɪŋ ˌbaɪk] Rennrad
⟨**racism**⟩ ['reɪsɪzəm] Rassismus
racist ['reɪsɪst] rassistisch
radio ['reɪdɪəʊ] Radio
clock radio [klɒk 'reɪdɪəʊ] Radiowecker
on the radio [ɒn ðə 'reɪdɪəʊ] im Radio, auf Sendung
radio collar ['reɪdɪəʊ ˌkɒlə] Sender am Hals
radio station ['reɪdɪəʊ ˌsteɪʃn] Rundfunkstation
white-water **rafting** [ˌwaɪt wɔːtə 'rɑːftɪŋ] Floßfahren auf reißenden Gewässern
railroad (AE) ['reɪlrəʊd] Eisenbahn
rain [reɪn] Regen
to **rain** [reɪn] regnen
to **raise** (money) [reɪz] Geld auftreiben, sammeln
Ramadan ['ræmədæn] moslemische Fastenzeit
ranch [rɑːntʃ] Ranch
to get around the ranch [get ə'raʊnd ðə rɑːntʃ] sich auf der Ranch fortbewegen
rancher ['rɑːntʃə] Rancher, Viehzüchter
ranger ['reɪndʒə] Ranger
rap [ræp] Rap (Sprechgesang)
rat [ræt] Ratte
rather ['rɑːðə] ziemlich
raw [rɔː] roh
R.E. = **Religious Education** [ɑː 'iː] Religion (Schulfach)
to **reach** [riːtʃ] erreichen
to reach out [riːtʃ ˈaʊt] die Hände ausstrecken
to **react** (to) [rɪ'ækt] reagieren (auf)

Dictionary

to **read*** [riːd] lesen
reading [ˈriːdɪŋ] Lesen
ready [ˈredi] fertig, startbereit
real [rɪəl] echt
reality [riːˈælɪti] Wirklichkeit
really [ˈrɪəli] echt
reason [ˈriːzn] Grund
for any **reason** [fɔːr‿ˈeni ˌriːzn] aus irgendeinem Grund
to **receive** [rɪˈsiːv] in Empfang nehmen, erhalten
receiver [rɪˈsiːvə] Hörer
recipe [ˈresɪpi] Rezept
record [ˈrekɔːd] Schallplatte
record player [ˈrekɔːd ˌpleɪə] Plattenspieler
to **record** [rɪˈkɔːd] aufnehmen
recording [rɪˈkɔːdɪŋ] (Ton-) Aufnahme
recording session [rɪˈkɔːdɪŋ ˌseʃn] Aufnahmetermin
to **recycle** [riːˈsaɪkl] wiederverwerten
to be **recycled** [riːˈsaɪkld] wiederverwertet werden
recycling [rɪˈsaɪklɪŋ] Wiederverwertung
recycling center [riːˈsaɪklɪŋ ˌsentə] Wiederaufbereitungsanlage
red [red] rot
to turn red [tɜːn ˈred] rot werden
reflector [rɪˈflektə] Reflektor, Rückstrahler
to **refuse** [rɪˈfjuːz] sich weigern
Registration [ˌredʒɪˈstreɪʃn] Anwesenheitskontrolle; Anmeldung
registration form [ˌredʒɪˈstreɪʃn fɔːm] Anmeldeformular
°**regular** [ˈregjələ] regelmäßig
to **reject** [rɪˈdʒekt] zurückweisen
relationship [rɪˈleɪʃnʃɪp] Beziehung
reliable [rɪˈlaɪəbl] verlässlich
religion [rɪˈlɪdʒn] Religion
religious community [rɪˈlɪdʒəs kəˈmjuːnəti] Religionsgemeinschaft
religious [rɪˈlɪdʒəs] religiös
remail [ˈriːmeɪl] Antwortmail
to **remember** [rɪˈmembə] sich erinnern
to **remind** [rɪˈmaɪnd] erinnern
removal man [rɪˈmuːvl ˌmæn] Möbelpacker
to **remove** [rɪˈmuːv] entfernen, beseitigen
to **repair** [rɪˈpeə] reparieren
repairer [rɪˈpeərə] Instandsetzer/in
°to **replace** [rɪˈpleɪs] ersetzen
reply [rɪˈplaɪ] Antwort
to **reply** [rɪˈplaɪ] antworten, erwidern
report [rɪˈpɔːt] Bericht; Zeugnis

to **report** [rɪˈpɔːt] berichten
reporter [rɪˈpɔːtə] Reporter/in, Journalist/in
junior reporter [ˈdʒuːnjə rɪˈpɔːtə] unerfahrener Reporter
representative [ˌreprɪˈzentətɪv] Vertreter/in
to **require** [rɪˈkwaɪə] benötigen, suchen
rescue [ˈreskjuː] Rettung
to **rescue** [ˈreskjuː] retten
resemblance [rɪˈzembləns] Ähnlichkeit
responsible [rɪˈspɒnsɪbl] verantwortlich
restaurant [ˈrestrɒŋ] Restaurant
°**result** [rɪˈzʌlt] Ergebnis
°to **rewrite** [ˌriːˈraɪt] neu schreiben
°**rhyme** [raɪm] Reim
⟨to **rhyme**⟩ [raɪm] reimen
⟨**rhythm**⟩ [ˈrɪðəm] Rhythmus
rice [raɪs] Reis
rich [rɪtʃ] reich
ride [raɪd] Fahrt
to **ride*** [raɪd] (mit dem Fahrrad) fahren; reiten
riding [ˈraɪdɪŋ] Reiten
riding a bike [ˌraɪdɪŋ‿ə ˈbaɪk] Fahrrad fahren
right [raɪt] Recht
civil right [sɪvl ˈraɪt] Bürgerrecht
to be right [biː ˈraɪt] Recht haben
right [raɪt] richtig; rechts
on the right [ˌɒn ðə ˈraɪt] rechts
right from the first moment [ˈraɪt frɒm ðə fɜːst ˈməʊmənt] vom ersten Moment an
right here [raɪt ˈhɪə] genau hier
right now [raɪt ˈnaʊ] jetzt sofort
°**right-hand** [ˈraɪt hænd] rechte/r/s
ring [rɪŋ] Ring
to **ring*** [rɪŋ] anrufen
risk [rɪsk] Risiko
⟨**ritual**⟩ [ˈrɪtʃuəl] Ritual
river [ˈrɪvə] Fluss
road [rəʊd] Straße
roadie [ˈrəʊdi] Roadie
to **rob** [rɒb] (aus)rauben
robber [ˈrɒbə] Räuber
robot [ˈrəʊbɒt] Roboter
rock [rɒk] Fels, Felsbrocken
rock climbing [ˈrɒk ˌklaɪmɪŋ] Klettern
role [rəʊl] Rolle
°role play [ˈrəʊl pleɪ] Rollenspiel
to **roll** [rəʊl] rollen
roller coaster [ˈrəʊlə ˌkəʊstə] Achterbahn
to **roller-blade** [ˈrəʊləbleɪd] Rollerblades fahren
roller-blading [ˈrəʊlə ˌbleɪdɪŋ] Inlineskating; Rollerblading
romance [rəʊˈmæns] Romanze, Liebesgeschichte

romantic [rəʊˈmæntɪk] romantisch
room [ruːm] Platz; Zimmer, Raum
changing room [ˈtʃeɪndʒɪŋ ˌruːm] Umkleideraum
round [raʊnd] rund, rund um
°**route** [ruːt] Strecke, Route
to do a paper route (AE) [duː‿ə ˈpeɪpə ˌruːt] Zeitungen austragen
rubber [ˈrʌbə] Gummi; Radiergummi
rubbish [ˈrʌbɪʃ] Quatsch
rucksack [ˈrʌksæk] Rucksack
rude [ruːd] unhöflich, unverschämt
to **ruin** [ˈruɪn] zerstören, ruinieren
rule [ruːl] Regel
ruler [ˈruːlə] Lineal
⟨**rum**⟩ [rʌm] Rum
to **run*** [rʌn] laufen, rennen
to run after [rʌn‿ˈɑːftə] hinterherlaufen
to run away [rʌn‿əˈweɪ] weglaufen, abhauen
to run into sb. [rʌn ˈɪntʊ ˈsʌmbədi] jdn. zufällig treffen
to **rush off** [rʌʃ ˈɒf] rasen, hetzen

S

sad [sæd] traurig
saddle [ˈsædl] Sattel
safari [səˈfɑːri] Safari
safe [seɪf] sicher, in Sicherheit
safety [ˈseɪfti] Sicherheit
⟨to **sail**⟩ [seɪl] segeln
sailing [ˈseɪlɪŋ] Segeln
sailor [ˈseɪlə] Matrose, Seemann
salad [ˈsæləd] Salat
sale [seɪl] Verkauf, Bazar
salesperson [ˈseɪlzpɜːsn] Verkäufer/in
salt [sɔːlt] Salz
the **same** [ðə ˈseɪm] der-/die-/dasselbe; °der/die/das Gleiche; gleich
sand [sænd] Sand
sandpit [ˈsændpɪt] Sandkasten
sandwich [ˈsænwɪdʒ] Sandwich (belegtes Brot)
Saturday [ˈsætədi] Samstag, Sonnabend
sausage [ˈsɒsɪdʒ] Wurst, Würstchen
to **save** [seɪv] retten; sparen
saxophone [ˈsæksəfəʊn] Saxophon
to **say*** [seɪ] sagen, sprechen
to **scare** [skeə] erschrecken
to scare away [ˈskeər‿əˈweɪ] verjagen
to be **scared** [bɪ ˈskeəd] Angst haben
scene [siːn] Szene
schedule [ˈʃedjuːl] Plan
scheme [skiːm] Programm

Dictionary

school [skuːl] Schule
  at school [ət ˈskuːl] in der Schule
  comprehensive school [kɒmprɪˈhensɪv ˌskuːl] Gesamtschule
  high school [ˈhaɪ skuːl] *amer.* Schulform ab Klasse 9
  middle school [ˈmɪdl skuːl] *amer.* Schulform (Klassen 7 und 8)
  off school [ɒf ˈskuːl] nicht in der Schule
  ⟨school fete⟩ [skuːl ˈfeɪt] Schulfest
  school holidays [skuːl ˈhɒlɪdeɪz] Schulferien
  school leaver [ˈskuːl ˌliːvə] Schulabgänger/in
  (school) playground [ˈpleɪgraʊnd] Schulhof, Spielplatz
Science [ˈsaɪəns] Naturwissenschaften (*Schulfach*)
  science fiction [ˌsaɪəns ˈfɪkʃn] Sciencefiction
score [skɔː] Punktestand, Spielstand
to score [skɔː] einen Punkt erzielen, ein Tor schießen
° **scrapbook** [ˈskræpbʊk] Sammelalbum
to scratch [skrætʃ] kratzen
to scream [skriːm] schreien
screen [skriːn] Bildschirm
screw [skruː] Schraube
to screw up [skruː ˈʌp] vermasseln
screwdriver [ˈskruːˌdraɪvə] Schraubenzieher
sea [siː] Meer
season [ˈsiːzn] Jahreszeit; Saison, Jahreszeit
seat [siːt] Sitz
second [ˈseknd] Sekunde
second [ˈseknd] zweite/r/s
secondly [ˈsekəndlɪ] zweitens
secretary [ˈsekrətrɪ] Sekretär/in
security guard [sɪˈkjʊərətɪ gɑːd] Sicherheitsangestellte/r
to see* [siː] sehen
  See you later! [ˌsiː jʊ ˈleɪtə] Bis bald!
  See you guys later. (*sl.*) [ˈsiː juː gaɪz ˈleɪtə] *ugs.* Bis bald.
  See you soon. [ˌsiː jʊ ˈsuːn] Bis bald.
  See you there! [siː jʊ ˈðeə] Bis bald! Bis dann!
to seek [siːk] suchen
to seem [siːm] scheinen
selfish [ˈselfɪʃ] egoistisch
to sell* [sel] verkaufen
seller [ˈselə] Verkäufer/in
semi-detached house [semɪdɪˌtætʃt ˈhaʊs] Doppelhaushälfte
to send* [send] schicken

sense of humour [sens‿əv ˈhjuːmə] Sinn für Humor
sensible [ˈsensəbl] vernünftig
° **sentence** [ˈsentəns] Satz
° sentence halves [ˈsentəns ˌhɑːvz] Satzhälften
separate [ˈsepəreɪt] getrennt
September [sepˈtembə] September
series (*sg.*) [ˈsɪəriːz] Serie
serious [ˈsɪəriəs] °ernst; ernsthaft
service [ˈsɜːvɪs] Dienst
° **session** [ˈseʃn] Laufzeit
  recording session [rɪˈkɔːdɪŋ ˈseʃn] Aufnahmetermin
to set up [set‿ˈʌp] aufstellen
seven [ˈsevn] sieben
seventeen [ˌsevnˈtiːn] siebzehn
seventy [ˈsevntɪ] siebzig
several [ˈsevrəl] mehrere
sex [seks] Geschlecht
sexy [ˈseksɪ] sexy
to shake* [ʃeɪk] schütteln; zittern
  to shake around [ʃeɪk‿əˈraʊnd] hin und her schütteln
shalwaar kameeze [ˌʃælvɑːkəˈmiːz] *pakistanisches Kleidungsstück*
to share [ʃeə] teilen
sharp [ʃɑːp] scharf
she [ʃiː] sie
shed [ʃed] Schuppen
sheep [ʃiːp] Schaf, Schafe
  sheep station [ˈʃiːp ˌsteɪʃən] Schaffarm
sheet [ʃiːt] Aufstellung
° sheet of paper [ʃiːt‿əv ˈpeɪpə] Blatt Papier
shelf-filling [ˈʃelfˌfɪlɪŋ] das Auffüllen der Regale
sheriff [ˈʃerɪf] Sheriff
shift [ʃɪft] Schicht
shinguard [ˈʃɪŋɑːd] Schienbeinschoner
ship [ʃɪp] Schiff
shirt [ʃɜːt] Hemd
shock [ʃɒk] Schock; °Schreck
shocked [ʃɒkt] schockiert
shoe [ʃuː] Schuh
to shoot [ʃuːt] schießen, erschießen
shooting [ˈʃuːtɪŋ] Schießerei
shop [ʃɒp] Laden, Geschäft
  paper shop [ˈpeɪpə ʃɒp] Zeitungsladen, -kiosk
  shop window [ˌʃɒp ˈwɪndəʊ] Schaufenster
  tuck shop [ˈtʌk ʃɒp] Schulkiosk
shopping [ˈʃɒpɪŋ] Einkaufen
  shopping centre [ˈʃɒpɪŋ ˌsentə] Einkaufszentrum
short [ʃɔːt] klein; kurz
° short form [ˈʃɔːt fɔːm] Kurzform
shorts [ʃɔːts] kurze Hose
shotgun [ˈʃɒtgʌn] Schrotflinte

should [ʃʊd] sollte/st/t/n
shoulder [ˈʃəʊldə] Schulter
to shout [ʃaʊt] rufen; schreien
to show* [ʃəʊ] zeigen
shower [ˈʃaʊə] Dusche
  to have a shower [hæv‿ə ˈʃaʊə] duschen
° **shrinking** [ˈʃrɪŋkɪŋ] die schrumpfen lässt
to shut sb. up [ʃʌt‿ˈʌp] jdn. zum Schweigen bringen
shut [ʃʌt] geschlossen
Shut up. [ˈʃʌt‿ʌp] Halt den Mund!
shuttle [ˈʃʌtl] (Raum-) Fähre
shy [ʃaɪ] schüchtern
sick [sɪk] krank
side [saɪd] Seite, Rand
sidewalk [ˈsaɪdwɔːk] Bürgersteig
to sigh [saɪ] seufzen
sight [saɪt] Anblick; °Ansicht; Sehenswürdigkeit
sign [saɪn] Schild; Zeichen
to sign [saɪn] unterschreiben
signal [ˈsɪgnəl] Signal, Zeichen
silence [ˈsaɪləns] Schweigen
⟨**silly**⟩ [ˈsɪlɪ] Dummkopf
silly [ˈsɪlɪ] albern, blöd
silver [ˈsɪlvə] Silber
since [sɪns] seit
to sing* [sɪŋ] singen
singer [ˈsɪŋə] Sänger/in
° solo singer [ˈsəʊləʊ ˌsɪŋə] Solosänger/in
single [ˈsɪŋgl] Single
  single parent [ˈsɪŋgl ˈpeərənt] ein Elternteil, Alleinerziehende/r
single [ˈsɪŋgl] einzeln
° **singular** [ˈsɪŋgjʊlə] Singular, Einzahl
sink [sɪŋk] Spüle
to sink [sɪŋk] sinken
to sip [sɪp] schlürfen
sister [ˈsɪstə] Schwester
to sit* [sɪt] sitzen
sitting fee [ˈsɪtɪŋ fiː] Platzgebühr
situation [ˌsɪtjʊˈeɪʃn] Situation
six [sɪks] sechs
sixteen [ˌsɪksˈtiːn] sechzehn
sixty [ˈsɪkstɪ] sechzig
size [saɪz] Größe
skate [skeɪt] Schlittschuh
° skate hire [ˈskeɪt ˌhaɪə] Schlittschuhausleihe
to skate [skeɪt] Schlittschuh laufen
skateboarding [ˈskeɪtbɔːdɪŋ] Skateboard fahren
  ice skating [ˈaɪs ˌskeɪtɪŋ] Schlittschuhlaufen
to go skiing [gəʊ ˈskiːɪŋ] Ski laufen gehen
skin [skɪn] Haut
skirt [skɜːt] Rock
sky [skaɪ] Himmel
⟨**slave**⟩ [sleɪv] Sklave, Sklavin
to sleep* [sliːp] schlafen

Dictionary

We've got to put Bonzo to sleep. [wɪv 'gɒt tʊ pʊt 'bɒnzəʊ tʊ 'sliːp] Wir müssen Bonzo einschläfern.
⟨sleepless⟩ ['sliːplɪs] schlaflos
slice [slaɪs] Scheibe
slim [slɪm] dünn, schlank
⟨slogan⟩ ['sləʊgən] Slogan
slow [sləʊ] langsam
small [smɔːl] klein
smart [smɑːt] clever; schick, fein
smell [smel] Geruch, Gestank
to smell [smel] riechen
smile [smaɪl] Lächeln
to smile [smaɪl] lächeln
smiling ['smaɪlɪŋ] lächelnd
to smoke [sməʊk] rauchen
°smoking ['sməʊkɪŋ] Rauchen
snack [snæk] Zwischenmahlzeit
snack bar ['snæk bɑː] Imbissstube
to snooze [snuːz] dösen
to snore [snɔː] schnarchen
snow [snəʊ] Schnee
to snow [snəʊ] schneien
snowboarding ['snəʊbɔːdɪŋ] Snowboarden
snowmobile ['snəʊməʊbiːl] Schneemobil
so [səʊ] so
soap [səʊp] Seife
soccer [sɒkə] Fußball
social worker ['səʊʃl ˌwɜːkə] Sozialarbeiter/in
society [sə'saɪətɪ] Gesellschaft
sock [sɒk] Socke, Strumpf
sofa ['səʊfə] Sofa
soft drink [sɒft 'drɪŋk] alkoholfreies Getränk
soft [sɒft] weich, zart
software ['sɒftweə] Software
soggy ['sɒgɪ] matschig
°solo singer ['səʊləʊ ˌsɪŋə] Solosänger/in
°solution [sə'luːʃn] Lösung
to solve [sɒlv] lösen
some [sʌm] einige, manche
somebody ['sʌmbɒdɪ] jemand
someone ['sʌmwʌn] jemand
something made him say ... ['sʌmθɪŋ meɪd hɪm 'seɪ] etwas zwang ihn zu sagen ...
something ['sʌmθɪŋ] etwas
something else [sʌmθɪŋ 'els] etwas anderes
sometimes ['sʌmtaɪmz] manchmal
somewhere ['sʌmweə] irgendwo
son [sʌn] Sohn
song [sɒŋ] Lied
song book ['sɒŋ ˌbʊk] Liederbuch
soon [suːn] bald
See you soon. [ˌsiː jʊ 'suːn] Bis bald.
to be sorry ['sɒrɪ] Leid tun
to feel sorry [fiːl 'sɒrɪ fɔː] Leid tun, bedauern

sorry ['sɒrɪ] Entschuldigung, tut mir Leid
sort [sɔːt] Art
I'm sort of lost. [aɪm 'sɔːt ˌəv lɒst] Ich habe mich irgendwie verlaufen.
sort of ['sɔːt ˌəv] irgendwie
to sort [sɔːt] sortieren, °ordnen
sound [saʊnd] Geräusch; °Laut
to sound [saʊnd] sich anhören (nach)
soup [suːp] Suppe
south [saʊθ] Süden
South-West [ˌsaʊθ'west] der Südwesten
southeast [ˌsaʊθ'iːst] Südosten
souvenir [ˌsuːv'nɪə] Souvenir, Mitbringsel
space [speɪs] ⟨Platz⟩; Weltraum
spacebus ['speɪsbʌs] Weltraumbus
spaceship ['speɪsʃɪp] Raumschiff
Spanish ['spænɪʃ] Spanisch
spanner ['spænə] Schraubenschlüssel
sparking plug ['spɑːkɪŋ plʌg] Zündkerze
to speak* [spiːk] sprechen
to speak out [spiːk 'aʊt] sich für/gegen etwas aussprechen
special ['speʃl] besondere/r/s
direct speech [daɪ'rekt spiːtʃ] direkte Rede
⟨speech bubble⟩ ['spiːtʃ ˌbʌbl] Sprechblase
speed [spiːd] Geschwindigkeit
speedboat racing ['spiːdbəʊt ˌreɪsɪŋ] Schnellbootfahren
to spell [spel] buchstabieren
spelling ['spelɪŋ] Schreibweise
to spend* [spend] verbringen; ausgeben
spice [spaɪs] Gewürz
spider ['spaɪdə] Spinne
spirit ['spɪrɪt] Geist, Teamgeist
to spit* [spɪt] spucken
splash [splæʃ] Spritzen, Platschen
to split [splɪt] sich teilen, sich spalten
spoke [spəʊk] Speiche
sport [spɔːt] Sport, Sportart
team sport ['tiːm spɔːt] Mannschaftssport
sports (pl.) [spɔːts] Sport(arten)
sports centre ['spɔːts ˌsentə] Sportzentrum
to do sports [duː 'spɔːts] Sport betreiben
spot [spɒt] Pickel
spotlight ['spɒtlaɪt] Scheinwerfer
sprayer ['spreɪə] Sprayer
spring [sprɪŋ] Frühling
°to spy [spaɪ] erspähen
square [skweə] Platz
St. Bernard [sn 'bɜːnəd] Bernhardiner

stadium ['steɪdɪəm] Stadion
ice stadium ['aɪs ˌsteɪdɪəm] Eislaufstadion
stage [steɪdʒ] Bühne
on stage [ɒn 'steɪdʒ] auf der Bühne
°stage fright ['steɪdʒ fraɪt] Lampenfieber
to stagger ['stægə] schwanken
stairs [steəz] Treppe
stall [stɔːl] Stand
white elephant stall [waɪt 'elɪfənt stɔːl] Gemischtwarenstand
stamp [stæmp] Briefmarke
stand [stænd] Stand
to stand* [stænd] stehen
I can't stand ... [aɪ ˌkɑːnt 'stænd] Ich kann ... nicht ausstehen.
to stand up [stænd 'ʌp] aufstehen
standing ['stændɪŋ] Stehen
star [stɑː] Stern; Star, Berühmtheit
to star [stɑː] die Hauptrolle spielen, glänzen
to stare [steə] starren
starmap ['stɑːmæp] Sternkarte
start [stɑːt] Beginn, Start
to start [stɑːt] anfangen, starten
°to start sb. off [stɑːt 'sʌmbədɪ ˌɒf] jdm. mit dem Anfang helfen
state [steɪt] Staat
station ['steɪʃn] Bahnhof; Haltestelle; °Station; Sender
police station [pə'liːs ˌsteɪʃn] Polizeirevier
sheep station ['ʃiːp ˌsteɪʃn] Schaffarm
statistics [stə'tɪstɪks] Statistik
statue ['stætʃuː] Statue, Denkmal
to stay [steɪ] bleiben, übernachten
to stay out late ['steɪ ˌaʊt 'leɪt] lange/spät wegbleiben
to stay up late [steɪ ˌʌp 'leɪt] (abends) lange/spät aufbleiben
to steal* [stiːl] stehlen
steep [stiːp] steil
step [step] Schritt
stepdad ['stepˌdæd] Stiefvater
stepfather ['stepˌfɑːðə] Stiefvater
stepmum ['stepˌmʌm] Stiefmutter
stepsister ['stepˌsɪstə] Stiefschwester
stick [stɪk] Stock
stick of gum [stɪk ˌəv 'gʌm] Streifen Kaugummi
sticker ['stɪkə] Aufkleber
still [stɪl] regungslos
still [stɪl] (immer) noch, trotzdem
stocking ['stɒkɪŋ] Strumpf
stomach ['stʌmək] Magen
bus stop ['bʌs stɒp] Bushaltestelle
to stop [stɒp] anhalten, stoppen, abhalten, aufhalten
Stop it! ['stɒp ˌɪt] Hör(t) auf!
°stopover ['stɒpəʊvə] Zwischenunit

store [stɔ:] Laden, Geschäft
department store [dɪ'pɑ:tmənt ˌstɔ:] Kaufhaus, Warenhaus
to store [stɔ:] speichern
⟨storm⟩ [stɔ:m] Sturm
story ['stɔ:rɪ] Geschichte
story-line ['stɔ:rɪlaɪn] Verlauf der Geschichte
straight away [streɪt ə'weɪ] sofort
to go straight on [ˌɡəʊ streɪt 'ɒn] geradeaus weitergehen
strange [streɪndʒ] fremd; seltsam, merkwürdig
stranger ['streɪndʒə] Fremde/r
strawberry ['strɔ:bərɪ] Erdbeere
stream [stri:m] Fluss, Strom
street [stri:t] Straße
street corner [stri:t 'kɔ:nə] Straßenecke
street musician [ˌstri:t mju:'zɪʃn] Straßenmusikant
streetball ['stri:tbɔ:l] Streetball
stretcher ['stretʃə] Tragbahre
strict [strɪkt] streng
striker ['straɪkə] Stürmer
⟨strip⟩ [strɪp] Streifen
strong [strɒŋ] stark
pretty strong [prɪtɪ 'strɒŋ] ziemlich stark
struggle ['strʌɡl] Kampf
to struggle ['strʌɡl] sich wehren
° stud [stʌd] Stecker (für Ohr, Nase, etc.)
student ['stju:dənt] Schüler/in (AE), Student/in (BE)
studio ['stju:dɪəʊ] Studio
study ['stʌdɪ] Arbeitszimmer
stuff [stʌf] ugs. Zeug
stuff like that (sl.) [ˌstʌf laɪk 'ðæt] ugs. so'n Zeug
stuntman ['stʌntmən] Stuntman
stupid ['stju:pɪd] dumm
subject ['sʌbdʒɪkt] (Unterrichts-)Fach
substitute ['sʌbstɪtju:t] Ersatz-
suburb ['sʌbɜ:b] Vorort
success [sʌk'ses] Erfolg
successful [sʌk'sesfʊl] erfolgreich
such [sʌtʃ] solch/e/er/es, so
suddenly ['sʌdnlɪ] plötzlich
to suffer ['sʌfə] leiden
⟨sugar⟩ ['ʃʊɡə] Zucker
to suggest [sə'dʒest] vorschlagen
suggestion [sə'dʒestʃən] Vorschlag
° summary ['sʌmərɪ] Zusammenfassung
summer ['sʌmə] Sommer
sun [sʌn] Sonne
sun cream ['sʌnkri:m] Sonnencreme
Sunday ['sʌndɪ] Sonntag
sunglasses ['sʌnɡlɑ:sɪz] Sonnenbrille
sunny ['sʌnɪ] sonnig

sunrise ['sʌnraɪz] Sonnenaufgang
⟨sunshine⟩ ['sʌnʃaɪn] Sonnenschein
super ['su:pə] super
supermarket ['su:pəˌmɑ:kɪt] Supermarkt
to suppose [sə'pəʊz] denken, annehmen
⟨Supreme Court⟩ [sʊ'pri:m kɔ:t] Oberstes Gericht
sure [ʃʊə] sicher
to surf the Internet ['sɜ:f ði: 'ɪntənet] im Internet surfen
surface ['sɜ:fɪs] Oberfläche
surfing ['sɜ:fɪŋ] Surfen
surfing the Internet ['sɜ:fɪŋ ði: 'ɪntənet] im Internet surfen
surprise [sə'praɪz] Überraschung
to surprise [sə'praɪz] überraschen
surprised [sə'praɪzd] überrascht
to surround [sə'raʊnd] umzingeln
° survey ['sɜ:veɪ] Umfrage
survival [sə'vaɪvl] Überleben
to survive [sə'vaɪv] überleben
suspect [sə'spekt] Verdächtige(r)
° to swallow up [ˌswɒləʊ 'ʌp] verschlingen
° to swap [swɒp] tauschen
to sweat [swet] schwitzen
sweatshirt ['swetʃɜ:t] Sweatshirt
sweet [swi:t] süß
sweets (pl.) [swi:ts] Süßigkeiten
to swim* [swɪm] schwimmen
swimmer ['swɪmə] Schwimmer/in
swimming ['swɪmɪŋ] Schwimmen
swimming pool ['swɪmɪŋ ˌpu:l] Schwimmbad
to go swimming [ɡəʊ 'swɪmɪŋ] schwimmen gehen
° symbol ['sɪmbl] Symbol
⟨system⟩ ['sɪstəm] System
systems engineer ['sɪstəmz endʒɪ'nɪə] Systemingenieur/in

T

T-shirt ['ti: ʃɜ:t] T-Shirt
table ['teɪbl] °Tabelle; Tisch
table tennis ['teɪbl ˌtenɪs] Tischtennis
tablet ['tæblɪt] Tablette
tail [teɪl] Schwanz
take-off ['teɪk ɒf] Start, Abflug
to take* [teɪk] kosten; mitnehmen, nehmen
Take it easy! (sl.) ['teɪk ɪt 'i:zɪ] ugs. Bleib ruhig.
to take a deep breath [teɪk ə 'di:p breθ] tief Luft einholen
to take a test [teɪk ə 'test] einen Test machen
to take for a walk [ˌteɪk fər ə 'wɔ:k] spazieren führen

to take off [teɪk 'ɒf] abnehmen, abmachen; auswechseln; ausziehen
to take over [teɪk 'əʊvə] beherrschen
to take part [teɪk 'pɑ:t] teilnehmen
to take photos [teɪk 'fəʊtəʊz] Fotos machen, fotografieren
to take place [teɪk 'pleɪs] stattfinden
to take to and from [teɪk 'tʊ ənd frɒm] hinbringen und abholen
to take to bed [ˌteɪk tə 'bed] ins Bett bringen
tale [teɪl] Geschichte, Erzählung, Märchen
to talk [tɔ:k] sprechen, reden
° to talk about ['tɔ:k əˌbaʊt] über … sprechen
to talk sb. out of sth. [tɔ:k … 'aʊt əv] jdm. etwas ausreden
tall [tɔ:l] groß
tank [tæŋk] Tank
tap [tæp] Wasserhahn, Zapfhahn
tape [teɪp] °Bandaufnahme; Tonband
° task [tɑ:sk] Aufgabe
to taste [teɪst] schmecken
° tattoo [tə'tu:] Tätowierung
taxi ['tæksɪ] Taxi
tea [ti:] Tee
to teach* [ti:tʃ] lehren, beibringen
to teach sb. a lesson ['ti:tʃ ˌsʌmbədɪ ə 'lesn] jdm. eine Lektion erteilen
teacher ['ti:tʃə] Lehrer/in
⟨head teacher⟩ ['hed ˌti:tʃə] Schuldirektor/in
team [ti:m] Team, Mannschaft
team sport ['ti:m spɔ:t] Mannschaftssport
technical ['teknɪkl] technisch
technician [tek'nɪʃn] Techniker/in
Technology [tek'nɒlədʒɪ] Technik (Schulfach)
technology [tek'nɒlədʒɪ] Technik, Technologie
teenager ['ti:nˌeɪdʒə] Teenager, Jugendliche/r unter 20 Jahren
tooth/teeth [tu:θ/ti:θ] Zahn/Zähne
telegram ['telɪɡræm] Telegramm
telephone ['telɪfəʊn] Telefon
telephone box ['telɪfəʊn ˌbɒks] Telefonzelle
telephone call ['telɪfəʊn ˌkɔ:l] Anruf
telephone line ['telɪfəʊn ˌlaɪn] Telefonleitung
to answer the telephone [ˌɑ:nsə ðə 'telɪfəʊn] ans Telefon gehen
telescope ['telɪskəʊp] Teleskop
television ['telɪˌvɪʒn] Fernseher

Dictionary

°to **tell*** [tel] sagen, erzählen, berichten
to tell the way [ˌtel ðə ˈweɪ] den Weg erklären
ten [ten] zehn
tennis [ˈtenɪs] Tennis
tennis court [ˈtenɪs kɔːt] Tennisplatz
tense [tens] Zeitstufe
tent [tent] Zelt
term [tɜːm] Schulhalbjahr
terraced house [ˈterəst haʊs] Reihenhaus
terrible [ˈterəbl] schrecklich
territory [ˈterətərɪ] Revier
test [test] Test
to **test** [test] testen, prüfen
to take a test [teɪk ə ˈtest] einen Test machen
°**text** [tekst] Text
textbook [ˈtekstbʊk] Schulbuch
than [ðæn] als
thank you [ˈθæŋk ju] danke
Thank God. [θæŋk gɒd] Gott sei Dank.
Thank heavens! [θæŋk ˈhevnz] Dem Himmel sei Dank!
that [ðæt] das
And that's that! [ænd ˌðæts ˈðæt] Schluss! Basta!
that way [ˈðæt weɪ] so, auf diese Art
the [ðə] der/die/das; die *(pl.)*
the aged [ðiː ˈeɪdʒɪd] die alten Menschen, die Alten
the big outdoors [ðə bɪɡ ˈaʊtdɔːz] die freie Natur
The fun they had [ðə ˈfʌn ðeɪ hæd] Was für einen Spaß sie hatten!
the pits [ðə ˈpɪts] das Allerletzte
the very last [ðə ˈverɪ lɑːst] der, die, das allerletzte
theft [θeft] Diebstahl
their *(pl.)* [ðeə] ihr/e
them [ðəm] ihnen/sie
theme park [ˈθiːm pɑːk] Freizeitpark
themselves [demˈselvz] sich selbst
then [ðen] dann
there [ðeə] dort, da
there are *(pl.)* [ðər ə] es gibt, da sind
there is *(sg.)* [ðər ɪz] es gibt, da ist
there was …, wasn't there? [ðeə ˈwɒz … ˈwɒznt ðeə] es gab …, nicht wahr?
these [ðiːz] diese (hier)
these days [ˈðiːz deɪz] heute, heutzutage
they [ðeɪ] sie
They can't …, can they? [ðeɪ ˈkɑːnt … ˈkæn ðeɪ] Sie können nicht …, nicht wahr?

thin [θɪn] dünn
thing [θɪŋ] Ding, Gegenstand
You know the kind of thing. [ju ˈnəʊ ðə kaɪnd ˌəv ˈθɪŋ] Man kennt das ja.
to **think*** [θɪŋk] denken, meinen
to think about [ˈθɪŋk əˌbaʊt] an … denken, über … nachdenken
to think of [ˈθɪŋk ˌəv] °an … denken, ausdenken; °halten von, denken über
I think so. [aɪ ˈθɪŋk səʊ] Ich glaube, ja. Ich denke, ja.
third [θɜːd] dritte/r/s
a third [ə ˈθɜːd] ein Drittel
thirsty [ˈθɜːstɪ] durstig
thirteen [ˌθɜːˈtiːn] dreizehn
thirty [ˈθɜːtɪ] dreißig
this [ðɪs] dies, das
This way. [ˈðɪs weɪ] Hier entlang.
those [ðəʊz] diese (da)
though [ðəʊ] obwohl
thought [θɔːt] Gedanke
to **threaten** [ˈθretn] bedrohen; °drohen
to threaten physically [ˈθretn ˈfɪzɪkəlɪ] mit roher Gewalt drohen
three [θriː] drei
three out of ten [ˈθriː ˌaʊt əv ten] drei von zehn
thriller [ˈθrɪlə] Thriller
through [θruː] durch
through *(sl.)* [θruː] *ugs.* fertig
to **throw*** [θrəʊ] werfen
to throw away [ˈθrəʊ əˌweɪ] wegwerfen
to throw out [ˌθrəʊ ˈaʊt] herausschmeißen
Thursday [ˈθɜːzdɪ] Donnerstag
ticket [ˈtɪkɪt] Eintrittskarte; Fahrschein
tidy [ˈtaɪdɪ] ordentlich
tie [taɪ] Krawatte
tiger [ˈtaɪɡə] Tiger
tight [taɪt] eng
till [tɪl] bis
time [taɪm] Zeit
after some time [ˈɑːftə ˌsʌm ˈtaɪm] nach einiger Zeit
all the time [ˈɔːl ðə taɪm] die ganze Zeit
at a time [æt ə ˈtaɪm] auf einmal
°each time [iːtʃ ˈtaɪm] jedes Mal
for a time [fɔːr ə ˈtaɪm] eine Zeit lang
for the first time [fə ðə ˈfɜːst taɪm] zum ersten Mal
How many times …? [ˈhaʊ menɪ ˌtaɪmz] Wie oft …?
°in five years' time [ɪn ˈfaɪv jɪəz taɪm] in fünf Jahren
in time [ɪn ˈtaɪm] rechtzeitig, pünktlich

most of the time [ˌməʊst əv ðə ˈtaɪm] die meiste Zeit
on time [ɒn ˈtaɪm] pünktlich
several times [ˈsevrəl taɪmz] mehrere Male
three times [ˈθriː taɪmz] dreimal
timetable [ˈtaɪmˌteɪbl] Stundenplan
tip [tɪp] Tipp, Hinweis; Trinkgeld
tired [ˈtaɪəd] müde
°**title** [ˈtaɪtl] Titel
to [tʊ] vor *(Uhrzeit)*; zu, nach, in
from … to [frɒm … tʊ] von … bis *(Wochentage)*
toaster [ˈtəʊstə] Toaster
tobacco [təˈbækəʊ] Tabak
today [təˈdeɪ] heute
together [təˈɡeðə] zusammen
toilet [ˈtɔɪlɪt] Toilette
toilet block [ˈtɔɪlɪt ˌblɒk] Toilettenanlage
tomato [təˈmɑːtəʊ] Tomate
tomorrow [təˈmɒrəʊ] morgen
dialling **tone** [ˈdaɪlɪŋ ˌtəʊn] Freizeichen
tongue [tʌŋ] Zunge
too [tuː] auch, zu
too many [tuː ˈmenɪ] zu viele
°too much [tuː ˈmʌtʃ] zu viel
tool [tuːl] Werkzeug; Werkzeug/Gerät
tooth/teeth [tuːθ/tiːθ] Zahn/Zähne
top [tɒp] Gipfel, Spitze; oberste(r), höchste(r), beste(r)
°at the top of [æt ðə tɒp əv] oben auf
torn [tɔːn] zerrissen
tornado [tɔːˈneɪdəʊ] Tornado, Wirbelsturm
°**total** [ˈtəʊtl] Summe
total [ˈtəʊtl] völlig
totally [ˈtəʊtlɪ] total, vollkommen
to **touch** [tʌtʃ] berühren
tough [tʌf] hart
°**tour** [tʊə] Tour
°tour dates [ˈtʊə deɪts] Tourdaten
tourist [ˈtʊərɪst] Tourist/in
towards [təˈwɔːdz] auf … zu
tower [ˈtaʊə] Turm
town [taʊn] Kleinstadt
toy [tɔɪ] Spielzeug
trace [treɪs] Spur
track [træk] Spur, Fährte
tracksuit [ˈtræksuːt] Trainings-, Jogginganzug
tractor [ˈtræktə] Traktor
⟨**trade**⟩ [treɪd] Handel
trade fair [ˈtreɪd feə] Messe
traffic [ˈtræfɪk] Verkehr
trailer [ˈtreɪlə] (Film-) Vorschau; Anhänger
train [treɪn] Zug
to **train** [treɪn] trainieren

Dictionary

trainee [treɪˈniː] Auszubildende/r
training [ˈtreɪnɪŋ] Training
to **translate** [trænsˈleɪt] übersetzen
translator [trænsˈleɪtə] Übersetzer/in
to **travel** [ˈtrævl] reisen
⟨to travel the world⟩ [ˌtrævl ðə ˈwɜːld] um die Welt reisen
treasure [ˈtreʒə] Schatz
to **treat** [triːt] behandeln
tree [triː] Baum
 palm tree [ˈpɑːm triː] Palme
trekking [ˈtrekɪŋ] Trecking
 trekking bike [ˈtrekɪŋ ˌbaɪk] Trekkingbike
trick [trɪk] Kunststück; Streich; Trick
 to play a trick [pleɪ ə ˈtrɪk] einen Streich spielen
trip [trɪp] Trip, Reise, Ausflug
⟨**troops**⟩ [truːps] Truppen
trouble [ˈtrʌbl] Ärger
 in trouble [ɪn ˈtrʌbl] in Schwierigkeiten
 to get into trouble [ɡet ˌɪntʊ ˈtrʌbl] Schwierigkeiten, Probleme bekommen
trousers (pl.) [ˈtraʊzəz] Hose
 pyjama trousers (pl.) [pəˌdʒɑːmə ˈtraʊzəz] Schlafanzughose
truck [trʌk] amer. Lastwagen
true [truː] wahr; richtig
°to come true [kʌm ˈtruː] wahr werden
to **trust** [trʌst] vertrauen
truth [truːθ] Wahrheit
truthful [ˈtruːθfʊl] ehrlich
to **try** [traɪ] versuchen, probieren
 to try out for (AE) [traɪ ˈaʊt fə] (für eine Rolle) vorsprechen
tube [tjuːb] Rohr; die Londoner U-Bahn
tuck shop [ˈtʌk ʃɒp] Schulkiosk
Tuesday [ˈtjuːzdɪ] Dienstag
tunnel [ˈtʌnl] Tunnel
to **turn** [tɜːn] biegen, drehen
 to turn around [tɜːn əˈraʊnd] umdrehen
 to turn left [tɜːn ˈleft] links abbiegen
 to turn off [tɜːn ˈɒf] ausschalten
 to turn on [tɜːn ˈɒn] anmachen
 to turn red [tɜːn ˈred] rot werden
 to turn right [tɜːn ˈraɪt] rechts abbiegen
 to turn round [tɜːn ˈraʊnd] wenden, drehen
TV [tiːˈviː] Fernseher
 on TV [ɒn ˌtiːˈviː] im Fernsehen
 to watch TV [wɒtʃ ˌtiːˈviː] fernsehen

twelfth [twelfθ] zwölfte/r/s
twelve [twelv] zwölf
twentieth [ˈtwentɪəθ] zwanzigste/r/s
twenty [ˈtwentɪ] zwanzig
twenty-first [ˌtwentɪ ˈfɜːst] einundzwanzigste/r/s
twenty-one [ˌtwentɪ ˈwʌn] einundzwanzig
twice [twaɪs] zweimal
two [tuː] zwei
°**type** [taɪp] Art, Sorte
typical [ˈtɪpɪkl] typisch
tyre [ˈtaɪə] Reifen

U

Ugh! [ɜːh] Igitt! Pfui!
ugly [ˈʌɡlɪ] hässlich
uncle [ˈʌŋkl] Onkel
uncool [ʌnˈkuːl] gar nicht cool
under [ˈʌndə] unter
°to **underline** [ˌʌndəˈlaɪn] unterstreichen
to **understand*** [ʌndəˈstænd] verstehen
to **undo** [ˌʌnˈduː] lösen
unemployed [ʌnɪmˈplɔɪd] arbeitslos
unemployment [ˌʌnɪmˈplɔɪmənt] Arbeitslosigkeit
unfair [ʌnˈfeə] unfair
unfortunately [ʌnˈfɔːtʃnətlɪ] unglücklicherweise
unfriendly [ˌʌnˈfrendlɪ] unfreundlich
unhappy [ʌnˈhæpɪ] unglücklich
unhealthy [ʌnˈhelθɪ] ungesund
unhurt [ʌnˈhɜːt] unverletzt
uniform [ˈjuːnɪfɔːm] Uniform
uninteresting [ʌnˈɪntrəstɪŋ] uninteressant
°**unit** [ˈjuːnɪt] Einheit, Lektion
⟨**university**⟩ [juːnɪˈvɜːsətɪ] Universität
⟨**unkind**⟩ [ʌnˈkaɪnd] gemein
to **unlock** [ˌʌnˈlɒk] aufschließen
unlucky [ʌnˈlʌkɪ] unglücklich
°**unnatural** [ʌnˈnætʃrəl] unnatürlich, künstlich
unpopular [ʌnˈpɒpjʊlə] unbeliebt
unsure [ˌʌnˈʃɔː] unsicher
until [ənˈtɪl] bis
unusual [ʌnˈjuːʒl] ungewöhnlich
unwanted [ˌʌnˈwɒntɪd] unerwünscht
unwelcome [ʌnˈwelkəm] unwillkommen
up [ʌp] oben
 to come up to [kʌm ˈʌp tə] zu jdm. kommen, auf jdn. zukommen
 to look up [lʊk ˈʌp] hochschauen, aufblicken; °nachschlagen
 to put up [pʊt ˈʌp] aushängen
 to wake up [weɪk ˈʌp] aufwachen
 up here [ʌp ˈhɪə] hier oben
 up to date [ˌʌp tə ˈdeɪt] auf dem neuesten Stand, modern
to **update** [ˈʌpdeɪt] aktualisieren
upset [ʌpˈset] verärgert
upside down [ˈʌpsaɪd daʊn] auf den Kopf gestellt
upstairs [ˌʌpˈsteəz] oben, nach oben (im Haus)
Urdu [ˈʊədu:] Urdu (indische Sprache)
urgent [ˈɜːdʒənt] dringend
us [ʌs] uns
to **use** [juːz] benutzen
 My parents used to take me everywhere. [maɪ ˈpeərənts juːst tʊ ˈteɪk mɪ ˈevrɪweə] Meine Eltern brachten mich früher überall hin.
 to get used to sth. [get juːzd] sich an etwas gewöhnen
useful [ˈjuːsfʊl] nützlich
user [ˈjuːzə] Anwender/in
usually [ˈjuːʒəlɪ] gewöhnlich, normalerweise

V

vacancy [ˈveɪkənsɪ] offene, freie Stelle
on vacation (AE) [ɒn vəˈkeɪʃn] im Urlaub, in den Ferien
vacuum cleaner [ˈvækjʊəm ˌkliːnə] Staubsauger
valley [ˈvælɪ] Tal
van [væn] Lieferwagen
vandal [ˈvændl] Rowdy
to **vanish** [ˈvænɪʃ] verschwinden
VCR (video cassette recorder) [viːsiːˈɑː] Videorekorder
vegetables (pl.) [ˈvedʒtəblz] Gemüse
verb [vɜːb] °Tätigkeitswort, °Verb
 modal verb [ˈməʊdl vɜːb] Modalverb
very [ˈverɪ] sehr
vet [vet] Tierarzt/-ärztin
 vet's assistant [vets əˈsɪstənt] Tierarzthelfer/in
⟨**via**⟩ [ˈvaɪə] über, durch
°**vice versa** [ˌvaɪsɪˈvɜːsə] umgekehrt
⟨**victim**⟩ [ˈvɪktɪm] Opfer
video [ˈvɪdɪəʊ] Video
 video arcade [ˈvɪdɪəʊ ɑːˈkeɪd] Videospielhalle
 video camera [ˌvɪdɪəʊˈkæmrə] Videokamera
°video jockey [ˈvɪdɪəʊ ˌdʒɒkɪ] Videojockey
view [vjuː] Aussicht

village ['vɪlɪdʒ] Dorf
vinegar ['vɪnɪgə] Essig
violence ['vaɪələns] Gewalt
violent ['vaɪələnt] gewalttätig
violin [ˌvaɪə'lɪn] Geige
°**visible** ['vɪzəbl] sichtbar
°**visit** ['vɪzɪt] Besuch
to **visit** ['vɪzɪt] besuchen
visitor ['vɪzɪtə] Besucher/in
voice [vɔɪs] Stimme
volleyball ['vɒlɪbɔːl] Volleyball
volume ['vɒljuːm] Band
vote [vəʊt] Abstimmung
to **vote** [vəʊt] abstimmen
⟨**voyage**⟩ ['vɔɪɪdʒ] Reise
vs (versus) ['vɜːsəs] gegen

W

wage [weɪdʒ] Lohn
waist [weɪst] Taille
to **wait** [weɪt] warten
  to wait for ['weɪt fɔː] warten auf
waiter ['weɪtə] Ober/Kellner
to **wake up*** [weɪk ˈʌp] aufwachen
to wake up* [weɪk ˈʌp] wecken
walk [wɔːk] Spaziergang
  to go for a walk [gəʊ fər ə 'wɔːk] spazieren gehen
  to take for a walk [teɪk fər ə 'wɔːk] spazieren führen
to **walk** [wɔːk] (zu Fuß) gehen
  to walk over [wɔːk ˈəʊvə] hinübergehen
wall [wɔːl] Wand
wanna = want to ['wɒnə] *ugs.* will
to **want (to)** [wɒnt] °sich wünschen; wollen
wanted ['wɒntɪd] gesucht; gewollt, erwünscht
wardrobe ['wɔːdrəʊb] Kleiderschrank
warehouse ['weəhaʊs] Lagerhaus
⟨to **warm**⟩ [wɔːm] erwärmen
warm [wɔːm] warm
to **warn** [wɔːn] warnen
warning ['wɔːnɪŋ] Warnung
⟨**warrior**⟩ ['wɒrɪə] Krieger
to **wash** [wɒʃ] waschen
  to wash off [wɒʃ ˈɒf] abwaschen
washbasin ['wɒʃbeɪsn] Waschbecken
washing-up [ˌwɒʃɪŋ ˈʌp] Abwasch
  to do the washing-up [duː ðə ˌwɒʃɪŋ ˈʌp] abwaschen
  washing machine ['wɒʃɪŋ məˌʃiːn] Waschmaschine
  washing-up liquid [ˌwɒʃɪŋ ˈʌp ˈlɪkwɪd] Spülmittel
wasn't ... either ['wɒznt ... 'aɪðə] war auch nicht
waste [weɪst] Müll, Abfall
to **waste** [weɪst] verschwenden

watch [wɒtʃ] Armbanduhr
to **watch** [wɒtʃ] schauen, ansehen
  to watch TV [wɒtʃ ˌtiːˈviː] fernsehen
water ['wɔːtə] Wasser
waterfall ['wɔːtəfɔːl] Wasserfall
wave [weɪv] Welle
to **wave** [weɪv] winken
way [weɪ] Art; Weg
  all the way [ɔːl ðə 'weɪ] den ganzen Weg
  By the way, ... [baɪ ðə 'weɪ] Übrigens, ...
  in a way [ɪn ə weɪ] in gewisser Weise
  It's the way wolves are. [ɪts ðə weɪ wʊlvz ɑː] So sind Wölfe.
  This way. ['ðɪs weɪ] Hier entlang.
  to find one's way around ['faɪnd wʌnz weɪ əˈraʊnd] sich zurechtfinden
  to tell the way [ˌtel ðə 'weɪ] den Weg erklären
we [wiː] wir
  We didn't have to ..., did we? [wiː 'dɪdnt hæv tuː: ... 'dɪd wiː] Wir mussten nicht ..., nicht wahr?
to **wear*** [weə] anziehen, tragen
weather ['weðə] Wetter
  weather warning ['weðə ˌwɔːnɪŋ] Unwetterwarnung
⟨**web**⟩ [web] Netz
website ['websaɪt] Seite im Internet
wedding ['wedɪŋ] Hochzeit
Wednesday ['wenzdɪ] Mittwoch
week [wiːk] Woche
  a week [ə 'wiːk] pro Woche
  days a week [deɪz ə 'wiːk] Tage pro Woche
  for a week ['fɔːr ə 'wiːk] eine Woche lang
  weeks a year [wiːks ə 'jɪə] Wochen pro Jahr
weekend [wiːk'end] Wochenende
  at the weekend [ət ðə ˌwiːk'end] am Wochenende
weekly ['wiːklɪ] wöchentlich, wöchentlich erscheinend
weight [weɪt] Gewicht
  weight-training ['weɪt treɪnɪŋ] Gewichtheben
to **welcome** ['welkəm] begrüßen, willkommen heißen
welcome ['welkəm] willkommen; °Herzlich willkommen
well-built [wel'bɪlt] gut gebaut
well [wel] gut
  to get on well with [get ɒn 'wel wɪð] gut auskommen mit
  to go well [gəʊ 'wel] gut gehen
  Well done! [wel 'dʌn] Gut gemacht!
°Well, ... [wel] Also, ...

west [west] Westen
western ['westn] Western
wet [wet] nass
what [wɒt] was; was für; °welche/r/s
  What about ...? [wɒt əˈbaʊt] Wie wäre es mit ...?
  What about you? [wɒt əˈbaʊt juː] Und du? Wie ist es bei dir?
  What are you having? [wɒt ɑː 'juː ˌhævɪŋ] Was nimmst du?
  °What colour is it? [wɒt ˈkʌlər ɪz ɪt] Welche Farbe hat es?
  What else? [wɒt 'els] Was sonst? Was noch?
  What time is it? [wɒt 'taɪm ɪz ɪt] Wie viel Uhr ist es?, Wie spät ist es?
  °What do they look like? [wɒt duː ðeɪ 'lʊk laɪk] Wie sehen sie aus?
  What's up? (*sl.*) [wɒts ˈʌp] *ugs.* Wie geht's?
whatever [wɒt'evə] was bloß
Whee! ['wiː] *Ausruf*
wheel [wiːl] Rad
wheelchair ['wiːlˌtʃeə] Rollstuhl
when [wen] wann; wenn
where [weə] wo; wohin
  where ... from [ˌweə ... 'frɒm] woher
which [wɪtʃ] welche/r/s
while [waɪl] während
white [waɪt] weiß
  white elephant stall [waɪt ˈelɪfənt stɔːl] Gemischtwarenstand
  the whites [ðə 'waɪts] die Weißen
  white-water rafting [ˌwaɪt wɔːtə 'rɑːftɪŋ] Floßfahren auf reißenden Gewässern
who [huː] wer
whole [həʊl] ganz
why [waɪ] warum
wide open spaces ['waɪd ˌəʊpn 'speɪsɪz] die Weite
wide-eyed [ˌwaɪd'aɪd] mit großen Augen
wife [waɪf] Ehefrau
wig [wɪg] Perücke
wild [waɪld] wild
  wild-looking ['waɪldˌlʊkɪŋ] wild aussehend
wilderness ['wɪldənɪs] Wildnis
will [wɪl] werden (*Zukunft*)
to **win*** [wɪn] gewinnen
wind [wɪnd] Wind
window ['wɪndəʊ] Fenster
  out the window (*AE*) [ˌaʊt ðə 'wɪndəʊ] aus dem Fenster
  window-shopping ['wɪndəʊˌʃɒpɪŋ] Schaufensterbummel
windy ['wɪndɪ] windig
wine [waɪn] Wein
winner ['wɪnə] Sieger/in, Gewinner/in

winning ['wɪnɪŋ] Gewinnen, Gewinn
winning [wɪnɪŋ] charmant
winter ['wɪntə] Winter
wire ['waɪə] Draht, Schnur, Kabel
wish [wɪʃ] Wunsch
  best wishes [ˌbest 'wɪʃɪz] herzliche Grüße
to **wish** [wɪʃ] (sich) wünschen
witchetty grubs ['wɪtʃətɪ 'grʌbz] Larven
with [wɪð] mit
witness ['wɪtnɪs] Zeuge/Zeugin
wolf/wolves [wʊlf, wʊlvz] Wolf/Wölfe
  It's the way wolves are. [ɪts ðə weɪ wʊlvz ˈɑː] So sind Wölfe.
woman ['wʊmən] Frau
  ambulance woman ['æmbjʊlns ˌwʊmən] Sanitäterin
women (*pl.*) ['wɪmɪn] Frauen
I wonder if you can … [aɪ 'wʌndə ɪf ju: kæn] Können Sie vielleicht …
wonderful ['wʌndəfʊl] wundervoll
won't [wəʊnt] wird nicht, werden nicht
wood [wʊd] Wald
word [wɜːd] Wort
° connecting word [kə'nektɪŋ wɜːd] Konjunktion, Bindewort
work [wɜːk] Arbeit
  at work [ət 'wɜːk] bei der Arbeit
to **work** [wɜːk] arbeiten; funktionieren
  social **worker** ['səʊʃl ˌwɜːkə] Sozialarbeiter/in
  oil rig worker ['ɔɪl rɪg ˌwɜːkə] Arbeiter/in auf dem Ölförderturm
° **working day** ['wɜːkɪŋ deɪ] Arbeitstag
  working place ['wɜːkɪŋ pleɪs] Arbeitsplatz
world [wɜːld] Welt
worm [wɜːm] Wurm
worried ['wʌrɪd] beunruhigt
to **worry** ['wʌrɪ] sich Sorgen machen
worse [wɜːs] schlechter; schlimmer (noch)
would [wʊd] würde, würden
Wow! [waʊ] Toll!, Klasse!
to **write*** [raɪt] schreiben
° to **write down** [raɪt 'daʊn] aufschreiben
writer ['raɪtə] Schriftsteller/in, Verfasser/in
writing paper ['raɪtɪŋ ˌpeɪpə] Briefpapier
wrong [rɒŋ] falsch
  to be wrong [bi: 'rɒŋ] Unrecht haben
  to get sb. wrong [get sʌmbədɪ 'rɒŋ] jdm. falsch verstehen
  to go wrong [gəʊ 'rɒŋ] kaputtgehen; schief laufen, daneben gehen

Y

to **yawn** [jɔːn] gähnen
year [jɪə] Jahr
  weeks a year [wiːks ə 'jɪə] Wochen pro Jahr
  yearbook ['jɪəbʊk] Jahrbuch
to **yell** [jel] schreien, brüllen
yellow ['jeləʊ] gelb
yes [jes] ja
yesterday ['jestədɪ] gestern
  not … yet [nɒt 'jet] noch … nicht; schon
Yo! (*sl.*) [jəʊ] *ugs.* Hallo!
yoghurt ['jɒgət] Joghurt
you [juː] dir/dich/euch/Sie/Ihnen; du/ihr/Sie
  You are …, aren't you? [juː ˈɑː … 'ɑːnt juː] Du bist …, nicht wahr?
  You know the kind of thing. [ju 'nəʊ ðə kaɪnd əv ˌθɪŋ] Man kennt das ja.
° You must be joking! [ju ˌmʌst bɪ 'dʒəʊkɪŋ] Du spinnst wohl!
young [jʌŋ] jung
  Young People's Club [jʌŋ 'piːplz ˌklʌb] Jugendklub
your [jɔː] dein/deine, euer/eure, Ihr/Ihre
You're welcome. [jʊə 'welkʌm] Gern geschehen.
yours [jɔːz] deiner, deine, dein, deins
Yours sincerely, … [jɔːz sɪn'sɪəlɪ] mit freundlichen Grüßen
yourself [jɔː'self] °dich, dir; dir/dich selbst
yourselves [jɔː'selvz] ihr/euch selbst
youth [juːθ] Jugend
  Youth Center ['juːθ sentə] Jugendzentrum
  youth club ['juːθ klʌb] Jugendklub
Yuk! [jʌk] Ätzend!; °Igitt!
Yum! [jʌm] Lecker!

Z

zoo [zuː] Zoo

Boys' names

Alan ['ælən]
Andrew ['ændruː]
Andy ['ændɪ]
Antanas ['æntənəs]
Ben [ben]
Bertie ['bɜːtɪ]
Bill [bɪl]
Bob [bɒb]
Brad [bræd]
Brett [bret]
Brian ['braɪən]
Buck [bʌk]
Bud [bʌd]
Calvin ['kælvɪn]
Carl [kɑːl]
Chiong [tʃɒŋ]
Chris [krɪs]
Colin ['kɒlɪn]
Crayk [kreɪk]
Dan [dæn]
Daniel ['dænjəl]
Darius ['dærɪəs]
David ['deɪvɪd]
Derek ['derɪk]
Ed [ed]
Eddie ['edɪ]
Eric ['erɪk]
Fabrizzio [fæ'brɪtsɪəʊ]
Frank [fræŋk]
Fudge [fʌdʒ]
Gary ['gærɪ]
Gavin ['gævɪn]
Gordon ['gɔːdn]
Greg [greg]
Hank [hæŋk]
Ian ['iːən]
Jack [dʒæk]
Jamar [dʒə'mɑː]
Jason ['dʒeɪsn]
Jassim ['dʒæsɪm]
Jeff [dʒef]
Jeremy ['dʒerəmɪ]
Jim [dʒɪm]
Joe [dʒəʊ]
John [dʒɒn]
Johnny ['dʒɒnɪ]
Keith [kiːθ]
⟨**Kemal**⟩ ['kemɑːl]
Kenny ['kenɪ]
Kevin ['kevɪn]
Lee [liː]
Lucas ['luːkəs]
Malcolm ['mælkəm]
Mario ['mɑːrɪəʊ]
Mark [mɑːk]
Martin ['mɑːtɪn]
Matt [mæt]
Michael ['maɪkl]
Nathan ['neɪθn]
Neal [niːl]
Neil [niːl]
Nick [nɪk]
Oscar ['ɒskə]
Paco ['pækəʊ]
Patrick ['pætrɪk]
Peter ['piːtə]
Phil [fɪl]
Pitt [pɪt]
Ramon [rə'mɒn]
Richard ['rɪtʃəd]
Ricky ['rɪkɪ]
Robert ['rɒbət]
Roger ['rɒdʒə]

Dictionary

Ryan [ˈraɪən]
Sam [sæm]
Sean [ʃɔːn]
⟨Sebastian⟩ [sɪˈbæstjən]
⟨Selim⟩ [seˈliːm]
Simon [ˈsaɪmən]
Smithie [ˈsmɪθɪ]
Steve [stiːv]
Steven [ˈstiːvn]
Terry [ˈterɪ]
⟨Thommy⟩ [ˈtɒmɪ]
Thorsten [ˈtɔːstn]
Tim [tɪm]
Tom [tɒm]
Tommy [ˈtɒmɪ]
Tony [ˈtəʊnɪ]
Trevor [ˈtrevə]
⟨Valentine⟩ [ˈvæləntaɪn]
Wayne [weɪn]

Girls' names

Abbey [ˈæbɪ]
Abigail [ˈæbɪgeɪl]
Aisha [ˈaɪʃə]
Alison [ˈælɪsn]
⟨Amina⟩ [ʌˈmiːnə]
Amy [ˈeɪmɪ]
Angela [ˈændʒələ]
Ann [æn]
Anna [ˈænə]
Audrey [ˈɔːdrɪ]
Barbara [ˈbɑːbərə]
Becky [ˈbekɪ]
Belinda [ˈbəlɪndə]
Bettina [beˈtiːnə]
Carol [ˈkærəl]
Caroline [ˈkærəlaɪn]
Catharine [ˈkæθrɪn]
Christine [krɪsˈtiːn]
Claire [kleə]
Claudine [klɔːˈdɪn]
Coralee [kɒrəˈliː]
Debbie [ˈdebɪ]
Debby [ˈdebɪ]
Edith [ˈiːdɪθ]
Elaine [eˈleɪn]
Emily [ˈemɪlɪ]
Emma [ˈemə]
Evelyn [ˈiːvlɪn]
Fiona [fɪˈəʊnə]
Georgia [ˈdʒɔːdʒə]
Hamida [həˈmiːdə]
Hannah [ˈhænə]
Helen [ˈhelən]
Jackie [ˈdʒækɪ]
Jane [dʒeɪn]
Janet [ˈdʒænet]
Jennifer [ˈdʒenɪfə]
Jenny [ˈdʒenɪ]
Jill [dʒɪl]
Jo-Ann [dʒəʊˈæn]
Joanne [dʒəʊˈæn]

Julia [ˈdʒuːljə]
Julie [ˈdʒuːlɪ]
Katherine [ˈkæθrɪn]
Kathleen [ˈkæθliːn]
Kati [ˈkeɪtɪ]
Katie [ˈkeɪtɪ]
Kiki [ˈkɪkɪ]
Kim [kɪm]
Kirsty [ˈkɜːstɪ]
Kristina [krɪsˈtiːnə]
Laura [ˈlɔːrə]
Leia [ˈliːə]
Lene [ˈleɪnə]
Lesley [ˈlezlɪ]
Letty [ˈletɪ]
Lila [ˈlaɪlə]
Linda [ˈlɪndə]
Lindy [ˈlɪndɪ]
Linh [lɪn]
Lisa [ˈliːzə]
Louise [luːˈiːz]
Lucy [ˈluːsɪ]
Lulu [ˈluːluː]
Mallory [ˈmælərɪ]
Mandy [ˈmændɪ]
Mareijka [məˈreɪkə]
Margie [ˈmɑːdʒɪ]
Maria [məˈriːə]
Marsha [ˈmɑːʃə]
Mary [ˈmeərɪ]
Meike [ˈmeɪkə]
Nandita [nænˈdiːtə]
Nathalie [ˈnætəlɪ]
Nikki [ˈnɪkɪ]
Pamela [ˈpæmələ]
Pat [pæt]
Patricia [pəˈtrɪʃə]
Penny [ˈpenɪ]
Pia [ˈpɪə]
Rachel [ˈreɪtʃəl]
Rosalind [ˈrɒzəlɪnd]
Rosie [ˈrəʊzɪ]
Sally [ˈsælɪ]
Sammia [ˈsæmjə]
Sarah [ˈseərə]
Shandi [ˈʃændɪ]
Sharra [ˈʃærə]
Sheena [ˈʃiːnə]
Sheila [ˈʃiːlə]
Sonia [ˈsɒnjə]
Stacey [ˈsteɪsɪ]
Sue [suː]
Susan [ˈsuːzn]
Svenja [ˈsvenjə]
Tatiana [ˌtætɪˈɑːnə]
Tootsie [ˈtʊtsɪ]
Tracey [ˈtreɪsɪ]
Trudy [ˈtruːdɪ]
Val [væl]
Vicky [ˈvɪkɪ]
Wendy [ˈwendɪ]
Yasmin [jæsˈmiːn]
Zoe [ˈzəʊɪ]

Surnames

Alexander [ˌælɪgˈzɑːndə]
Anderson [ˈændəsn]
Barber [ˈbɑːbə]
Barker [ˈbɑːkə]
Barnes [bɑːnz]
Baxter [ˈbækstə]
Bennett [ˈbenɪt]
Benson [ˈbensn]
Bettingham [ˈbetɪŋəm]
Bradley [ˈbrædlɪ]
Brown [braʊn]
Burton [ˈbɜːtn]
Carpenter [ˈkɑːpəntə]
Castle [ˈkɑːsl]
Chowdury [ˈtʃaʊdrɪ]
Clausell [ˈklɔːzəl]
Collin [ˈkɒlɪn]
⟨Columbus⟩ [kɒˈlʌmbəs]
Croft [krɒft]
Cromwell [ˈkrɒmwəl]
Dane [deɪn]
Davis [ˈdeɪvɪs]
Dixon [ˈdɪksn]
Dodd [dɒd]
Evans [ˈevənz]
Farelli [fæˈrelɪ]
Ferraro [fəˈrɑːrəʊ]
Fisher [ˈfɪʃə]
Foster [ˈfɒstə]
Frazer [ˈfreɪzə]
Garner [ˈgɑːnə]
Greenwood [ˈgriːnwʊd]
Guntrie [ˈgʌntrɪ]
Hancox [ˈhæŋkɒks]
Harding [ˈhɑːdɪŋ]
Hayes [heɪz]
Hooper [ˈhuːpə]
Jenkins [ˈdʒenkɪnz]
Jones [dʒəʊnz]
Lambert [ˈlæmbət]
Lewinsky [ləˈwɪnskɪ]
Maclean [məˈkleɪn]
Match [mætʃ]
McAllister [məˈkælɪstə]
Monroe [mənˈrəʊ]
Murdstone [ˈmɜːdstəʊn]
Murray [ˈmʌrɪ]
Narayan [ˈnærəjæn]
Nazeer [nəˈzɪə]
Nixon [ˈnɪksn]
Olesen [ˈɒlezən]
Ortiz [ɔːˈtiːz]
Parker [ˈpɑːkə]
Penrose [ˈpenrəʊz]
Peters [ˈpiːtəz]
Philips [ˈfɪlɪps]
Pinday [ˈpɪndeɪ]
Pokorney [pəˈkɔːnɪ]
Porter [ˈpɔːtə]
Powell [ˈpaʊəl]
Prigg [prɪg]
Purdie [ˈpɜːdɪ]

Queredo [kweˈreɪdəʊ]
Quinion [ˈkwɪnjən]
Richards [ˈrɪtʃədz]
Richardson [ˈrɪtʃədsn]
Ridgeway [ˈrɪdʒweɪ]
Roberts [ˈrɒbəts]
Rosco [ˈrɒskəʊ]
Sanders [ˈsændəs]
Singer [ˈsɪŋə]
Sitaram [ˈsɪtærəm]
Smith [smɪθ]
Stevens [ˈstiːvnz]
Tompkins [ˈtɒmkɪnz]
Velardi [vəˈlɑːdɪ]
Voyance [ˈvɔɪəns]
Wang [wæŋ]
Williams [ˈwɪljəmz]
Wilson [ˈwɪlsn]
Winters [ˈwɪntəs]
Wright [raɪt]

Geographical names

Africa [ˈæfrɪkə]
Ala. (= Alabama) [ˌæləˈbæmə]
Alabama [ˌæləˈbæmə]
⟨Alaska⟩ [əˈlæskə]
Alassio [əˈlæsɪəʊ]
Alice Springs [ˌælɪs ˈsprɪŋz]
Alligator River [ˈælɪgeɪtə ˈrɪvə]
America [əˈmerɪkə]
Arizona [ˌærɪˈzəʊnə]
⟨Arkansas⟩ [ˈɑːkənsɔː]
Arndale Road [ˌɑːndeɪl ˈrəʊd]
Arnot Hill Park [ˌɑːnət hɪl ˈpɑːk]
Asia [ˈeɪʃə]
Australia [ɒˈstreɪljə]
Austria [ˈɒstrɪə]
Baker Street [ˈbeɪkə striːt]
Bakerloo Line [ˈbeɪkəluː laɪn]
Barrow-in-Furness [ˌbærəʊˌɪn ˈfɜːnɪs]
Berlin [bɜːˈlɪn]
Big Ben [bɪg ˈben]
Blackpool [ˈblækpuːl]
Bournemouth [ˈbɔːnməθ]
Bradford [ˈbrædfəd]
Brazil [brəˈzɪl]
Bristol [ˈbrɪstl]
Britain [ˈbrɪtn]
Bromley [ˈbrɒmlɪ]
Bromley Place [ˌbrɒmlɪ ˈpleɪs]
Buckingham Palace [ˌbʌkɪŋhəm ˈpælɪs]
Ca. (= California) [ˌkælɪˈfɔːnjə]
California [ˌkælɪˈfɔːnjə]
Calle Ocho [ˌkæje ˈɒtʃəʊ]
Camden [ˈkæmdən]
Camden Market [ˌkæmdən ˈmɑːkɪt]
Camden Town [ˌkæmdən ˈtaʊn]
Canada [ˈkænədə]
Canberra [ˈkænbərə]
Canterbury [ˈkæntəbərɪ]

the Caribbean [ˌkærɪˈbiːən]
Castle Boulevard [ˌkɑːsl ˈbuːləvɑːd]
Castle Gate [kɑːsl ˈgeɪt]
Castle Museum [ˌkɑːsl mjuːˈzɪəm]
Castle Road [kɑːsl ˈrəʊd]
Chicago [ʃɪˈkɑːgəʊ]
China [ˈtʃaɪnə]
⟨Chris Colón⟩ [krɪs kɒˈlɒn]
Co. (= Colorado) [ˌkɒləˈrɑːdəʊ]
Cobar [ˈkəʊbɑː]
Colchester [ˈkɒltʃɪstə]
Collin Street [ˈkɒlɪn striːt]
Cologne [kəˈləʊn]
Colorado [ˌkɒləˈrɑːdəʊ]
Coltswood Terrace [ˈkəʊltswʊd ˈterəs]
Coniston [ˈkɒnɪstən]
Costume Museum [ˈkɒstjuːm mjuːˌzɪəm]
Crewe Road [kruːˈrəʊd]
Cromwell Road [ˈkrɒmwel ˈrəʊd]
Cumberland [ˈkʌmbələnd]
Cumberland Place [ˌkʌmbələnd ˈpleɪs]
Denmark [ˈdenmɑːk]
Dinosaur National Monument [ˈdaɪnəsɔː næʃnl ˈmɒnjʊmənt]
Docklands [ˈdɒkləndz]
Dover [ˈdəʊvə]
Dublin [ˈdʌblɪn]
Durango [dʊˈræŋgəʊ]
Edwards Lane [ˌedwədz ˈleɪn]
Embankment [ɪmˈbæŋkmənt]
Empire State Building [ˌempaɪə steɪt ˈbɪldɪŋ]
England [ˈɪŋglənd]
Essex [ˈesɪks]
Europe [ˈjʊərəp]
Exclose Lane [ˌeksklaʊs ˈleɪn]
Exeter [ˈeksətə]
Falls Church [ˌfɒls tʃɜːtʃ]
° Fantasy Land [ˈfæntəsɪ ˌlænd]
Flagstaff Park [ˈflægstɑːf ˈpɑːk]
Flagstaff Road [ˈflægstɑːf ˈrəʊd]
Florida [ˈflɒrɪdə]
France [frɑːns]
Frankfurt [ˈfræŋkfət]
Fresno [ˈfreznəʊ]
Friar Lane [fraɪə ˈleɪn]
Germany [ˈdʒɜːmənɪ]
Glasgow [ˈglɑːzgəʊ]
Grand Junction [grænd ˈdʒʌŋtʃən]
Green Park [griːn ˈpɑːk]
Gretna Green [ˌgretnə ˈgriːn]
Haldens [ˈhɔːldnz]
Hamburg [ˈhæmbɜːg]
Harrisburg [ˈhærɪsbɜːg]
Hillcrest [ˈhɪlkrest]
Hollywood [ˈhɒlɪwʊd]
Huntsville [ˈhʌntsvɪl]
Ill. (= Illinois) [ɪlɪˈnɔɪ]
⟨India⟩ [ˈɪndɪə]
⟨Ireland⟩ [ˈaɪələnd]
Italy [ˈɪtəlɪ]

⟨Jackie Robinson⟩ [ˌdʒækɪ ˈrɒbɪnsən]
Jamaica [dʒəˈmeɪkə]
Japan [dʒəˈpæn]
° Kakadu National Park [ˈkækədu: ˌnæʃnl ˈpɑːk]
Kalispell [ˈkælɪspel]
Kendal [ˈkendəl]
Keswick [ˈkezɪk]
King's Reach Tower [kɪŋz riːtʃ ˈtaʊə]
L.A. (= Los Angeles) [lɒsˌˈændʒɪliːz]
the Lake District [ˈleɪk dɪstrɪkt]
Larwood Grove [ˌlɑːwʊd ˈgrəʊv]
Latin America ! [ˈlætɪnˌəˈmerɪkə]
Lawson Street [ˈlɔːsən striːt]
Lister Gate [lɪstə ˈgeɪt]
⟨Little Rock⟩ [lɪtl ˈrɒk]
Liverpool [ˈlɪvəpuːl]
London [ˈlʌndən]
London Dungeon [ˌlʌndən ˈdʌnʒn]
Long Beach [lɒŋ ˈbiːtʃ]
Long Row [lɒŋ ˈrəʊ]
Long Row West [ˌlɒŋ rəʊ ˈwest]
Low Pavement [ˌləʊ ˈpeɪvmənt]
° Lyon [ljɔ̃]
Madame Tussaud's [ˌmædəm təˈsɔːdz]
Madrid [məˈdrɪd]
Maid Marian Way [meɪd ˌmærɪən ˈweɪ]
Majorca [məˈdʒɔːkə]
Manchester [ˈmæntʃɪstə]
Manhattan [mænˈhætn]
Mansfield Road [ˌmænsfiːld ˈrəʊd]
McGucken Park [məˌgʊkən ˈpɑːk]
Mesa Verde National Park [mesa ˌvɜːdə næʃnl ˈpɑːk]
Mexico [ˈmeksɪkəʊ]
MGM Cinema [emdʒɪˈem ˈsɪnəmə]
Middle Hill [mɪdl ˈhɪl]
Milan [mɪˈlæn]
Mississippi [ˌmɪsɪˈsɪpɪ]
Montana [mɒnˈtænə]
Mount Street [ˈmaʊnt ˌstriːt]
Nebraska [nɪˈbræskə]
New York City [njuː jɔːk ˈsɪtɪ]
New Zealand [ˌnjuːˈziːlənd]
North London [nɔːθ ˈlʌndən]
the North of England [nɔːθˌ əv ˈɪŋglənd]
Northern Line [ˈnɔːðn laɪn]
Notting Hill Gate [ˌnɒtɪŋ hɪl ˈgeɪt]
Nottingham [ˈnɒtɪŋəm]
Nottingham Road [ˌnɒtɪŋəm ˈrəʊd]
N.Y. (= New York) [ˌnjuːˈjɔːk]
Odeon Cinema [ˌəʊdɪən ˈsɪnəmə]
Oxclose Lane [ˌɒksləʊs ˈleɪn]
Oxford Circus [ˌɒksfəd ˈsɜːkəs]
Oxford Street [ˈɒksfəd striːt]
Pacific Avenue [pəˌsɪfɪkˌˈævənjuː]
Paddington [ˈpædɪŋtən]
Pakistan [ˌpɑːkɪˈstɑːn]
Paris [ˈpærɪs]

Dictionary

Park Row [pɑːk 'rəʊ]
Parkway City Mall [,pɑːkweɪ sɪti 'mɔːl]
Pennsylvania (P.A.) [,pensɪl'veɪnjə]
Penrith ['penrɪθ]
Piccadilly [,pɪkə'dɪli]
Potrero Hill [pɒ'treərəʊ ,hɪl]
Queensland ['kwiːnzlənd]
Richmond Park [,rɪtʃmənd 'pɑːk]
River Thames [,rɪvə 'temz]
Riverside Junior High School [,rɪvəsaɪd dʒuːnjə 'haɪ skuːl]
Rochester ['rɒtʃɪstə]
Rock Circus [rɒk 'sɜːkəs]
Rocky Mountains [,rɒkɪ 'maʊntɪnz]
⟨Rosa Parks⟩ [,rəʊsə 'pɑːks]
Rufford Road [,rʌfəd 'rəʊd]
Russia ['rʌʃə]
Salamanca [,sælə'mæŋkə]
San Diego [sæn dɪ'eɪgəʊ]
San Francisco [sæn fræn'sɪskəʊ]
San Jose [sæn ,həʊ'zeɪ]
Sandringham House [,sændrɪŋəm 'haʊs]
Scotland ['skɒtlənd]
Sherwood ['ʃɜːwʊd]
Silverton ['sɪlvətən]
⟨South Africa⟩ [,saʊθ 'æfrɪkə]
South Parade [,saʊθ pə'reɪd]
Southend [,saʊθ'end]
Spain [speɪn]
St. James's Terrace [snt ,dʒeɪmzɪz 'terɪs]
St. Nicholas Church [snt ,nɪkələs 'tʃɜːtʃ]
St. Peter's Church [snt ,piːtəz 'tʃɜːtʃ]
St. Peter's Gate [snt ,piːtəz 'geɪt]
Stamford Street ['stæmfəd striːt]
Swansea ['swɒnzi]
Sydney ['sɪdnɪ]
⟨Sydney Cove⟩ [,sɪdnɪ 'kəʊv]
Tales of Robin Hood [,teɪlz ˌəv ˌrɒbɪn 'hʊd]
Taunton Way [,tɔːntən 'weɪ]
Texas ['teksəs]
Toronto [tə'rɒntəʊ]
Tourist Information Centre [,tʊərɪst ˌɪnfə'meɪʃn ˌsentə]
Tower Bridge [taʊə 'brɪdʒ]
Tower Hill [taʊə 'hɪl]
Tower of London [,taʊə ˌəv 'lʌndən]
UK (=United Kingdom) [juː'naɪtɪd ˌkɪŋdəm]
U.S.A. [juːes'eɪ]
Van Diemen's Land [væn 'diːmnz lænd]
Venice ['venɪs]
Verona [ve'rəʊnə]
Virginia [vɜː'dʒɪnɪə]
Wales [weɪlz]
Waterford ['wɔːtəfəd]
Westminster ['westmɪnstə]
Wheeler Gate [,wiːlə 'geɪt]

Whitby Harbour [,wɪtbɪ 'hɑːbə]
Whitehaven ['waɪtheɪvn]
Wimbledon ['wɪmbldn]
Windermere ['wɪndəmɪə]
Woodthorpe Grange Park [,wʊdθɔːp greɪndʒ 'pɑːk]
Woodthorpe Road [,wʊdθɔːp 'rəʊd]
World Trade Center [,wɜːld 'treɪd sentə]
Wyomimg [waɪ'əʊmɪŋ]
York [jɔːk]
the Yorkshire Moors [,jɔːkʃə 'mɔːz]

Other names

Aborigine [æbə'rɪdʒəniː]
°Ace Club ['eɪs klʌb]
American Adventure [ə,merɪkən əd'ventʃə]
Angela Bennett ['ændʒələ 'benɪt]
Ann M. Martin ['æn ˌem 'mɑːtɪn]
Annalena McAfee [ænə'liːnə 'mækəfi:]
⟨Armada⟩ [ɑː'mɑːdə]
Arnold Schwarzenegger ['ɑːnld 'ʃwɑːtsnegə]
Arsenal ['ɑːsənl]
Barbie ['bɑːbɪ]
°Benwood School ['benwʊd ,skuːl]
⟨Billy Bragg⟩ [,bɪlɪ 'bræg]
Biscuit ['bɪskɪt]
Blue Moon Cafe [,bluː muːn 'kæfeɪ]
Bonzo ['bɒnzəʊ]
Brighton Middle School [,braɪtn 'mɪdl skuːl]
Bruce Willis ['bruːs 'wɪlɪs]
Camden Allstars [,kæmdn 'ɔːlstɑːs]
Captain Cook ['kæptɪn 'kʊk]
Catford Cannons [,kætfəd 'kænəns]
Catford Gazette [,kætfəd gə'zet]
C.D. Spearman ['spɪəmən]
Center Radio [,sentə 'reɪdɪəʊ]
Central Hollywood Junior High [sentrl ,hɒlɪwʊd dʒuːnjə 'haɪ]
Central Library [,sentrl 'laɪbrərɪ]
Chad Forward ['tʃæd 'fɔːwəd]
Challenger Middle School [,tʃælɪndʒə 'mɪdl skuːl]
°Challenger Space Shuttle ['tʃælɪndʒə 'speɪs ʃʌtl]
Changing of the Guard [,tʃeɪndʒɪŋ ˌəv ðə 'gɑːd]
Chat Radio London [tʃæt ˌreɪdɪəʊ 'lʌndən]
Christa McAuliffe ['krɪstə mək ˌ'ɔːlɪf]
Chronicle Herald Sun [,krɒnɪkl 'herəld sʌn]
Circle Line ['sɜːkl laɪn]
Civil Rights Act [sɪvl 'raɪts ˌækt]
Clifton Middle School [,klɪftn 'mɪdl skuːl]

Clinton ['klɪntən]
Crocodile Dundee ['krɒkədaɪl dʌn'diː]
David Copperfield ['deɪvɪd 'kɒpəfiːld]
⟨Declaration of Independence⟩ [deklə'reɪʃn ˌəv ɪndɪ'pendəns]
Demi Moore ['demɪ 'mɔː]
Dennis Miller ['denɪs 'mɪlə]
Denny's ['deniːz]
Department of Motor Vehicles [dɪ'pɑːtmənt ˌəv 'məʊtə 'vɪəklz]
District Line ['dɪstrɪkt laɪn]
DIY Direct [,diː aɪ waɪ daɪ'rekt]
⟨Donna Summer⟩ [,dɒnə 'sʌmə]
Dr Champion ['dɒktə 'tʃæmpjən]
⟨Drake⟩ [dreɪk]
°Dum-Dum plant ['dʌm dʌm ,plɑːnt]
Eagle Quest [iːgl 'kwest]
Elizabeth II (the Second) [ɪ,lɪzəbəθ ðə 'seknd]
Felix ['fiːlɪks]
Flying Doctor Service [flaɪɪŋ 'dɒktə ˌsɜːvɪs]
⟨Gary Moore⟩ [gærɪ 'mʊə]
⟨Great Famine⟩ [greɪt 'fæmɪn]
Harley Davidson ['hɑːlɪ 'deɪvɪdsn]
Haywood School ['heɪwʊd ˌskuːl]
Heartline ['hɑːtlaɪn]
Help the Aged [help ðiː ˌ'eɪdʒɪd]
Homecoming Dance ['həʊm ˌkʌmɪŋ dɑːns]
Homecoming Week ['həʊm ˌkʌmɪŋ wiːk]
Homestead Hotel [,həʊmsted həʊ'tel]
⟨Industrial Revolution⟩ [ɪn'dʌstrɪəl revə'luːʃən]
Isaac Asimov ['aɪsek 'æsɪməf]
Jack Devlin [dʒæk 'devlɪn]
James Dean [,dʒeɪmz 'diːn]
Jason Crazy [,dʒeɪsn 'kreɪzɪ]
Jeremy Norton [,dʒerəmɪ 'nɔːtn]
Johnny Depp [,dʒɒnɪ 'dep]
Judy Blume [,dʒuːdɪ 'bluːm]
Just Jeans [dʒʌst 'dʒiːnz]
Kindergarten Cop ['kɪndəgɑːtn 'kɒp]
⟨King Philip⟩ [kɪŋ 'fɪlɪp]
Lakeside High [,leɪksaɪd 'haɪ]
Langston Hughes [,læŋstən 'hjuːz]
Larry Liar ['lærɪ 'laɪə]
Last Action Hero ['lɑːst ˌækʃn 'hɪərəʊ]
Letty Chubb [,letɪ 'tʃʌb]
Liana [lɪ'ɑːnə]
the London Underground [,lʌndən ˌ'ʌndəgraʊnd]
Mania ['meɪnjə]
Marks and Spencer [,mɑːks ˌənd 'spensə]
Martin Luther King [,mɑːtɪn luːθə 'kɪŋ]
Maxi ['mæksɪ]

Dictionary

⟨**Melba Pattillo Beals**⟩ [ˈmelbə ˌpəˈtɪləʊ biːls]
Metallica [meˈtælɪkə]
Midnight Oil [ˌmɪdnaɪt ˈɔɪl]
MIZZ [mɪz]
Monny [ˈmɒnɪ]
Motor Museum [ˈməʊtə mjuːˌzɪəm]
Mountain Rescue [ˌmaʊntɪn ˈreskjuː]
Mr Fixit [ˌmɪstə ˈfɪksɪt]
Nazeer's Discount [nəˈzɪəz ˈdɪskaʊnt]
Notting Hill Carnival [ˌnɒtɪŋ hɪl ˈkɑːnɪvl]
Old Smith [ˌəʊld ˈsmɪθ]
Olly [ˈɒlɪ]
Park Foot Trekking [ˌpɑːk ˈfʊtˌtrekɪŋ]
Paul Hogan [ˈpɔːl ˈhəʊgn]
⟨**Pet Shop Boys**⟩ [ˈpet ʃɒp bɔɪz]
⟨**President Clinton**⟩ [ˌprezɪdənt ˈklɪntən]
°**Radio Nottingham** [ˌreɪdɪəʊ ˈnɒtɪŋəm]
Real Life Radio [ˌrɪəl laɪf ˈreɪdɪəʊ]
Redbridge Secondary School [ˈredbrɪdʒ ˈsekəndrɪ skuːl]

Ritchie McMadd [ˌrɪtʃɪ məkˈmæd]
Robin Hood [ˌrɒbɪn ˈhʊd]
Ronald Keen [ˌrɒnəld ˈkiːn]
Rookin House Farm [ˌrʊkɪn haʊs ˈfɑːm]
Ros Asquith [ˌrɒz ˈæskwɪθ]
Ruth Marx [ˌruːθ ˈmɑːks]
Sandra Bullock [ˈsændrə ˈbʊlək]
School of the Air [ˈskuːl əv ðɪ ˈeə]
7C [sevən ˈsiː]
the **Sheriff of Nottingham** [ˈʃerɪf]
Sherlock Holmes [ˌʃɜːlɒk ˈhəʊmz]
Signor Santoni [siːnˈjɔː sænˈtəʊnɪ]
Signora Nencini [siːnˈjɔːrə nenˈtʃiːnɪ]
Silver City [ˌsɪlvə ˈsɪtɪ]
Starlight Express [ˌstɑːlaɪt ɪkˈspres]
°**Starship 7** [ˌstɑːʃɪp ˈsevn]
Superfudge [ˈsuːpəfʌdʒ]
Superman [ˈsuːpəmæn]
Sylvester Stallone [sɪlˌvestə stəˈləʊn]
Tetra [ˈtetrə]
The Band [ðə ˈbænd]
The Righteous Brothers [ðə ˈraɪtʃəs ˌbrʌðəz]

Thorsten Grothe [ˈtɔːstn ˈgrəʊtə]
Tiddles [ˈtɪdlz]
Tiger [ˈtaɪgə]
Tina Goodnow [ˌtiːnə ˈgʊdnəʊ]
Toby Sweet [ˌtəʊbɪ ˈswiːt]
⟨**Tracy Chapman**⟩ [ˌtreɪsɪ ˈtʃæpmən]
⟨**Triangular Trade**⟩ [traɪˈæŋgjʊlə treɪd]
TV Times [tiːviː ˈtaɪmz]
Under 16s [ˈʌndə ˌsɪksˈtiːnz]
United [jʊˈnaɪtɪd]
United States Space and Rocket Center [juːˌnaɪtɪd steɪts speɪs ənd ˈrɒkɪt sentə]
U.S. Mail [juː es ˈmeɪl]
U16s [ˈʌndə ˌsɪksˈtiːnz]
⟨**Valentine's Day**⟩ [ˈvæləntaɪnz deɪ]
Victoria Centre [vɪkˈtɒrɪə ˌsentə]
°**Viking Centre** [ˈvaɪkɪŋ ˌsentə]
4WD = four-wheel drive [ˌfɔːwiːl ˈdraɪv]
⟨**William the Conqueror**⟩ [ˈwɪljəm ðə ˈkɒŋkərə]
Willy Shironsky [ˈwɪlɪ ʃɪˈrɒnskɪ]

DICTIONARY (GERMAN-ENGLISH)

A

abbiegen to turn
abbrennen to burn down
Abend evening, night *(Ausgang)*
heute Abend tonight
Abendessen dinner
Abenteuer adventure
aber but
Abfall waste
abfliegen to fly off
Abflug take-off
in Flaschen abfüllen to bottle
Abgase fumes
abhalten to stop
Abhang slope
abhängen von to depend on
abhauen to run away *(wegrennen)*; to get lost *(schimpfen)*
abholen to collect
Abkürzung abbreviation
abnehmen to lift *(Telefonhörer)*; to take off *(Hut)*
abprallen to bounce off
Absatz paragraph
abschicken to post
Abschluss certificate *(Prüfung)*
Abschnitt paragraph
abschreiben to copy
Abstimmung vote
absturzen to crash
Abwasch washing up
abwaschen to do the washing up *(spülen)*; to wash off
zur Abwechslung for a change
einen Schuss abwehren to make a save *(Fußball)*
Abwesenheit absence
acht eight
achte/r/s eighth
Achterbahn roller coaster
achtzehn eighteen
achtzig eighty
addieren to add
Adjektiv adjective
Adresse address
Adverb adverb
Afrika Africa
Agent agent
Agentur agency
aggressiv aggressive
Ähnlichkeit resemblance
Ahnung clue
keine Ahnung no idea
Aktivität activity
aktualisieren to update
aktuell latest
albern silly
Alkohol alcohol
alkoholfrei soft *(Getränk)*
alkoholisch alcoholic
alle all, everybody, everyone
alle anderen everyone else
alle Arten von every kind of
allein alone
Alleinerziehende/r single parent

das Allerletzte the pits
der/die/das allerletzte the very last
alles all, everything
Alligator alligator
Alltags- everyday
Alphabet alphabet
alphabetisch alphabetical
als as; when; than
mehr als more than
als Erste/r/s first
als Nächste/r/s next
als ob as if
also so; well, …
alt old
wie alt how old
die Alten the aged
Alter age
Alternative alternative
Altglascontainer bottle bank
Aludose can
am Ende by the end
am Morgen in the morning
am Samstag on Saturday
am Wochenende at the weekend
Amerika America
Amerikaner/in American
amerikanisch American
denken an to think of, to think about
an Bord on board
Rücken an Rücken back to back
an Stelle von instead of
an … vorbei past
anbieten to offer
Anblick sight
andere other, others
die anderen the others
anderer Meinung sein to disagree
ändern to change
anders different
Anfang beginning, start
jdm. mit dem Anfang helfen to start sb. off
anfangen to begin, to start; to have a go *(den Anfang wagen)*
Angebot offer
angehören to join
Angelegenheit matter
Angewohnheit habit
angezogen dressed
angreifen to attack
Angst haben to be afraid, to be scared
ängstlich afraid
anhalten to stop
Anhänger pendant *(Schmuck)*; trailer *(Wagen)*
anhören to listen (to)
anklopfen to knock
ankommen to arrive; to land *(Flugzeug)*
Anlage equipment *(elektronisch)*
anmachen to turn on
jdn. anmachen to chat sb. up *(flirten)*
Anmeldeformular registration form

Anmeldung registration
annehmen to guess, to suppose
Anorak anorak
Anruf (telephone) call
einen Anruf tätigen to make a telephone call
Anrufbeantworter answering machine
anrufen to call, to phone, to ring
Anrufer/in caller
ans Telefon gehen to answer the phone
anschauen to look at
Anschrift address
ansehen to have a look, to look at; to watch *(Fernsehen, Spiel)*
Ansicht sight
Anspitzer pencil sharpener
ansprechen to contact
anstarren to gaze at, to stare
anstatt instead of
anstellen to turn on *(Gerät)*
anstreichen to paint
Anstrich paint
Antwort answer, reply
antworten to answer, to reply
Antwortmail remail
Anwender/in user
Anwesenheitskontrolle Registration
Anzeige ad (= advertisement)
Anzeigetafel noticeboard
anziehen to put on, to wear; to pull on *(Stiefel)*
anzünden to light
Apfel apple
April April
Arbeit work, job
arbeiten to work
Arbeiter/in worker
Arbeitsanzug overalls
Arbeitskleidung working clothes
arbeitslos unemployed
Arbeitslosigkeit unemployment
Arbeitsplatz working place
Arbeittstag working day
Arbeitszimmer study
Ärger trouble
ärgerlich angry
Argument argument
Arm arm
arm poor
Armbanduhr watch
Armut poverty
Art way *(wie etwas gemacht wird)*; kind, sort, type
Artikel article
Arzt/Ärztin doctor
beim Arzt at the doctor's
Arzthelferin receptionist
Asiat/in Asian
asiatisch Asian
Asien Asia
Asphalt asphalt
Athletik athletics
Atmosphäre atmosphere
attraktiv attractive

Dictionary

auch also, too
kann auch nicht can't ..., either
auch keine Jobs no jobs either
auch wenn even if
auf onto; upon; on; at
auf ... zu towards
auf dem neuesten Stand up to date
auf dem Weg on the way
auf den Kopf gestellt upside down
auf der Bühne on stage
Auf die Plätze ... On your marks ...
auf diese Art that way
auf einmal at a time
auf Englisch in English
auf jdn. zukommen to come up to sb.
auf jeden Fall anyway
auf Urlaub on holiday
auf Wiedersehen! Goodbye!
aufbewahren to keep
lange aufbleiben to stay up late
aufblicken to look up
aufführen to perform
Auffüllen der Regale shelf-filling
Aufgabe job, task
aufgeben to give up
aufgeregt excited
aufgeschlossen open-minded
aufhalten to stop
aufheben to pick up
aufholen to catch up with
aufhören to end, to finish
aufkleben to stick on
Aufkleber sticker
aufladen to charge
auflisten to list
aufmachen to open
aufmuntern to cheer up
Aufnahmetermin recording session
aufnehmen to record
Kontakt aufnehmen to contact
aufpassen auf to look after
aufräumen to clean up
aufregend exciting
Aufregung drama
aufschlagen to turn to *(Seite)*
aufschließen to unlock
aufschreiben to note down
aufstehen to get up, to stand up
aufsteigen to get on *(Bus)*
aufstellen to put up, to set up
aufwachen to wake up
aufwachsen to grow up
aufwecken to wake up
Auge eye
Augenblick moment
im Augenblick at the moment
in diesem Augenblick at that moment
August August
Auktion auction
Auktionator/in auctioneer
Aula (assembly) hall
aus from
aus irgendeinem Grund for any reason

aus ... heraus out of
ausbrechen to break out
ausdenken to think of
Ausdruck expression, phrase
ausdrucken to print out
Auseinandersetzung argument
ausfallen to fail
Ausflug trip
ausführlich full
Ausgang ending *(Geschichte)*; a night out *(freier Abend)*
ausgeben to spend *(Geld)*
mit jdm. ausgehen to go out with sb.
ausgezeichnet excellent
aushängen to put up
aushelfen to help out
miteinander auskommen to get on with each other
Ausländer/in foreigner
ausländisch foreign
ausleihen to borrow
ausliefern to deliver
Auslieferung delivery
ausmachen to arrange *(Termin)*
ausprobieren to try out
ausrauben to rob
jdm. etwas ausreden to talk sb. out of sth.
Ausreißer/in runaway
ausrüsten to equip
Ausrüstung equipment
Aussage statement
ausschalten to turn off
ausschneiden to cut out
aussehen (wie) to look (like)
Außenseiter/in outsider
Außenbordmotor outboard motor
außer but, except
Äußere outside
außerhalb outside
Außerirdische/r alien
Aussicht view
Ich kann ... nicht ausstehen. I can't stand ...
aussteigen to get off
aussuchen to choose, to pick
Austausch exchange
austeilen to deliver
austragen to deliver
Australien Australia
Australier/in Australian
auswählen to choose, to decide on, to pick
auswechseln to take off *(Spieler)*
Ausweis pass, identity card
Ausweispapiere identification
ausziehen to move out *(Wohnung)*; to take off *(Kleidung)*
Auszubildende/r trainee
Auto car
Autobahn motorway
Autogramm autograph
Automat machine
automatisch automatic

B

Baby baby
Babysitter/in baby-sitter
Babysitting baby-sitting
Bäcker baker
Badewanne bath
Badezimmer bathroom
Bahn lane *(Aufteilung des Schwimmbeckens)*; length *(Schwimmstrecke)*
Bahnhof station
Bahnsteig platform
bald soon
Balkon balcony
Ball ball; ball *(Tanz)*
einen Ball schießen to kick
Ballabwehr save
Ballett ballet
Ballonfahren ballooning
Ballonfahrt flight
Band volume *(Buch)*
Bandaufnahme tape
Bande band, gang
Banjo banjo
Bank bank
Bankangestellte/r bank clerk
Bankkarte cash card
Bar bar
Bär bear
Barbiepuppe Barbie doll
Barkeeper barman
Barriere barrier
Bart beard
Basar sale
Baseball baseball
Baseballplatz ball park
Basketball basketball
Bassgitarre bass guitar
Batterie battery
bauen to build
Bauer farmer
Bauernhof farm
Baum tree
Baumaschinenvermietung plant hire
Baustelle building site
Beamter/-tin official
beantworten to answer
Becken pool
(etwas) bedauern to feel sorry (about sth.)
bedecken to cover
bedeuten to mean
Bedeutung meaning
Bedingung condition
bedrohen to threaten
sich beeilen to hurry (up)
beenden to end, to finish
befragen to interview
befriedigen to satisfy
Begierde desire
Beginn beginning, start
beginnen to begin, to start
begrüßen to welcome
behalten to keep

Dictionary

Behälter container
behandeln to treat
behaupten to claim
beherrschen to take over
behindert disabled
bei at
mitmachen bei to join
Wie ist es bei dir? What about you?
bei der Arbeit at work
beibringen to teach
beide both
beige cream
beim Arzt at the doctor's
Bein leg
beinahe nearly
Beispiel example
zum Beispiel for example
bejahend positive
bekommen to get
Belgien Belgium
beliebt popular
bellen to bark
Belohnung reward
bemerken to notice
benoten to mark
benötigen to require
benutzen to use
Benzin petrol
bequem comfortable
Berater/in consultant
Berg hill *(klein)*, mountain *(groß)*
Bergwacht Mountain Rescue
Bericht article, report
berichten to report, to tell
über etwas berichten to report
berichtigen to correct
Bernhardiner St. Bernard *(Hund)*
berufliche Laufbahn career
Berufsberater/in careers officer
sich beruhigen to calm down
berühmt famous
Berühmtheit star
berühren to touch
beschädigen to damage
beschäftigt busy
Beschäftigung activity
beschimpfen to call sb. names
beschreiben to describe
Beschreibung description
beschriften to label
beschützen to protect
beseitigen to remove
besetzt busy
besitzen to own
Besitzer/in owner
besondere/r/s special
besser better
in etwas besser werden to get better at sth.
beste/r/s best, top
bestellen to order
bestimmt certain, sure
Besuch visit
besuchen to visit
Besucher/in visitor
Beton concrete

Betonmischer cement mixer
betont stressed
Betonung stress
Sport betreiben to do sports
betrogen cheated
betrunken drunk
Bett bed
ins Bett bringen to take to bed
ins Bett gehen to go to bed
beunruhigt worried
Beutel bag
Bevölkerung population
bevor before
bewegen to move
Bewegung action, movement
sich bewerben to apply
Bewunderung admiration
bezahlen to pay
Bezahlung pay
bezaubernd adorable
Beziehung relationship
Bier beer
Bierdeckel beer mat
Bikini bikini
Bild picture; image *(Vorstellung)*
bilden to form
Bilderbuch picture book
Bildschirm screen
Bildung education
billig cheap
binden to tie up
Bindewort connecting word
Biologie Biology
bis before; by; till, until
Bis bald! See you later!, See you soon!, See you there!
bis dahin by then
bis dann by then
Bis dann! See you there!
bis jetzt so far
ein bisschen a bit
bitte please
bitten um to ask for
bitter bitter
Blase bubble *(Luft, Seife)*
Blatt/Blätter leaf/leaves
Blatt Papier sheet of paper
Blattsalat lettuce
blau blue
blauäugig blue-eyed
Blechdose can
Bleib ruhig! Take it easy! *(ugs.)*
bleiben to stay
stecken bleiben to get stuck
stehen bleiben to stop short
Bleistift pencil
Bleistiftspitzer pencil sharpener
Blick look
(Häuser)block block
blöd silly
Blödsinn rubbish
blond blond, fair
bloß just
Blume flower
Bluse blouse
Blut blood

blutig bloody
Boden bottom *(eines Gegenstandes)*; ground *(Erde)*
Bogen bow
Bohne bean
Boot boat
Bord shelf
an Bord on board
borgen to borrow
böse bad
böse (werden) (to get) nasty
die Bösen the bad
Boss boss
Botschaft message *(Information)*; embassy *(Vertretung eines Landes)*
Boxershort boxer shorts *(pl.)*
Boykott boycott
brasilianisch Brazilian
Brasilien Brazil
brauchen to need
nicht brauchen needn't
braun brown
brav good
brechen to break
breit wide
Bremse brake
bremsen to brake
Brett shelf
Brief letter
Brieffreund/in pen pal
Briefkasten letterbox
Briefmarke stamp
Briefpapier writing paper
Briefträger postman
bringen to bring
bringen nach, zu to take to
britisch British
Broschüre brochure
Brot bread
Brötchenverdiener breadwinner
Brücke bridge
Bruder brother
brüllen to yell
Brust chest
brustschwimmen to do the breast stoke
Buch book
Bücherei library
Bücherwurm bookworm
Buchhandlung bookshop
Buchstabe letter
buchstabieren to spell
Bucht bay
Bügelwäsche ironing
Bühne stage
Bumerang boomerang
Bungalow bungalow
bunt colourful
Bürgerrecht civil right
Bürgersteig pavement
Büro office
Büroangestellte/r clerk
Bürogehilfe/-gehilfin office junior
Bursche lad
Bus bus
im Bus on the bus

Dictionary

mit dem Bus by bus
mit dem Bus fahren to go by bus
Busch outback *(in Australien)*
Buschmann bushman
Bushaltestelle bus stop
Butler butler
Butter butter

C

Café cafe
Camper camper
Camping camping
Campingplatz camping site
CD-Player CD player
CD-ROM CD-ROM
Champion champion
Chance chance
Charakter character
charmant winning *(Lächeln)*
Charts chart, charts
Chatline chat line
Checkliste checklist
Cheerleader cheerleader
Cheerleading cheerleading
Chef boss
Chemie Chemistry
Chihuahua chihuahua
China China
Chinese/in Chinese man, boy/woman, girl
chinesisch Chinese
Chor choir
Christ/in Christian
christlich Christian
clever smart
Clown clown
Club club
Code code
Cola cola
Comic cartoon
Comic(heft) comic
Compactdisc CD (= compact disc)
Computer computer
Computerspiel computer game
cool cool
Cornflakes cornflakes
Cousin/e cousin
Cowboy cowboy
Cursor cursor

D

da there
da draußen out there
da drüben over there
dalassen to leave
Dame lady
meine Damen und Herren ladies and gentlemen
danach after that
Däne/Dänin Danish man, boy/woman, girl
daneben gehen to go wrong

dänisch Danish
Gott sei Dank! Thank heavens!, Thank God!
dankbar grateful
danke thank you, thanks
dann then
darstellen to act
Darstellung portrait *(Bild)*; presentation *(Vorstellung)*
darunter below
das the; that, this
Das macht mir nichts aus. I don't mind.
Das macht Spaß! That's fun!
Das wollte ich gerade erzählen I'm coming to that.
Datei file
Datum date
Dauer duration
dauern to take
Dealer dealer
Deck deck
Deckel lid *(auf Topf usw.)*; cover
dein/e your
dein/e/er/s yours
Dem Himmel sei Dank! Thank heavens!
den ganzen Tag (lang) all day long
den ganzen Weg all the way
Den Haag The Hague
denken to think, to suppose
denken über to think of
Denkmal statue
der-/die-/dasselbe the same
der/die/das Gleiche the same
der/die/das the
der/die/das meiste most
Design design
Detail detail
Detektiv detective
deutlich clearly
deutsch German
Dezember December
Diagramm diagram
Dialog dialogue
dich you
dich selbst yourself
dick fat
die/die *(pl.)* the
Dieb robber
Diebstahl theft
Dienst service
Dienstag Tuesday
dies this
diese (da) those
diese (hier) these
Diesel diesel
diesmal this time
Ding thing
Dinosaurier dinosaur
dir you
dir selbst yourself
direkt direct, straight *(unmittelbar)*; live *(Sendung)*
direkte Rede direct speech
Disco disco

Diskette (floppy) disc
Diskjockey DJ (= disc jockey)
Diskountladen discount
diskriminieren to discriminate
Diskriminierung discrimination
Diskussion discussion
diskutieren to discuss
Do-it-yourself DIY, do-it-yourself
Dokumentarfilm documentary
Dollar $ (= dollar)
Dom cathedral
Donnerstag Thursday
Doppeldeckerbus double-decker bus
Doppelhaushälfte semi-detached house
doppelt double
Dorf village
dort there
dort drüben over there
dort hinkommen to get there
dort oben up there
dösen to snooze
Drachenfliegen hang gliding
Draht wire
Drama drama
Jetzt bin ich dran. Now it is my turn.
draußen outside, outdoors
nach draußen outside
drehen to turn round
drei three
dreimal three times
dreißig thirty
dreizehn thirteen
dringend urgent
dritte/r/s third
ein Drittel a third
Droge drug
Drogendealerei drug-dealing
drohen to threaten
Druck pressure
drucken to print
drücken to push
Dschungel jungle
du you
dumm stupid
Dummkopf fool
dunkel dark
dunkelhaarig dark haired
Dunkelheit darkness
dünn thin
durch through
durcheinander in a muddle
durchkommen to get through
Durchschnitt average
durchschnittlich average
jdn. durchstellen to put sb. through
dürfen to be allowed to, may
fort dürfen to be allowed out
nicht dürfen must not
durstig thirsty
Dusche shower
duschen to have a shower
Dussel goon, idiot

E

E-Mail e-mail
echt real, really
Ecke corner
Egal, ... Anyway, ...
egoistisch selfish
Ehe marriage
Ehefrau wife
Ehemann husband
ehrlich honest, truthful
Ei egg
Eichhörnchen squirrel
Eid Eid *(moslemisches Fest)*
eifersüchtig jealous
eigene/r/s own
Eigenschaftswort adjective
eigentlich actually, really
in Eile sein to be in a hurry
eilen to hurry, to race
ein für allemal once and for all
ein paar a couple of, a few
ein/e a, an *(vor Vokalen)*
noch ein/e another, one more
einbrechen to break into
Einbruch robbery
Eindruck impression, image
einen guten Eindruck machen to make a good impression
eine Art a kind of
eine Fahrradtour machen to go on a bike trip
eine Menge a lot, a lot of, lots of, many
eine Woche lang for a week
einen Streich spielen to play a joke/trick
einfach easy; just *(bloß)*; primitive
einführen to introduce
Eingang doorway
eingebildet big-headed
eingeschlafen asleep
einholen to catch up
einhundert one hundred
einige a few, some
sich auf etwas einigen to agree on sth.
Einkaufen shopping
Einkaufsliste shopping list
Einkaufszentrum shopping centre
einladen to invite
Einladung invitation
einloggen to log in
einmal once
einpacken to wrap up
eins one
einsam lonely
einschlafen to fall asleep
einschläfern to put to sleep
einschüchtern to bully
einsetzen to put in
einstecken to post *(Brief)*
einsteigen to get on *(bus)*
eintragen to fill in *(Formular)*; to enter *(Angabe)*
Eintritt entry
Eintrittskarte ticket
einundzwanzig twenty-one
einundzwanzigste/r/s twenty-first
Einwanderer immigrant
einwerfen to insert *(in Automaten)*; to post *(Brief)*
Einzahl singular
Einzelheit detail
einzeln single
einziehen to move in
einzige/r only
Eis ice; ice cream
Eisdisco ice disco
Eisenbahn railway
Eislaufstadion ice stadium
Elefant elephant
Elektriker/in electrician
elektrisch electric
Elektrizität electricity
elend miserable
elf eleven
Eltern parents *(pl.)*
Emu emu
End- final
Ende end; ending *(Geschichte)*
am Ende by the end
endlich finally
Energie energy
eng tight, narrow
England England
Engländer/in Englishman/woman, English boy/girl
englisch English
Enkelkinder grandchildren
entfernen to remove
entführen to kidnap
entgegen towards
enthalten to contain
entladen flat *(Batterie)*
entscheiden to decide
entschließen to decide
Entschuldigung note *(geschrieben)*
Entschuldigung (bitte). Excuse me., Sorry.
enttäuscht disappointed
entweder ... oder either ... or
entwerfen to design
entwickeln to develop
Enzyklopädie encyclopedia
er he
er selbst himself
Erbse pea
(er)hängen to hang
Erdbeere strawberry
Erde earth
Erdgeschoss ground floor
Erdkunde Geography
Erdling Earthling
Ereignis event
Erfahrung experience
erfinden to invent
Erfinder/in inventor
Erfindung invention
Erfolg success
erfolgreich successful
erfreut pleased
Ergebnis result
in Empfang erhalten to receive
erinnern to remind
Erinnerung memory
erklären to explain
jdm. etwas erlauben to allow sb. to do sth.
erleben to experience
ernst(haft) serious
erraten to guess
erreichen to get to, to reach
einen Bus erreichen to catch a bus
Ersatz substitute
erscheinen to appear
erschießen to shoot
erschrecken to scare
ersetzen to replace
erspähen to spy
erstaunlich amazing
erste Hilfe first aid
erste/r/s, als Erste/r/s first
erstens first of all
jdm. eine Lektion erteilen to teach sb. a lesson
Erwachsene/r adult
erwarten to expect
er kann es kaum erwarten zu he can't wait to
erwidern to reply
erwünscht wanted
erzählen to tell
Erzähler/in narrator, reader
Erzählung tale
es it
es gibt there is, there are
Es macht ihr nichts aus. She doesn't mind it.
es schaffen to make it
es selbst itself
essen to eat
Essen food
Essig vinegar
Esszimmer dining-room
Etage floor
Etikett label
etliche quite a few
Etui pencil case
etwa about
etwas any, anything, something
etwas anderes anything/something else
etwas bedauern to feel sorry about sth.
etwas eilig tun to do sth. in a hurry
gegen etwas fahren to hit
euch selbst yourselves
Eule owl
Europa Europe
europäisch European
Eurotunnel Channel Tunnel
seit einer Ewigkeit for ages
Experte/-tin expert
explodieren to explode
Explosion explosion

F

Fabrik factory
Fach subject
Fähre ferry
fahren to cycle; to drive; to go
mit dem Bus fahren to go by bus
mit dem Fahrrad fahren to cycle, to ride
Fahrer/in driver
Fahrgast passenger
Fahrrad bicycle, bike
mit dem Fahrrad by bike
Fahrradfahren riding a bike
eine Fahrradtour machen to go on a bike trip
Fahrschein ticket
Fahrt ride
Fährte track
fair fair
Fairplay fair play
Fakt fact
Fall case
fallen lassen to drop
Fallrohr drainpipe
falls if
Fallschirm parachute
falsch false, wrong
jdn. falsch verstehen to get sb. wrong
Familie family
Fan fan, freak
fangen to catch
fantastisch brilliant, fantastic
Farbe colour; paint *(Lack)*
Welche Farbe hat es? What colour is it?
färben to colour
farbenprächtig colourful
fast almost, nearly
faul lazy
Faust fist
Fax fax
Faxgerät fax machine
Februar February
Federmäppchen pencil case
Fehlen absence
fehlend missing
Fehler fault, mistake
Feier celebration, party
feiern to celebrate, to party
Feigling coward
fein fine, smart
Feld field
Felsbrocken rock
Felsen cliff
Felsvorsprung ledge
Fenster window
Ferien holiday(s)
in den Ferien on holiday
Ferienwohnung holiday flat
Fernsehen television, telly, TV
fernsehen to watch TV
im Fernsehen on TV
Fernseher television, TV
Fernsehzeitschrift TV guide

fertig ready, through *(ugs.)*; finished *(fertiggestellt)*
jdn. fertig machen to clobber sb.
fesseln to tie up
Fest celebration, party
fest fast
fest zugeschraubt done up tight
Fest(tag) festival
festhalten to hold onto
festnehmen to arrest
fett fat
Feuer fire
Feuer fangen to catch fire
Feuerwehr fire service
Feuerwehrwagen fire engine
Feuerwerk fireworks *(pl.)*
Feuerzeug lighter
Figur character *(Film, Buch)*; figure *(Körper)*
Film film, movie
Filmvorschau trailer
Filter filter
finden to find
Finger finger
Firma business, company, firm
Fisch/Fische fish *(sg.)*/fish *(pl.)*
Fischburger fishburger
Fischstäbchen fish finger
Fitness fitness, keeping fit
Fitnessstudio fitness studio
Flasche bottle
flauschig fluffy
Fleisch meat
Fleischpastete meat pie
Fliege fly
fliegen to fly
Fließband conveyor belt
Flirten flirting
Flohmarkt bring-and-buy sale
Floß float
Floßfahren white-water rafting
Flucht escape
flüchten to escape
Flug flight
Flügel wing
Flughafen airport
Flugzeug plane
Flur hall
Fluss river *(groß)*, stream *(klein)*
Flussbett river bed
Flüssigkeit liquid
folgen to follow
Fön hairdryer
Form form
formell formal
Formular form
fort dürfen to be allowed out
sich fortbewegen to get around
fortfahren to continue
fortkommen to get away
Foto photo, photograph
Fotoapparat camera
Fotograf/in photographer
fotografieren to take photos
Fotos machen to take photos
Frage question

Fragebogen questionnaire
sich fragen to wonder
fragen (nach) to ask (for)
Frankreich France
Französisch French
Frau/en woman/women; Mrs, Ms *(Anrede)*
Fräulein Ms *(Anrede)*
frech cheeky
frei free
freie Stelle vacancy
im Freien outdoor
die Freien the free
ein freier Abend a night out
Freiheit freedom
Freiluft- outdoor
Freitag Friday
Freizeichen dialling tone *(Telefon)*
Freizeit free time, leisure time
Freizeitbeschäftigung activity
Freizeitpark theme park
fremd foreign, strange
Fremde/r foreigner, stranger
Freude enjoyment
sich freuen auf to look forward to
Freund/Freundin (boy)friend/(girl)friend
Freunde finden to make friends
freundlich friendly
Mit freundlichen Grüßen Yours, ...
Freundschaft friendship
frisch fresh
Frisur hairstyle
fröhlich cheerful
Fröhliche Weihnachten! Merry Christmas!
Frosch frog
früh early
Frühling spring
Frühstück breakfast
frühstücken to have breakfast
Frühstücksfernsehen breakfast television
Frühstückspension bed and breakfast place
fühlen to feel
Führer guide
Führerschein driving licence
Führung guided tour
füllen to fill
Füller pen
Füllwort filler
fünf five
fünfte/r/s fifth
fünfzehn fifteen
fünfzig fifty
funktionieren to work
für for
für den Fall in case
für etwas bezahlt werden to get paid for sth.
für sich alleine on his/her/its own
furchtbar awful, horrible
ich fürchte I'm afraid
fürchterlich awful
fürchterlicher Zustand mess

Dictionary

furchterregend frightening
zu Fuß on foot
Fuß/Füße foot/feet
Fuß foot *(30,5 cm)*
(zu Fuß) gehen to walk
Fußball football, soccer
Fußballplatz football ground
Fußballspiel football match
Fußballspieler footballer
Fußboden floor
Fußgänger/in pedestrian
füttern to feed

G

Gabel fork
gähnen to yawn
Gang gear
Gangschaltung gears
ganz quite *(ziemlich)*; whole *(vollständig)*
die ganze Nacht all night
die ganze Zeit all the time
den ganzen Tag all day
gar nicht cool uncool
Garage garage
Garten garden
Garten hinter dem Haus back garden
Gas gas
Gasse alley
Gast guest
Gastfamilie host family
Gastgeber host
Gaststätte pub
Geächtete/r outlaw
Gebäude building
geben to give
geboren werden to be born
gebraten fried
Gebrauchsartikel article
Geburt birth
Geburtsdatum date of birth
Geburtstag birthday
Gedächtnis memory
Gedanke thought
Gedicht poem
Geduld haben to be patient
Gefahr danger
gefährlich dangerous
Gefangene/r prisoner
Gefängnis prison
gefroren frozen
Gefühl feeling
gefüllt mit filled with
gegen against, vs (versus)
Gegend area, countryside
Gegenstand article, object, thing
Gegenteil opposite
gegenüber opposite
Gegenwart present
einfache Gegenwart present simple
Verlaufsform der Gegenwart present progressive
geheimnisvoll mysterious

Geheimschrift code
gehen to go
(zu Fuß) gehen to walk
schwimmen gehen to go swimming
zu jdm. gehen to go over to sb.
Gehen wir! Come on!
Das geht sie nichts an. It's none of her business.
Mir geht's gut. I'm fine.
Geige violin
Geist ghost, spirit
gekränkt hurt
gelangen to get
in ein Programm gelangen to get into a program
gelangweilt bored
gelb yellow
Geld money
Geld auftreiben to raise money
Geldbörse purse
Gelegenheit chance
Gelegenheitskauf bargain
Geliebte/r lover
gelingen to manage
gemein mean, unkind
Gemeinschaft community
gemischt mixed
Gemischtwarenstand white elephant stall
Gemüse vegetables *(pl.)*
genau close
genau hier right here
genießen to enjoy
genug enough
geöffnet open
Gepäckträger carrier *(auf Fahrrad)*
gerade straight *(unmittelbar, Linie)*; at the moment *(im Augenblick)*
geradeaus weitergehen to go straight on
Gerät gadget
Geräusch noise, sound
gerecht fair
Gerechtigkeit justice
Gericht dish
ich würde gerne I'd (= I would) like to
Geruch smell
Gesamtschule comprehensive school
Geschäft shop, store
geschehen to go on, to happen
Geschenk gift, present
Geschichte History *(Schulfach)*; story, tale *(Erzählung)*
geschichtlich historical
geschieden divorced
Geschirr dishes *(pl.)*
Geschirrspülmaschine dishwasher
Geschlecht sex
geschlossen closed, shut
geschockt shocked
Geschwindigkeit speed
Gesellschaft society
Gesetz act
Gesicht face

Gespenst ghost
Gespräch conversation, discussion
Gestank smell
gestern yesterday
gestresst werden to get stressed
gesucht wanted
gesund healthy, fit
Getränk drink
alkoholfreies Getränk soft drink
getrennt separate
Gewalt violence
mit roher Gewalt drohen to threaten physically
gewalttätig violent
Gewicht weight
Gewichtheben weight-training
Gewinn(en) winning *(Wettkampf)*
gewinnen to win
Gewinner/in winner
jdm. ein schlechtes Gewissen machen to make sb. feel guilty
sich an etwas gewöhnen to get used to sth.
gewöhnlich ordinary, usual
gewollt wanted
Gewürz spice
Gipfel top
Gitarre guitar
1. Gitarre lead guitar
Gitarre spielen to play the guitar
glänzend bright
Glas glass
Glaube belief
glauben to believe
an etwas glauben, to believe in sth.
gleich alike, equal, the same
Ja, gleich. Just a moment.
der gleichen Meinung sein to agree
Gleitschirmfliegen paragliding
Glocke bell
Glück luck
Glück haben to be lucky
glücklich happy, lucky
Herzlichen Glückwunsch zum Geburtstag! Happy Birthday!
Gokart go-kart
Gokart-Fahren go-karting
Gold gold
Gold waschen to pan for gold
Goldgräber gold miner
Goldmine gold mine
Gott Lord
Gott sei Dank. Thank God., Thank heavens.
Götterspeise jelly
Graffiti graffiti
Grafik graph
Grammatik grammar
Gras grass
das Gras mähen to cut the grass
grau grey
Grenze border *(zwischen Ländern)*; edge
Grieche/in Greek man, boy/woman, girl
griechisch Greek

Grill grill
Grillparty Bar-B-Q (= barbecue)
Grimassen schneiden to make funny faces
grinsen to grin
Grinsen grin
groß big, great, large; tall *(in der Höhe)*
großartig brilliant
Großbritannien (Great) Britain
Größe size
Großeltern grandparents
Großmutter grandmother
Großstadt city
Großvater grandfather, grandad
grün green
Grund ground *(Boden)*; reason *(Begründung)*
Grundsatz policy
Gruppe group
Gruppenarbeit groupwork
gruppieren to group
herzliche Grüße best wishes
Liebe Grüße … Love …
Mit freundlichen Grüßen … Yours, …
Gummi rubber
Gummiband elastic band
gut fine, good, well
gut auskommen mit jdm. to get on well with sb.
gut aussehend good-looking, handsome
gut gebaut well-built
gut gehen to go well
Gut gemacht! Well done!
etwas gut können to be good at sth.
gut sein in to be good at
Er spielt gut. He plays well.
Mir geht's gut. I'm fine.
Gute Nacht Good night
die Guten the good
Guten Abend Good evening
Guten Morgen Good morning
Guten Tag Hello
jdm. einen Gutenachtkuss geben to kiss sb. goodnight
gutgelaunt cheerful

H

Haar/Haare hair *(sg./pl.)*
haben have got
Hacker hacker
Häftling prisoner
Hähnchen chicken
Hai shark
halb half past *(Uhrzeit)*
Halbzeit half-time
Halfpipe halfpipe
Hälfte half
Hallo! Hello., Hi., Yo! *(ugs.)*
Halt den Mund! Shut up.
halten to hold *(greifen)*; to keep *(behalten)*

halten von to think of
Haltestelle station
Hamburger hamburger
Hammer hammer
Hamster hamster
Hand hand
eine Hand ausstrecken to reach out
Händchen halten to hold hands
Handschuh glove
Handtasche handbag
Handwerk craft
Handy mobile phone
hänseln to tease
Hanukkah Hanukkah *(jüdisches Fest)*
Hardware hardware
hart hard, tough
hassen to hate
hässlich ugly
Haube cover *(Deckel)*
Haupteingang main entrance
die Hauptrolle spielen to star
Hauptstadt capital
Haus house
Hausarbeit housework
Hausaufgabe homework
Hausaufgaben machen to do homework
nach Hause home
zu Hause at home
Häuserblock block
Hausfrau housewife
hausgemacht home-made
Haushaltshilfe home help
Hausmann househusband
Haustier pet
Haustür front door
Haut skin
Heavymetal-Band heavy metal band
heben to lift
Heiligabend Christmas Eve
Heim home
Heimatstadt hometown
heimlich undercover
Heimweh haben to be homesick
Heimwerkermarkt do-it-yourself store
heiraten to get married, to marry
heiß hot
Heißluftballon balloon
Held/in hero
helfen to help
jdm. mit dem Anfang helfen to start sb. off
Helfer/in helper
hell bright
Helm helmet
Hemd shirt
herausfallen to fall out
herausfinden to find out
Herausforderer/-forderin challenger
Herausgeber/in editor
herausholen to get out, to take out
herauslegen to put out

herausschmeißen to throw out
herausstellen to highlight
Herbst autumn
Herd cooker
hereinkommen to come in
Herr Mr *(Anrede)*
herrlich lovely
herübergehen to go over
herum around
herumdrehen to turn around
herumfahren to cruise
herumhängen to hang around
herumkommen to get around
herunter down
herunterfallen to fall off
heruntergehen to go down
herunterspringen to jump off
hervorheben to highlight, to mark
hervorragend brilliant, excellent
Herz heart
Herzinfarkt heart attack
Herzlich willkommen. Welcome.
Herzliche Grüße Best wishes
Herzlichen Glückwunsch zum Geburtstag! Happy Birthday!
hetzen to rush off
heulen to howl
heute today; these days *(heutzutage)*
heute Abend tonight
heute Morgen this morning
heutzutage these days
hier here
Hier bitte. Here you are.
Hier entlang. This way.
hier oben up here
Hightech- hi-tech
Hilfe help
um Hilfe bitten to ask for help
hilfreich helpful *(Person)*; useful *(Gegenstand)*
hilfsbereit helpful
Himmel heaven; sky
hinbringen und abholen to take to and from
Hindu Hindu
hinduistisch Hindu
hinein inside
hineingehen to go in
hineingelangen to break into
hineinkommen to get in
hinfallen to fall, to fall over, to fall down
dort hinkommen to get there
sich hinlegen to lie down
hinreißend adorable
sich hinsetzen to sit down
hinten at the back
hinter behind
Hintergrund background
hinterher afterwards
hinterherlaufen to run after
eine Nachricht hinterlassen to leave a message
hinterste Reihe back row
Hintertür back door

Dictionary

hinübergehen to walk over
hinunter down
hinunterfallen to fall down
Hinweis clue, tip
hinzufügen to add
historisch historical
Hit hit
Hitliste chart
Hobby hobby
hoch high, large, tall
hoch halten to hold up
hoch oben high up
Hochgeschwindigkeits- high-speed
hochgucken to look up
hochheben to pick up
Hochrad penny farthing
hochschauen to look up
höchste/r top
Hochzeit marriage, wedding
Hockey hockey
hoffen to hope
Hoffnung hope
höflich polite
Höhle cave
holen to fetch, to get
Holland The Netherlands
holländisch Dutch
Hölle hell
Hör(t) auf! Stop it!, Cut it out! *(ugs.)*
hören to hear
Hörer receiver *(Telefon)*
Horoskop horoscope
Horror horror
Hörspiel radio play
Hose trousers
Hotel hotel
hübsch lovely, pretty
Hügel hill
Hund dog
(ein)hundert one hundred
hunderte von ... hundreds of ...
hungrig hungry
hurra! hurrah
husten to cough
Hut hat

I

ich I
Ich auch. Me, too.
Ich denke/glaube, ja. I think so.
ich selbst myself
ideal ideal
Idee idea
Identifikation identification
die Identität feststellen to identify
Idiot idiot
Idol idol
Igitt! Ugh!, Yuk!
ihm him, it
ihm selbst himself, itself
ihn him, it
Ihnen you
ihnen them
ihr selbst herself, yourselves
ihr/ihre her, its, your, their
illegal illegal
im Augenblick at the moment
im Ausland abroad
im Bus on the bus
im Fernsehen on TV
im Freien outdoors
im Haus indoors
im Internet on the Internet
im Internet surfen surfing the Internet, to surf the Internet
im Kino at the cinema
im Nu in no time
im Radio on the radio
im Urlaub on holiday
im Weg stehen to be in the way
Imbissstube snack bar
immer always
immer noch still
in in; to; into
in den Ferien on holiday
in der Nähe nearby
in der Schule at school
in die Luft gehen to explode
in diesem Augenblick at that moment
in Eile sein to be in a hurry
in fünf Jahren in five years' time
in gewisser Weise in a way
in Not in need
in Ordnung okay
in Sicherheit safe
in Schwierigkeiten in trouble
in seinem Kopf on his mind
in Übergröße oversized
inbegriffen included
Inch inch *(engl. Maßeinheit, = 2,4 cm)*
Inder/in Indian
Indianer/in Native American
Indien India
indisch Indian
Industrienation industrial nation
Informatik Computers *(Schulfach)*
Information information
Ingenieur engineer
inklusive included
Inlineskating roller-blading
innen (drin) inside; indoors *(im Haus)*
Innenstadt city centre
Innentasche inside pocket
Innere inside
innerstädtisch inner-city
ins Bett bringen to take to bed
ins Bett gehen to go to bed
Insekt insect
insgesamt altogether
Installateur/in plumber
installieren to put in
Instandsetzer/in repairer
Instrument instrument
interessant interesting
Interesse interest
interessiert sein an to be interested in
international international
Internet Internet
Interview interview
interviewen to interview
Interviewer/in interviewer
irgendein/e any
irgendetwas (anderes) anything
irgendjemand anybody, anyone
irgendwie kind of, sort of
Ich habe mich irgendwie verlaufen. I'm sort of lost.
irgendwo anywhere, somewhere
irisch Irish
Irrtum fault, mistake
Italiener/in Italian
italienisch Italian

J

ja yes
Ja, gleich! Just a moment!
Jacke(tt) jacket
jagen to chase, to hunt
Jäger hunter
Jahr year
Jahrbuch yearbook
Jahreszeit season
Jamaika Jamaica
jamaikanisch Jamaican
Januar January
Japan Japan
japanisch Japanese
Jazz jazz
je ever
je mehr ... desto mehr the more ... the more
Jeans jeans *(pl.)*
Jeans- denim
jede zweite Zeile every other line
jede/r everybody, everyone
jede/r/s each, every
jeden Morgen in the mornings, every morning
jeden Tag every day
jedenfalls anyway, at least
jedes Mal each time
Jedoch ... However, ...
jemals ever
jemand someone, somebody
jetzt (sofort) (right) now
joggen to jog
Jogginganzug tracksuit
Jogurt yoghurt
Journalist/in reporter
Jude Jew
jüdisch Jewish
Jugend youth
Jugendklub youth club, Young People's Club
Jugendzentrum Youth Centre
Juli July
jung young
Junge boy
Jungs fellas = fellows *(ugs.)*
Juni June

Dictionary

K

Kabel cable, cord; wire *(Draht)*
Kabelfernsehen cable TV
Kaffee coffee
Käfig cage
Kaktus cactus
Kalender calendar
kalt cold
Kamera camera
Kamin open fire
Kampf battle, fight, struggle
kämpfen to fight
Kämpfer/in fighter
Kanada Canada
kanadisch Canadian
Känguru kangaroo
Kaninchen rabbit
kann nicht cannot
Kantine cafeteria
Kanu canoe
Kanufahren canoeing
Kapitän captain
Kappe cap
kaputt broken (down)
kaputtgehen to go wrong
Karaoke karaoke
Karibik the Caribbean
Karotte carrot
Karren cart
Karte card
Karteikasten file
Kartoffel potato
Kartoffelchips crisps
Karton carton *(Tüte)*; Box *(Schachtel)*
Käse cheese
Kasse box office *(Theater, Kino)*
Kassette cassette
Kassettenrekorder cassette recorder
Kästchen box
Kasten box
Katze cat
kaufen to buy
Kaufhaus department store
kaum hardly
Kegel pin
Kegelbahn bowling alley
kein Glück haben to be unlucky
kein/e not … any, no
keine … mehr no more
keine/n/s none
Keks biscuit
Keller cellar
kennen to know
Kennwort password
kennzeichnen to highlight, to mark
Kerl guy
Kerze candle
Kette chain
Keyboard keyboard
KFZ-Werkstatt garage
kicken to kick
Kilogramm kilogramme
Kilometer kilometre, km
Kind/Kinder child, kid *(ugs.)*/ children
Kindergarten kindergarten
Kinderkrankenschwester nursery nurse
Kindheit childhood
Kino cinema
im Kino at the cinema
Kirche church
Kiste crate
klar clear
(Schul)klasse class
Echt klasse! Brilliant!
Klassenlehrer/in tutor
Klassenzimmer classroom
Klatsch gossip
klatschen to clap
Kleid dress
Kleider/Kleidung clothes
Kleiderschrank wardrobe
Kleidungsvorschrift dress code
klein little, small; short *(Körpergröße)*
Kleinigkeit detail
Kleinstadt town
klettern to climb
Klettern (rock) climbing
Klick click
Klima climate
klimpern to jingle
Klingel bell
klingeln to ring
klingen to sound
Klippe cliff
klönen to chat
klopfen to knock, to tap
klug clever
Knall explosion
Kneipe pub
Knie knee
Knochen bone
Knopf button
Koalabär koala bear
Koch/Köchin cook
kochen to cook
Kochen cooking
Kofferraum boot
Kohl cabbage
Kolonie colony
komisch funny
Komma comma
kommen to come
Kommunikation communication
Komödie comedy
Konflikt conflict
König/in king/queen
Konjunktion connecting word
können can, to be able to
Können Sie vielleicht … I wonder if you can …
konnte could
könnte could, might
Kontakt contact
Kontakt aufnehmen to contact
Kontrolle control
kontrollieren to control
sich konzentrieren (auf) to concentrate (on)
Konzern organization
Konzert concert
Koordinator/in coordinator
Kopf head
in seinem Kopf on his mind
Kopfhörer headphones
kopieren to copy
Korb basket
koreanisch Korean
Körper body
Körpergröße height
körperlich physical
korrekt correct
korrigieren to correct
Kosten cost
kosten to cost; to take *(Zeit)*
Kostüm costume
Kraft energy, power
Kragen collar
krank ill, sick
Krankenhaus hospital
Krankenpfleger male nurse
Krankenschwester nurse
Krankenwagen ambulance
kratzen to scratch
Krawatte tie
kreativ creative
Kreide chalk
Kreis circle
Kreuz cross
kriegen to get
einen Bus kriegen to catch a bus
Kriminelle/r criminal
Kroatien Croatia
Krokodil crocodile
Kubaner/in Cuban
kubanisch Cuban
Küche kitchen
Kuchen cake
kühl cool
Kühlschrank fridge
Kummerkastentante agony aunt
Kumpel mate
Kunde/-din customer
Kunst Art
Kunstgewerbe craft
Künstler/in artist
künstlich unnatural
Kunststück trick
Kurier messenger
Kurs class
kurz short
kurz ansehen to have a look
kurze Hose shorts *(pl.)*
Kurzform short form
Kuss kiss
jdm. beim Abschied einen Kuss geben to kiss sb. goodbye
küssen to kiss
Küste coast

L

Labor laboratory, lab
Lächeln smile

Dictionary

lächeln to smile
lächelnd smiling
lachen (über) to laugh (at)
jdm. lächerlich machen to make a fool of sb.
Laden shop, store
laden to load
Lagerhaus warehouse
Lampe light
Lampenfieber stage fright
Land country; land *(Nation)*
landen to land
Landkarte map
Landschaft countryside
lang long
Länge duration
lange aufbleiben to stay up late
lange wegbleiben to stay out late
Langeweile boredom
langsam slow
Languste crawfish
langweilig boring
Lärm noise
Lass mich in Ruhe. Leave me alone.
lass/lasst uns ... let's (= let us) ...
lassen to leave, to let
lässig casual
lästig annoying
Lastwagen lorry, truck
Latino Hispanic
laufen to run
gegen etwas laufen to hit
Schlittschuh laufen to skate
Laune mood
laut loud
Laut sound
laut noisy
Leadgitarre lead guitar
Leben life
leben to live
von etwas leben to live off sth.
Leben im Alltag everyday life
lebend(ig) alive
Lebensmittelgeschäft grocery store
lecker delicious
leer empty
Leerkassette blank cassette
legen to put
sich legen to lie
Lehre apprenticeship
lehren to teach
Lehrer/in teacher
Lehrling apprentice
leicht easy *(einfach)*; light *(Gewicht)*
Leid tun to be sorry, to feel sorry
Es tut mir Leid. I'm sorry.
leiden to suffer from
Leidenschaft passion
leihen to borrow, to hire
sich leisten to afford
Leiter ladder
Leitung line
Lektion lesson
jdm. eine Lektion erteilen to teach sb. a lesson

Lenkrad wheel
lernen to learn
lesen to read
letzte/r/s last
Leute people *(pl.)*
Licht light
lieb dear
Liebe love
Liebe Grüße ... Love ...
Liebe/r ... Dear ...
lieben to love
lieber haben to prefer
Liebesgeschichte romance
liebeskrank lovesick
Liebhaber/in lover
Liebling darling, dear
Lieblings- favourite
Lied song
Liederbuch song book
Lieferant/in deliverer
Lieferung delivery
Lieferwagen lorry, van
liegen to lie
lila purple
Limonade lemonade
Lineal ruler
linke/r/s left, left-hand
links left, on the left
Lippe lip
Lippenstift lipstick
Liste list
live live
Loch hole
logisch logical
Lohn wage
lokal/Lokal- local
Los geht's. Off they/we go.
lösen to solve *(Problem)*; to undo *(Schraube)*
losfliegen to fly off
loslegen to begin; to have a go *(etwas versuchen)*
Lösung solution
Löwe lion
Lücke gap
Luft air
tief Luft einholen to take a deep breath
in die Luft gehen to explode
Luftkissenboot hovercraft
Luftpumpe pump
Lüge lie
lügen to lie
Lunchpaket packed lunch
Lust haben, etwas zu tun to fancy doing sth.
lustig funny
sich über jdn. lustig machen to make fun of sb.
Luxus- luxury

M

machen to make, to do
Fotos machen to take photos

Macht force, power
Macht nichts. Never mind.
Das macht Spaß! That's fun!
Mädchen girl; maid *(Dienstmädchen)*
Magd maid
Magen stomach
das Gras mähen to cut the grass
Mäher mower
Mahlzeit meal
Mai May
Mais maize
Make-up make-up
(nächstes) Mal (next) time
malen to paint
Maler decorator
man you
Manager/in manager
manche some
manchmal sometimes
Mandarine tangerine
Mann/Männer man/men
männlich male
Mannschaft team
Mannschaftssport team sport
Mantel coat
Märchen tale
markieren to highlight, to mark
Markt market
Marktplatz market square
März March
Maschine machine
Maschinenbaufirma engineering firm
Maskottchen mascot
Match match
Material material
Mathematik Maths
Matrose sailor
matschig soggy
Matte mat
Mauer wall
Maurer bricklayer
Maus/Mäuse mouse/mice
Mechaniker/in mechanic
Medaille medal
Medien media
Meer sea
mehr more
keine mehr no more
nicht mehr not ... any more
viel mehr lots more
mehr als more than
mehrere several
Mehrzahl plural
Meile mile *(1,609 km)*
mein/e/er/s mine
mein/e my
meine Damen und Herren ladies and gentlemen
meine Liebe love *(Anrede)*
meinen to mean *(sagen wollen)*; to think *(Meinung haben)*
Meinung opinion
der gleichen Meinung sein to agree
die meiste Zeit most of the time

Dictionary

die meisten most
Meisterkoch/köchin mastercook
eine Menge a lot, a lot of, lots of, many
Menge crowd
Mensch person
Menschen people
merkwürdig funny, strange
Messe trade fair
Messer knife
Metall metal
Meter meter
Mexikaner/in Mexican
mexikanisch Mexican
mich me
mich selbst myself
mies miserable (Stimmung)
mieten to hire
Mikrofon microphone
Mikrowelle microwave
Milch milk
Milchmann milkman
Milchshake milkshake
Million million
Millionär/in millionaire
mindestens at least
Mine mine
Mini- mini
Minigolf crazy golf
Minute minute
mir me
Mir geht's gut. I'm fine.
mir selbst myself
mischen to mix
missverstanden misunderstood
Mist rubbish
mit with
Mit freundlichen Grüßen Yours, Yours sincerely
mit großen Augen wide-eyed
mit jdm. ausgehen to go out with sb.
mit roher Gewalt drohen to threaten physically
Wie wäre es mit …? What about …?, How about …?
mitbringen to bring
Mitbringsel souvenir
miteinander auskommen to get on
Mitglied member
mitnehmen to bring
Mittag midday, noon
zu Mittag essen to have lunch
Mittag(szeit) lunch-time
Mittagessen lunch
Mitte middle
Mittelklasse- middle-class
mitten in der Nacht in the middle of the night
Mitternacht midnight
Mittwoch Wednesday
Möbel furniture
Möbelpacker removal man
Möbeltischler furniture maker
Möchtest du/
Möchten Sie …? Would you like …?
Ich möchte… I'd (= I would) like …

Modalverb modal verb
Modedesigner fashion designer
Model model
Modell(-) model
Modenschau fashion show
modern modern, up to date
mogeln to cheat
mögen to like, to fancy
Möhre carrot
Mohrrübe carrot
Moment moment
vom ersten Moment an right from the first moment
Moment mal! Just a moment!
Monat month
Mond moon
Monster monster
Montag Monday
Moped moped
Mörder/in killer, murderer
morgen tomorrow
Morgen morning
heute Morgen this morning
jeden Morgen in the mornings, every morning
morgens a.m. (0–11:59 Uhr)
Moslem Muslim
moslemisch Muslim
Motor motor
Motorboot motor boat
Motorrad motorbike
Mountainbike mountain bike
müde tired
Müll rubbish, waste
Mülleimer waste bin
multikulturell multi-cultural
Mund mouth
Münze coin
Museum museum
Musical musical
Musik music
musikalisch musical
Musikband band
Musikbranche music business
Musiker/in musician
Muskel muscle
Müsli muesli
ein Muss a must
müssen to have to, must
Muster design
mutig brave
Mutter mother, mum
Mütze cap

N

nach after; past (Uhrzeit); to (Richtung)
nach draußen outside
nach einiger Zeit after some time
nach Hause home
nach Westen west
nach … fragen to ask for
Nachbar/in neighbour
Nachbarschaft neighbourhood

Nachmittag afternoon
nachmittags p.m. (Uhrzeiten)
Nachricht message
eine Nachricht hinterlassen to leave a message
Nachrichten news
nachrufen to call after
nachschlagen to look up
nachschulisch after-school
Nachsitzen detention
nächste/r/s next
Nacht night
Nachteil disadvantage
nachts at night
nah close
nah bei close to
in der Nähe nearby
in der Nähe von near
Nähkurs Dressmaking (Schulfach)
nahegelegen nearby
Name name
Narr/Närrin fool
Nase nose
die Nase voll haben von jdm./etwas to be/get fed up with sb./sth.
nass wet
Nationalitätenschild nationality plate
Natur nature
die freie Natur the big outdoors
natürlich of course (selbstverständlich); natural; genuine (Charakter)
Naturwissenschaften Science (Schulfach)
neben beside, next to
nebenan next door
negativ negative
nehmen to take
in Empfang nehmen to receive
nein no
nennen to name, to call
nervig annoying
nervös nervous
nett kind, nice
Netz net
neu new
neueste latest
neugierig curious
neulich the other day/night
neun nine
neunte/r/s ninth
neunzehn nineteen
neunzig ninety
nicht not
Ich kann … nicht ausstehen. I can't stand …
nicht brauchen/müssen needn't
nicht dürfen must not
nicht mehr not … any more
nicht mögen to dislike
nicht müssen need not
Nichte niece
Nichtraucher non-smoker
nichts nothing
Nichts, was ich tue, … Nothing I do …

Dictionary

nicken to nod
nie never
niederreißen to break down
niedlich cute
niemand nobody, no one
Nikolaus Father Christmas
nirgendwo nowhere
(immer) noch still
noch ein/e another, one more
noch einmal again
noch zehn Minuten ten minutes to go
noch … nicht not … yet
nonstop non-stop
Norden North
Nordengland the North of England
Nordpol North Pole
Nordsee North Sea
normal normal, ordinary
normalerweise usually
in Not in need
Notdienst emergency service
Note mark
Notfall emergency
notieren to note down
Notiz note
Notruf emergency call
notwendig necessary
November November
im Nu in no time
Nudel noodle
null oh *(bei Telefonnummern und Uhrzeit)*
die Nummer 1 werden to get to no.1
nun now
nun also anyway
nur only, just
nützlich useful

O

ob if
als ob as if
oben above; up *(Richtung)*; upstairs *(im Haus)*
dort oben up there
hier oben up here
oben auf at the top of
Ober waiter
Oberfläche surface
oberste/r top
Objekt object
Obst fruit
obwohl although, though
öd barren
oder or
offen open-minded
offene Stelle vacancy
öffentlich public
öffentliche Toilette public convenience
öffnen to open
oft often
wie oft … how often …
öfter more often

ohne without
ohne Unterbrechung non-stop
Ohr ear
Ohrstecker stud
okay okay
Oktober October
Öl oil
Ölbohrinsel oil rig
Ölförderturm oil rig
ölverschmiert oily
Oma gran, Grandma
Omelette omelette
Onkel uncle
online gehen to go on-line
Opa grandad
optimistisch optimistic
orange orange
Orangenmarmelade marmalade
Orangensaft orange juice
Orchester orchestra
ordentlich tidy
ordnen to sort
Ordner file
in Ordnung okay
Ordnung order
Organisation organization
Organisator/in coordinator
organisieren to organize
Original original
Ort place
örtlich local
Osten East
Österreich Austria
Österreicher/in Austrian
österreichisch Austrian
Outfit outfit

P

Paar pair
ein paar a few, a couple of
packen to grab *(mit der Hand)*; to pack *(Koffer)*
Packung pack
paddeln to paddle
Pakistan Pakistan
Pakistani Pakistani
pakistanisch Pakistani
Panik panic
Keine Panik. Don't panic.
Papier paper
Stück Papier piece of paper
Pappschachtel carton *(Tüte)*; box
Paradies paradise
Paragliding paragliding
Park park
Parken parking
Parkhaus/-platz car park
Partizip Perfekt past participle *(3. Form des Verbs)*
Partner/in partner
Party party
Pass pass
Pass auf! Be careful!
Passagier passenger

passen zu to fit, to go with
passieren to happen to
Pasta pasta
(in der) Pause (at) break
Pech haben to be unlucky
Pedal pedal
Pence p, pence *(brit. Währung)*
Penny p, penny *(brit. Währung)*
Perfekt present perfect
perfekt perfect
Person character, person
Personalausweis identity card
persönlich personal
Persönlichkeit personality
Perücke wig
pessimistisch pessimistic
Pfanne pan
Pfeil arrow
Pferd horse
Pfirsich peach
Pflanze plant
pflücken to pick
Pfund pound, £1 = 1 pound *(brit. Währung)*; pound *Gewicht)*
Phrase phrase
Physik Physics *(Schulfach)*
Pickel spot
Picknick picnic
Pilot pilot
pink pink
Pinnwand pinboard
Piste slope
Pistole gun
Pizza pizza
Pizzeria pizzeria
Plakat poster
Plan plan, schedule
planen to plan
Planet planet
Plastik plastic
Plastikbehälter plastic container
Platschen splash
Plattenspieler record player
Platz ground *(Fußball)*; place, room, square *(in der Stadt)*
Plätzchen biscuit
Platzgebühr sitting fee
Platzwart groundsman
plaudern to chat
plötzlich suddenly
Plural plural
Podest block, podium
Polier foreman
Politik policy
Polizei police
Polizeirevier police station
Polizeiwagen police car
Polizist/in policeman/woman, cop *(ugs.)*
polnisch Polish
Pommes Frites chips
Pony pony
Poolbillard pool
Popcorn popcorn
Popgruppe pop group
Popmusik pop music

Dictionary

Popstar pop star
Portmonee purse
Portrait portrait
Portugal Portugal
Portugiese/in Portuguese man, boy/woman, girl
portugiesisch Portuguese
Position position
positiv positive
Postamt post office
Postbote postman
Poster poster
Postkarte postcard
Präsentation presentation
Präsentationsmappe portfolio
präsentieren to present
Präsident/in president
Praxis surgery
Preis price *(den man bezahlt)*; prize *(den man gewinnt)*
prima great
primitiv primitive
Prinz prince
pro Woche a week
probieren to try
Problem problem
Probleme kriegen to get into trouble
Produzent producer
Programm programme *(TV, radio)*; program *(Computer)*; scheme *(Projekt)*
Programme schreiben programming
Programmierer/in programmer
Projekt project
Prospekt brochure
Prostitution prostitution
Prozent percent
prüfen to check, to test
Pullover jumper, pullover
Punker/in punk
Punkt dot *(Pünktchen)*; point
einen Punkt erzielen to score
Punktestand score
pünktlich on time
Pyjama pyjamas

Q

quadratisch square
Quadratmeile square mile
Quatsch rubbish
quatschen to chat
Querflöte flute
Quiz quiz

R

Rabauke bully
Rad wheel
Radfahren cycling
Radfahrer/in cyclist
Radiergummi rubber
Radio radio
im Radio on the radio
Radiosender radio station
Radiowecker clock radio
Radweg cycle path
Ramadan Ramadan
Ranch ranch
Rancher rancher
Rand edge; side *(Straße)*
Ranger ranger
Rap rap *(Sprechgesang)*
rasen to rush (off)
rasend furious
Rasenmäher mower
Rasse race
rassistisch racist
Raster grid
Rat advice
raten to guess
Ratschlag advice, tip
Rätsel riddle, quiz
rätselhaft mysterious
Ratte rat
Raub robbery
rauben to rob
Räuber robber
Räuberbande band of robbers
Rauchen smoking
rauchen to smoke
Raum room
Raumfähre shuttle
Raumschiff spaceship
reagieren to react
Rebell rebel
Rechnung bill
Recht right
Recht haben to be right
rechte/r/s right, right-hand
rechts right, on the right
Rechtsanwalt/-wältin lawyer
rechtzeitig in time
Redakteur/in editor
reden to say, to speak, to talk
Redewendung phrase
Reflektor reflector
Regalbrett shelf
Regel rule
regelmäßig regular
Regen rain
Regenbogen rainbow
Reggae reggae
Regie führen to direct
Regierung government
regnen to rain
heftig regnen to rain cats and dogs
regungslos still
reich rich
Reifen tyre *(Auto)*; hoop *(Metall)*
Reihe queue *(Personenschlange)*; line
hinterste Reihe back row
Jetzt bin ich an der Reihe. Now it's my turn.
Reihenfolge order
Reihenhaus terraced house
Reim rhyme
rein pure
Reis rice
Reise journey, trip
Reisebus coach
Reisemagazin travel show
reisen to travel
Reisepass passport
reiten to ride
Reiten riding
Rektor/in principal
Religion religion
Religionsgemeinschaft religious community
religiös religious
rennen to run
Rennen race
Rennrad racing bike
reparieren to fix, to repair
Reporter/in reporter
Restaurant restaurant
retten to rescue, to save
Rettung rescue
Rettungsdienst ambulance service
Revier territory
Rezept recipe *(Kochen)*; prescription *(für Medizin)*
richtig correct, right; proper *(passend)*; true *(wahr)*
richtig stellen to put right
Richtung direction
riechen to smell
Riegel bar
Rindfleisch beef
Ring ring
Risiko risk
Roadie roadie
Roboter robot
Rock skirt
Rock 'n' Roll rock 'n' roll
roh raw
Rohr pipe *(Sanitär)*; tube
Rolle role
für eine Rolle vorsprechen to try out for a part
rollen to roll
Rollenspiel role play
Rollerblades fahren to roller-blade
Rollerblading roller-blading
Rollstuhl wheelchair
romantisch romantic
Romanze romance
rosa pink
rot red
rot werden to turn red
Route route
Rowdy vandal
Rücken back
Rücken an Rücken back to back
Rückenschwimmen backstroke
Rucksack rucksack
Rückstrahler reflector
Rudel pack
rufen to call, to shout
Lass mich in Ruhe! Leave me alone!
ruhig calm, quiet
ruinieren to ruin
rund (um) round
Rundfahrt tour

Dictionary

Rundfunkstation radio station
die Stirn runzeln to frown

S

Sache matter
Sack bag, sack
Sackgasse dead end
Safari safari
Saft juice
sagen to say, to tell
Saison season
Salat lettuce *(Kopfsalat)*; salad *(Gericht)*
Salz salt
Sammelalbum scrapbook
sammeln to collect; to raise *(Geld)*
Sammlung collection
Samstag Saturday
samstags on Saturday(s)
Sand sand
Sandkasten sandpit
Sandwich sandwich
Sänger/in singer
Sanitäter/in ambulance man/woman
Satellit satellite
Satellitenstation satellite station
Sattel saddle
Satz sentence
Satzteil phrase
sauber clean
sauber machen to clean up
Saxophon saxophone
Schachtel box, packet
Schaf sheep
Schaffarm sheep station
schaffen to manage
es schaffen to make it
Schale pan
Schallplatte record
scharf hot *(Essen)*; sharp *(Messer)*
Schatten shadow
Schatz treasure *(den man findet)*; darling, dear *(Liebling)*
Schätzchen honey
schätzen to guess
Schaubild diagram
schauen to watch, to look
Schaufenster shop window
Schaufensterbummel window-shopping
schaukeln to rock
Schauspieler/in actor/actress
Scheck cheque
Scheibe slice *(Brot)*
Scheidung divorce
scheinen to seem *(aussehen)*; to shine *(glänzen)*
Scheinwerfer spotlight
scheußlich (werden) (to get) nasty
Schicht shift *(Arbeit)*
schick smart
schicken to send
schieben to push

schief laufen to go wrong
Schienbeinschoner shinguard
schießen to shoot
Schießerei shooting
Schiff boat, ship
schikanieren to bully
Schild sign
Schlafanzug pyjamas
Schlafanzughose pyjama trousers
schlafen to be asleep, to sleep
schlafend asleep
schlaflos sleepless
Schlafzimmer bedroom
schlagen to beat, to hit
Schläger bully
Schlagzeile headline
Schlagzeug drums
Schlange snake *(Tier)*; queue *(Personen)*
Schlange stehen to queue
schlank slim
schlau clever
schlecht bad
schlechter worse
schließen to close
schließlich at last, finally
schlimmer (noch) worse
Schlittschuh skate
Schlittschuh laufen to skate
Schlittschuhausleihe skate hire
Schlittschuhlaufen ice skating
Schlittschuhläufer/in skater
Schloss castle *(Gebäude)*; lock *(zum Abschließen)*
schlummern to slumber
schlürfen to sip
Schluss(teil) ending
Schluss machen to break up
Schlüssel key
Schlüsselwort key word
schmecken to taste
schmelzen to melt
Schmerz pain
Schminke make-up
Schmuck jewellery
schmücken to decorate
Schmutz dirt
schmutzig dirty
Schnäppchen bargain
schnarchen to snore
Schnee snow
Schneemobil snowmobile
schneiden to cut
Grimassen schneiden to make funny faces
Schneider/in dressmaker
schneien to snow
schnell fast, quick
schnell laufen to hurry
etwas schnell und schmerzlos tun to do sth. clean
Schnellbootfahren speedboat racing
schneller als ich faster than me
Schnellimbiss fast-food place
Schnur wire *(Draht)*
Schock shock

schockiert shocked
Schokolade chocolate
Schokoriegel candy bar
schon already, yet
schön beautiful, lovely
schon einmal before, ever
Hast/Bist du schon einmal ...? Have you ever ...?
Schön, dich zu sehen. Nice to see you.
Schottland Scotland
Schrank cupboard
Schraube screw
Schraubenschlüssel spanner
Schraubenzieher screwdriver
Schreck shock
schrecklich horrible, terrible
Schrei cry, scream
schreiben to write
neu schreiben to rewrite
Schreibtisch desk
Schreibweise spelling
schreien to cry, to scream, to shout, to yell
Schriftsteller/in writer
Schritt step
Schrotflinte shotgun
Schublade drawer
schüchtern shy
Schuh shoe
Schulabgänger/in school leaver
Schulabschluss school leaving certificate
Schulamt education office
Schulbuch textbook
schuldig guilty
Schule school
in der Schule at school
Schüler/in pupil
Schulferien school holidays
Schulhalbjahr term
Schulhalle assembly hall
Schulhof (school) playground
Schulkiosk tuck shop
Schulklasse class
Schulleiter/in head teacher
Schulstunde lesson, period
Schultasche bag
Schulter shoulder
schummeln to cheat
Schuppen shed *(einfache Hütte)*
schütteln to shake
hin und her schütteln to shake around
Schutz protection
Schutzblech mudguard
(sich) schützen to defend (oneself)
schützen vor to shelter from
schwanger pregnant
schwanken to stagger, to wobble
Schwanz tail
schwänzen to cut classes
schwarz black
schwarzes Brett notice board
Schwatz gossip
Schweigen silence

Schweinefleisch pork
schwer difficult, hard *(nicht einfach)*; heavy *(Gewicht)*
Schwert sword
Schwester sister
schwierig difficult
Schwierigkeit conflict
Schwierigkeiten kriegen to get into trouble
in Schwierigkeiten in trouble
Schwimmbad swimming pool
Schwimmbecken pool
schwimmen to swim
Schwimmen swimming
Schwimmen gehen to go swimming
Schwimmer/in swimmer
schwitzen to sweat
Sciencefiction science fiction
sechs six
sechzehn sixteen
sechzig sixty
(der) See lake
(die) See sea
Seele soul
Seemann sailor
Segel sail
Segeln sailing
sehen to see, to look
Sehenswürdigkeit sight
sehr very
Seife soap
Seifenoper soap (opera)
sein/e his, its
seit for, since
seit einer Ewigkeit for ages
Seite page *(Buch)*; side
Seite im Internet website
Sekretär/in secretary
Sekretariat office
Sekunde second
selbstsüchtig selfish
selbstverständlich of course
seltsam strange
senden to send
Sender channel
Sender am Hals radio collar
Sendung programme
senken to lower
September September
Serie series *(sg.)*
Sessel armchair
setzen to put
seufzen to sigh
sexy sexy
Sheriff sheriff
sich abstoßen to push off
sich abwechseln to take turns
sich ändern to change
sich anhören (nach) to sound
sich anlehnen to lean
sich anstellen to queue
sich auf den Weg machen zu/nach to head for
sich ausdenken to make up, to think up
sich aussuchen to choose

sich bedroht fühlen to feel threatened
sich beeilen to hurry (up)
sich benehmen to behave
sich beschweren to complain
sich bewegen to move
sich die Zeit vertreiben to hang out
sich engagieren to get involved
sich entscheiden für to decide on
sich entschließen to decide
sich erinnern to remember
sich fit halten to exercise
sich fragen to wonder
sich fühlen to feel
sich für/gegen etwas aussprechen to speak out
sich gegenseitig each other
sich hinlegen to lie down
sich hinsetzen to sit down
sich kümmern to care
sich leihen to borrow
sich leisten to afford
sich links halten to keep to the left
sich mit jdm. verabreden to ask sb. out
sich niederknien to kneel down
sich öffnen to open
sich schämen to be/feel ashamed
sich schützen to defend oneself
sich selbst herself, himself, itself, yourself, yourselves, themselves
sich Sorgen machen to worry
sich streiten to argue
sich treffen to meet
sich umdrehen to roll over
sich umsehen to look around
sich unterhalten to communicate
sich verabreden to date
sich verlaufen to get lost
sich verlieben to fall in love
sich vermischen to mingle
sich verstecken to hide
sich vorbereiten to get ready
sich vorstellen to imagine
sich (jdm.) vorstellen to introduce oneself (to sb.)
sich wehren to struggle
sich weigern to refuse
sich wünschen to want, to wish
sich zurechtfinden to find one's way around
sicher safe, sure
Sicherheit safety
in Sicherheit safe
Sicherheitsangestellte/r security guard
sicherlich surely
sichtbar visible
Sie you
sie she, her, they, them
sie selbst herself
sieben seven
siebzehn seventeen
siebzig seventy
Sieger/in winner
Signal signal

Silber silver
singen to sing
Single single
Singular singular
sinken to sink
Sinn für Humor sense of humour
Situation situation
Sitz seat
sitzen to sit
Skateboardfahren skateboarding
Ski laufen gehen to go skiing
Skizze plan
Snackbar bar
Snowboarden snowboarding
so like this, so, such, that way
So sind … . It's the way … are.
so tun, als ob to pretend
so viel … wie as much … as
so … wie as … as
so'n Zeug stuff like that *(ugs.)*
Socke sock
Sofa sofa
sofort at once, immediately, straight away
Software software
sogar even
Sohn son
solch/e/er/es such
Soll das ein Scherz sein? Are you kidding?
sollte/st/t/n should
Solosänger/in solo singer
Sommer summer
Sonnabend Saturday
Sonne sun
Sonnenaufgang sunrise
Sonnenbrille sunglasses
Sonnencreme sun cream
Sonnenschein sunshine
sonnig sunny
Sonntag Sunday
sonst else
sich Sorgen machen to worry
sorgfältig careful
Sorte type
sortieren to sort
Soße gravy
Souvenir souvenir
soweit so far
sowieso anyway
Sozialarbeiter social worker
Sozialwohnung council flat
Spalte column
spanisch Spanish
spannend exciting
sparen to save
Spaß fun
Spaß haben to enjoy
Das macht Spaß! That's fun!
Viel Spaß! Have fun!
(zu) spät late
Wie spät ist es? What time is it?
spät wegbleiben to stay out late
später later
spazieren führen to take for a walk
spazieren gehen to go for a walk

Dictionary

Spaziergang walk
Speiche spoke
speichern to store
Speisekarte menu
Spiegel mirror
Spiel game
spielen to act, to perform *(Schauspiel)*; to play *(Spiel)*
Gitarre spielen to play the guitar
einen Streich spielen to play a joke/trick
spielen gegen ... to play (against) ...
Spieler/in player
Spielhalle arcade
Spielkarte card
Spielplatz (school) playground
Spielrunde turn
Spielshow game show
Spielstand score
Spielzeug toy
Spinne spider
Du spinnst wohl! You must be joking!
Spitze top
Sport sport
Sport betreiben to do sports
Sportart sport
Sportplatz playing field
Sportunterricht P.E. = Physical Education
Sportzentrum sports centre
Sprache language
Sprayer sprayer
sprechen to speak
springen to jump
Sprung jump
spucken to spit
Spüle sink
Spülmittel washing up liquid
Spur clue, sign *(Indiz)*; trace; track *(Tier)*
Staat state
Stadion stadium
Stadt town, city
Stadtmitte city centre
Stadtplan map
Stammbaum family tree
stampfen to stamp
Stand stall, stand
Star star
stark fit, strong
starren to stare
Start start *(Beginn)*; take-off *(Flugzeug)*
startbereit ready
starten to start *(beginnen)*, to take off *(Flugzeug)*
Station station
Statistik statistic *(einzeln)*; statistics *(Tabelle usw.)*
statt instead of
stattdessen instead
stattfinden to take place
Statue statue
Staubsauger vacuum cleaner
Steckbrief wanted poster

stecken bleiben to get stuck
stehen to stand
im Weg stehen to be in the way
stehen bleiben to stop short
stehlen to steal
steil steep
stellen to put
richtig stellen to put right
sterben to die
Stern star
Sternenlicht starlight
Sternkarte starmap
Steuerrad (steering) wheel
Stewardess air hostess
Stichwort note
Stiefel boot
Stiefmutter stepmother, stepmum
Stiefschwester stepsister
Stiefvater stepfather, stepdad
Stier bull
still quiet
stilvoll stylish
Stimme voice
Stimmung atmosphere
die Stirn runzeln to frown
Stock stick
Stockwerk floor
stöhnen to moan
Stolz pride
stolz proud
stolz auf sich sein to be proud of oneself
stoppen to stop
Strafgefangene/r convict
Sträfling convict
Strand beach
Strandball beachball
Straße street
Straßenecke street corner
Strecke route
Streetball streetball
Streich trick
einen Streich spielen to play a joke/trick
Streichholz matchstick
Streifen stick *(Kaugummi)*
Streit argument, quarrel
(sich) streiten to argue *(mündlich)*; to fight *(Schlägerei)*
streng strict, tough
Strickjacke cardigan
Strom stream
Strumpf sock, stocking
Strumpfhose tights
Stück piece
Stück Papier piece of paper
Student/in student
Studio studio
Stuhl chair
Stunde hour *(Uhr)*; lesson *(Schule)*
Stunden ausfallen lassen to cut classes
Stunden pro Tag hours a day
Stundenplan timetable
Stuntman stuntman
Sturm storm

Stürmer striker
suchen to look for, to seek; to require *(benötigen)*
Süden south
Südosten southeast
Südwales South Wales
Südwesten south-west
Summe total
super great, super
Supermarkt supermarket
Suppe soup
süß sweet *(Person, Essen)*; cute *(Person)*
Süßigkeiten sweets
Sweatshirt sweatshirt
Symbol symbol
System system
Systemingenieur/in systems engineer
Szene scene

T

T-Shirt T-shirt
Tabak tobacco
Tablette tablet
Tafel board
Tag day
den ganzen Tag all day
jeden Tag every day
Tage pro Woche days a week
Tagebuch diary
Tagesausflug day out, day trip
täglich everyday
tagsüber in the daytime
tagträumen to daydream
Taille waist
Tal valley
Talkshow talk show
Tank tank
Tante aunt
Tanz dance
Tanzball ball
tanzen to dance
Tanzen dancing
Tänzer/in dancer
Tasche pocket
(Schul)tasche bag
Taschengeld pocket money
Taschenlampe torch
Tasse cup
Tätigkeitswort verb
Tätowierung tattoo
Tatsache fact
tatsächlich in fact
weiße Taube dove
tauschen to swap
tausend (one) thousand
Taxi taxi
Team team
Teamgeist spirit
Technik technology
Techniker/in technician
technisch technical
Technologie technology

Tee tea
Teenager teenager
Teigware pasta
Teil part
teilen to divide, to share
teilnehmen to take part
Teilzeit part-time
Telefon phone, telephone
ans Telefon gehen to answer the phone
Telefongespräch call
Telefonkarte phonecard
Telefonleitung telephone line
Telefonzelle callbox, telephone box
Telegramm telegram
Teleskop telescope
Teller plate
Tennis tennis
Tennisplatz tennis court
Teppich carpet
Test exam, test
einen Test machen to take a test
testen to test
teuer expensive
Text text
Theater drama
Theaterstück play
Theke bar
Thema topic
Themenbereich topic
Thriller thriller
tief deep
tief Luft einholen to take a deep breath
Tier animal
Tierarzt/-ärztin vet
Tierarzthelfer/in vet's assistant, veterinary nurse
Tierheim animal home
Tiger tiger
Tipp tip
Tisch table
Tischtennis table tennis
Titel title
Toast toast
Toaster toaster
Tochter daughter
Tod death
tödlich deadly
Toilette toilet
Toilettenanlage toilet block
toll great
Tomate tomato
Tonaufnahme recording
Tonband tape
Toningenieur sound engineer
Tonne drum
Tor gate; goal *(Fußball)*
ein Tor schießen to score
Torhüter/in goalkeeper
Tornado tornado
Torwart keeper
tot dead
total totally
töten to kill
Tour tour

Tourdaten tour dates
Tourist/in tourist
Tragbahre stretcher
tragen to carry *(in den Händen)*; to pull on *(Stiefel)*; to put on, to wear *(Kleidung)*
trainieren to be in training, to train
Training training
Trainingsanzug tracksuit
Traktor tractor
Träne tear
trauern to mourn
Traum dream
träumen to dream
Träumer/in dreamer
traurig sad
Trecking trekking
Treckingbike trekking bike
treffen to meet
Verabredungen treffen dating
Treffen meeting
Treppe stairs
treten to step
Trick trick
trinken to drink
Trinkgeld tip
Trip trip
trocken dry
trocknen to dry
Trompete trumpet
trotzdem still
Tschüs! Bye!
tun to do
Tunnel tunnel
Tür door
Türglocke doorbell
türkisch Turkish
Türklingel doorbell
Turm tower
Turnhalle gym
Tüte bag
Typ bloke, guy
typisch typical

U

U-Bahn underground, tube
üben to practise
über about; over
lachen über to laugh about
nachdenken über to think about
sprechen uber to talk about
über Bord overboard
überall all around, all over, everywhere
nicht übereinstimmen to disagree
überfüllt crowded
in Übergröße oversized
überhaupt anyway, at all
Überleben survival
überleben to survive
übernachten to stay
überprüfen to check
überqueren to cross
überraschen to surprise

überrascht surprised
Überraschung surprise
Überschrift heading
übersetzen to translate
Übersetzer/in translator
überstehen to get over sth.
überstreichen to paint over
Überstunden long hours
üblich usual
übrig left
übrigens by the way
Übung exercise
Übungsheft exercise book
Uferpromenade boardwalk
Uhr clock *(Wanduhr)*; o' clock *(Uhrzeit)*
um around
um die Hälfte by half
um ... bitten to ask for
um ... Uhr at ... o' clock
Umarmung hug
umdrehen to turn around, to turn over
Umfrage survey
umgekehrt vice versa
Umkleideraum changing room
umsteigen to change
Umwelt environment
Umweltgruppe environmental group
Umweltschützer/in environmentalist
umwerfen to push over
umziehen to move
umzingeln to surround
Umzug moving
unbeliebt unpopular
und and
und so weiter and so on
unerwünscht unwanted
unfair unfair
Unfall accident
unfreundlich unfriendly
ungefähr about
ungesund unhealthy
ungewöhnlich unusual
Unglaube disbelief
unglücklich unhappy
unglücklicherweise unfortunately
unhöflich impolite, rude
Uniform uniform
uninteressant uninteresting
unmöglich impossible
unnatürlich unnatural
unpopulär unpopular
Unrecht haben to be wrong
unregelmäßig irregular
uns us
uns selbst ourselves
unser/e ours
unsicher unsure
unten below; downstairs *(im Haus)*
unter among; below; under
unterbrechen to interrupt
unterhalb below
Unterhaltung conversation

Dictionary

Unternehmen business
Unterrichtsfach subject
Unterrichtsstunde lesson, period
Unterschied difference
unterschreiben to sign
unterstreichen to underline
Untersuchung survey
unterwegs on the way
unterwegs sein zu to be off to
unverletzt unhurt
unverschämt rude
unwillkommen unwelcome
Ur-Ur-Großeltern great-great-grandparents
Urdu Urdu
Urlaub holiday
im Urlaub on holiday
ursprünglich original
Urwald jungle
USA U.S. A.

V

v. Chr. BC (= Before Christ)
Vater father, dad
Verabredung date *(Rendezvous)*; meeting *(geschäftlich)*
Verabredungen treffen dating
verändern to change
Veränderung change
Veranstaltung event
für etwas verantwortlich sein to be responsible for sth.
jdn. veräppeln to make a fool of sb.
verärgert upset
Verb verb
verbessern to correct
verbinden to connect
Verbindung connection
verbrauchen to consume
Verbrechen crime
verbringen to spend
Verdächtige/r suspect
Verdammt! Damn it!
Verdammt nochmal! God damn!
verdecken to cover up
verdienen to earn
Verein club
vereinbaren to arrange
Vereinigte Staaten von Amerika U.S. A.
Vereinigtes Königreich United Kingdom
Verfasser/in writer
verfehlen to miss
verfolgen to follow
Vergangenheit past
einfache Vergangenheit past simple
Vergangenheitsform past form
vergehen to go by
vergessen to forget
vergleichen to compare
Verhältnisse conditions
verheiratet married
ein Tor verhindern to make a save

verjagen to scare away
Verkauf sale
verkaufen to sell
Zu verkaufen. For sale.
Verkäufer/in salesperson/assistant *(im Laden)*; seller
Verkehr traffic
Verkehrsbüro information centre
Verkehrsstau traffic jam
verlassen to leave
verlässlich reliable
Verlauf einer Geschichte story-line
Verlaufsform der Vergangenheit past progressive
verlegen embarrassed
verletzen to hurt
verletzt hurt
verliebt in love
verlieren to lose
Verlierer/in loser
vermasseln to screw up
vermeiden to avoid
vermissen to miss
vermuten to guess
verneinend negative
vernünftig sensible
verpassen to miss
verprügelt werden to get a beating
verregnet rainy
verreisen to go away, to travel
verrückt crazy, mad
verrückt nach etwas sein to be mad about sth.
Versammlung assembly
verschieden different
verschlingen to swallow up
verschlossen locked
Verschmutzung pollution
verschwenden to waste
verschwinden to disappear, to vanish; to get lost *(abhauen)*
verstecken to hide
versteckt hidden
Versteckspiel hide-and-seek
verstehen to understand
Versteigerung auction
versuchen to have a try, to try
Vertrag contract
vertrauen to trust
verträumt dreamy
Vertreter/in representative
verursachen to cause
vervollständigen to complete
verwechseln to mix up
verwickelt werden to become involved
auf etwas verzichten to give up sth.
Verzweiflung desperation
Video video
Videojockey video jockey
Videokamera video camera
Videorekorder VCR (= video cassette recorder)
Videospielhalle video arcade
Vieh cattle
Viehzüchter rancher *(in USA)*

zu viel too much
viel mehr lots more
viel Spaß haben to have a good time
Viel Spaß! Have fun!
so viel … wie as much … as
viel/e a lot of, lots of, many
vielleicht maybe, perhaps
Können Sie … vielleicht I wonder if you can …
vier four
vierte/r fourth
Viertel nach quarter past
Viertel vor quarter to
vierzehn fourteen
vierzig forty
violett purple
Vogel bird
Vokabelliste vocabulary list
voll full
sehr voll crowded
die Nase voll haben to be fed up
voll von filled with
volle Geschwindigkeit voraus full speed ahead
Volleyball volleyball
völlig total
vollkommen pure, total
vollständig complete
Vollzeit full-time
vom ersten Moment an right from the first moment
von of; from
von der Schule verwiesen werden to get expelled
Von mir aus. I don't mind.
drei von zehn three out of ten
von … bis from … till, from … to
vor before *(zeitlich)*; in front of *(örtlich)*; to *(Uhrzeit)*; ago *(Zeitangabe)*
vor sich gehen to go on
vorbei over
es ist vorbei it's over
an …vorbei past
vorbeigehen, -laufen to walk past, to pass
vorbeikommen to come round
Vorfall incident
Vorhaben programme
vorher before
vormittags a.m. *(0–11:59 Uhr)*
vorne at the front
vornehm fine, stylish
Vorort suburb
Vorschau trailer
Vorschlag suggestion
vorschlagen to suggest
vorsichtig careful
Vorsilbe prefix
vorsprechen to try out for
Vorsprung ledge *(Felsen)*
Vorstellung idea
Vorteil advantage
Vorurteil prejudice
vorziehen to prefer

W

Wache guardsman
wachsen to grow
Wachtposten guardsman
wackeln to wobble
Wackelpudding jelly
Wagen cart; float *(elektr. Lieferwagen)*
Wahl choice
wählen to choose *(aussuchen)*; to dial *(Telefon)*; to vote *(Stimme abgeben)*
Wahlmöglichkeit option
wahr true
wahr werden to come true
während during, while
Wahrheit truth
wahrscheinlich probably
Wald forest *(groß)*, wood *(klein)*
Wand wall
Wanderschuhe hiking boots
Wange cheek
wann when
Wann ...? What time ...?
war ... auch nicht wasn't ... either
Warenhaus department store
warm warm
warnen to warn
Warnung warning
Warte, ... Hang on, ...
warten to wait; to hold the line *(während eines Telefonats)*
Warteschlange queue
warum why
was what
was ... bloß whatever
was für what
Was in aller Welt ...? What on earth ...?
Was ist los? What's the matter?
Was noch/sonst? What else?
Waschbecken washbasin
waschen to wash
Waschmaschine washing machine
Wasser water
Wasserfall waterfall
Wasserhahn tap
wechseln to change
wecken to wake up
weg away
Weg lane, way
auf dem Weg on the way
den Weg erklären to tell the way
im Weg stehen to be in the way
wegblasen to blow off
wegen about
wegfahren to drive off
weggehen to go away, to leave, to walk off
wegkommen to get away
weglaufen to run away
wegwerfen to throw away
wehtun to hurt
weiblich female
weich soft

Weihnachten Christmas
Fröhliche Weihnachten! Merry Christmas!
1. Weihnachtstag Christmas Day
weil because
Wein wine
weinen to cry
weiß white
weiße Taube dove
die Weißen the whites
weit far
die Weite wide open spaces
und so weiter and so on
(geradeaus) weitergehen to go (straight) on
weitermachen to continue, to go on
Weitsprung long jump
welche/r/s what, which
Welle wave
Wellensittich budgie
Welt world
er kam auf die Welt he was born
Weltraum space
Weltraumbus spacebus
wenden to turn round
weniger (als) fewer (than), less (than)
wenigstens at least
wenn when, if
wer who
werben to advertise
Werbespot commercial
Werbung advert
ich werde ... anschauen I'm going to watch ...
werden to become; to get *bekommen)*; will *(+ Inf.)*
rot werden to turn red
werfen to throw
Werken Woodwork *(Schulfach)*
Werkzeug tool
Wesen being
Westen west
Western western
Wettbewerb competition
wetten to bet
Wetter weather
Wettkampf competition, match
wichtig important
wie how, like
wie alt how old
Wie geht's (dir)? How are you doing? *(ugs.)*, What's up? *(ugs.)*
Wie ist es bei dir? What about you?
Wie ist es? What is it like?
Wie oft ...? How many times ...?, How often ...?
Wie sehen sie aus? What do they look like?
Wie spät ist es? What time is it?
Wie viel kostet/kosten ...? How much is/are ...?
Wie viel Uhr ist es? What time is it?
wie viel/e how much/how many
Wie wäre es mit ...? How about ...?, What about ...?

wieder again
wieder erkennen to recognize
Wiederaufbereitungsanlage recycling center
wiederverwerten to recycle
Wiederverwertung recycling
Wiese meadow
wild wild
wild aussehend wild-looking
Wildnis wilderness
willkommen welcome
willkommen heißen to welcome
Wind wind
windig windy
winken to wave
Winter winter
wir we
wir selbst ourselves
Wirbelsturm tornado
wirklich real
Wirklichkeit reality
wissen to know
Witz joke
witzig funny
wo where
Woche week
Wochen pro Jahr weeks a year
Wochenende weekend
Wochentag weekday
wöchentlich (erscheinend) weekly
woher where ... from
wohin where
Wohltätigkeitsverein charity
wohnen to live
Wohngegend neighbourhood
Wohnheim hostel
Wohnung flat, place *(ugs.)*
Wohnwagen caravan
Wohnzimmer living-room
Wolf/Wölfe wolf/wolves
Wolke cloud
wollen to want (to)
Wort word
Wörterbuch dictionary
wunderbar wonderful
wunderschön lovely
wundervoll beautiful, wonderful
Wunsch wish
(sich) wünschen to want, to wish
ich würde gerne I'd (= I would) like to
würde/n would
würdevoll graceful
Wurm worm
Wurst sausage
Wüste desert
wütend angry, furious

Z

Zahl number
zählen to count, to number
Zahlenkette number chain
Zählwerk counter
Zahn/Zähne tooth/teeth

Dictionary

Zahnarzthelferin dental nurse
Zapfhahn tap
zart fragile *(zierlich)*; soft *(weich)*
Zaun fence
zehn ten
Zeichen sign, signal
Zeichentrickfilm cartoon
zeichnen to draw
zeigen to point *(hinweisen)*; to hold up, to show *(hochhalten)*; to present
Zeile line
Zeit tense *(Verb)*; time
die meiste Zeit most of the time
nach einiger Zeit after some time
eine Zeit lang for a time
Zeitform tense
Zeitschrift magazine
Zeitstufe tense
Zeitung newspaper, paper
Zeitungen austragen to do a paper round
Zeitungskiosk paper shop
Zelt tent
zelten gehen to go camping
Zentimeter centimetre, cm
zerbrechen to break (up)
zerrissen torn
zersprungen cracked
zerstören to destroy, to ruin
Zeug stuff
Zeuge witness
Zeugnis certificate *(Urkunde)*; report *(Schule)*
ziehen to pull

zielen to aim *(Waffe)*
ziemlich quite, rather, pretty *(+adj.)*
Zigarette cigarette, fag *(ugs.)*
Zimmer room
Zirkus circus
zischend hissing
zittern to shake
Zoo zoo
zu to; too
zu Boden gehen to go down
zu Fuß on foot
zu Fuß gehen to walk
zu Hause at home
zu jdm. kommen to come up to sb.
zu Mittag essen to have lunch
zu spät late
zu teuer too expensive
Zu verkaufen. For sale.
zu viele too many
zuallererst first of all
Zucker sugar
zudecken to cover up
zuerst at first, first
zufällig by chance
jdn. zufällig treffen to run into sb.
zufrieden pleased
zufriedenstellen to satisfy
Zug train
fest zugeschraubt done up tight
Zuhause home
zuhören to listen (to)
Zuhörer/in listener
Zukunft future
zuletzt last of all
zum Beispiel for example

zum ersten Mal for the first time
zum Narren halten to fool
jdn. zum Schweigen bringen to shut sb. up
zumachen to close
zumindest at least
Zündkerze sparking plug
Zunge tongue
zuordnen to match
zur Abwechslung for a change
zurück back
zurückkehren to get back
zurückkommen to get back
zurückweisen to reject
zusammen together
zusammen passen to get on
zusammenbrechen to break down
Zusammenfassung summary
zusammenschlagen to beat up
zusammenstoßen mit to walk into
Zustand condition
zustimmen to agree
nicht zustimmen to disagree
zuvor before
zwanzig twenty
zwanzigste/r/s twentieth
zwei two
zweimal twice
zweite/r/s second
zweitens secondly
zwischen between
Zwischenmahlzeit snack
zwölf twelve
zwölfte/r/s twelfth

Dictionary

Bildquellen
Umschlag: Dennis Junor/Mauritius, Stuttgart. Vorderer Vorsatz: Scivos/Klett Perthes, Gotha. S. 10: re. o.: Photodisc; re. mi.: Mauritius, Stuttgart; re. u.: Christian Dekelver, Weinstadt. S. 11: li.o., re. o.: PictureQuest; re. mi.: Phyllis Cohen-Edwards; u. mi.: PictureQuest; re. u.: Bill Luster/Focus, Hamburg. S. 13: li. o.: Dieter Gebhardt; li. u.: PictureQuest. S. 14: Dieter Gebhardt, Asperg. S. 24: Mark Borrill, Stuttgart-Hofen. S. 26: Grundig. S. 29: li. o.: Corbis/Bettmann; mi. o., re. o.: PictureQuest; mi. re.: AKG-Photo, Berlin; re. u.: Francis Miller/Life. S. 30, 31: Ray Jeanotte, Washington. S. 34: Hintergrund: Christian Dekelver, Weinstadt.; li. o.: Paul Almasy/AKG-Photo, Berlin; re. o.: Ossinger/dpa, Frankfurt; li. u.: dpa, Frankfurt; re. u.: J. Beck/Mauritius, Stuttgart. S. 35: Hintergrund: Christian Dekelver, Weinstadt.; li. mi.: Joachim Ladefoged/dpa, Frankfurt. S. 37, 38, 46, 47: Dieter Gebhardt, Asperg. S. 48-51: Illustrations © Ros Asquith, from **The Teenage Worrier's Guide to Lurve** and **I Was a Teenage Worrier** by Ros Asquith. By arrangement with Transworld Publishers, a division of the Random House Group Ltd. S. 53: li. u.: The Sammarish, 1995. S. 54, 55, 58-63, 65: Dieter Gebhardt, Asperg. S. 71: Dorothea Nadzeika-Humbaraci, Elmshorn. S. 75: PictureQuest. S. 76: o.: Ullstein Bilderdienst, Berlin; mi.: dpa, Frankfurt; mi. u.: National Cable Satellite Corp.; re. u.: **Warriors don't cry** by Melba Pattillo Beals, Pocket Books, New York 1995. S. 77: Dorothea Nadzeika-Humbaraci, Elmshorn. S. 78: li. o.: Noel Tatt Ltd.; mi. o.: Ling's cards. S. 80, 81: Dieter Gebhardt, Asperg. Hinterer Vorsatz: Scivos/Klett Perthes, Gotha.

Textquellen
S. 48/49/50 **All about love**, **A love-hate letter** by Ros Asquith, from **I Was a Teenage Worrier** © 1992 Ros Asquith and **The Teenage Worrier's Guide to Lurve** © 1996 Ros Asquith, Corgi Books, London; S. 68 **Dreams** from COLLECTED POEMS by Langston Hughes. © 1994 by the Estate of Langston Hughes. Reprinted by permission of Alfred A. Knopf, a Division of Random House, Inc. **Reach out** by Ronald Keen, from Departures, Reflections in Poetry. © 1991 by Nelson Canada, a Division of Thomson Canada, Limited; S. 180 **Friday on my mind** T+M: Harry Vanda, George Young. © 1966 J Albert & Son Pty Ltd/EMI United Partnership Ltd, EMI Music Publishing Limited, London WC2H 0EA, Reproduced by permission of International Music Publications Ltd; **Behind the wall** T+M: Tracy Chapman. © 1988 by EMI April Music Inc/Purple Rabbit Music, Rechte für D/A/CH und Osteuropa außer Baltikum: EMI Songs Musikverlag GmbH, Hamburg; S. 181 **Single** T+M: Neil Tennant, Chris Lowe. © 1996 by EMI 10 Music Ltd/Cage Music Ltd, für D/A/CH und Osteuropa außer Baltikum: EMI Virgin Music Publishing Germany GmbH, Hamburg; S. 182 **Love's unkind** T+M: Giorgio Moroder, Peter Bellotte, Donna Summer. © 1977 Sweet Summernight Music/Justin Music, Rolf Budde Musikverlag GmbH, Berlin/Intro Meisel GmbH/Axxis Musikverlag GmbH; S. 183 **To have and to have not** T+M: Billy Bragg. © BMG Music Publishing Ltd, Musik-Edition Discoton GmbH (BMG UFA Musikverlage), München.

Every effort has been made to trace owners of copyright material. However, in a few cases this has not proved possible and repeated enquiries have remained unanswered. The publishers would be glad to hear from the owners of any such material reproduced in this book.

SONG LYRICS

TOPIC 1

Friday On My Mind by Gary Moore   Text and music: Harry Vanda, George Young

Monday morning feels so bad
Everybody seems to nag me
Come on Tuesday I feel better
Even my old man looks good
Wednesday just won't go
Thursday goes too slow
I've got Friday on my mind

Gonna have fun in the city
Be with my girl she's so pretty
She looks fine tonight
She is outa' sight to me

Tonight, I'll paint it red
Tonight, I'll lose my head
Tonight, I've got to get tonight
Monday I have Friday on my mind

Do the five day drag once more
No one, nothing else that bugs me
Now I'm working for the rich man
But I'll change his tune one day

Tonight I'll get mad
Tomorrow I'll be glad
'Cause I've got Friday on my mind

Gonna have fun in the city
Be with my girl she's so pretty
She looks fine tonight
She is outa' sight to me

Tonight, I'll paint it red
Tonight, I'll lose my head
Tonight, I've got to get tonight
Monday I have Friday on my mind

Yeah

Gonna have fun in the city
Be with my girl she's so pretty
Gonna have fun in the city
Gonna have some fun
Be with my girl she's so pretty
Gonna have some fun

Gonna have fun in the city
Gonna have some fun
Be with my girl she's so pretty
In the city tonight
Gonna have fun in the city

on my mind [ˈɒn maɪ ˈmaɪnd] in meinen Gedanken; **to nag** [næg] an jdm. herumnörgeln; **my old man** mein Vater; **gonna = going to**; **outa sight = out of sight** [ˈaʊtə ˈsaɪt] *hier:* phantastisch; **I'll paint it red** ich werde einen tollen Abend verbringen; **drag** [dræg] langweilige Routine; **to bug** [bʊg] ärgern; **I'll change his tune** [aɪl ˈtʃeɪnʒ hɪz ˈtjuːn] ich werde sein Verhalten mir gegenüber ändern; **glad** [glæd] froh; **'cause = because**

TOPIC 2

Behind The Wall by Tracy Chapman   Text and music: Tracy Chapman

Last night I heard the screaming
Loud voices behind the wall
Another sleepless night for me
It won't do no good to call
The police
Always come late
If they come at all

Last night I heard the screaming
Loud voices behind the wall
Another sleepless night for me
It won't do no good to call
The police
Always come late
If they come at all

And when they arrive
They say they can't interfere
With domestic affairs
Between a man and his wife
And as they walk out the door
The tears well up in her eyes

Last night I heard a screaming
Then a silence that chilled my soul
I prayed that I was dreaming
When I saw the ambulance in the road

And the policeman said
"I'm here to keep the peace
Will the crowd disperse
I think we all could use some sleep"

Last night I heard the screaming
Loud voices behind the wall
Another sleepless night for me
It won't do no good to call
The police
Always come late
If they come at all

screaming [skriːmɪŋ] Schreien; **sleepless** ['sliːplɪs] schlaflos; **it won't do no good** = it won't do any good [ɪt 'wəʊnt duː nəʊ 'gʊd] es wird nichts nutzen ; **at all** [æt‿ɔːl] überhaupt; **to interfere** [ˌɪntəˈfɪə] sich einmischen; **domestic affairs** [dəʊˈmestɪk‿əˈfeəz] private Angelegenheiten; **out the door** *AE* = out of the door; **tear** [tɪə] Träne; **to well up** [wel‿ʌp] in die Augen steigen; **silence** ['saɪləns] Stille; **to chill** [tʃɪl] gefrieren lassen; **soul** [səʊl] Seele; **to pray** [preɪ] beten; **to keep the peace** ['kiːp ðə 'piːs] Ruhe schaffen; **to disperse** [dɪˈspɜːs] sich auflösen; **sleep** [sliːp] Schlaf

TOPIC 3

Single   by Pet Shop Boys

Text and music: Neil Tennant, Chris Lowe

They call this a community
I like to think of it as home
Arriving at the airport
I'm going it alone
Ordering a boarding pass
Travelling in business class
This is the name of the game
I'm single bilingual
Single bilingual
I come to the community from U.K. p.l.c.
Arriving at my hotel there are faxes
    greeting me
Staying in a junior suite
so there's room to meet and greet and
    after work explain how I feel
'Perdoneme me llamo Neil'¹
I'm single bilingual
Single bilingual

In Brussels
Bonn or Barcelona
I'm in demand and quite at home there 'Adelante'²
Through the door
'Un momento por favor'³
This is what I get paid for
'Muchas gracias senor'⁴

I'm a player in the continental game with unlimited
    expenses to reclaim
Information's easy
Tapping at my PC
That is the frame of the game
I'm single bilingual

Single bilingual
I'm single bilingual
Single bilingual

'¿Hay una discoteca por acqui?'⁵

¹Excuse me, my name is Neil.   ²Come in.   ³One moment, please.
⁴Thank you very much, sir.   ⁵Is there a disco near here?

go it alone [gəʊ‿ɪt‿əˈləʊn] alles alleine machen; **to order** ['ɔːdə] bestellen; **boarding pass** ['bɔːdɪŋ pɑːs] Bordkarte; **bilingual** [baɪˈlɪŋgwəl] zweisprachig; **to greet** [griːt] begrüßen; **U.K.** = United Kingdom Vereinigtes Königreich; **p.l.c.** A.G.; **junior suite** ['dʒuːnjə 'swiːt] kleine Suite; **to be in demand** [biː‿ɪn dɪˈmɑːnd] sehr gefragt sein; **continental** [ˌkɒntɪˈnentl] Festlands-; **unlimited** [ʌnˈlɪmɪtɪd] unbegrenzt; **expenses** [ɪkˈspensɪz] Spesen; **to reclaim** [rɪˈkleɪm] zurückerstattet bekommen; **to tap** [tæp] *hier:* tippen; **frame** [freɪm] Rahmen

TOPIC 4

Love's Unkind by Donna Summer

Well I see him every morning in the schoolyard when the ♦ rings
And when he passes in the hallway, well he doesn't seem to notice me
He's got a crush on my best friend
But she don't care, 'cause she ♦ someone else
I'm standing on the outside, not the inside where I wanna be

Chorus:
Love's unkind, love's unkind
Love's unkind, 'cause he's not ♦

Just the other day I was praying that he'd give me a chance
Hoping he would choose me for his partner for the ♦ dance
I was standing outside the ♦
But it wasn't me, but my ♦, he asked
I went running back inside teary-eyed and left the two of them behind

Text and music:
Giorgio Moroder, Peter Bellotte, Donna Summer

Chorus:

Spoken:
Oh how I love him so, but I can't even let him know.
'Cause he loves my best friend.
But she don't care, she loves someone else.
And I asked my mama, and she said: Love's unkind.
Love's so unkind.
She said: Just keep it alive.
'Cause you may find love's unkind.

Love's unkind, love's unkind, love's unkind

Spoken:
Oh, why did I have to love him so.
Why did I have to love him so.

© 1977 Sweet Summernight Music/Justin Music Rolf Budde Musikverlag GmbH, Berlin/ Intro Meisel GmbH/Axxis Musikverlag GmbH

---

unkind [ʌnˈkaɪnd] gemein; **schoolyard** [ˈskuːljɑːd] Schulhof; **to ring** [rɪŋ] klingeln; **to pass** [pɑːs] vorbeigehen; **hallway** [ˈhɔːlweɪ] Flur, Korridor; **to have a crush on sb.** [krʌʃ] in jemanden verschossen sein; **he don't care = he doesn't care** [keə] es ist ihm egal; **'cause = because**; **wanna = want to**; **on the outside** [ˈɒn ðiːˌˈaʊtsaɪd] draußen; **the other day** [ðiːˌˈʌðə deɪ] neulich; **to pray** [preɪ] beten; **to run back** [rʌn ˈbæk] zurückrennen; **teary-eyed** [tɪəɪˌˈaɪd] mit tränen in den Augen; **can't even** [kɑːntˌˈiːvn] kann nicht einmal; **to know** [nəʊ] wissen; **alive** [əˈlaɪv] lebendig; **may find** [meɪ ˈfaɪnd] vielleicht finden können

TOPIC 5

To Have And To Have Not   by Billy Bragg

Text and music: Billy Bragg

Up in the morning and out to school
Mother says there'll be no work next year
Qualifications once the Golden Rule
Are now just pieces of paper

Just because you're better than me
Doesn't mean I'm lazy
Just because you're going forwards
Doesn't mean I'm going backwards

If you look the part you'll get the job
In last year's trousers and your old
    school shoes
The truth is, son, it's a buyers' market
They can afford to pick and choose

Just because you're better than me
Doesn't mean I'm lazy
Just because I dress like this
Doesn't mean I'm a communist

The factories are closing and the army's full –
I don't know what I'm going to do
But I've come to see in the Land of the Free
There's only a future for the Chosen Few

Just because you're better than me
Doesn't mean I'm lazy
Just because you're going forwards
Doesn't mean I'm going backwards

At twenty-one you're on top of the scrapheap
At sixteen you were top of the class
All they taught you at school
Was how to be a good worker
The system has failed you, don't fail yourself

Just because you're better than me
Doesn't mean I'm lazy
Just because you're going forwards
Doesn't mean I'm going backwards

---

qualification [ˌkwɒlɪfɪˈkeɪʃn] Qualifikation; **forwards** [ˈfɔːwədz] vorwärts; **backwards** [ˈbækwədz] rückwärts; **to look the part** [ˈlʊk ðə ˈpɑːt]*hier:* entsprechend aussehen; **truth** [truːθ] Wahrheit; **buyer** [ˈbaɪə] Käufer; **to afford** [əˈfɔːd] sich leisten; **to pick and choose** [ˈpɪk ənd ˈtʃuːz] wählerisch sein; **to dress** [dres] sich kleiden; **communist** [ˈkɒmjʊnɪst] Kommunist; **army** [ˈɑːmɪ] Armee; **the free** [ðə ˌfriː] die Freien; **chosen few** [ˈtʃəʊzən fjuː] wenige Auserwählte; **scrapheap** [ˈskræphiːp] Schrotthaufen; **system** [ˈsɪstəm] System; **to fail** [feɪl] im Stich lassen

(BMG UFA Musikverlage), München

List of irregular verbs

Die Liste umfasst alle unregelmäßigen Verben, die in *Password Orange 1–6* vorkommen.

infinitive (1st form)	past tense (2nd form)	past participle (3rd form)	German
be [i:]	was/were [ɒ/ɜ:]	been [i:]	sein
beat [i:]	beat [i:]	beaten [i:]	schlagen
become [ʌ]	became [eɪ]	become [ʌ]	werden
begin [ɪ]	began [æ]	begun [ʌ]	anfangen, beginnen
bet [e]	bet [e]	bet [e]	wetten
blow [əʊ]	blew [u:]	blown [əʊ]	blasen
break [eɪ]	broke [əʊ]	broken [əʊ]	(zer)brechen
bring [ɪ]	brought [ɔ:]	brought [ɔ:]	(her)bringen
build [ɪ]	built [ɪ]	built [ɪ]	bauen
buy [aɪ]	bought [ɔ:]	bought [ɔ:]	kaufen
catch [æ]	caught [ɔ:]	caught [ɔ:]	fangen
choose [u:]	chose [əʊ]	chosen [əʊ]	wählen
come [ʌ]	came [eɪ]	come [ʌ]	kommen
cost [ɒ]	cost [ɒ]	cost [ɒ]	kosten
cut [ʌ]	cut [ʌ]	cut [ʌ]	schneiden
do [u:]	did [ɪ]	done [ʌ]	tun, machen
draw [ɔ:]	drew [u:]	drawn [ɔ:]	zeichnen
drink [ɪ]	drank [æ]	drunk [ʌ]	trinken
drive [aɪ]	drove [əʊ]	driven [ɪ]	fahren
eat [i:]	ate [e]	eaten [i:]	essen
fall [ɔ:]	fell [e]	fallen [ɔ:]	fallen
feel [i:]	felt [e]	felt [e]	fühlen
fight [aɪ]	fought [ɔ:]	fought [ɔ:]	kämpfen
find [aɪ]	found [aʊ]	found [aʊ]	finden
fly [aɪ]	flew [u:]	flown [əʊ]	fliegen
forget [e]	forgot [ɒ]	forgotten [ɒ]	vergessen
forgive [ɪ]	forgave [eɪ]	forgiven [ɪ]	vergeben
get [e]	got [ɒ]	got [ɒ]	bekommen; werden; holen
give [ɪ]	gave [eɪ]	given [ɪ]	geben
go [əʊ]	went [e]	gone [ɒ]	gehen, fahren
grow [əʊ]	grew [u:]	grown [əʊ]	wachsen
hang [æ]	hung [ʌ]	hung [ʌ]	hängen
have [æ]	had [æ]	had [æ]	haben
hear [ɪə]	heard [ɜ:]	heard [ɜ:]	hören
hide [aɪ]	hid [ɪ]	hidden [ɪ]	(sich) verstecken
hit [ɪ]	hit [ɪ]	hit [ɪ]	schlagen, treffen
hold [əʊ]	held [e]	held [e]	(fest)halten
hurt [ɜ:]	hurt [ɜ:]	hurt [ɜ:]	verletzen
keep [i:]	kept [e]	kept [e]	(be)halten
kneel [i:]	knelt [e]	knelt [e]	knien
know [əʊ]	knew [u:]	known [əʊ]	wissen, kennen
lay [eɪ]	laid [eɪ]	laid [eɪ]	liegen
lead [i:]	led [e]	led [e]	führen, leiten
leave [i:]	left [e]	left [e]	(ver)lassen, weggehen
let [e]	let [e]	let [e]	lassen
lie [aɪ]	lay [eɪ]	lain [eɪ]	liegen
light [aɪ]	lit [ɪ]	lit [ɪ]	anzünden
lose [u:]	lost [ɒ]	lost [ɒ]	verlieren
make [eɪ]	made [eɪ]	made [eɪ]	machen
mean [i:]	meant [e]	meant [e]	bedeuten; meinen
meet [i:]	met [e]	met [e]	(sich) treffen; kennen lernen
pay [eɪ]	paid [eɪ]	paid [eɪ]	bezahlen
put [ʊ]	put [ʊ]	put [ʊ]	setzen; stellen; legen
read [i:]	read [e]	read [e]	lesen
ride [aɪ]	rode [əʊ]	ridden [ɪ]	reiten; fahren
ring [ɪ]	rang [æ]	rung [ʌ]	klingeln, läuten
run [ʌ]	ran [æ]	run [ʌ]	laufen, rennen
say [eɪ]	said [e]	said [e]	sagen
see [i:]	saw [ɔ:]	seen [i:]	sehen
seek [i:]	sought [ɔ:]	sought [ɔ:]	suchen
sell [e]	sold [əʊ]	sold [əʊ]	verkaufen
send [e]	sent [e]	sent [e]	schicken, senden
set [e]	set [e]	set [e]	setzen, stellen
shake [eɪ]	shook [ʊ]	shaken [eɪ]	schütteln
shoot [u:]	shot [ɒ]	shot [ɒ]	(er)schießen
show [əʊ]	showed [əʊ]	shown [əʊ]	zeigen
shut [ʌ]	shut [ʌ]	shut [ʌ]	zumachen, schließen
sing [ɪ]	sang [æ]	sung [ʌ]	singen
sink [ɪ]	sank [æ]	sunk [ʌ]	sinken
sit [ɪ]	sat [æ]	sat [æ]	sitzen
sleep [i:]	slept [e]	slept [e]	schlafen
speak [i:]	spoke [əʊ]	spoken [əʊ]	sprechen
spend [e]	spent [e]	spent [e]	verbringen; ausgeben
stand [æ]	stood [ʊ]	stood [ʊ]	stehen
steal [i:]	stole [əʊ]	stolen [əʊ]	stehlen
swim [ɪ]	swam [æ]	swum [ʌ]	schwimmen
take [eɪ]	took [ʊ]	taken [eɪ]	nehmen; hinbringen; dauern
teach [i:]	taught [ɔ:]	taught [ɔ:]	beibringen, unterrichten, lehren
tear [ɪ]	tore [ɔ:]	torn [ɔ:]	zerreißen
tell [e]	told [əʊ]	told [əʊ]	erzählen, sagen
think [ɪ]	thought [ɔ:]	thought [ɔ:]	denken, meinen
throw [əʊ]	threw [u:]	thrown [əʊ]	werfen
understand [æ]	understood [ʊ]	understood [ʊ]	verstehen
wake [eɪ]	woke [əʊ]	woken [əʊ]	aufwachen, aufwecken
wear [eə]	wore [ɔ:]	worn [ɔ:]	tragen (Kleidung)
win [ɪ]	won [ʌ]	won [ʌ]	gewinnen
write [aɪ]	wrote [əʊ]	written [ˈrɪtn]	schreiben

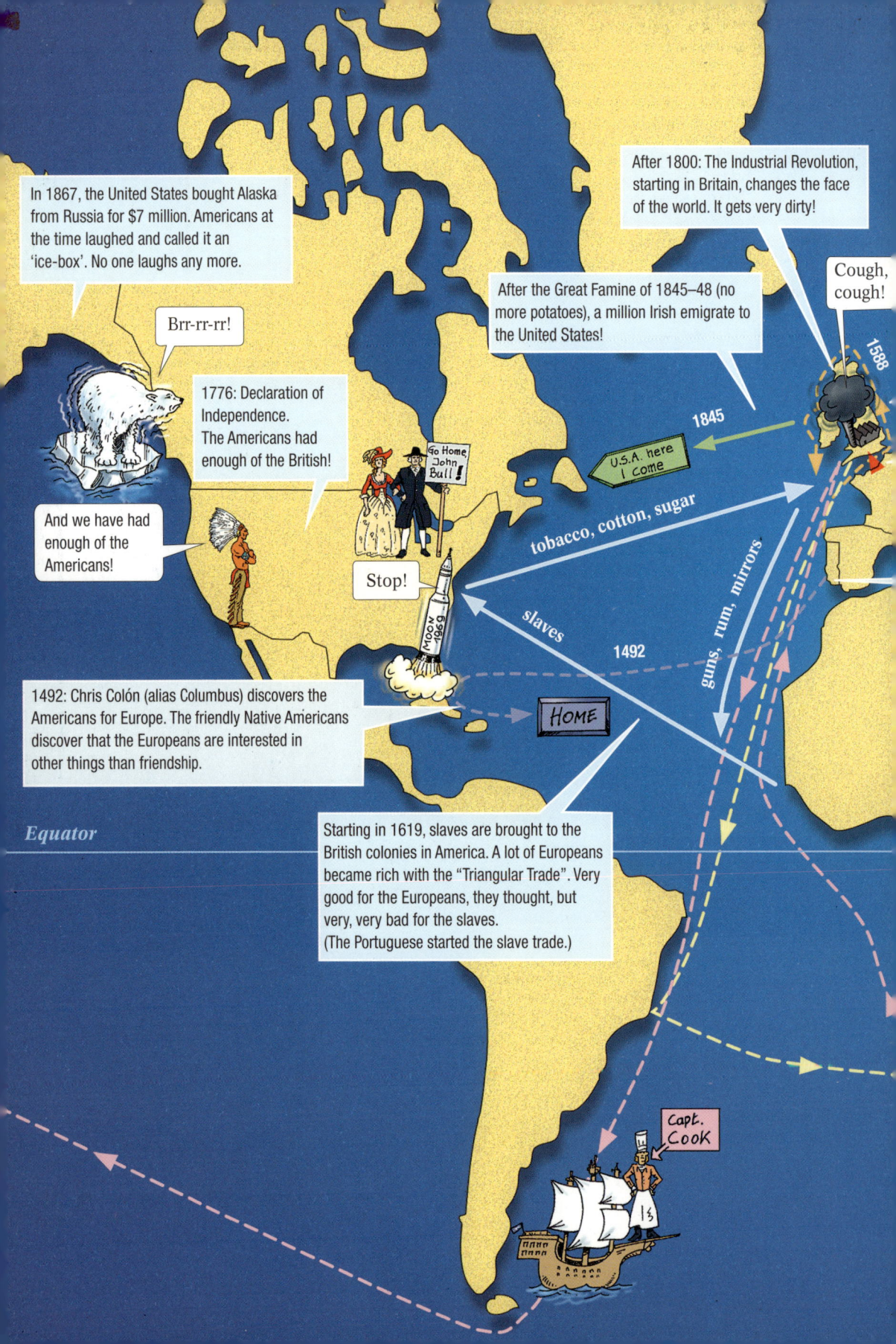

In 1867, the United States bought Alaska from Russia for $7 million. Americans at the time laughed and called it an 'ice-box'. No one laughs any more.

After 1800: The Industrial Revolution, starting in Britain, changes the face of the world. It gets very dirty!

Cough, cough!

Brr-rr-rr!

After the Great Famine of 1845–48 (no more potatoes), a million Irish emigrate to the United States!

1776: Declaration of Independence. The Americans had enough of the British!

Go Home John Bull!

1588

U.S.A. here I come

1845

And we have had enough of the Americans!

Stop!

tobacco, cotton, sugar

slaves

1492

guns, rum, mirrors

MOON 1969

1492: Chris Colón (alias Columbus) discovers the Americans for Europe. The friendly Native Americans discover that the Europeans are interested in other things than friendship.

HOME

Equator

Starting in 1619, slaves are brought to the British colonies in America. A lot of Europeans became rich with the "Triangular Trade". Very good for the Europeans, they thought, but very, very bad for the slaves.
(The Portuguese started the slave trade.)

Capt. Cook